Standards-Based &
Responsive
Evaluation

to Dubhe

Robert E. Stake
University of Illinois, Urbana-Champaign

Standards-Based &
Responsive
Evaluation

SAGE Publications
International Educational and Professional Publisher
Thousand Oaks ▪ London ▪ New Delhi

Cover photographs by Dale McClung and Lonnie Graham.

For information:

 Sage Publications, Inc.
2455 Teller Road
Thousand Oaks, California 91320
E-mail: order@sagepub.com

Sage Publications Ltd.
6 Bonhill Street
London EC2A 4PU
United Kingdom

Sage Publications India Pvt. Ltd.
B-42, Panchsheel Enclave
Post Box 4109
New Delhi 110 017 India

Printed in the United States of America

Library of Congress Cataloging-in-Publication Data

Stake, Robert E.
Standards-based and responsive evaluation / Robert E. Stake.
    p. cm.
Includes bibliographical references and index.
ISBN 0–7619–2664–X–ISBN 0–7619–2665–8 (pbk.)
   1. Evaluation research (Social action programs) 2. Evaluation. I. Title.
H62.S738 2004
001.4—dc22

                        2003014865

03   04   05   06   10   9 8 7 6 5 4 3 2 1

Acquisitions Editor:	Lisa Cuevas Shaw
Editorial Assistant:	Margo Beth Crouppen
Production Editor:	Melanie Birdsall
Copy Editor:	Margaret C. Tropp
Typesetter:	C&M Digitals (P) Ltd.
Proofreader:	Cheryl Rivard
Indexer:	Julie Grayson
Cover Designer:	Michelle Kenny

Contents

First Words ix

1. Criterial and Interpretive Evaluation 1
   The Ubiquitous Search for Quality 3
   Standards 7
   Criterial and Episodic Thinking 15
   Roles and Styles of Evaluation 16
   Formative and Summative Evaluation 17
   The Evaluand 18
   The Evaluator 19

2. Roles, Models, and Dispositions 27
   Models 29
   Dispositions 30
   Roles 31

3. Standards-Based Evaluation 54
   Standards-Based 57
   Bias 59
   Factors 60
   Criteria and Standards for Comparisons 64
   Needs Assessment 66
   Goals 71
   Costs 76
   Representations of Performance 78
   What Goes Wrong 82

4. Responsive Evaluation 86
   Issues as Conceptual Structure 89
   Observations and Judgments 90
   Perceptions 92

Combining Responsive and Standards-Based Evaluation   94
Experience as Knowledge   95
Organizing and Reporting   100
Procedures   102
What Goes Wrong   104

5.   Data Gathering   108
Choosing Data Sources   110
Instrumentation   112
Recipient Responses   113
Staff and Management Responses   123
Stakeholder and Public Responses   127
Data Coding and Records Processing   129
Surveys   137
Observation Schedules   142
Interviewing   146
Histories and Artifacts   155

6.   Analysis, Synthesis, and Meta-evaluation   159
Analysis   160
Synthesis   169
Experiential and Probative Inferences   175
Meta-evaluation   180
An Ethic of Continuous Self-Challenge   186

7.   Clients, Stakeholders, Beneficiaries, and Readers   190
Participatory Evaluation   193
Stakeholding   195
Utilization   197
Democratic Evaluation   199
Negotiation of a Contract   203
Writing Reports   206
Styles of Reporting   211
Representations of the Evaluand   212
Names and Labels   213
Cutting Edge   218
Offering Recommendations   219

8.   Issues Needing Interpretation   223
Complexity   226
Program Standardization   227
Program Fairness   228
Staff Development   235

9.	Evidence-Based Evaluation	245
	Is Evaluation Science?	246
	Petite and Grand Generalizations	247
	Policy Evaluation	250
	Bias	253
	Skepticism as a Commitment	255
10.	Doing It Right	260
	Quality Work Is Ethical Work	261
	Personal Standards	263
	Professional Standards	265
	Human Subjects Protection	267
	Confidentiality and Anonymity	268
	The Business of Evaluation	270
	Personnel Evaluation	272
	Product Evaluation	276
	Political and Cultural Contexts	278
	Last Words	285
	References	289
	Bibliography	301
	Index	305
	About the Author	329

Web Appendix: Sample Designs, Proposals, and Other Evaluation Statements

Issues to Study as Part of Evaluation Work
4. Standardized Student Achievement Testing
5. Possible Bias in Committee Work (RELS)

Designs for Evaluation
1. Chicago Teachers Academy for Mathematics and Science
2. Girls' Education in Guinea
3. Six Indianapolis Elementary Schools

Proposals
1. Milwaukee Alternative Teacher Training (Chandler)
2. Escola Ativa, Federal Program for Rural Schools in Brazil
3. A Study of the Scaling-Up Problem

Reports
  1. WMU Evaluation of Ke Aka Ho'ona
  2. Evaluation of Training for Reader Focused Writing
  3. Meta-Evaluation of Evaluation of School to Work Transition
  4. Meta-Evaluation of Training, Veterans Benefits Administration (Greene)

Miscellaneous
  1. Methods Chapter, Middle School Technical Education (Harnisch)
  2. Methods Statement as a Footnote
  3. Teachers Academy for Mathematics and Science, Principal's Interview

Available at http://www.sagepub.com/stake/evaluation/webappendix

First Words

To the Student

Hello. I am Bob Stake. I have written a rather personal book about the formal evaluation of educational and social programs. It is a fascinating topic stretched across a troubled time.

I invite you to enjoy reading this book but to be troubled by it as well. Some of the time it says we don't know how to do what we must do. We often cannot recognize the quality of the actions we take to educate our children, care for our elderly, reengineer our organizations, and be ourselves. It is not easy to do any of these things well. And it is hard to demonstrate to others how well we are doing them.

Life is complex, and we work to complicate it further. We have become masters at communicating. My cell phone rings and I hear my wife say, "Are you still in the basement?" And we have become masters at miscommunicating. There are two opposite ways of interpreting the phrase, "You can't put too much emphasis on quality."

Before he became president of Czechoslovakia, Vaclav Havel was a writer. The concrete poetry shown in Figure 1 is his. Before you look at the title, note how obvious it is that the linkage between A and J is complicated. It's a roundabout way to get them connected. Are they having trouble connecting? Havel (1971) titled it *Estrangement*. When I first saw it, I thought it was the track A was taking to find J. I decided that A stood for Access and J stood for Judgment, and that it was a long way from Access to a program to Judgment of it. Instead of Estrangement, I called it Perseverance.

I couldn't make up my mind. It would have been nice to put this "concrete poem" on the cover of the book, but I had two prior choices. I wanted a cover showing a glass half-full, possibly a cut-glass crystal tumbler from the Czech Republic. I wanted the spectrum to glow at each bevel. With our eyes, we usually see the tumbler in black and white. With the lens of insight, the colors appear. But I also wanted to capture the transformation of chrysalis to

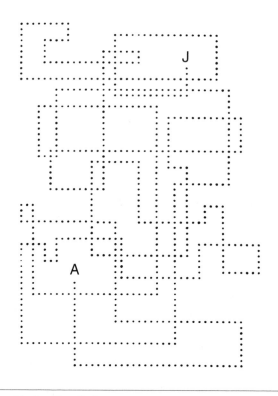

Figure 1   Vaclav Havel's *Estrangement*

SOURCE: Reprinted from *Modulo* by Vaclav Havel. Reprinted with permission.

butterfly. Here too the colors emerge, but in a burst of activity. Which is the better metaphor for the realization of quality?

One of the main messages of this book is that valuing is ubiquitous. We may not see all the value, but we always see some of it. Every time we look at something, judgment mixes with perception. The theme of some evaluation textbooks is that the value messages of those first impressions are not to be trusted, that they need to be wiped clean so that portrayals of value can be unbiased. Well, we do need unbiased portrayals, but we also need to take those early impressions and refine them, stretch them, challenge them, polish them—for the values of the human encounter, however biased, reveal some deep and complex meanings that surface no other way. It is a message of listening to experience.

Speaking at the World Economic Forum in Davos, Switzerland, on February 4, 1992, Havel said, "We must try harder to understand than to explain." We evaluators start with audiences that know quite a bit about what we are trying to evaluate. Our job is to help them add to that understanding.

As pointed out by Finnish philosopher Georg Henrik von Wright (1971), explanation is the aim of science, to relate ordinary happenings to abstract theory. Understanding, however, comes from mixing knowledge with social experience. Personal happenings over time provide a critical structure for the meaning of all that is encountered. The stories of our lives are filled with personal knowledge of what is good and bad. Sometimes we misperceive good and bad, but there is no knowledge of complex activity in society that does not carry the coloration of personal experience, wise and foolish. The task for the evaluator is to tease one from the other.

This is a book on methods for the formal evaluation of programs in education and the social services. It is a textbook for an introductory course for students of some advanced standing, usually graduate students, especially persons who have had some practical experience in such programs. I anticipate that the course will be useful for students in Departments of Education, Communications, Leisure Studies, Social Work, Kinesiology, Psychology, Sociology, Anthropology, and maybe others.

The main theme of the book is that there are two grand ways of approaching the task of evaluation, a measurements-oriented way and an experience-oriented way. They each enrich an inquiry differently. Both deserve to be included in most searches for program quality, even when they do not join smoothly and even when they contradict. But measurements and experience seem too simple a distinction between the two ways of inquiry. So do quantitative and qualitative. I have chosen *standards* and *criteria* as key concepts for the measurements way and *evaluator responsiveness* and *interpretation* as key concepts for the other. I have not set out to describe the work of professional evaluators as more complex and abstract than it really is, and I will resist making it simpler than it is.

To relieve the humidity, I've put some dry humor in this book. I hope I don't offend you. At some moments, you may wonder why I would lead you into a forest of metaphors. In my own practice as an evaluator, I have passed through lots I haven't understood, and I sometimes do not know if the path we are taking leads the right way. Here, part of that is up to you.

As I write this, I am Robert Stake, Emeritus Professor of Education and Director of the Center for Instructional Research and Curriculum Evaluation (CIRCE) at the University of Illinois. I am a specialist in the evaluation of educational programs. My students of forty-five years have made me proud of their work in many educational responsibilities, particularly for research on student assessment and curriculum analysis on campuses, in government agencies, and in schools around the world.

I came to the University of Illinois in 1963 to become Associate Director of the Illinois Statewide Testing Program. Following the lead of Thomas Hastings and Lee Cronbach, I assisted in the founding of CIRCE, and in 1975 I became its director. This center is widely recognized in educational research circles as a site for the designing of innovative and ethical evaluation. CIRCE people have collaborated with distinguished practitioners and theorists around the world.

Most of my evaluation work has been done in the United States, a small bit in Britain, Sweden, and Brazil. Among topics of the evaluative studies I have directed are science and mathematics in U.S. elementary and secondary schools, education of the gifted and model art teaching, development of teaching with sensitivity to sex equity, education of teachers for the deaf, and alternative teacher education; also, environmental education, the training of Veterans Benefits Administration personnel, urban social services, and youth sports. I have been active in the development of what has been called "responsive evaluation," where inquiry is focused on problems faced by educators, sponsors, and students in a particular program context. The techniques of ethnography, case study, and investigative reporting have been prominent in my work in addition to the traditional psychometric data gathering of testing, surveys, and attitude scaling. At one time or another, I have described my evaluation approach as interpretive, naturalistic, responsive, particularistic, and qualitative, yet I continue to take pride in developing quantitative instruments, standards, scoring procedures, and other criterial forms.

As for professional activities, I have been active in the American Educational Research Association, particularly regarding curriculum and research methods. I participated in the organization of two professional groups, the Evaluation Research Society and the Evaluation Network, that later joined to become the American Evaluation Association. Originally from Nebraska, I got my Ph.D. in 1958 with a specialization in psychometrics at Princeton University. My doctoral dissertation was published as a *Psychometric Monograph* under the title "Learning Curve Parameters and Aptitudes." In 1988, I received the Lazarsfeld Award from the American Evaluation Association and, in 1994, an honorary doctorate from the University of Uppsala.

Throughout the late seventies, eighties, and nineties, I planned to write a book on "responsive evaluation." I have been advocating more use of qualitative methods over the years. But I know that if there had been as much emphasis on qualitative evaluation methods as there was on quantitative methods, I would have remained a promoter of quantitative methods. So by the time I wrote this book, the most frequent thing I have to say is "You have to use some of both."

There is advocacy in this book for a collection of ideas. Lee Cronbach (1980) called his collection "95 theses." Michael Scriven (1993) called his "Hard-won Lessons." I haven't thought of my name yet. I want to spread these ideas before you in as many ways as I can. I have borrowed one way from Galileo. You may know that he sometimes set forth his theories in fictitious conversations. According to *Galileo's Daughter* by Dava Sobel (1999), the great astronomer's ideas were voiced by Filippo Salviati. His antagonist was Giovanfrancesco Sagredo. Here, in a running narrative at the end of each chapter of this book, I have put forth my ideas, voiced by the evaluator, Phyllis, who faces the challenges of her boss, Mr. Sagredo.

There is still more to the book than meets the eye. I have provided an electronic appendix at the Web site http://www.sagepub.com/stake/evaluation/webappendix. I have placed there for your examination several longer pieces, as shown in the Contents. The pieces amplify nicely, I think, the concepts and stories of the chapters.

I hope this book draws you into some new thinking. And also gives you opportunities to say, "I knew that." You already know lots about what you need to know.

Acknowledgments

To Bernadine, who, long peering the depths, knew I had this book in me and helped bring it out. To C. Deborah Laughton, who gave me sage advice and every editorial encouragement. To Rita Davis, my alter ego and eager alto, probably the very only person who understands everything in this book. To students and colleagues, who stimulated me and reflected my ideas with chromatics I never imagined . . . .

To those who red-penciled drafts: Charles Secolsky, Katherine Ryan, David Balk and his Oklahoma State students, Sheryl Gowen and her Georgia State students, Izabel Savickiene, Brinda Jegatheesan, Gordon Hoke, Henry Braun, Liora Bresler, Aysel Tufeksi, Chryso Mouzourou and Pepe Arostegui . . . . To Ernie Olson, who sketched cartoons . . . .

To those on my branches of the evaluation genealogy, to be read about in Marvin Alkin's forthcoming book on who got what from whom. To my bosses, from Rupert Evans and Mike Atkin on to Tom Hastings and Lizanne DeStefano, who made CIRCE a habitat for musing, evaluating, and writing . . . .

To the Instructor

Some of you faculty members will find this a good book to teach with. It provides a range of ideas at the heart of program evaluation, each of them needing further explanation and development. The book will serve as background for what's most important for you to teach. You can teach within the book or outside. It sets up lots of opportunities for discussion, bridging to your examples and interpretations as well as mine.

For most students, it will be a fun read, a vicarious experience, but not much of an experience in the mechanics. It leaves plenty of room for your exercises and projects, if that is your suit. You may get students into projects growing out of the issues here, or of their choosing, or yours. Some of your colleagues will find teaching with this book not so much fun because of its indecision about what is right as to conceptual definition and practice. These ten chapters say over and over that novice and expert evaluators alike have many choices to make. Evaluation is situational. There is no one best way.

Some instructors will use this book as supplementary to a text on experimental method, or participatory evaluation, or to readings from the literature. Even though I have written it for setting foot in the specialization, your students will think of it as a reference work as they make their way along. I think you will see possibilities also of using it with workshops or short courses for experienced professionals wanting to acquaint themselves with responsive evaluation.

We probably agree that it is important for students to be acquainted with actual evaluation studies. I have provided snippets of many of those in the boxes of the text, and a few at greater length in the Web appendix. I have included the full report of Daniel Stufflebeam's evaluation of Ke Aka Ho'ona, a values-based self-help housing and community development project for low-income families in Hawaii. Another possibility is CIRCE's evaluation of the National Youth Sports Program at www.ed.uiuc.edu/CIRCE/NYSP/Index. You probably have others in mind. The Web is a godsend. It helps to walk students through some of the decisions, some of the problems, and some of the accomplishments.

While writing (and teaching), I have been thinking a lot about international students, mine and yours. I find great differences among students, those within any country as well as those from across the seas. We all know a bit about research cultures in some places, but seldom enough to teach directly for those cultures (Smith, 2002). I think we should not try to prescribe the practices best suited out there, however suitable they seem where we are. We need to provide some experience with practice, as we do in projects, theses, and dissertations, but we need to emphasize principles, choices, and risks. Those are emphasized in this book.

Even as our cultures vary, I find universal pressures on evaluators to concentrate on outcomes and to be protective of the program. Both are common in evaluation practice around the world. Returning to existing assignments or going for new jobs, our students need to expect to fit in. And yet it is always their responsibility to cast a critical eye, to see the bad with the good, to rock the boat, sometimes only a little, sometimes a lot. Student personalities will vary. The situations they move into will vary. Most will move to conditions appearing stable, and they will contribute to the stability, but also to the change. Some will move toward upheavals, and they need some readiness to protect what is good and to replace what is not. May we serve them well.

Standards-Based and Responsive Evaluation

One of the pressing motivations of this book is the need for evaluators to combine two kinds of thinking and two research paradigms that don't much mix. Often they are called qualitative and quantitative. It's fine to call them that.

Figure 2   The Young Lady and the Old Woman

I choose to call the one "responsive" or "interpretive" and the other "standards-based" or "criterial." Too many names? Perhaps, but a lot more than numbers keeps them apart. And they should not be kept too far apart. With Jennifer Greene, Yvonna Lincoln, Sandra Mathison, Donna Mertens, and Kathryn Ryan (1998) showing the way, qualitative and quantitative can be joined. They can both be used nicely in a single project, as Daniel Stufflebeam did in the appendix example (see also Reichardt & Rallis, 1994). It is rather difficult, however, to be simultaneously deeply involved in these two kinds of thinking about program quality.

I am calling the one kind of thinking *criterial* to build upon the analysis of descriptive variables and the other *interpretive* to build upon experiential, personal knowing in real space and real time and with real people. A personal narrative is likely to mention criteria, but its take on merit will be known to audiences through vicarious experience. An analytic statement often will make reference to personal experience, but its take on merit will be known to audiences through propositional statements implying standards. These two ways of thinking may stand side by side, but like an optical illusion (Figure 2), only one is seen at a time.

Evaluation studies that rely mostly on numbers and criterial thinking are recognizable as *standards-based* studies. Not only do they emphasize criteria for description and judgment, but they allude to explicated standards of merit. They often construe merit and shortcoming in terms such as productivity and effectiveness and the ratio of cost and benefit.

Evaluation studies that rely from beginning to end on interpretive thinking are also steadfastly responsive to the chronological activity, the perceptions, and the voices of people associated with the evaluand. I call these studies *responsive* because many of the important meanings of organization and accomplishment and goodness are situational, reflecting and responding to the locality of the evaluand. Responsive evaluation studies emphasize social issues and cultural values as well as personal and programmatic dilemmas.

But the differences are neither mainly in the choice of research question nor in the choice of method; they are differences in mind-set. Is merit the attaining of a measurement standard, or is it the attaining of human esteem? Yes, it can be both. And we do a better job if we seek both, not to merge them into a single judgment but to let their differences stimulate us to deeper thinking.

In the early chapters of this book, I will develop these two perspectives slowly. You may need to help the students tolerate the redundancy. You may need to help the students understand and challenge my duality. Hopefully, together we will encourage them to develop additional skill in both camps. These perspectives are not, of course, something I have dreamed up; they have been well recognized by philosophers of science and experienced evaluators for many years. One of the primary sources of my own departure from strictly quantitative, psychometric research was von Wright's (1971) *Explanation and Understanding*. But many young and old evaluators do not see the worldview difference that von Wright discusses. You may have seen the interesting debate in the *American Journal of Evaluation* by two leading theorists, Mark Lipsey and Tom Schwandt (2000). Both were persuasive, but to many readers, they appeared to fail to engage each other. Each put his case rationally, persuasively. I am going to insert the first exchange here so that you will be brought fresh into the difference and separation between criterial and interpretive thinking. Let's wait until later in the semester to have the students try to catch these two winds a-blowing.

Meta-Analysis and the Learning Curve in Evaluation Practice[1]

Mark W. Lipsey

Progress, far from consisting in change, depends on retentiveness. Those who cannot remember the past are condemned to repeat it.

George Santayana

---

[1]From the *American Journal of Evaluation*, 21(2) 2000, 207–212. Mark W. Lipsey is Professor of Public Policy, VIPPS, Vanderbilt University. Reprinted with permission from Elsevier.

Is every social program unique? Well, yes, in many ways each is, just as every person has a unique mix of characteristics. At the same time, family resemblances among programs make it fairly easy to categorize them according to the type of social problem they address, the intervention approach they use, and the social and political context within which they operate. We can view social programs, therefore, as variations on recognizable themes with only an occasional innovation so distinct that it defies categorization. Evaluators, service providers, and policy makers thus converse comfortably about family preservation programs, services for domestic violence victims, anti-smoking campaigns, needle exchange programs, outpatient psychotherapy, reduced class size in elementary schools, and numerous other such program types without great confusion about what they mean.

It follows from these family resemblances that there are common themes in the issues evaluators must consider in evaluating programs of a particular type and telling policy makers how well they work. Correspondingly, it would be an advantage to the evaluator to know a great deal about the research and evaluations that have already been conducted on similar programs. This information might tell the evaluator if this type of program is generally effective for ameliorating the target problem, what variations in client population, program process, and intervention mode are most critical to success, what intended and unintended outcomes might occur, and so forth. Even with very distinctive, innovative programs it is likely that insights from the most similar known program situations would be useful in focusing and designing an evaluation.

These observations are, admittedly, rather straightforward and mundane. What makes them worth discussing is the curious fact that the evaluation field gives remarkably little attention to the systematic cumulation of knowledge from evaluation studies and the use of that knowledge in designing evaluations and informing policy makers. It is not at all unusual in evaluation practice to see planning documents and final reports that make little or no reference to anything learned from evaluation of similar programs elsewhere.

It is not altogether clear why evaluators so often take a de novo approach to evaluation. Perhaps the exigencies of practice do not provide time to assemble relevant information from other studies in a form useful for evaluation purposes. Or, it may be that many practicing evaluators believe that the differences among programs are more important than their commonalities and thus presume there is little generalizability from what is known about other programs. Whatever the reason, it seems that evaluators most often rely on their own experience and judgment to identify the important features of the programs they evaluate rather than turn to the lessons to be gleaned from prior evaluation of similar programs.

Despite limited development and application, I want to argue that systematic summaries of evaluation studies in a form useful to program design, evaluation, and communication with policy makers is an important part of the evaluation field. Such systematic summaries can come in many forms—quantitative (as in meta-analysis), qualitative, and "mixed methods" as may be appropriate for different issues and different sources of information. In the remaining portion of this paper I will develop this argument by identifying some of the contributions such systematic summaries might provide to the field, with meta-analysis illustrations from my work and my colleagues.

WHAT WE MIGHT LEARN

Taxonomy and terminology. The family resemblances that allow us to talk generically about various program approaches are easily recognized but not well identified, labeled, and organized in the field. Systematic review of evaluation studies could lead to clarification of the major dimensions along which programs vary and the ways of categorizing their similarities and differences. Such a taxonomy—a sort of periodic table of the elements for social programs—could be useful in various ways. For instance, a good taxonomy would provide a framework for organizing information from prior evaluation studies so that an evaluator assessing a particular program could quickly locate the most relevant instances of previous work.

The meta-analysis studies my colleagues and I have conducted over the last decade on juvenile delinquency programs give some illustration of the kind of dimensions along which useful program taxonomies might be organized. In analyses with various subsets of the over 500 intervention studies represented in our database, certain distinctions among programs have regularly asserted themselves either conceptually or in relation to program effects on delinquent behavior.

For example, program effects are consistently stronger for structured, behavioral, and/or skill-building interventions than for those using a more insight-oriented approach, such as counseling, group therapy, and casework (Lipsey, 1995). We also find many differences in personnel, organization, and context between programs provided to institutionalized delinquents (in custodial facilities) and those on probation and participating in community-based programs.

Another critical variable relates to whether the program is an ongoing "practical" program routinely provided in the relevant institutional or community context or a "demonstration" program organized primarily for research purposes and/or administered by researchers (Lipsey, 1999). In short, the analyses we have done on descriptive and outcome data from hundreds of evaluations identify certain key characteristics that are generally important in relation to program functioning. A classification of programs based on those characteristics makes more meaningful practical distinctions than the labels customary in this area, most of which focus narrowly on the treatment modality, such as, token-economy, vocational training, social casework, tutoring, family counseling, and so forth.

Critical factors. Aside from the general distinguishing characteristics of programs, there also may be more specific features that are critical to the effectiveness of particular program types. It is only by examining variation across programs within an intervention area that we are able to see the differential effects of some of these characteristics. Once identified, however, knowledge of these critical factors sensitizes the evaluator to aspects of the program that may warrant special attention and that may explain success or failure.

One of our meta-analysis projects, for instance, revealed that the effectiveness of wilderness challenge programs for delinquent youth depended critically on the intensity of the physical activities involved and whether they were accompanied by therapeutic enhancements such as individual or group counseling (Wilson & Lipsey, 2000). Another meta-analysis of studies of rehabilitation treatment for institutionalized juvenile offenders unexpectedly highlighted program personnel as a critical factor (Lipsey & Wilson, 1998). The effects were considerably larger when the treatment was administered by mental health personnel than when administered by juvenile justice personnel. An evaluator working with programs of these types will be better informed about potentially important program characteristics with the benefit of such insights from prior evaluation studies.

Generalizability and robustness. One of the difficulties in evaluating a specific program is that the evaluator often has little basis for knowing which aspects of the program work in relatively predictable ways and which are very distinctive to that particular program situation. A given intervention, for instance, may be known to have positive effects when used with some client populations but it may be uncertain whether those effects generalize to a different population of current concern to the evaluator. Similarly, one variation of a service may be effective, but that may not be true of another variation, especially when applied in a different program situation.

One contribution systematic summaries of evaluation findings can make to practice is to provide a basis for assessing how generalizable or robust the effects of various program features are. If we find that a type of intervention generally has positive effects on certain outcomes over a range of variations in its implementation, target populations, and the like, the evaluator has some assurance that similar effects are likely in a program not yet evaluated.

A finding from our meta-analyses of delinquency intervention is that effects on reoffense rates do not differ greatly according to the characteristics of the juveniles receiving treatment. In particular, the age, gender, and ethnic mix of the client samples are not related to the magnitude of the program effects (Lipsey, 1992). This does not mean that evaluators working with a program of this type should ignore the possibility of differential response to intervention among these groups. But, knowing of this pattern in hundreds of prior studies, an evaluator with limited resources has some assurance that it would be reasonable to design the evaluation with the expectation that there will not be large interactions involving client demographic characteristics.

What effects to expect. Over a number of evaluation studies in a particular program area, evaluators will generally examine a broad range of outcome variables. Some of these may show program effects and some may not. Knowing this will help the evaluator determine what effects warrant assessment and, hence, should be built into the evaluation design. At the same time, prior studies give some indication of the magnitude of those effects as they appear on various measures and guide the evaluator toward a design sensitive enough to detect such effects if they occur.

An important finding from our meta-analyses of delinquency programs, for instance, is that the effect sizes for subsequent delinquent behavior are much smaller than those on virtually all other outcome domains examined, including psychological (attitudes, self-esteem), interpersonal (peer or family relations), school attendance, academic performance, and vocational accomplishment (Lipsey, 1995). The lesson for the evaluator of such a program is twofold. First, if it is important to determine effects on re-offense rates, care must be taken to ensure that the design is sufficiently sensitive to detect a modest statistical effect (note that the practical significance may be greater than the statistical effect suggests). Second, the evaluator who examines only effects on offense rate may miss large, important effects in the other domains.

Choice of method and procedure. One of the more interesting aspects of systematic cumulation of evaluation research is the contribution it makes to our understanding of the strengths and weaknesses of the methods evaluators use. With sufficient methodological information in a database of evaluation studies, it is possible to make an empirical examination of the relationship between observed intervention effects and the various evaluation designs, outcome measures, and data collection procedures used by evaluators to generate those observations.

A dramatic and sobering finding from meta-analysis concerns the amount of variation in observed intervention effects across studies that is associated with methodological and procedural characteristics of the studies. That portion is about equal to the portion associated with the substantive aspects of the intervention—type of treatment, dose, quality of implementation, recipient characteristics, and the like (Wilson, 1995). In other words, the evaluator's finding about program effects on a given outcome variable seems to be influenced as much by the evaluator's methodological choices as by the actual effectiveness of the intervention. Clearly, this situation requires the evaluator to exercise great care in those choices and draw as much as possible on existing knowledge about method effects in designing an outcome evaluation.

Several specific results of our meta-analytic examinations of the role of method in evaluation are potentially useful to evaluators. Among the more general are indications of the widespread use of statistically underpowered designs with little capability to detect meaningful effects (Lipsey, 2000). An important implication is the inadequacy of statistical significance as a basis for deciding if effects are found and the relative advantages of other decision criteria. Other meta-analysis work has shown that the evaluator's choice of outcome measures and the timing of measurement can be as important to the findings as the selection of control groups or assignment to treatment conditions (Lipsey, 1992). Similarly, meta-analyses of prior evaluation studies have cast light on the degree to which various impact designs (e.g., nonrandom assignment, prepost) may be biased in different applications (Lipsey & Wilson, 1993). Indeed, what cumulative synthesis of prior evaluation studies can teach us about evaluation methods would, by itself, justify the effort of conducting such syntheses.

CONCLUSION

Meta-analysis and other forms of systematic synthesis of evaluation studies provide the information resources for a continuous improvement program for evaluation practice itself. By examining the patterns and relationships revealed by meta-analysis, an evaluator will better understand what program characteristics, outcome domains, and research methods are most likely to be important for a particular evaluation effort. As new evaluation studies are completed and added to cumulative syntheses, the knowledge resources of the evaluation field will become richer and more differentiated and their potential contribution to practice, in turn, will become more useful.

At present it is apparent that the field is well short of an effective integration of research synthesis and evaluation practice. As noted earlier in this paper, evaluators do not routinely review prior evaluation work in any great detail when planning an evaluation. Meta-analysis of evaluation studies, in turn, is not available for many program areas and, when available, these meta-analyses may provide only global information, such as mean effect sizes, which is of limited use for planning or interpreting an evaluation study.

Meta-analysis is developing at a rapid rate, however, and differentiated, focused syntheses are increasingly available in the program domains of interest to evaluators. The time is ripe to encourage both the production of more useful meta-analysis and more use of meta-analysis products in the evaluation field.[2]

REFERENCES

Lipsey, M. W. (1992). Juvenile delinquency treatment: A meta-analytic inquiry into the variability of effects. In T. D. Cook, H. Cooper, D. S. Cordray, H. Hartmann, L. V. Hedges, R. J. Light, T. A. Louis, & F. Mosteller (Eds.), *Meta-analysis for explanation: A casebook* (pp. 83–127). New York: Russell Sage Foundation.

---

[2]An especially interesting and promising development in this regard is the recent launching of a "Campbell Collaboration" at the University of Pennsylvania to foster the synthesis of research on social intervention. This endeavor is modeled on the successful Cochrane Collaboration, which has produced hundreds of useful research syntheses in medical and health domains over the last decade.

Lipsey, M. W. (1995). What do we learn from 400 research studies on the effectiveness of treatment with juvenile delinquents? In J. McGuire (Ed.), *What works? Reducing reoffending* (pp. 63–78). New York: John Wiley.

Lipsey, M. W. (1999). Can rehabilitative programs reduce the recidivism of juvenile offenders? An inquiry into the effectiveness of practical programs. *Virginia Journal of Social Policy & the Law, 6*(3), 101–129.

Lipsey, M. W. (2000). Statistical conclusion validity for intervention research: A significant (p < .05) problem. In L. Bickman (Ed.), *Validity and social experimentation: Donald Campbell's legacy,* Vol. I (pp. 101–120). Thousand Oaks, CA: Sage Publications.

Lipsey, M. W., & Wilson, D. B. (1993). The efficacy of psychological, educational, and behavioral treatment: Confirmation from meta-analysis. *American Psychologist, 48*(12), 1181–1209.

Lipsey, M. W., & Wilson, D. B. (1998). Effective intervention for serious juvenile offenders: A synthesis of research. In R. Loeber & D. P. Farrington (Eds.), *Serious and violent juvenile offenders: Risk factors and successful interventions.* Thousand Oaks, CA: Sage.

Wilson, D. B. (1995). The role of method in treatment effect estimates: Evidence from psychological, behavioral, and educational treatment intervention meta-analyses. Doctoral dissertation, Claremont Graduate School, Claremont, California.

Wilson, S. J., & Lipsey, M. W. (2000). Wilderness challenge programs for delinquent youth: A meta-analysis of outcome evaluations. *Evaluation and Program Planning, 23,* 1–12.

Meta-Analysis and Everyday Life: The Good, the Bad, and the Ugly[3]

Thomas A. Schwandt

Professor Lipsey offers an important argument for using meta-analysis to provide information on the efficacy of various social interventions as well as insight into the design of evaluation research on those interventions. The following is less a response to Professor Lipsey's paper per se than a second opinion based on a brief meta-theoretical investigation of the technique of meta-analysis. By subjecting the method, its assumptions, what it takes as "givens," and the methodology in which it acquires meaning to some careful scrutiny, I hope to reveal the good news, the

[3]This response to Mark Lipsey appeared in the *American Journal of Evaluation, 21*(2) 2000, pp. 213–219. Thomas Schwandt was at the University of Illinois at Urbana-Champaign.

bad news, and the potentially really objectionable news that attends the deployment of this method.

Meta-analysis, cluster evaluation, integrative research reviews, Foucault's archaeology and genealogy, and the like, are methods that make it possible for us to talk about human experience in general. Thinking and talking about experience in general is patently necessary simply to get along in everyday life. If we could not conceive of and speak about roses, tires, bread, pain, success, fear, health, families, violence, and so on in general, we would have a very hard time communicating with one another and we would face the impossible task of remembering every event and instance in particular. Thus, the good news about a method such as meta-analysis is that it makes possible (and assumes) a kind of general knowledge that, as Professor Lipsey says, allows us to "converse comfortably" about a variety of social phenomena "without a great deal of confusion about what they mean." Thus, we can talk about your family and my family, even though the notion means very different things to each of us—what the family actually is or was in each case is most likely constituted in very different ways.

The potential bad news about the use of a method like meta-analysis is that one begins to forget that in fact there *is* a great deal of confusion about what social phenomena mean. This mistake usually follows from forgetting that (a) there is no idiom in which reality prefers to be described, and (b) meta-analysis is part of a particular idiom (or language of methodology) that dictates how social reality is to be perceived, comprehended, described, and represented (Gubrium & Holstein, 1997). That idiom makes it possible to describe the essentially intentional phenomena that constitute social life (e.g., being a member of a family, marrying, joining, healing, teaching, participating, negotiating, evaluating, etc.) in general non-intentional ways. Consider the following example, which I have adapted from Fay (1996).

Suppose we describe an event as follows: "Beginning on May 3, 1997, Mary Smith, a long-time user of heroin and other hard drugs, enrolled in the sixteen-week Mt. Sinai drug rehabilitation program. She participated for the full 16 weeks and was discharged." To explain this event, *as described in this way,* we would need to understand what "enrolled," "participated," and "discharged" meant. That, in turn, would require that we either grasp the intentions of the actor(s) involved or the intentionality of the acts of "enrollment," "participation," and "discharged" themselves. But if this same event is described in a non-intentional manner as "a drug addict completed a drug treatment program," then, *as described in this way,* this event is amenable to an explanation requiring general information about drug addicts and drug treatment programs. The first kind of explanation is idiographic and reflects an abiding interest in the particularity, specificity, and uniqueness of the event.

The second kind of explanation is (more or less) nomological and treats all unique events such as this in terms of what they have in common—as an instance of a class of events—so that it is possible to talk generally about a recurring pattern.

There are two important points to be seen here: First, social reality does not demand a certain idiom by which to be described. We may all readily (and quite correctly) acknowledge that human action is clearly intentional in nature (versus, for example, the nonintentional behavior of natural phenomena), that its meaning is open and heterogeneous. But we can choose to describe, represent, and interpret social actions *as* intentional phenomena (as, for example, is done in interpretive anthropology, ethnomethodology, symbolic interactionism, etc.) or we can choose to describe social action in general, non-intentional ways (as is done in meta-analysis). The "bad" news about meta-analysis arises when we mistake efforts to *describe and represent* social phenomena in general, non-intentional ways for the belief that this is precisely the way social phenomena *are.* The possibility of describing human action so as to eliminate its intentional, language-impregnated, discursive, historical character is often too easily confused with assuming that human action is *necessarily* arranged in something like a "periodic table of the social elements." This is an error of reification: treating our language of description and representation *as if* it denoted a material and concrete reality.

For the sake of argument, let us assume that we understand that meta-analysis is a means of generating general knowledge, as described above, and that its users are mindful of the danger of reification inherent in mistaking the application of the method for the way the world really is. We must now address the following questions: What do we do with this kind of knowledge in evaluation? In what kind of framework is it deployed? What do we think having this kind of knowledge means for the human activity we call doing evaluation?

I believe an even greater peril, a truly objectionable state of affairs, lurks just ahead. This becomes apparent in examining the association of meta-analysis as method with evaluation as a technical project—an activity dedicated to managing the social world through objective knowledge obtained by method. (Please note that in what follows I am not claiming that Professor Lipsey makes this association in his paper.)

Of course, by no means is the technical view of evaluation associated only with perspectives that endorse the merits of meta-analysis as a technique. Virtually all forms of evaluation practice in contemporary society (whether they are so-called quantitative, qualitative, participatory, or mixed-method approaches) both constitute and are constituted by this view.

There is a long line of thought stretching from the prewar period in Europe to the present day in which thinkers as diverse as Bergson, Husserl, Nietzsche, and Heidegger, and closer to the present, Gadamer, Arendt, Adorno, Habermas, Taylor, and Bauman share a broadbased criticism of modern technicism and the hegemony of method in the study of human affairs. All argue that there is something seriously amiss in a society that assumes that technical mastery of human action through objective knowledge is a viable project.

Even a cursory glance at any major statement of the purpose and role of evaluation in society will reveal that evaluation is a thorough manifestation of this modern project. Evaluation is a technology for assigning value to objects, events, processes, and people. It is a practice built around the assumptions that (a) evaluative information makes possible the improvement of society through the rationalization of various kinds of social practices, such as, the formation of social policy, the implementation of educational programs, social services, and medical and psychological treatments, the administration of these programs, and so forth, and (b) there is a best means of generating and delivering this information to clients, administrators, or managers to ensure the realization of their goal of an ordered society.

The aim of the modernist project of evaluation is to tame the unruly social world, to bring order to our way of thinking about what does and does not work for improving social life. As currently conceived, evaluation is one of those human endeavors like administration, management, health care, and education that reflect the mistaken belief in the manageability of everything human, and in which method is increasingly allowed to define and circumscribe our entire view of the world (Schwandt, 1998).

This attitude or posture of bringing everyday life under control, of managing it and ordering it, is captured in the following observation: As human beings we give ourselves to—or find ourselves in—projects through which we shape our environments and our relationships with each other.

In the history of this projecting, particularly since the rise of modern science in the seventeenth century, we have moved more and more into a position where, as "subjects," we confront a world which is ours to objectify and control. And, increasingly, the substance of our human lives has become part of this objectified world over which we exercise mastery. Our lives are resolved into a series of projects—all our "wanting and doing," our "making, producing and constructing"—occur within this overall project or "frame" of mastery itself.

It is this frame which defines the scope of our ambitions and the meaning of success; our attitudes, our modes of thought, the very questions which are our problems arise already within this framework or else are smoothly, and inexorably, assimilated to it (Dunne, 1993, p. 366).

As a modern technological project, evaluation practice begins with the reasonable assumption that the activity of evaluation is a type of moral-political social interaction conducted by ordinary folks in a variety of settings and circumstances where these people invariably both know and act. In these settings (classrooms, administrative offices, social service agencies, etc.), actors' evaluation knowledge is intimately connected with ordinary ways of conducting themselves, with relating to others, and with getting things done.

However, evaluation practice assumes that these highly contingent ways of evaluating and judging that occur in the course of everyday life can be and ought to be brought within the scope of a more scientifically managed view. That is, there ought to be both a body of knowledge and a set of explicit methods and rules that will supplant (or, at the very least, significantly reduce) the contingent, unreliable evaluation understanding and judgment of everyday practitioners and thereby ensure the success of their performance.

Meta-analysis is but one of many techniques used in the service of this goal. The aim of the modernist evaluation project is thus to convert the rationality implicit in evaluation practices associated with teaching, managing, providing health care, offering social welfare services, and so on into technical rationality and thereby to overcome as much as possible the contingencies and conditionality of human life (Dunne, 1993).

The guiding knowledge-constitutive interest of evaluation practice is what Habermas (1974 [1971]) and others have identified as the technical cognitive interest—an interest grounded in the notion of purposive-rational action and directed at controlling and manipulating the natural and social worlds. There is nothing inherently "evil" in this interest in technique, means-end rationality, and productive, method-driven knowledge. The problem lies in the fact that this interest and its associated conception of knowledge have increasingly come to characterize all of human life in modern societies.

Gadamer (1992 [1965]) makes this point in the following way: It would be no exaggeration to claim that we owe the modern phase of the industrial revolution not so much to the advances in the natural sciences as to the rationalization of their technical and economic application. What appears to me to characterize our epoch is not the surprising control of nature we have achieved, but the development of scientific methods to guide the life of society. . . . The scientific tendencies of thought underlying our civilization have in our time pervaded all aspects of social praxis. Scientific market research, scientific warfare, scientific diplomacy, scientific rearing of the younger generation, scientific leadership of the people—the application of science to all these fields gives expertise a commanding position in the economy and society. And so the problem of an ordered world assumes primary importance (p. 165).

This does not mean that society is deformed simply because experts in evaluation, management, and so on are consulted for their knowledge. The danger lies in the mistaken belief that we can *apply* this conception of knowledge to the "concrete life situation of people and the practical exercise of their commonsense rationality" (Gadamer, 1992 [1965], p. 171).

The more we believe that it is both possible and desirable to transform the kind of knowledge and rationality suited to moral-political human interaction (i.e., praxis) into a kind of technical knowledge and means-end rationality, the more we risk our responsibility to ourselves and as citizens of a society to reflect on and criticize our practices. This deformation of praxis—bringing its unique kind of knowledge and rationality within the frame of technical mastery—aided by, among other developments, the modern technologies of evaluation, electronic communication, and practices of administrative coordination is readily evident in all aspects of human interaction. Consider, for example, efforts to rationalize the practice of education by focusing on measurement of student achievement and other "output" indicators, to manage the delivery of care for the health of others in terms of indicators of cost-effectiveness and efficiency, and to develop the science of public administration.

None of this means that knowledge of the kind that Professor Lipsey explains can be generated by meta-analytic techniques is without merit or value. The issue is not to confuse the production of general knowledge generated via such methods with the kind of knowledge necessary for actors in classrooms, meeting rooms, and board rooms to make wise evaluation judgments. Even a perfect evaluation technology of society will not guarantee wise practical choices when evaluation is called for because the knowledge required in the concrete situations of everyday life is a different kind of practical knowing.

As a modern professional practice, evaluation is a scientific undertaking, the technical province of a particular kind of expert. It is an activity that has to do with making or production—an activity designed to bring about and terminate in a product or result, namely, an evaluation judgment of the merit, worth, or significance of some person, policy, program, and so on. The product/result (the evaluation outcome as reported by the evaluator) is separable from the one who produces it; the knowledge required for (or which governs) this activity also is separable from the user of that knowledge. In other words, it is a kind of activity in which one can decide to willfully participate or not participate: Monday through Friday, the evaluation expert "puts on" her evaluation knowledge to make the "product" of an evaluation. On the weekends, that knowledge is set aside when the evaluator is not engaged in "making" evaluations.

This mode of productive activity is associated with a kind of practical knowledge called *techne*. This is knowledge possessed by an expert in a specialized craft—a person who understands the principles underlying the production of an object or state of affairs, such as, a house, a table, a safe journey, a state of being healthy, or an evaluation. This kind of knowledge fits smoothly into a means-end framework: The materials and tools (including methods) of this kind of practical knowledge are means used by the maker to bring about the end product/result. Practical knowledge itself is a means to the achievement of the final product as the end of the activity. Evaluation as a productive activity is thus under the firm control of an objective, impersonal method (whether qualitative, quantitative, or "mixed").

The professional practice of evaluation as this kind of expert productive activity fails to make sense of and relate to evaluation as a dimension of praxis. Praxis is a form of human activity that has to do with the conduct of one's life and affairs as a member of society. The distinct mode of practical knowledge associated with praxis is *phronesis*. This is neither a technical nor a cognitive capacity that one has at one's disposal, but rather is bound up with the kind of person that one is and is becoming. This kind of knowledge characterizes a person who knows how to live well; it is acquired and deployed in one's actions with one's fellow human beings. This kind of knowledge is variously referred to as deliberative excellence, practical wisdom, or practical reason. Associated cognitive virtues are understanding, judgment, and interpretation.

The kinds of evaluative decisions that we make as a part of our everyday life (in our interactions with our children, colleagues, spouses, significant others, friends) and as part of the practices to which we belong and the associated responsibilities that we have as teachers, health care professionals, social workers, public managers, and so on are moral-political actions. They are a kind of human interaction and activity that leaves no separate identifiable outcome as its "product"—hence, the end (aim) of the activity is realized in the very doing of the activity itself.

In conversation with my daughter I evaluate her reasons for wanting me to lend her money to buy a car. The aim of the evaluative activity here is to make a wise judgment. The evaluative decision that I take as a result shapes both her and my own sense of my being a father.

In conversation with a student, we review a recent paper submitted by the student for a seminar that I led. I offer my evaluation of the paper; the aim of the activity is to help the student develop and strengthen her perspective and to offer criticism in a constructive way. The evaluative decision that I take as a result shapes my sense of being a teacher of a particular kind. The "outcome" is about formation of self (hers and mine) in the encounter with others.

The same kind of phenomenon occurs when a manager and team of service providers together evaluate whether their agency is effective in helping their clients. The "outcomes" of these evaluation activities are not decisions about which "program components" are "working," what to do about changing "client demographics," or what to do about "differential responses to the treatment." Rather, the "result" of the evaluation is a particular way of being toward and interacting with these clients, conceiving of their needs, regarding them as persons of a particular kind, and grappling with the question "are we doing the right thing and doing it well?"

The contingency, situational specificity, inherent openness, and ambiguity of evaluating cannot be eliminated, reduced, or made more manageable by having the "right" kind of technical knowledge. Evaluation is not a decision-making process that can be rationalized by *applying* better technologies. It is a human activity, a social interaction requiring moral political judgment. It requires general knowledge of all kinds—knowledge of concepts and relations between concepts involved in various practice situations (health care versus education, for example) as well as knowledge of techniques of communication, case-based knowledge of strategies previously used and found successful in particular circumstances, unformulated knowledge of pitfalls and difficulties to be anticipated and avoided, knowledge of the aims of the practice and what both fosters and subverts and transforms those aims, and so on (Dunne, 1993). But the judgment required to make use of those stocks of knowledge in the situation at hand—deploying that understanding in relation to right person(s), to the right extent, at the right time, given the right aim, and in the right way—is simply not a kind of knowledge that is forthcoming from the application of method and a conception of evaluation as a technique.

Modernist conceptions of evaluation supplant rather than develop this kind of wisdom and intelligence in practitioners by divorcing the activity of evaluation from the kind of knowing and acting that constitute evaluative interactions with others in everyday life. Thus, the truly objectionable move potentially associated with meta-analysis (and with all efforts to find method-driven solutions to the "problem" of praxis) is assuming that evaluation is a technology for managing human affairs and believing that somehow practice will be less ambiguous or more rational if we can only find the right ways to generate and apply evaluation knowledge. (Of course, effective resistance to this move will not be forthcoming from a neo-romantic, unrealistic longing for a premodern society. Nor will the modernist project of eclipsing praxis by technique be obstructed by so-called third paradigm or mixed-methods approaches that continue to unfold within the frame of mastery, or by postmodern approaches to evaluation that retreat into the aesthetic and the play of language, deny the concrete reality of everyday life, and elevate the contingency and concrete situatedness of choice-making into a radical, universal perspectivism.)

General knowledge is an important way of thinking about ourselves and our actions. Of course, then, we should do meta-analyses and other forms of evaluation synthesis (e.g., cluster evaluation, integrative literature reviews, etc.). But we should not invest in these tools on the mistaken technicist assumption that better technical or craft knowledge (better methods, rules, or procedures) will eliminate the interpretive challenges of evaluative praxis and thereby yield a science of human action.

We must learn to become responsible to and for ourselves and our circumstances. The activity of evaluating does not lie outside ourselves in the effectiveness of objects (e.g., programs, treatments, interventions, projects, and their components) and actions divorced from our ways of being in the world. Decisions about the merit, worth, or significance of our actions are about our own self-formation and responsibility to others. We must help practitioners see themselves as students and researchers of their own evaluative practices rather than consumers of evaluation aided by outside experts.

REFERENCES

Dunne, J. (1993). *Back to the rough ground: "Phronesis" and "techne" in modern philosophy and in Aristotle.* Notre Dame, IN: University of Notre Dame press.

Fay, B. (1996). *Contemporary philosophy of social science.* Oxford: Blackwell.

Gadamer, H.-G. (1992). Notes on planning for the future. In D. Misgeld & G. Nicholson (Eds.), and L. Schmidt & M. Reuss (Trans.), *Hans-Georg Gadamer on education, poetry, and history: Applied hermeneutics* (pp. 165–180). Albany, NY: SUNY Press (Originally appeared in *Daedalus, Journal of the American Academy of Science, 95,* 572–589 [1965]).

Gubrium, J. F., & Holstein, J. A. (1997). *The new language of qualitative method.* Oxford: Blackwell.

Habermas, J. (1974). *Theory and practice* (abridged version of *Theorie und praxis,* 4th ed. Frankfurt am Main: Suhrkamp Verlag, 1971). J. Viertel (Trans.). London: Heinemann.

Schwandt, T. A. (1998). The interpretive review of educational matters: Is there any other kind? *Review of Educational Research, 68*(4), 405–408.

Issue 21, Number 2 of the *American Journal of Evaluation* also carried the next round of the debate. Each continued speaking from his own world view. Lipsey moved again to make standards-based evaluation more integrated into social science and existing quantitative research. Schwandt pleaded for a further move away from criterial thinking and toward practice-based experience as a foundation for evaluation.

In this book, we will not analyze the debate. It is out there. But the two realities of which they speak are also out there, and the new evaluator needs to know there is language and practice for both. The languages and thinking of the two will remain separate, as will the methods. Each new evaluator will choose more of one than the other, but whether by plan or not, each will use both. It is in our nature to be both criterial and interpretive. This book should help the student feel comfortable using both.

I hope that you enjoy teaching with this book. You will have opportunities to make this a formative experience, hopefully not a summative experience, for the students.

1

Criterial and Interpretive Evaluation

The earth brought forth vegetation, plants yielding seed according to their own kinds, and trees bearing fruit in which is their seed, each according to its own kind. And God saw that it was good.

Genesis 1.12

And the Lord God commanded the man, saying, "You may freely eat of every tree of the garden; but of the tree of the knowledge of good and evil you shall not eat, for in the day that you eat of it, you shall die."

Genesis 2.16–17

Accordingly, evaluation has been with us for a long time. And there is much more to come. It goes without saying that God knew the difference between good and evil but provided no indication here how they can be distinguished. When He saw the vegetation was good, He may have had criteria in mind, but such were not recorded in the Scriptures.

God indicated that Adam should not know what is good and evil but exposed him to the opportunity to know—an opportunity that, with the help of Eve and the Serpent, Adam took. It is a knowledge handed down generation to generation. We are born evaluators but not necessarily good evaluators. And although we also know Good and Evil, that alone does not put us on the side of Good.

You aren't reading this book to learn about informal evaluation. In academic and organizational settings, the term *evaluation* implies a formal, deliberative procedure. That is what this book is about. But formal evaluation always has informal, intuitive, casual, self-serving sides to it. So it behooves us to do a lot of thinking about how formal and informal evaluation are related.

Informal evaluation might argue that it is better than formal evaluation because we (Homo sapiens) as a species have survived. We are the fittest, or at least fitter than those who did not survive. Luck was probably involved, but it is safe to say that survival meant making a lot of the right choices. And choosing is a matter of evaluation. Since there wasn't much formal evaluation, as we know it today, before 1950, and even the courts, hospitals, priestly councils, and sciences are modern inventions, we might well conclude that it was informal evaluation, not formal evaluation, that got us this far.

For formal evaluation to be better than informal, we need to be satisfied that it helps us to recognize goodness better—and without costing too much. Is it okay if formal evaluation causes us to change our minds as to what goodness is? We will be wondering about that throughout this book.

But even if we persuaded ourselves that usually it would be better to evaluate our programs informally rather than formally, much of this world expects formal evaluation to be more trustworthy, more likely to provide reliable evidence of quality. It is usually a good idea to think carefully as to whether formal or informal evaluation fits better, but when it is said that a program evaluation is needed, it probably means formal evaluation. Most of the writing of this book is about formal evaluation, but we will take time to consider informal evaluation too.

Formal and informal are important, but much more important for strategic thinking in evaluation is the distinction between *criterial evaluation* and *interpretive evaluation*. Criterial evaluation is the determination and representation of quality using numbers and scales—that is, with criteria. It is quantitative evaluation—more objective, analytic, and standards-based. Interpretive evaluation is the determination and representation of quality through subjective experience, using verbal description and vicarious experiencing of merit and shortcoming. It is qualitative evaluation—more episodic and holistic. The teenager who describes a basketball slam dunk as "a perfect ten" is using criterial evaluation; one who describes it as "like Michael Jordan" is using interpretive evaluation. In Chapter 3, under the title of Standards-Based Evaluation, we will dig deeply into the meanings, procedures, and merit of criterial evaluation. A chapter later, under the title of Responsive Evaluation, we will dig deeply into the meanings, procedures, and merit of interpretive evaluation. A strong connection will be made between interpretive evaluation and responsive evaluation, but they are not the same.

The Ubiquitous Search for Quality

We look for merit and shortfall all the time, consciously and unconsciously. We manage to ignore it when it's trivial. We sometimes fail to see it when it would embarrass us, such as the skill of a rival or the illogic of our own argument. But we are constantly sensitive to thousands of ways things can go wrong. Our survival has depended on things going right. We are self-correcting mechanisms, internally wired to correct what we do. In the world of communications, we depend on having good receptors, decoders, and review mechanisms to evaluate the messages coming in and going out. Many of these messages are extremely complex. Most of them are part of the domain of informal evaluation.

In the world of duties, contracts, assignments, and supervision, there is great need for formal evaluation. Monitoring is made explicit, grades are assigned, billing codes used. Sometimes a policy, decision, or problem requires formal review procedures. They may be as brief as a glance or may last years. Informal evaluation is a big part of both primitive life and modern life; formal evaluation is a big part of modern life, especially corporate and institutional life. We have to rate the evaluand.

I cannot avoid using the word *evaluand*. It is not a pretty word, but talking about evaluation is just too awkward without it. The thing measured is the

Morning Scene, by Ernest Olson

Reprinted with permission of the artist.

evaluand. If we evaluate a training program, the program is the evaluand. If we evaluate shampoo, shampoo is the evaluand. If we evaluate a candidate for a job opening, the candidate is the evaluand. In the cartoon above, there are three evaluands. It may irritate other people to talk such jargon, but while talking among ourselves, we will talk about the evaluand.

> **evaluation** *n* the comparison of the condition or performance of something to one or more standards; the report of such a comparison

One definition of our business reads something like the "dictionary" definition given here. The standard indicates how good it ought to be. People have to set the standard. There is no other source of standards than people's ideas of quality. Sometimes the evaluator sets the standard. Often, different people set different standards. Sometimes it is useful to try to get them to agree on a single standard, but evaluators have no choice but to work with multiple standards.

To evaluate a training program, we would examine the training procedures and the performance of the trainers and perhaps the performance of the trainees during and after training. We need separate standards for each comparison. Evaluation might be a pretty simple business if we had standards that everyone agreed on. But we often cannot find standards that even the same persons continue to agree on as conditions change. Setting standards is an extremely difficult task.

When I first started theorizing about evaluation,[1] I proposed that one should gather data to show what people considered to be relevant standards for our evaluands. But I found such information almost impossible to draw from authoritative sources. And the questions about standards I put to staff members and stakeholders[2] were seldom answered in useful ways. Well, what would you say if I asked you your standard for a good textbook? You might give an example, such as Richard Jaeger's (1993) statistics book. You might point out some criteria by which you evaluate books, including this book—criteria such as readability, informativeness, being up-to-date, and usefulness as a reference book. But those are criteria, not standards. It is far easier to identify

---

[1] I wrote a paper in 1967 called "The Countenance of Educational Evaluation," in which I proposed many different data useful for program evaluation. To some people it became known as the "countenance model," but it was not a model for doing evaluation. The categories of evaluation data I proposed are in Figure 5.1 in Chapter 5.
[2] Stakeholders are people having some investment in or benefit from the program, including sponsors, operators, beneficiaries, and maybe taxpayers.

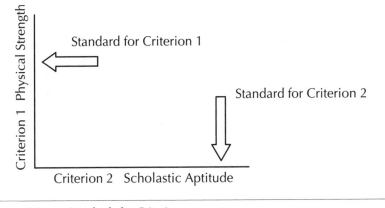

Figure 1.1   Standards for Criteria

some of the criteria we use than the standards that mark the different *levels of quality.*

The terms *criteria* and *standards* are not used in the same way by everyone, but most evaluators use *criterion* to mean an important descriptor or attribute and *standard* to mean the amount of that attribute needed for a certain judgment. Height and stubbornness are personal attributes. Scholastic aptitude is considered to be an attribute of students—a score of 28 on a scholastic aptitude test might be the standard used to decide whether or not the student will be given special education. Those of us who like graphic representations use a line to represent a criterion, and we use a point or range on that line to represent the standard. For example, the two lines (or scales) in Figure 1.1 represent two criteria, physical strength and scholastic aptitude—let's say, for admission to a security officer training program—with the cutoff standards for each criterion represented by points marked by the arrows. It's something you need to know.

Let's spend a few minutes thinking about the concept of *quality.* The word is commonly used in two ways. The word *qualities* refers to the characteristics of something, such as the qualities of a musical comedy or the qualities of Nelle's teaching. Speaking of these qualities is more a matter of description than judgment. To describe the qualities of music, we use such terms as lyrical, sonorous, earthy, conventional. To describe the qualities of teaching, we use terms such as creative, conventional, child-centered, and lacking focus. Here's a phrase from John Dewey (1939): "self interest and sympathy, opposites in quality." These uses of the word *quality* refer to the nature or content of something, not its goodness.

The other meaning of quality *is* about goodness. The quality of a music performance is its degree of excellence. The quality of a training episode is its merit and shortcoming. This is the sense in which we usually use the term in evaluation work. We are looking for program quality, meaning its merit and worth. But that leaves much unsaid. Just what the quality or merit or excellence is is usually hard to specify and agree upon.[3] The standards we set in words or measurements are often simpler, less complicated, than what we experience personally. When we say that the quality of a student's writing is mediocre, we are sensitive to many aspects: its coherence, topicality, grammar, creativeness, penmanship, timeliness, word play, conformity to assignment, even to some qualities that we do not think about in advance—but not all of these every time and not weighted the same from time to time. Criterial thinking is important, but so is interpretation.

I am one evaluator who does not find it necessary to be highly explicit as to the quality I am looking for. Some evaluators try hard to be explicit. But I am wary of using a single or even just a few criteria, wanting to become experientially acquainted with the collection of aspects of the program. Some evaluators prefer to devote their resources to measuring the best single or the best several criteria they can. We will examine both strategies in the chapters ahead, linking criteria to standards-based evaluation and linking interpretation to responsive evaluation—but neither exclusively.

Another difference among some of us evaluators is the "epistemological" perception of quality. When you think of the quality of the cantaloupe you are eating, you may think of goodness as a property of the melon. Or you may think of quality as defined by your response to eating the melon. Does the quality belong to the melon or to the experience? Notice that the latter requires more attention to who is doing the eating. Evaluators differ as to how much attention they give to who is experiencing the evaluand. When you think of the quality of a performance in performance testing, you may think of it as a property of the performer or some kind of interaction between the performer and the judges.

You don't have to agree with me, but I like to think of the origin of quality as found in human experience. I see little use for the concept of quality without human experience. There is quality because people experience quality. And over the ages, the positive experiences that have counted most are comfort, contentment, and happiness; and the negative experiences, discomfort, anger, and fear. What we quickly recognize as high-quality teaching or cantaloupe is rooted, I think, in present and past experience with them. By now, we may have developed formal or informal standards, conventions, or traditions to grade melons and teaching, but the roots of the meaning of quality are in the emotional experience it has evoked over time. A watch is of high quality partly because it keeps good time and has finely tooled parts, but also because people find it highly

---

[3]Robert Persig (1974) wrote *Zen and the Art of Motorcycle Maintenance* to examine the philosophical and practical difficulties in defining quality. It contrasts the quality of experience in cycling the open road with the quality of calibration that has the motor purring like a kitten.

satisfying and superior to other watches they have known. What this makes us evaluators sensitive to, as we go about the business of evaluating things, is to recognize that quality depends a lot on who has been experiencing it.

Standards

A girl says that she won't go out with a boy shorter than herself. Her goal is to be the shorter. The criterion she is talking about is height. Her standard is five foot seven, her own height.

A *standard* is how good a boy or a book—or anything else—needs to be. How readable does the book need to be to be satisfactory? How up-to-date does it need to be? Can a single book be good for all readers? Those are hard questions. And we would not necessarily agree on how we should measure those qualities. Should an expert on textbooks decide? Should the evaluator decide? Should the evaluator spend much of the evaluation budget trying to get stakeholders to reveal the levels at which the product changes from unacceptable to acceptable or from good to excellent? Sometimes it will be useful to do so; usually not. Sometimes it will be useful for the evaluator to set arbitrary standards, and watch to see how they work. Often it will be useful not to define what is good until after the condition or performance is closely examined.

Speaking from special knowledge about artistic performances and productions, Elliot Eisner (1969) spoke of *expressive* objectives or standards—standards and criteria that are not realized by the evaluator as relevant until well into the evaluation. Upon observing nurses at work, even if we know quite a bit about nursing, we might wait until after studying their special responsibilities and local constraints to decide what the standards are—as well as how the evaluation information is to be used. And even then, we might make decisions as to the quality of their work without referring to any explicit standards.[4]

> The State of Texas wanted to assure that every public school teacher could read English above the fifth grade level for students. But when they tested the teachers, that standard failed too many teachers, and certainly too many teachers of pre-school, special education, auto mechanics, and bilingual students (Popham & Kirby, 1989, p. 5).

---

[4]One problem is that people change standards. And sometimes they change because the evaluation has exposed new information about standards. Evaluators like to think that they are opening people's eyes to new thinking. But isn't it possible sometimes that people are being attracted to bad standards?

It is a tricky business. On many occasions we evaluators would like to be explicit about the criteria and standards we are using. But the standards do not materialize when we need them.

The problem is similar for student assessment. The cutting scores (standards) for state-mandated standardized student testing (discussed in the Web appendix, http:// www.sagepub.com/stake/ evaluation/webappendix, as Issue 4) result from political sensitivities. They are based less on the qualification needed than on what standard won't raise too much fuss. In almost all the program evaluation work we do, there are no fixed standards and no good ways of fixing them. In one fashion or another, we need to hold up the performance for people to examine and then decide, "Is this good enough?"

Personnel evaluation and product evaluation, as we will see in the final chapters, are different from program evaluation. With persons, more often than not we have many persons, and we can compare them among themselves rather than hold them up to an absolute standard. With products, we can compare several examples of the same product to others and decide which is the best in terms of certain criteria. Direct comparison is more useful there than in program evaluation.

For its product comparisons, *Consumer Reports* identifies a number of criteria and compares relative "performance" on those criteria. It works fine if the comparisons are based on criteria relevant to the reader, if *CR* does a good job of measuring performance, and if the evaluation task is identifying which product should be purchased. Evaluation is a quite different process if there is only a single evaluand to be evaluated.

With program evaluation, we usually have but one program needing evaluation. We raise questions like "Is this program working well?" "What are the strengths and weaknesses in this program?" "Does this program meet professional standards?" Sometimes, the organization has some alternative programs to chose among, such as with training programs or quality control programs, but usually a program exists alone, even with many parts. Its merit and accomplishment need to be better understood, and grounds for improving the program or replacing it need to be set forth. This is not a natural situation for comparison of programs.

We have two strategic choices: to try to compare it to another program, a model program; or to try to compare it to a set of criteria that represents a model program, with standards marking different levels for each of the criteria. Let's talk about the more holistic comparison, program to program. Probably the most attractive idea of evaluation is to compare the program to an ideal, to what the evaluand ought to be or ought to become. Here is the evaluand; there is the ideal we are comparing it to. The ideal is the standard. But an "ideal" program never exists. For ourselves, we can imagine an ideal, but an imaginary standard is hard to describe to other people. Sadly, there is almost

(Text continued on page 13)

Table 1.1   *Consumer Reports* Comparisons of Brands of Ice Cream

Product	Per Half-Cup Serving			Comments
	Cost (cents)	Calories	Fat (grams)	
Vanilla				
Excellent				
Dreyer's/Edy's Dreamery	74	260	15	Balanced, full, and creamy, with real vanilla flavors. Denser than most.
Häagen-Dazs	80	270	18	Balanced, full, and creamy, with real vanilla flavors. Denser than most.
Ben & Jerry's World's Best	81	250	16	Balanced, full, and creamy, with real vanilla flavors. Denser than most.
Very Good				
Breyers Natural	28	150	9	Balanced dairy and real vanilla flavors. Icy texture detracts.
Breyers Calcium Rich	27	130	7	Balanced dairy and real vanilla flavors. Icy texture detracts. Supplies up to triple the calcium of others.
Good				
Dreyer's/Edy's Grand Vanilla Bean	27	140	8	Decent. Slightly icy.
Kirkland Signature Super Premium (Costco)	25*	270	18	Eggnoglike flavor. Slightly gummy and slick. Denser than most.
Blue Bell Homemade	28	180	8	Eggnoglike flavor. Variable quality.
Turkey Hill Vanilla Bean	24	140	8	Mild flavor. Slightly gummy and slick.
Private Selection Premium Vanilla Bean (Kroger)	31	160	9	Mild flavor. Slightly gummy and slick.
Lactaid Premium Classic	38	160	9	Mild flavor. Slightly gummy and slick. Reduced lactose.

(Continued)

Table 1.1   (Continued)

Product	Per Half-Cup Serving			Comments
	Cost (cents)	Calories	Fat (grams)	
America's Choice Premium Vanilla Bean (A&P stores)	20	140	8	Low flavors and lack of freshness. Slightly gummy and slick.
Prestige Premium (Winn-Dixie)	17	160	9	Cloying sweetness. Slightly gummy and slick.
Albertson's Premium	21	150	9	Muted dairy flavor. Slightly gummy and slick.
Dreyer's/Edy's Homemade	27	130	7	Not a clean vanilla flavor, with chocolate notes and artificial impression. Slightly gummy and slick.
Blue Bunny Premium Homemade	28	160	8	Big imitation vanilla impression, with a cloying, commercial sweetener flavor. Slightly gummy and slick.
Dreyer's/Edy's Grand Light	33*	100	3.5	Mild, with lower dairy flavor than most. Slightly gummy and slick.
Breyer's Light	28	110	3	Nonfat dry milk impression, with mild vanilla. Icy.
Dreyer's/Edy's No Sugar Added	28	90	3	Imitation vanilla impression with a slight chemical aftertaste. Gummy and slick.
Sam's Choice Homemade (Wal-Mart)	17*	150	8	Sweet, with big imitation vanilla flavor and chocolate and alcohol notes. Gummy and slick.

Chocolate

Excellent

Godiva Belgian Dark	81	280	17	Intense, rich, and complex high-quality bittersweet-chocolate flavor. Creamy smooth. Denser than most.

(Continued)

Table 1.1   (Continued)

| Product | Per Half-Cup Serving | | | Comments |
	Cost (cents)	Calories	Fat (grams)	
Häagen-Dazs	80	270	18	Balanced big-dairy and high-quality chocolate flavors. Creamy smooth. Denser than most.
Very Good				
Prestige Premium (Winn-Dixie)	18	160	9	Full dairy and complex chocolate flavors. A bit chalky.
Dreyer's/Edy's Grand	28	150	8	High-quality chocolate balanced by dairy flavors
Good				
Breyers	27	160	9	Frozen chocolate-malted flavor. Icy.
Turkey Hill Dutch Chocolate	24	150	8	Typical basic chocolate. Slightly gummy.
Blue Bell Dutch Chocolate	28	160	8	Typical basic chocolate. Somewhat icy.
Private Selection Premium Classic (Kroger)	31	150	8	Bitter chocolate flavor, with a harsh note. Slightly gummy.
Blue Bunny Premium Homemade	27	150	8	Slightly fruity and malt flavors, otherwise basic chocolate. Slightly gummy.
Albertson's Premium Chunky Chocolate	21	160	9	So-so, but decent chocolate chips. Slightly gummy.
America's Choice Premium (A&P stores)	20	150	9	Low on flavor. Somewhat icy and slightly gummy.
Sam's Choice Homemade (Wal-Mart)	17*	150	7	Imitation chocolate impression, with nonchocolate flavors. Cloying, lingering sweetness. Gummy.
Dreyer's/Edy's Light No Sugar Added Triple Chocolate	28	100	3	Low chocolate flavor, not enhanced by bits and swirls with an imitation chocolate impression.

(Continued)

Table 1.1   (Continued)

| Product | Per Half-Cup Serving | | | Comments |
	Cost (cents)	Calories	Fat (grams)	
Healthy Choice Premium Low-Fat Chocolate Chunk	26	120	2	Lower chocolate flavor than most, with nonchocolate flavors. Waxy chips.
Butter Pecan *Very Good*				
Häagen-Dazs	80	310	23	High-quality vanilla with nuts, but without butter-pecan character. Denser than most.
Breyers	26	170	12	Mild vanilla with big, flavorful, crunchy nuts, but without butter-pecan character.
Dreyer's/Edy's Grand	26	160	10	A respectable maple-flavored butter pecan with decent nuts. Slightly gummy.
Good				
Turkey Hill	23	170	11	Mild butterscotch flavor with slightly soft nuts. Slightly gummy.
Blue Bunny Premium	27	170	10	Imitation butter impression and few nuts. Gummy and slick.
Blue Bell	28	180	11	Tropical fruit notes and cloying sweetness. Icy and slightly gummy.

SOURCE: Consumer Reports Ice Cream Ratings Report, http://www.consumerreports.org/static/0207ice1.html

NOTES: Comments give detail on flavor, texture, and density. Our trained taste panel expected a creamy, smooth product with definite dairy flavor (less so for chocolate ice creams), little iciness, and no texture defects such as gumminess, slickness, or grittiness. Chocolate ice creams were expected to have a touch of bitterness and astringency, without harshness. Butter-pecan ice creams should have a buttery quality.

Products lost points for medicinal, artificial, or other off-notes. Cost per half-cup serving is generally based on the national average price for the most common package size—a pint for the products that were rated excellent plus *Häagen-Dazs* butter pecan, a half gallon for others except *Kirkland Signature* vanilla (a gallon) and *Lactaid vanilla* (a quart). An asterisk (*) denotes the price paid. Nutrition information comes from labels. Some store-brand products are made by more than one manufacturer; we may not have tested all version of those products.

never a real program that even approximates the ideal. It is the same for the "minimally satisfactory" condition or performance. An example of a border-line program seldom actually exists, and if it did, it would take all our evaluation resources to establish the fact. Again, seldom is there an actual program, and certainly not several different equivalent programs, to serve as a tangible standard for directly evaluating our evaluand.

To evaluate samples of penmanship or air quality, we can set up a reference bank of graded samples. Each new sample can be placed somewhere on the graduated scales. With programs having many complexities and without anything close to a storehouse of graded samples, we cannot evaluate programs in this classical way.

> **standard** *n* 1. a conspicuous object at the top of a pole to mark a rallying point esp. in battle or to serve as an emblem 2. Something established by authority, custom, or general consent as a model or example: criterion

What we usually do is shift away from the idea of a single ideal totality to the idea of a collection of criteria for rating the evaluand. On each important variable, we set cutting scores or zones of quality, and we check the condition or performance of the evaluand to see what criterial standards it surpasses. The problem was mentioned earlier: It is very difficult even for experts to agree on the criterial cutting scores.

Often there will be several "reference programs" that could be used for comparison purposes. One can be called a *control group*. In a theory-testing experiment or pharmaceutical trial, cases are assigned randomly to the experimental and control groups, and both are monitored closely so that the only difference between them is the critical treatment or programming. In policy evaluation, as we shall discuss in Chapter 9, such assignment to the two groups can be a workable strategy; but for educational and social programs in the real world, assignment of cases belongs to program operators and communities, not to researchers. Efforts to create a second program as a control group are usually doomed to fail. It has been tried many times, seldom successfully.

Another common design sets up a comparison to the performance of the previous group. Last year's results become the standard. Still another design calls for comparing performance at the end of the programming with performance at the outset. The mean scores on key criteria will sometimes be found to be different, and sometimes the difference will be statistically significant. Statistical significance indicates the two groups should not be thought of as being drawn from one and the same population. In evaluation studies, however, we want to know whether the evaluand performance is a high-quality performance. An external standard is not easy to find. To make it worthwhile to bring in a comparison group as the standard, we either have to have very good advance information on how good that reference group is or we have to study both groups, doubling the work of the evaluation study.

Recognizing standards is an essential idea in evaluation. But stating what the standards are, either for comparison of groups or as a set of reference scales, is far more difficult than just being aware of them. Luckily, we have a solution. We can use the implicit standards people have in their heads. We can measure and describe. We can display the performance or condition of the evaluand to individuals or panels, lay stakeholders or experts, to obtain their ratings. We can interpret and reconfirm the ratings and judgments made. In this way, we can do a pretty decent job of indicating the merit and shortfall of the program. We rely on standards, but mostly the standards that have been built up in the minds of persons by all the experience they bring to the task.

To repeat, the most central idea of evaluation is comparing the program's performance to a standard[5]—or to several standards, such as the ratings "Barely minimal acceptability, General acceptability, and Acceptability so strong that we had better work hard to protect it." Or if the scale of acceptability is multidimensional, we may need several scales to describe everything that matters and then add them up to get a single score of merit for that program. Everything that matters might make a very long list. Some examples of characteristics of a program worth considering are productivity, ease of use, cost, demands for special resources, clarity of purpose, mood, facilitation of communication, public image, absence of negative side effects, and adaptation to local conditions. Each of the characteristics, and perhaps a number of sub-characteristics, needs to be conceptualized as part of the common scale of acceptability. Then the weighted score can be seen to fall short of or exceed any of the standards set by the staff, its patrons, and its stakeholders.

If we use a weighted score in this way, we will be using what is called a *compensatory model:* We will allow a weakness in one aspect, such as a lower physical strength score for security office candidates, to be compensated for by strength in another aspect, such as a higher scholastic aptitude score. Or we will allow a program's ineffective communication to be tolerated because of strength in other aspects, such as almost complete freedom from negative public criticism plus a very low cost. A different approach is called a *multiple cutoff model,* in which a standard must be met on each of several criteria or the whole thing fails. We may set such a standard by saying that no program that

---

[5]Evaluation's venerable scholar Michael Scriven (1994b) placed explicated standards in a central role in evaluation, much as I have presented it in Chapter 3, saying that the synthesis leading to value statements requires two basic tasks: measuring program performance and comparing performance to standards.

requires staffing costs exceeding $50,000 or that fails to get unanimous support of its own trustees will be considered acceptable. Each characteristic can have its own standard or cutoff score.

These comparisons may be done formally, with rather precise measurement, or they may be just a way of thinking. That is, in the back of our minds, we may think of the different characteristics, separately or together, as acceptable or excellent. We may work through the program's strengths and weaknesses intuitively and in conversation with others, but not make any record of the inner workings. Or we may use a checklist, marking each of the characteristics on a scale of acceptability, and use it as the final indication of merit, or as input to further discussion of how good the program is.

Almost everyone expects that in order to evaluate quality, you are going to need to compare performance to a standard. And it is true. But there are lots of ways to behold the evaluand to ascertain quality. And some ways work better than others some of the time.[6]

Criterial and Episodic Thinking

The dictionary doesn't require it, but in research circles—as you probably noticed in the previous section—we conventionally think of a *criterion* as a descriptor of the evaluand, such as its effectiveness, durability, cost, or aesthetic value. And we think of a *standard* as the amount of that criterion that differentiates the evaluand between acceptable and unacceptable, or some other discriminative boundaries or grounds for action. It is jargon, but very useful.

Forty-eight years ago I was in graduate school in a Psychology Department. One day, sitting at my desk, I suddenly realized there is a Social Science of Education because educational psychologists and sociologists were able to transform the phenomena into variables. They had invented the constructs of education, building blocks for disciplined thinking about education, and those constructs they called *variables*. These same descriptive constructs were also called attributes, properties, traits, characteristics, facets, and dimensions. Much of the time they were called *criteria*. By reducing the complex phenomena of classroom, boardroom, history, and community aspiration to variables, one could get a handle on things. Translating happenings into variables is called *criterial thinking*.

A variable is an attribute that takes on more than one value. It can vary in various ways, but social scientists decided to emphasize variables that vary in

---

[6]I wonder if this is boring you. I hope not. These seem to me important things to be thinking about. I am aware that some of your fellow readers just want to be told what to do to carry out an evaluation.

quantity. Amounts vary up and down a scale. So once we identified the construct as a scale, the important thing was to measure the quantity. We can use these quantities to describe, to distribute, to compare, even to make like we are finding causes, and to interpret the identified causes as bases of control, of improvement, of reform. It looked to me like harnessing the atom. With criteria, with *criterial thinking,* we could measure, and with measurement scales, we could move mountains.

With criterial thinking and sampling as our entree, the study of education could be precise, generalization-producing, and useful. Any doubts I had were blown away. I enlisted in the science of testing. I devoted myself to becoming a "measurements man," and I am one still. I am a measurement man. My work is program evaluation. I try to measure the quantity and quality of Education, or of Training, or of Social Service, the merit and shortcoming, the elusive criteria of teaching and learning.

My psychology tells me that the alternative to criterial thinking is *episodic thinking.* Educational phenomena come to be known through episodes, happenings, activities, events. The phenomena have a time period and a context. They are populated with people having personalities, histories, aspiration, frailty. We sometimes talk about personality and frailty, contexts and episodes, in terms of variables. The more the episode is important as a life event, the more the criteria remain in the background. Almost anything can be converted into variables. The problem is, conversion often oversimplifies and underrepresents. We may gain a handle and lose our grip on the situation.

Criterial thinking and episodic thinking exist, side by side, in our communication and in our brains. With some kind of binocular resolution, we resolve the disparity, unconsciously, into a unity not attainable from either criterial or episodic thinking alone. In Chapter 9 we will refer to it as a *dialectic.*

Roles and Styles of Evaluation

Evaluation is the pursuit of knowledge about value. Much of that knowledge emerges from personal experience, often from our own awareness. I know that Allopurinol is good medicine for me because without it I have kidney stones, and with it I do not. What the doctor tells me is important, and I can read about stones in *The Wellness Encyclopedia* (1991), but I pay a lot of attention to my own experience. I can't always depend on experience, but I will use it regularly—and the experience of people I know, and the indirect experience and reasoning and research of people I do not know. I put all of the knowledge together, and with crudeness and precision, I know the value. It helps also to drink lots of water.

Evaluation is always a determination of merit and shortcoming. Sometimes it is a lot more, but the essential function is the determination of merit. That is the first purpose. That is the definition. That is the *sine qua non*. I overheard a woman in the waiting room telling an acquaintance she was an evaluator. "What do you do?" "I help people lose weight." "Why do you call yourself an evaluator?" "People are more inclined to do what I say if I'm an evaluator rather than a dietician." Dieticians are evaluators too, but if she primarily helped people with weight loss, she was misleading people by passing as an evaluator. Can people call themselves whatever they want? Pretty much, they can. But we will communicate better if we speak of an evaluator as someone who, within some sphere of activity, seeks out and reports the merit and shortcoming of an evaluand. I will develop ideas about the roles of evaluation and predilections of evaluation in the next chapter.

The value determined can be used for lots of different purposes, such as improving a process, awarding a prize, assigning remedial teaching, or recognizing contracts fulfilled. These are some of the many roles in which evaluation is used.

Formative and Summative Evaluation

One of the key distinctions among roles for evaluation is the distinction between formative and summative evaluation. Michael Scriven drew everybody's attention to these in his 1967 essay, "The Methodology of Evaluation." Most readers interpret the distinction as between intermediate and final efforts to evaluate a program, but a more valuable distinction is between evaluation that serves new program development and evaluation that serves day-to-day program operation. My interpretation is that when the chef tastes the soup, it's formative evaluation, and when the guest tastes the soup, it's summative evaluation.

Both the developer and the program manager have questions such as "Are the explanations too complicated?" and "Is the material up-to-date?" But the developer, ever redesigning programs, seeks information to create them better. So he or she asks, "How long should this phase be applied?" and "Should we require participants to have access to the Web?" An evaluator studies alternative length phases and Web-based versus Web-free use to find the merit of the alternatives. The formative evaluator thinks of evaluation as part of a change process, providing information that helps change the developing evaluand. Most internal evaluators spend more time on formative than summative evaluation.

On the other hand, when the question is "How well did the evaluand work in this particular situation?" it is summative evaluation. The evaluator here is not looking at ways of modifying the package as much as finding out its quality, its productivity, its defects, its costs—given certain staffing, program recipients, and stakeholders. The summative evaluator is likely to try to measure the effects of the evaluand. In product evaluation, where the consumer is trying to decide which software or rotary mower to purchase, it is summative evaluation. The consumer chooses among alternative models, sometimes each having its own formats, materials, personnel, and service agreements—and wants to know the relative merits of the packages.

It is not uncommon for an evaluation study to include both formative and summative components. A faculty development program is evaluated to measure change in instructor awareness and disposition to use new guidelines, but also to help decide how to run the training next time. A teacher and a photocopy machine repairman both evaluate what they are doing because they need to know the results, but almost at the same time, they consider modifying their next work. Formative and summative evaluation can happen together, but the roles of formatively looking forward and summatively looking back are worth keeping separate.

The Evaluand

Earlier in this chapter we identified the thing that is being evaluated as the evaluand. But already we need to expand that definition. Programs to be evaluated are ill-defined in the sense that it is often not easy to agree upon what is inside and outside the boundaries of the evaluand. If the evaluand is the training of agency personnel to write better correspondence, we may need to decide on whether that includes more effective composition of e-mail, memoranda, and oral exchanges. We need to decide whether that includes the coaching that the mentors subsequently give their mentees. We may need to decide whether the program advocates the omission of relevant information in order to reduce the reader's confusion. Just what the evaluand is is seldom adequately described in its authorization, its budget, its technical manuals, or the evaluation contract. Part of the ongoing work of the evaluation is to improve understanding of what the evaluand is.

Psychologists have a concept they call *stimulus error*. If experimenters think it is just an ordinary teddy bear with which they are stimulating the subject (a person), but the subject sees the stimulus and recalls a personal trauma, then the subject's responses may well be misinterpreted. If the evaluation client (the one who arranges for the evaluation) thinks the evaluand is X and the evaluator studies X without considering the part of X called X_1, then the evaluation may be at risk. If a reader of the evaluation report presumes that no mention of the fiscal responsibility of program managers means that the program is fiscally sound, then we may have a problem. Getting a good specification of the evaluand is an important step, but additional steps may be needed to minimize the chances of stimulus error.

Often, only a part of a program is to be evaluated; thus, the evaluand is not the whole program. Still, the evaluator may need to look into the rest of the program to understand the merit of the evaluand. Or the evaluand may be a family of programs. It may be a particular intervention that is implemented in different ways at different sites—and the qualities and the quality of each may be different. The evaluator's report should include definition and description of the evaluand.

The Evaluator

There is no one personality type or collection of skills or methodological inclination that makes the best evaluator—old and young, men and women, city people and rural folks, measurement specialists and interpreters of experience. Of course it helps in most tasks to be intelligent, logical, and well-read—and for some tasks, genial and stubborn and with a sense of humor. Of course there are many different ways to do good work, and the profession is better because it has a diversity of approaches and role models. Diversity is good not only because the situations needing evaluation are of many kinds, but also because we learn how to do things better by seeing how others do it differently.

In much earlier times, strengths and weaknesses in a scientific field (e.g., psychometrics) or professional specialization (e.g., radiology) were evaluated by colleagues, fellow members of the guild. People attended small scientific meetings and published their works in a small number of periodicals. Today, thousands meet at conventions,[7] and the journals are highly specialized. In spite of an ever-growing ease of communication shrinking the world, the number of practitioners has so expanded that most remain out of touch with all but a few others. Most evaluation reports are not circulated. Books and journals are reviewed too slowly to have a strong corrective effect on how we carry out our evaluations. If strengths and weaknesses are not examined while the evaluation is being carried on, they often go unrecognized. This ongoing evaluation is partly carried out by members of a team or by visitors who do "their thing" in a different way.

Only a few evaluators are on their own; most work for an organization. Their boss has a boss who has a boss. Even though there are lots of choices to make in carrying out an evaluation, you as an evaluator have to abide by someone else's choice. There are evaluation offices, corporations, consultancies, and

---

[7]The American Evaluation Association is an affiliation of 3,000 evaluation practitioners and administrators from around the world. Its annual meeting in 2001 was held in St. Louis and had 1,200 registered participants. On the Net it is www.eval.org.

> **culture** *n* 1. cultivation of the soil 2. the ideas, customs, skills, arts, etc. of a people or group, that are transferred, communicated or passed along to succeeding generations

shops—big and little. Most of the research corporations that do program evaluation, such as Rand Corporation, SRI International, World Bank, and KPMG Peat Marwick, employ large numbers of technical specialists who work tasks and routines seldom decided by the individual evaluator. One of the best evaluation shops in the 1990s was the evaluation division of the U.S. General Accounting Office headed by Eleanor Chelimsky. Although the staff was large, many of her evaluation studies were designed by one or two people and carried out by one or two others.

To some extent, sometimes to a great extent, the evaluator is operating out-of-culture. Cultures have their own traditions, languages, values, organizational structures, aesthetics, and mannerisms. The evaluator belongs to one or more cultures, ethnically but also to the culture of a department, a coterie, a profession. The evaluand's staff and stakeholders share some cultures, yet subdivide into subcultures and sub-subcultures.

The campus culture is different from the business culture, which is different from the government culture; there are subcultures within each of these three, and even a subculture varies over time and place.

Evaluators, even internal evaluators, will seldom know thoroughly the customs and values of the cultures of the evaluand. The evaluation consultant to another country can expect to be insensitive to many expectations. The instructor in an evaluation class should expect "foreign students" to be skeptical that recommended procedures and illustrated reports would be acceptable back home. The same may be true for any student feeling outside the current classroom culture. Part of carrying out an evaluation contract is an examination of cultural expectations in and around the evaluand.

A common cultural conflict occurs when the evaluator expects to examine a problem broadly and the program manager considers that to be outside the territory to be evaluated, or when the evaluator expects to inform a number of audiences and the manager considers the information privileged. The evaluator sometimes expects greater access to meetings, personnel, and files than the organization allows. The evaluator may have a research background, bringing expectations that the pursuit of knowledge should be open and forthright. Beyond protecting private knowledge, many organizations, including families and ministries, with reason, discourage inquiry into what has not been made public. As part of negotiating a contract, gathering data, and making preliminary reports, the evaluator tries to be sensitive to the informal boundaries of acceptable conduct.

An evaluator from Singapore is on assignment to evaluate a UNESCO program in India. Program specifications call for an external objective evaluation, but she recognizes that there is staff reluctance to provide access to program activities and records. Her requests that the recipients provide evaluative information are met with objection. The evaluator has studied evaluation in the Netherlands as well as at home. Although the expectation of her Dutch colleagues for openness and access appeals to her, she is constrained by her experiences over the years, including at the Ministry of Social Service in Singapore. She finds the constraint at this site in India even greater. In terms of what she studies and what she reports, she needs to take positions somewhere within these forces:

- Her self-perception as an evaluator
- The perception of her by the program people and Indian officials
- The customs and operations of the evaluand hosts
- The ethics and expectations of the profession
- The need to help those responsible for the program
- Her desire to have opportunities for future evaluation assignments

These forces will affect her performance as issues of gender, class, and ethnicity come into focus. If she were to follow her instructions blindly, she would gather little data and be of little help to the authorities and program recipients. She needs to fit into the expectations of her hosts, but not completely—compromising, finding a few critical ways, often small ways of moving, toward the ideology of her profession.

That does not mean that the evaluator will comply with all rules and expectations. The task of the evaluator is to come to help the audiences comprehend the quality of the program being evaluated.[8] Each evaluator needs

---

[8]That usually happens by the evaluator's first coming to understand program quality and then informing others. But audiences also learn some things about program quality from what the evaluator does that are too subtle or contextual for the evaluator to understand. The accomplished evaluator seeks ways of helping audiences enhance their own understanding. More of this in Chapter 4.

to find compromises, neither being entirely oneself nor masquerading as a member of other groups and cultures.[9]

As to technical expertise, some evaluators specialize in the work of evaluation but apply themselves to a range of topics, programs, contents, and fields. We call them independent or external evaluators—independent if they have no affiliation with the evaluand, external if they are outside the organization. Other evaluators are internal or topical evaluators—internal because they are inside the organization, topical if they claim expertise only in the topic being evaluated. They tend to stick to a particular field, or even to a small range of topics, such as water quality or highway safety or power point presentations. Many of them do other things besides evaluation: administration, teaching, promotion, research, customer relations. Some evaluators spend a great portion of their work soliciting contracts—writing proposals to compete with others for contracts. Some professional evaluators wait to be asked or assigned to evaluation projects.

An evaluator makes mistakes. Making mistakes is not bad. Making mistakes and finding it out and not doing anything about it is bad. We humans, including the experts too, start to make mistakes all the time, but those who have a good self-evaluation mechanism, lots of self-challenge, a self-correcting system—those people can keep mistakes at a minimum. Of course, too much self-doubt, too much inhibition, keeps one from doing what needs to be done. So we look for a balance between self-confidence and self-challenge.

A thermostat is a self-correcting control device. So is cruise control on your car. When your car starts to slow, it automatically pumps more gasoline; going downhill, automatically, it brakes. You set the standard speed, and the car stays at that speed. In most of our behavior, we don't know what speed we want. We don't know numerically what standard to set, but we have good sensitivities as to what is too much and what is too little. As long as we are paying attention and have some control, we can correct the mistakes. We can be pretty good self-correcting mechanisms.

A manager plays that role for an organization. An evaluator temporarily plays part of that role for a program, providing feedback information that may

---

[9]*Participant observation* is an approach to field study practiced particularly by ethnographers studying distant cultures. It is their intent to inquire by playing an active role in the communities they study, adopting the local language, activities, and mores as best they can. It is an artifice, serving the purpose of research, not a real entry into the culture. The researcher is expected to understand that he or she will continue to interpret the meanings of things largely in terms of his or her home culture. A few professional evaluators use participant observation in their field study, but seldom have the time and other resources to carry it very far.

be used for exercising control. There are always questions as to which criteria to be monitoring, what issues to be sensitive to. If neither the manager nor the evaluator nor the stakeholders are sensitive to dangers, the crash may not be avoided.

The evaluator needs to rely on a personal sense of program well-being. But that intuition or impression will not be sufficient. The well-designed evaluation program will incorporate various checks and balances to recognize that the program is veering off course or endangering its riders. The question "What may be going wrong?" needs raising again and again. The evaluator cannot rely on his or her own sensitivities alone, or on the sensitivities of others on the evaluation team. The evaluator needs to set up review mechanisms to validate observations, to reanalyze data, to challenge interpretations. Representations of program quality need to be examined again and again. Thomas Jefferson said, "The price of liberty is eternal vigilance." The evaluator says, "The price of valid evaluation is eternal vigilance."

We sometimes call it *meta-evaluation*—the evaluation of evaluation. Sometimes meta-evaluation is thought of as an extra, external study to authenticate the process or product of the evaluation. It is that, but it is also all the informal reviewing and even the self-corrective monitoring that checks for mistakes in evaluation along the way. We will examine the construct of meta-evaluation in Chapter 6, but suffice it for the moment to recognize that the price of validity is eternal vigilance.

Whether vigilant or not, an evaluator is usually working on several assignments or contracts at the same time. There is too little time to do the work the way he or she would like to do it. There is too little time to pilot the instruments right. There are too many sites to be visited. Feedback from *member checking* and review panels is slow in returning. The project probably wasn't budgeted to do it right in the first place. Proposals are often underbudgeted to submit a more competitive bid. It is a wise boss or client who knows how to protect against the crunch. Part of the work of the evaluator is coming to know the implication of cutting corners on validation and interpretive writing, and being able to argue effectively for an extension. That isn't what most of us enjoy doing, but for many evaluators, it is the real world.

Nevertheless, the satisfactions of evaluation work can be deep and joyous. Coming to understand the program and its complexities is deeply rewarding. So is it to prepare a report that will be examined with pride for years. Becoming familiar with what program connoisseurs recognize as quality gives one a sense of great personal accomplishment. This is a line of work that has great challenges and great rewards. There is no limit to the depth of understanding that one can aspire to in the evaluation of even some pretty ordinary programs.

Narrative

Mr. Sagredo calls Phyllis in.

Sagredo: I was thinking of a new assignment for you for a while. Could you do an evaluation of our Senior Mentor Training?

Phyllis: Maybe. I have some familiarity with it, but it would help if you describe the training to me.

Sagredo: Well, in order to get our senior people mentoring more effectively, we got Vivani Associates to set up these computer programs for self-instruction, with some group activity. It takes about six hours, preferably at three sittings. The main idea is to help the mentor know what to do and what not to do. The trainees joke about it, saying, "Can't we learn some of the mistakes on our own?"

Phyllis: Does that mean they think the training is trivial?

Sagredo: Well, I don't know. They are really busy at their work, and they may see it as not the kind of training that could help them the most.

Phyllis: So the evaluation would need to consider not just whether the program is working but whether it's a good use of staff time?

Sagredo: I hadn't thought of that. We mostly want to know if they are giving good advice. The evaluation should show how good this training is.

Phyllis: A randomized experiment might provide the greatest certainty. Do you want mainly to find out if this training approach works well in general?

Sagredo: Let's not spend our money to find out if the approach would work elsewhere.

Phyllis: Could we limit the measurement of positive and negative effects to a few criteria?

Sagredo: I want to know all the benefits—and the problems.

Phyllis: Who gets trained?

Sagredo: All the senior professionals, including managers. Not the support personnel. Especially in CS (the customer service group), everyone is expected to mentor the new employees. They are expected to e-mail each participant at least once a week. Most of them paste in paragraphs of technical information, or they adapt standard memos. They are the people for whom the training is targeted.

Phyllis: Do you think they already knew how to be a mentor but didn't have the time or inclination?

Sagredo: That's a good question. I suppose a lot has to do with motivation.

Phyllis: Did your consultants from Vivani talk about that when they set up the program?

Sagredo: Yes, they assured us that the training materials would increase the sense of importance of communicating well with the new people. I wonder about personal attitude. Isn't coaching first an interpersonal matter, then a matter of the technicalities of the organization?

Phyllis: As you know, I am not a specialist in organization development or in mentoring skills. It could be that you need further help from task analysis more than evaluation, but that is one thing an evaluation study could help you decide. Are you satisfied the program was designed for such a group?

Sagredo: Won't we know that when we see the increase in quality of advice the mentors give?

Phyllis: Well, we should find out how well they *can* coach people as well as how well they *are* coaching them. It could be that the training approach is excellent but the staff is not properly prepared for it. And it could be that the senior staff people mentor in a way that ignores other things but best meets deadlines. If we simply look at the outcomes of the training, we might fail to learn what you need to know.

Sagredo: Would you just have them tell us if they took the training seriously?

Phyllis: Yes, we should ask. Under some circumstances, they might not be candid. Still, it's important to ask.

Sagredo: These are really fine people. Why wouldn't they be candid?

Phyllis: They might worry that someday today's low enthusiasm might hold back their promotion. Or they may want to avoid embarrassing someone. I don't presume they have an inclination to deceive us. I just like to be wary.

Sagredo: Do you understand the goals?

Phyllis: We probably should look at what is stated in writing, but we should also suppose that different people see the purposes of the training project somewhat differently. Or did you mean the goals of the evaluation?

Sagredo: Yes, of course, there are goals for each, and there, too, different people will have different expectations. Wouldn't that be your responsibility, to write down the goals of the evaluation?

Phyllis: Yes, I could prepare a draft, and you could indicate how they ought to be changed.

Sagredo: How can I learn more about how you would carry out the evaluation?

Phyllis: I would prepare a proposal, a design. Since evaluations sometimes need to change along the way, it might be useful for you to look at some evaluation reports prepared in the past. This will give you some idea of how evaluators deal with problems as they come along.

Sagredo: Could we count on you to be favorably disposed to the aims of the training?

Phyllis: I can tell you now that I support such training generally, but I will have to consider the present circumstances. I think you will be able to tell from the proposal what I consider to be the promise and the risks of the training. We can expect to need to negotiate some things. Once we have agreed on the proposal, it would serve as an assignment for me—more or less a contract, until the contract needs to be renegotiated.

(To be continued)

2

Roles, Models, and Dispositions

The world will little note nor long remember what we say here . . .

Abraham Lincoln

Gettysburg Address

One of the roles for evaluation is *action research*. Action research is evaluative self-study, either by an individual or an organization, usually with the intent to improve things. Or it can be done just to understand things better. Or it can be done to support a protest. For teachers, social workers, and nurses, it sometimes is a form of professional development, presuming that some of their obstacles or ineffectiveness may be reduced if the right information is found. For them, questions of what is competence and what is of merit are highlighted. Action research can be a personal and institutional effort to evaluate the practices.

Sara, a labor and delivery nurse, is concerned about how she deals with the companion of the mother-to-be (husbands are rarely the problem, lesbian partners and mothers sometimes, drunk lovers always, she says), a companion present in the delivery room at the time of the baby's delivery. With all else going on, she realizes that their feelings are often ignored, and in moments of crisis, she has thought they were in the way. But she recognizes that this

(Continued)

important time sets the stage for the new family unit and a course for the mother's and baby's lifelong health and well-being. So Sara wonders about the anguished and helpless looks on the companion's face during the laboring process and wonders what actions and statements would include and empower the partner (while still keeping him/her out of the way).

Sara's staff development coordinator suggests doing a little action research: observing a delivery or two when she is not on duty, audiotaping and analyzing tapes of deliveries for which she is on duty, and interviewing some of the partners a few weeks after the baby is born. She does it and studies the information. She carefully rereads hospital policy (which states that two people may be present, but nothing about their significance or treatment) and an article in the *American Journal of Maternal and Child Nursing*. Sara discusses her data with the coordinator and a fellow nurse. That's it. She does not need to count up critical incidents or write a report, but she could. This is action research[1] and can contain all the elements of a good evaluation.

Action research is the study not only of one's practice but of oneself. To become a good evaluator, it is important to understand yourself as others know you. Are you predisposed to support authorities, whistle-blowers, advocates of prespecification, free spirits? What are your strengths and your biases? Who you are affects how you evaluate. Sigmund Freud insisted that to become psychoanalytic psychiatrists, students needed to go through psychoanalysis themselves. It was not just to learn the procedure and the experience of a patient but also to gain self-knowledge. One learns something about oneself by conducting evaluations and meta-evaluations, but it is important also to reflect, to inquire into how others see you, and to seek counsel. More on this in Chapters 6 and 9. It is impossible to completely know yourself, and it is important to know that you do not completely understand yourself. You will continue to change, even some from week to week, and so an evaluator's self-study goes on all through life.

Action research is one of the many roles for evaluation. *Role* is both a situation and a purpose. In what situation will you evaluate? And what will you use the evaluation for? A *model* is a particular method of doing the evaluation.

---

[1]More about action research is to be found in Kemmis and McTaggart (1992).

It is expected to be general across situations and purposes. A *disposition* is a value orientation of an evaluator. Some evaluators are disposed to remediate, to help improve the evaluand. Some evaluators are disposed to be explicit about standards. Some evaluators are disposed to make contributions to social science. Others are not. Roles, models, and dispositions overlap; yet it is useful to try to categorize some of their main differences in evaluation studies.

Models

To design evaluations of any kind, one may get advice from experienced colleagues, or find a guide or model in a journal or textbook, or just do what makes sense to learn more about the activity and its worth. The actual work and report of an evaluation study serve as a model for subsequent work. No matter how detailed the design others have written, no matter how well a plan worked somewhere else, a lot has to be done to adapt it to fit another evaluand. It is our purpose in this chapter to look at some of the alternatives. There is no model or approach that drives on cruise control. It has to be thought through.

Many evaluators call the alternative approaches "models." I seldom do. I think of a model as a prototype or template or recipe or ideal. I think the models put forward by us evaluation theorists are too incomplete and idealistic to be called a model. It is not that the model builders are negligent.

The decisions a practicing evaluator has to make are voluminous, far-ranging, and unpredictable. The model builder just cannot provide the guidance I expect of a model. You should feel free to call Daniel Stufflebeam's CIPP Model[2] a model, because he does. We refer to the experimental model, implying a concern for controlled treatments, random sampling, and statistical comparison of dependent variables. Some people call my approach to evaluation the

In 2002, in the Kili region of Tanzania, prepping for her dissertation research, Namkari Msangi evaluated three new private elementary schools on the Kenya border. Children had been sent to these schools from both sides of the border because their parents wanted the "quality education" of an English medium school for them. The perceptions of owners/ managers, teachers, parents, and children were obtained through face-to-face interviews and field observations.

[2]An update on the CIPP Model is to be found in Stufflebeam, Madaus, and Kellaghan (2000). A detailed example is shown as " The Spirit of Consuelo" in our Web appendix.

Countenance Model or the Responsive Model—but I do not. I want newcomers to realize that they may like some things about Responsive Evaluation, but each evaluator will have to make a very different adaptation to suit each situation.

Dispositions

Clearly, there are general orientations or styles or dispositions of evaluators that shape evaluation studies. For example, the predisposition to include patients or trainees actively in designing the study will make it a different study. Another disposition is investing heavily in data-gathering instruments. Another is the evaluator's disposition to study policy questions in addition to technical questions. In particular, some evaluators are fixated on using goal statements to define the limits of the study. Still others lean toward being of maximum help to the sponsor of the evaluation. And still others, like myself, think of our reports as contributing to the literature of exemplars that may guide future evaluators in their work. One cannot do all these things well at the same time. I sometimes refer to these choices not as models but as dispositions—the dispositions of program evaluation. I sometimes call them persuasions. Most evaluators have several of these dispositions, not compelling them to follow a single, rigid design, but a style. No evaluator participates in all the styles. That is partly because a strong disposition to one or two leaves little energy for other dispositions.

Here are some common dispositions I find among my colleagues:

- An accountability disposition, aiming at assuring program obligations are honored
- A case study disposition, concentrating on a particular case and its complexity
- A connoisseurship disposition, honoring scholarship and expert judgment
- A democratic disposition, active in extending personal protection and choice
- An ethnographic disposition, emphasizing cultural relationships and activity
- An experimental disposition, valuing precise and objective knowledge
- An illuminative disposition, providing what readers might see themselves
- A judicial disposition, emphasizing presentation of arguments for and against
- A naturalistic disposition, valuing ordinary activities in their settings
- A responsive disposition, fixing on issues and values held by stakeholders

Dispositions tell us about the evaluator's preferences for main questions and data-gathering methods. Like all people, evaluators have more than one disposition, and the strengths of those dispositions wax and wane. Sometimes the dispositions are inconsistent with one another. Together they express the evaluator's ideology, his or her dedication to reach a higher understanding, as in the next cartoon. Dispositions tell us about the evaluator, but not much about what the evaluation will be used for. For that, we look at roles.

Roles

For some clients, the evaluator's role should be merely one of data collection. For them it is not a professional role, merely a clerical role. Such was illustrated well in Halldór Laxness' (1968) Icelandic novel *Under the Glacier*. The hero is a young assistant in the bishop's office being sent as his emissary to a distant parish to report how the local pastor carries out his duties. Would the bishop's instructions be appropriate for evaluation fieldwork?

When the [emissary] had eventually agreed to make the journey, the bishop said: The first thing is to have the will; the rest is technique.

The [emissary] continued, for appearance's sake, to protest his youth and lack of authority to scrutinize a venerable old man's discharge of his pastoral duties or to reform Christianity in places where the words of even the bishop himself were disregarded; or what kind of "technique" could one expect from an ignorant youth in such a predicament? What am I to say? What am I to do?

Bishop: One should simply say and do as little as possible. Keep an eye on things. Talk about the weather. Ask what sort of summer they had last year, and the year before that. Say that the bishop has rheumatism. If anyone else has rheumatism, ask where it affects them. Not try to put anything right—that's our business in the Ministry of Ecclesiastical Affairs, provided that we know what's wrong. We're asking for a report, that's all. No matter what credos or fables they come up with, you're not to convert them. Not reform anything or anyone. Let them talk, not argue with them. And if they are silent, what are they silent about? Note down everything that's relevant—I'll give you the framework in the brief. Not be personal—be dry! We don't want to hear anything funny from the west, we laugh at our own expense here in the south. Write in the third person as much as possible. Be academic, yes, but in moderation. Take a tip from the phonograph.

(Continued)

(Continued)

Emissary: If the pastor is always patching up old engines or mending saucepans and forgets to bury the dead, so that corpses are taken to the glacier, well, can a farce be made less comical than it actually is?

Bishop: I'm asking for facts. The rest is up to me.

Emissary: Am I not even to say what I think about it then?

Bishop: No, no, no, my dear man. We don't care in the slightest what you think about it. We want to know what you see and hear, not how the situation strikes you. Do you imagine we're such babies here that people need to think for us and draw conclusions for us and put us on the potty?

Emissary: But what if they start filling me up with lies?

Bishop: I'm paying for the tape. Just so long as they don't lie through you. One must take care not to start lying oneself!

Emissary: But somehow I've got to verify what they say.

Bishop: No verifying! If people tell lies, that's as may be. If they've come up with some credo or other, so much the better! Don't forget that few people are likely to tell more than a small part of the truth; no one tells much of the truth, let alone the whole truth. Spoken words are facts in themselves, whether true or false. When people talk they reveal themselves, whether they're lying or telling the truth.

Emissary: And if I find them out in a lie?

Bishop: Never speak ill of anyone in a report. Remember, any lie you are told, even deliberately, is often a more significant fact than a truth told in all sincerity. Don't correct them, and don't try to interpret them either. That's our responsibility. He who would hold his own against them, let him take care not to lose his own faith.

For most of this chapter I want to concentrate on six common roles for the professional evaluation of programs. These tell us of the function and central purpose of the evaluation:

1. Assessing goal attainment

2. Aiding organization development

3. Assessing contextual quality

4. Studying policy

5. Aiding social action

6. Legitimating the program and deflecting criticism

There are other roles, such as assuring accountability, accrediting programs, estimating cost-effectiveness, and granting awards or standings, but these six predominate in the work of educational and social program evaluators. Most evaluation designs fit at least one of the six, often more than one, but a few evaluation studies in the literature fit none of them. Any particular evaluator may have a disposition or preference for working at one of these purposes. Long-experienced evaluators use a variety of methods, but most are rather consistent as to purpose across their many studies. It is important to think carefully about roles and dispositions because each tends to devour evaluation resources and each pulls the interpretation of data in particular ways, leaving little time and money for other interests. I want to describe each of the six roles in detail. Then, in the following chapters, I will describe how evaluation theorists and practitioners draw upon these roles and their personal dispositions.

GOAL ATTAINMENT EVALUATION

The classical approach to formal program evaluation is to orient around the question "Have the program goals been fulfilled?" Here we are talking mostly about evaluating programs designed to change people in certain ways, such as through schooling, training, or therapy. Some researchers speak of a treatment's having effects that need to be measured. Many clients presume or require that every evaluation study will concentrate on stated program goals—goals as stated by those who funded or manage the program.

> A district school board has received complaints about the way one middle school teacher is teaching his course, saying he encourages his students to be overly critical of local traditions and institutions.[3] The district curriculum guide states the course goals but indicates that it is the teacher who will decide how the goals will be met.
>
> *(Continued)*

---

[3]This hypothetical situation faced the fictional Radnor, Pennsylvania, School Board, and Ron Brandt (1981) got eight real evaluators to respond.

The teacher has stated his goals in the course syllabus. These goal statements do not look the same, but the teacher argues that his goals fit within the district's goals. The superintendent asks you, since you are taking an evaluation course, if you would evaluate the teacher's course to see if it fulfills the district goals. What do you do? You may recognize three questions: the question of goal compatibility, the merit of the teacher's goals, and whether or not his students are achieving the district's goals. And alone or with help, you study the materials and existing test results. Perhaps you include data from other teachers. Perhaps you examine some of the students yourself, but that would be pretty ambitious.

Goal-based evaluation is usually thought to be an evaluation structured by the already expressed goals of the program sponsors or staff. But sometimes it is the task of evaluators to figure out what the sponsor's goals or staff goals are and to compose goal statements for them. It gets more complicated when the sponsor and the program staff have different goals, or when different members of the staff have different priorities. The evaluator does not expect that everyone will have equal enthusiasm for any of the goals. Further complicating the situation, there always will be some unstated goals, such as the goals of helping youngsters mature socially and preserving teaching jobs. There usually will be more goals than can be given high priority in the design, so one of the tasks of the evaluator is to identify the attention that different goals will get, perhaps negotiating the priorities with the client, and perhaps with some of the stakeholders.

client *n* a person or company employing an evaluator, a contracting agency

As commonly pursued, goal attainment evaluation shows much more attention to the goals of clients, administrators, sponsors, and the staff than to the goals of other stakeholders, such as students, other teachers, parents, and other community members. But that need not be so. Most evaluators are sensitive to the expectations, hopes, and fears held by some stakeholders and can treat these as additional goals to be incorporated into the study.

In some situations it is important for the evaluator to remain really independent, to be seen as not a lackey of the program sponsors. When the evaluator chooses not to be swayed at all by these interests, he or she avoids interacting with the sponsors and staff and may even avoid reading their operational and promotional literature, including their statements of purpose. This disposition has come to be called "goal-free evaluation" (introduced to the field by Michael Scriven[4]). It still organizes its data gathering around commonly accepted purposes for such a program, as implied by program title and activity. Thus, a goal-free evaluation of a remedial algebra course would pay attention to what is generally expected of algebra courses for such students, but not to the stated goals of this particular course. Evaluators are seldom that much concerned about avoiding the bias of talking about goals with clients and staff, so goal-free evaluation remains a valuable reminder of that potential bias rather than a viable work plan for most evaluators.

Among the approaches having a strong disposition toward measuring goal attainment are those called instrumentalist evaluation, discrepancy evaluation, outcome evaluation, impact evaluation, purposive evaluation, regression-equation evaluation, and logic-model evaluations. All of these usually have in common a high concern for the measurement of student or trainee accomplishment, whatever the outcomes specified in goal statements. It is important to note that in addition to outcome goals, programs sometimes have input and process goals, and the attainment of these goals would also fit under goal attainment evaluation. But most of the time, goal statements emphasize outcomes and goal attainment evaluation seeks outcome data.[5] Outcomes are often quantified as the difference between pretest scores and posttest scores. If we presume that the trainees have no pertinent knowledge at the outset, then the pretest probably can be omitted.

Goal attainment evaluations are widely respected because they concentrate on client values and they provide aggregates of quantitative evidence of trainee performance. It is often presumed that the quality of what is happening in the classrooms and the quality of the management do not need to be studied if outcome performances are satisfactory. (You might want to question that.) Trainee or patient needs are sometimes studied, but often in goal attainment studies it is presumed that their needs have already been adequately determined. Goal attainment evaluation is not particularly diagnostic; that is, it is not seeking to find how the teaching should be improved. So these goal attainment evaluations are not satisfying to evaluators and educators who want to know what the treatment has been or should be.

---

[4]Goal-free evaluation is described in Scriven's *Evaluation Thesaurus* (1991).
[5]Evaluators sometimes gather *impact data* showing how attainments from the program are actually utilized in work and further study.

EVALUATION FOR ORGANIZATIONAL DEVELOPMENT

In 2001, the American Evaluation Association (AEA), the primary professional organization for program evaluators, used for its annual meeting in St. Louis the theme of "Mainstreaming Evaluation." In his welcome, President James Sanders (2002) said,

> The problem of developing an evaluation culture in organizations remains perplexing. Organizations talk about it and say they want it, but evaluation frequently becomes a secondary activity, appearing when there is pressure, problems, or mandates. For those of us who are true believers in the benefits of evaluation, the question of what we can do to make it part of the everyday life of organizations remains unanswered.

I said in Chapter 1 that evaluation plays a big part in the everyday life of individuals and organizations but formal program evaluation does not. Sanders and many evaluators believe that organizations would function better if formal evaluation of activities, processes, personnel, and products were more frequently part of the organization's planning, supervision, measuring, and analysis. Clearly, sometimes they would, but sometimes some things would get worse. Some of the speakers at St. Louis indicated that meta-evaluation was needed to decide which evaluations improved the organizations and which did not.

Organizations exist to do a job, many jobs. Hospitals exist to treat serious injuries and illnesses. Symphony orchestras exist to do concerts and recordings. Hospitals and symphonies are alike in that many things can go wrong for them. Chances of mishap are reduced if the doctors and violinists are really good and if patients and patrons pay well for the services. Along the way, policies and practices are evaluated. And many of them could be evaluated more effectively, more fairly, and to the greater enhancement of the organization. The officers and some specialists have been hired to know what's good and what's bad about what they do. Most administrators are not inclined to think that people trained in evaluation would do a better job than they are doing, except when it comes to a facet of the work highly technical or specialized. They hire consultants to give them advice—advice based on special experience. Sometimes they have a study group look into a problem. On rare occasions, they get certain specialists within the organization or some outsiders to do a study. And if they do the job well, it becomes a small step toward "mainstreaming evaluation."

In this way of thinking about evaluation, the internal operation of the organization is the focus rather than its production or its goals. The staff maintains a capacity for reflecting upon itself, recognizing problems, and preventing problems from happening. Typically it sees itself as a hierarchical, purposive community, dependent on competence, communication, and work ethic. Officers

In the late 1990s, the National Science Foundation was charged by Congress to create assistance for community colleges across the United States to upgrade a range of technical training programs, particularly those needed by local industry, business, and governmental agencies. Among the technical fields needing modernization were global positioning, water purification, waste management, and nursing. The two-year colleges used their grants for course development, bringing in consultants, recruitment, staff development, and the like, trying to assure that the new courses would have state-of-the-art technology and be suitable both for students without jobs and those already on-the-job. A team headed by Arlen Gullickson of the Evaluation Center at Western Michigan University was contracted to evaluate the program. Their primary attention was on the quality of the preparation of new instructional materials and courses at the more than 100 colleges participating. They created an annual survey and analyzed the data. To a sample of 13 of the campuses, they sent a team (two evaluators, plus sometimes a faculty specialist) to interview the principal investigator and pertinent project members. The teams followed a standard protocol. And they observed some teaching. They looked for the uniqueness of the site, the local story. And they prepared a case report on each site to accompany the survey reports from all the sites. Across several years, working with NSF people and consultants, they clarified the needs of the projects, eventually recognizing eight categories—namely, Collaboration, Dissemination, Materials Development, Program Improvement, Recruitment and Retention, Sustainability, The Role of Advisory Committees, and The Use of Evaluation. In other words, they did a needs assessment, seeking ways the organization, these loosely connected colleges, could do the job better. In their reports to the NSF, they (Gullickson, Lorenz, & Keiser, 2002) wrote a bit about goal attainment, about impact, but mostly about "capacity building"—about being better able to offer high-quality technical courses to students and local employers. As meta-evaluators for Gullickson's work, Chris Migotsky and I (2001) spoke highly of this organizational development evaluation.

and workers recognize that changes in technology, markets, public relations, and lots of things change the suitability of the organization for its jobs. So sometimes they need studies—sometimes, evaluation studies. Of course, the evaluators have some of their own ideas as to what needs to be studied.

Among the evaluation approaches having a disposition toward organization development are those called decision-based evaluation, utilization-based evaluation, client-centered evaluation, organization self-study, action research, empowerment evaluation, and institutional accreditation. They have in common a high concern for the protection and enhancement of the organization, sometimes maintaining the status quo against challenges, but often seeking a higher level of functioning.

Some evaluation theorists, such as Michael Patton (1997) and Saville Kushner (2000), say they contribute best to the development of the organization by helping make the study more a self-evaluation. There, with help, staff members design, carry out, and make judgments about the quality of the organization's structure and activities. I agree that the best-spent money for program evaluation can be for internal evaluation that draws the staff into self-reflection and dedication to action. Self-evaluation often will do more good for an agency, company, or project than independent, external evaluation. But the self-study may be seen by critics as biased and inappropriately self-serving. At any rate, when the staff, as a whole or in part, takes major responsibility for the evaluation, the assisting external evaluator may cease to be an evaluator, assuming the role of consultant on evaluation.

SEEKING HOLISTIC QUALITY

Sometimes the attention of the evaluators is not so much on impact and improvement as on understanding the nature of the evaluand—particularly, of course, its merit and worth, sometimes portraying its quality of life. Of course, this curiosity may accompany efforts to improve the organization, to declare a contract fulfilled, or to serve any other evaluative function. The evaluand here tends to be seen as some sort of creature, more or less with habitat, family, lifestyle, aspirations, and risks. In other words, the program or organization is seen as having human qualities. Some would say it is "anthropomorphized." Here the purpose of evaluation is not so much to make a summary judgment of the quality of this creature but to recognize the good and bad of its situation and of its responses to that situation. Constituent parts and behaviors can be of major attention, but the evaluative view is broad, acknowledging the interactions of many of its functions.

The U.S. Veterans Benefits Administration has long been accused of sending incomprehensible letters to veterans of military service applying for medical benefits needed for service-related injuries. Letter writing

(Continued)

in this situation has not been an easy task because both injuries and benefits are complex, defined by legislation and medical and legal practice, and situations often are emotional and life-ending. Furthermore, a long backlog of claims worked against Rating Specialists' giving much personal consideration to their letters. VA officers decided that the raters and many other staff members should be trained to write better letters. A half-week training program titled Reader Focused Writing was developed in-house and administered by satellite communication at the fifty-eight regional offices nationwide. An evaluation of the training was contracted. Instead of limiting attention to whether or not training improved the competence of staffers to write accurate, pertinent, and comprehensible letters, the evaluators went out to examine the conditions of daily letter writing, the attitudes of the staffers toward veterans, and attitudes of the staffers toward training generally. Interpersonal relations within the regional offices and with the veterans service agencies, such as the American Legion, were examined. Raised also was the perception of training as lifelong learning. The evaluators found the training well done, but only a partial solution to the problem. By taking a broad view of the context of the letter writing, the evaluators tried to increase understanding of the problem, the training, and the constraints on effective communication. A meta-evaluation of the project appears in the Web appendix.

Holistic quality is the target of many evaluators. Many are disposed to study the process of the evaluand and to emphasize personal interactions and group relationships. The quality of life at the Veterans Benefits Administration was pretty good—good people to work with, most having a deep conviction that the veteran deserved every effort to find the legitimacy of his/her claim.

Among the evaluation approaches used by evaluators having a disposition toward finding holistic quality are those called naturalistic evaluation, responsive evaluation, interpretive evaluation, transactional evaluation, and constructivist evaluation. They have in common a high concern for understanding the nature of the evaluand and the contexts in which it exists, such as the historical, economic, political, aesthetic, sociological, and cultural contexts.

Investigation of holistic quality requires lots of data, both quantitative and qualitative. Criterial measurements can be important; so can subjective

(Ask questions in bold font, probe with other questions)

Greetings and introduction; mention CIRCE letter sent earlier.

Indicate that the letters you got from VA is the focus of questions today.

Confirm benefit topic: Loan, Insurance, Disability, Pension, Rehab, Other.

How many letters did you write to the Veterans Administration?

How many did they send to you?

Indicate our interest in only the most recent letters received.

(To learn about comprehensibility of VBA letters)

In the letter(s) you got back, was the meaning clear?

Was the VA letter(s) relatively easy, or hard, to understand?

(To learn about completeness of VBA letters)

Did the letter(s) contain all the information that you needed?

Did it tell you how to proceed toward a solution to your problem?

Did it leave out important information that you needed?

Did the letter(s) contain information that wasn't useful or necessary?

(Continued)

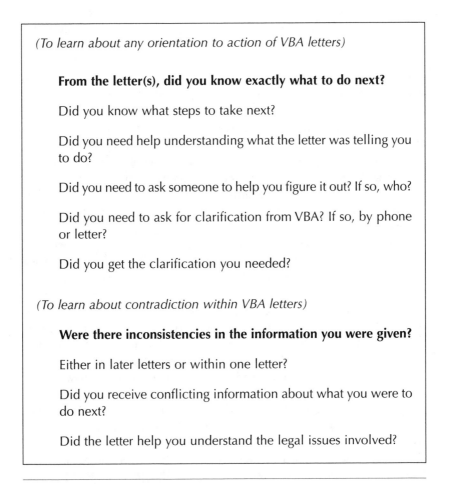

(To learn about any orientation to action of VBA letters)

From the letter(s), did you know exactly what to do next?

Did you know what steps to take next?

Did you need help understanding what the letter was telling you to do?

Did you need to ask someone to help you figure it out? If so, who?

Did you need to ask for clarification from VBA? If so, by phone or letter?

Did you get the clarification you needed?

(To learn about contradiction within VBA letters)

Were there inconsistencies in the information you were given?

Either in later letters or within one letter?

Did you receive conflicting information about what you were to do next?

Did the letter help you understand the legal issues involved?

Figure 2.1   Guide for Telephone Interview of Veterans

perceptions. Holistic quality is understood partly from statistical means and variability in the measurements, particularly as that variability correlates with temporal, geographic, demographic, social, and political conditions. Holistic quality is understood partly in the narratives of conversations and the responses to interviews.

Understanding the veterans frustrated with letters from the Veterans Benefits Administration (VBA) needed a well-rounded set of data. Understanding the problems in writing to these veterans needed another well-rounded set of data. Figure 2.1 is the protocol for a telephone interview of veterans making claims for benefits. For our evaluation of VBA training in letter writing, we needed to understand the problem holistically. We used interview responses from veterans to gain some of that understanding.

Please read the interview protocol. Notice that relatively simple questions were asked, calling for answers that could be easily coded or recorded, but also that follow-up questions were asked to get a more holistic picture. What were the categories of problems? Notice the effort made to get the interviewee to describe in some detail his or her perceptions of the letter-writing problem. The interviewer is trying to get historical perspective—a sense of what this means in the life of the veteran. Holistic quality provides a feeling that the problem and the accomplishment are becoming understood in depth.

For many descriptions, and for personal meanings of conditions, the evaluator relies on personal accounts. Some such accounts may be biased and inaccurate, but when handled carefully, they can be useful. All evaluators pay attention to holistic quality, but some seek to minimize it and others seek to pursue it.

Although formal evaluation of assembly lines, gymnastic competitions, and schools was in practice long before that, the decade of the 1960s saw the first burgeoning of evaluation studies. The National Science Foundation response to Sputnik (Kilpatrick & Stanic, 1995), as well as the programs of Lyndon Johnson's War on Poverty (Beschloss, 2001) and Robert MacNamara's management of the Vietnam War by formal evaluation (Halberstam, 1972), created the need for an academic and professional discipline of evaluation. Already then, and especially in the decade to follow, the merits of qualitative study were compared to the merits of quantitative study. In an early debate between Ellis Page (1979) and myself (1979), the issue was "Should educational evaluation be more objective or more subjective?" The 2000 *American Journal of Evaluation* debate between Mark Lipsey and Tom Schwandt (presented in First Words) represents more recent thinking about criterial and interpretive evaluation.

In 1979, I was supportive—and am still—of the growth of the subjective side of formal evaluation because, trained in quantitative methods, I had seen how incomplete were the studies relying on large numbers of people performing on a small number of criteria, with low attention to situational variables. The positions of Page and Lipsey are rooted in a respected research tradition and are supported by a majority of professional evaluators today. The typical contemporary AEA member is admiring of the contributions of qualitative studies but recognizes the demand for objectivity and criterial thinking. Today's evaluators have their persuasions, and many of them are correlated with their positions on the question of need for qualitative data.

POLICY AND GENERALIZATION STUDIES

The question is sometimes asked, "What is the difference between evaluation and research?" Those are common terms in our language, and the difference will vary with the speakers, the occasion, and the place. As I said in the previous chapter, much evaluation (judgment of quality) is informal, even unconscious. We seldom want to call that research. It is evaluation because it is finding the value of something. Formal evaluation can be merely procedural, such as polling; or deliberative, such as jury trials; or investigative, such as social science research. When it is merely the collection of judgments, however procedural, let's not call that research. But when we make a systematic effort to discover the activity, meanings, and values of an entity (evaluand), then it is both evaluation and research. Much research is not focused on the merit or worth of an entity; let's not call that evaluation.

There is a category of studies called evaluation research that looks for the value not of a single evaluand but of an entire class. Product evaluation is evaluation research when one studies Macintosh G4 computers as a class. Institutional research is evaluation research if the collective teaching across campus is evaluated. Instructional research is evaluation research when evaluating such a pedagogy as the case method of law school teaching. *Evaluation research* is a name given by many people to that simultaneous search for quality and generalization. All formal evaluation studies are research, but only those seeking generalization to a population of cases goes by the special name *evaluation research.*

A common dissertation topic for doctoral students specializing in program evaluation is research on evaluation. Many undertake an evaluation study in the field but make a scholarly study of some aspect of evaluation methods at the same time. Ólafur Proppé (1983) studied a Habermasian approach to evaluation as he was evaluating the use of standardized tests in Iceland. Jeri Ridings (now Nowakowski) (1980) studied the development of the *Joint Standards* (Joint Committee, 1994) as a matter of audit and accountability. These studies simultaneously deal with the singularity of an evaluand and the generalizability of a certain approach to program evaluation. We will return to this differentiation in Chapter 9.

Among the evaluation approaches having a disposition toward finding and assessing the quality of a strategy or policy are those called theory-based evaluation, experimental studies, social-science-based evaluation, and causal modeling evaluation. They have in common a high concern for understanding the nature, implications, and effectiveness of the policy, and the contexts in which it exists, such as those mentioned earlier. Here the evaluator is tempted to emphasize the question "What does it all mean?"

EVALUATION AID TO SOCIAL ACTION

There is a strong disposition among evaluators to leave the evaluand in healthier condition than when they found it. Some evaluators even define evaluation as formative or remedial or democratic. Strictly speaking, evaluation is

"You do the hokeypokey and you turn yourself around—that's what it's all about."

SOURCE: *The New Yorker*. Reprinted with permission.

the finding of merit and shortcoming, whether or not anyone works on improvement, but most evaluators want their findings to be useful. Most believe that their findings will be useful for improvements in the evaluand. And some even hope to contribute to management decisions or institutional pressures that lead not only to a more effective, considerate, and ethical evaluand but to the improvement of the community and society.

A strong disposition of many evaluators is toward being more rational. They often imply that the organization would be more effective or worth more if it would be more explicit in its goals, more reasonable in its decisions, and more precise in measuring what it does. Communication is usually something that could be better. Rosalie Torres, Hallie Preskill, and Mary Piontek (1996) wrote,

> Organizations will succeed through the sharing of information. It is critical that evaluators help demystify communication processes and increase opportunities for individuals to express attitudes, feelings, intentions and opposing views. (p. 28)

Part of the goodness of being an evaluator is the contribution that one can make to helping people, programs, and organizations be more open, communicative, and deliberative. That is their disposition, and many choose approaches such as democratic evaluation and participatory evaluation to further those ends.

Democratic evaluation is a way for evaluators to serve the interests of the public, or a limited public such as the workers of an industry or the stakeholders of a youth organization (more on this in Chapter 7). It maintains the evaluative function of search for merit and shortcoming in the evaluand, but through either process or findings, or both, serves to assist the standing of people. The usual process assistance is through participation. People other than managers, bureaucrats, and experts are drawn into the design, data gathering, and interpretation of the findings. Barry MacDonald advanced the idea of democratic evaluation in the early 1970s. Ernest House (1980), a longtime colleague of MacDonald's, developed his own ideas of a democratic evaluation approach that emphasizes public deliberation:

MacDonald headed the evaluation of UNCAL, a national effort to increase the role of computers in British higher education. The funding agency representatives were explicit in what the evaluation should measure in the way of improvement in teaching, especially laboratory and field assignments, but MacDonald also pursued such issues as whether or not a principal intent of the government was to subsidize the British computer industry. His argument was that use of taxpayer money required consideration of the political and economic issues discussed openly and covertly during the passing of the legislation. It was democratic evaluation, but not participatory evaluation, because, however negotiative in approach and solicitous of campus and public views, the evaluation team made the decisions as to the conduct of the study and the interpretations in its reports.

Participatory evaluation was mentioned a few pages earlier as it relates to organizational development evaluation (also see Chapter 7). It is sometimes called collaborative evaluation (O'Sullivan, in press). Getting involved with stakeholders makes the evaluation more relevant to the human issues of the program. Getting stakeholders involved in doing the evaluation goes further to enhance their station, to empower them, to focus on their problems, and to give them respect. As good civic practice, there is much to be said for charging stakeholders with the design, data gathering, and interpretation of findings. When the stakeholders under consideration are the members of an organization or staff members of a company, it is often good organizational practice to make an annual review or the evaluation of innovations or troubled processes some form of participatory evaluation.

Two Austrian evaluators, Markus Grutsch and Markus Themessl-Huber, were engaged by a company in Innsbruck to evaluate the functioning of their workforce (Grutsch & Themessl-Huber, 2002; Themessl-Huber & Grutsch, 2003). They spent extensive time at the plant getting acquainted with managers and the staff. To design the data gathering, they drew on writings about responsive evaluation, structuring their thinking about issues or problems, and seeking the multiple perspectives expected in any large group of people. Increasingly, they found little willingness on the part of managers to disclose company plans and administrative priorities. And increasingly, they participated in worker meetings where grievances and demands were expressed. It was their belief that the well-being of the company and the workers would be served if increasing responsibility for fact finding and evaluation were vested with the workers, and they drew more heavily for guidance from the literature on collaborative evaluation. Eventually, their evaluation was officially terminated, but they continued to provide advice to those who asked for it.

Among the evaluation approaches having a disposition toward studying human issues and aiding social action, in addition to participatory evaluation, collaborative evaluation, and democratic evaluation, are those called empowerment evaluation by David Fetterman (1994) and personalistic evaluation by Saville Kushner (2000). Critical studies can be fitted into this category as well. Critical studies are studies in which the investigator starts with an ideological frame of reference, such as a feminist perspective or a global market advocacy, and holds the evaluand up to sharp scrutiny. Literary and other forms of artistic criticism are related to this disposition and can be guides to improving evaluation practice. There is a special kind of critical study that is called "whistle-blowing." It is usually a set of claims made by a member of the organization who finds practices in violation of law, trust, or contract. He or she speaks out, not only to restrain or redirect the organization but to protect the public. Sooner or later, every evaluator will find conditions so bad that promises of confidentiality will need to be broken (more about that in Chapter 10).

ADVOCACY

This is a good time to raise the question of the propriety of the evaluator as advocate. We will return to it in Chapters 7 and 9. Advocacy is ever present. Most clients hope to use evaluation findings as advocacy for support. Given supportive findings, many expect the evaluator to testify in their behalf. Most evaluators are respectful of the evaluand at the outset, become increasingly caught up in its good work, and are not uncomfortable making statements supporting the program.

Jennifer Greene (1995), stepping off in a different direction, has taken the position that evaluators should more vigorously advocate for the program's target groups—who are sometimes allied with their clients, but sometimes not:

> Evaluation inherently involves advocacy, so the important question becomes advocacy for whom. The most defensible answer to this question is that evaluation should advocate for the interests of program participants. (p. 1)

Michael Scriven (1997), however, has urged evaluators to reject any advocate role that goes beyond testifying as to what was found in the evaluation. Is it a matter of choice? Part of the educational evaluator's plight is that of being caught in a field (such as education) losing professional authority. Less and less are professionals, researchers, teachers, and support people trusted to guide education to serve the public interest. Most educational programs subjected to formal evaluation are under increasing scrutiny, their accountability challenged, and for many, their future cloudy. Education remains a championed virtue, but educators everywhere are under fire. Although we seldom allow it to rise into consciousness, unconsciously we are aware that advertising is a more persuasive medium than teaching or research. Salesmanship sells better than teaching teaches. Politics gets into it, often with deceit.[6] Campaigns and legislation push the boundaries of disregard for the facts. Advocacy often overcomes truth.

Research tries to fight fire with fire. Given the good causes of our clients and their stakeholders, evaluative research distressingly mimics the media world of sound bites. We seek the quotable quote, the executive summary, the deciding graphic, the bottom-line indicator, even the cartoon, to stand for quality in the moving, complex, and contextual evaluand. We ourselves are reluctant to separate epistemology from ideology, findings from yearnings. We consciously seek those expressions of findings that persuade the reader of our points of view. We too are advocates, some more than others. Linda Mabry (1995) pointed out that "Natural variation among evaluators along these dimensions guarantees that proactive advocacy must always be an uneven current in our field. . . (p. 7).

---

[6]In *The Nation*, January 28, 2002, Stephen Metcalf wrote:
When [President George W. Bush] invited a group of "education leaders" to join him for his first day in the White House, the guest list was dominated by Fortune 500 CEOs. One, Harold McGraw, the publishing scion and current chairman of McGraw-Hill, summed up: "It's a great day for education, because we now have substantial alignment among all the key constituents— the public, the education community, business and political leaders—that results matter." As a leading publisher of tests, he was, of course, speaking about test results.

My CIRCE[7] colleagues and I published *Restructuring* (Stake et al., 1995), the Year II evaluation report of the Chicago Teachers Academy for Mathematics and Science. The Academy was a free-standing professional-development institution devoted to improved teaching and reform in Chicago's elementary schools. Our findings told of good curricular and pedagogical bases in Academy work-shops for teachers in the more than sixty participating schools. We told of consequential change in some classrooms. We told of a School Improvement Unit (an Academy department) dedicated to helping schools define and solve their problems themselves—but also giving them too little help connecting with problem-solving efforts at other schools and with the "change literature."[8] And so on. But it is not findings I want to point to here—rather, the ideological stance to be found in *Restructuring*, that year's final report submit-ted to the Academy to be used as it wished.

The Academy existed in a fragile state financially, not greatly aided by cross-institutional support. We saw the Academy as a pos-itive force for education in Chicago, notwithstanding occasional mistakes, inefficiencies, and political indulgences. It clearly was a positive force for assisting teachers—and without a serious com-petitor institution, without a successor, in sight.

Some observers pointed out that our underlying ethic here was protective, even paternalistic. That attitude grew over time with increased familiarity with the teachers and schools that we case-studied. The ethic is stated this way: "We try not to allow our eval-uation study to make it more difficult for the staff to discharge its responsibilities." In practice, it meant forgoing judgment about some important practices in the schools, especially those not directly the responsibility of the evaluand. Contractually, we were not evaluating the teachers, the classrooms, and the schools, but the Academy. We saw ourselves as guests in the schools we visited, inquiring sometimes into the teachers' personal affairs. We wanted it to be done with empathy and care, with discretion.

(Continued)

---

[7]CIRCE is the Center for Instructional Research and Curriculum Evaluation at the University of Illinois.

[8]We at CIRCE endorsed the professional development views found in Little (1993) and such school restructuring views as found in Newmann & Wehlage (1995).

Yet we were evaluators. We worked to find and understand quality. We did not come to assist in remediation. We did not think of ourselves as collaborators in reform. We promised to help the Academy staff understand itself, particularly in terms of the quality of its operations. We provided details of merit and shortcoming. We interpreted and discussed the issues. Among the CIRCE ideological positions discernible in our report were the following:

- Teaching that emphasizes problem solving, experiential learning and constructivist epistemology is generally more educationally valuable than direct teaching of basic skills.
- Professional development programs basically dependent on face-to-face teaching by expert instructors seldom extend to the bulk of teachers needing it; thus, the traditional in-servicing strategy is inadequate.
- Reform standards and expectations for Chicago schools set by central authorities, however popular and legitimate, actually divert schools and teachers from improvements that they and the Academy desire.

And there were others. It should be noted that these three positions, these standards of quality for Academy operation, were not agreed upon. Although shared by many educators and evaluators, they were opposed by others. In using these standards in our evaluation, we were expressing a parochial ideology. We were supporting reform—as we defined it.

Where responsibility to schools ends and responsibility to the Academy begins was not clear. Operating under an ethic of minimized disruption, and given an Academy rationale with curricular values we shared, we emphasized Academy strengths in our reporting. Weaknesses were not as clearly stated. Of Academy misdirections, we spoke more privately; of good moves, we spoke more publicly. Going beyond the stated ethic, we tried not to author a final report that, if distributed, might add to the Academy's insecurity.

Michael Scriven and Jane Kramer (1994, p. 15) advised that after an evaluation is finished, the evaluator may "advocate on the merits of the case." But when subsequent evaluation work is anticipated, as it was here, the report-distributing evaluator is not newly free to advocate. And does "advocate on the merits" mean one can downplay shortcomings? What is advocacy if it's not to apply a favorable gloss?

Advocacy within program evaluation is not new. Twenty years ago Ernest House (1980) urged us to think of program evaluation as argumentation. Regularly unchallenged, we evaluators have argued for objectivity, explication, historical perspective, and rational thinking, each traditionally considered a virtue, even an obligation, in research. Advocacy for educational reform, curricular remediation, and pedagogical change has been almost as common. Those advocacies are fundamental to our work. We have long been sympathetic to the values of our colleagues and our clients. But we seem to be moving further and further into advocacy of little agreed-upon values. And of course we know that some advocacies will not be acceptable to some stakeholders. Are we justified in vigorous protection of teachers, opposition to home schooling, and tolerance of kids dropping out of school? As of now, we have few guidelines for examining distinctions between advocacies good and bad.

LEGITIMATION AND PROTECTION

I am not aware of evaluators who encourage clients to engage in evaluation services or employ an evaluation specialist because of the authentication that act alone may provide. I am aware of apocryphal advice to a manager, "If you are in trouble, appoint a committee. If you're in real trouble, do an evaluation." The implication is that this will buy time, keep the attackers at bay. Increasing security is one of the roles of an evaluation, although seldom admitted.

It is common, however, for a manger to say "We know we are good, and we expect the evaluation to prove it." I have no trouble with that, but I will say that any evaluation that I conduct will be interested as much in shortcomings as in merit. Often the contractor for an evaluation wants the study to bolster a request for continuation funding. The evaluation should indicate the expectation that if the evaluation report is submitted to the funding agency, it will be submitted in its entirety. A program evaluation is sometimes required by a funding agency. Or opponents of the program may manage to call for an evaluation in order to substantiate its weaknesses. And so, of course, we will say we look at strengths as well.

These comments underplay the social and political situation. Whoever approaches the evaluator first and whoever will decide to have the evaluation is likely to win some empathy from the evaluators. They get together and talk about the program and the need for continuation or change. It makes sense, they are nice people, and there is likely to develop a study that will be particularly attentive to their needs. Most evaluators want to be accurate, honest, and fair. They also want to be helpful. Being honest and being helpful are not one and the same thing, as we shall see in our look at Professional Standards in Chapter 10.

The evaluator cannot ignore the effect that the evaluation will have on the program. A program providing good services may be jeopardized by a particular negative finding. Shall we say "Let the chips fall where they may"? Usually, yes. But the social injury of full honesty can for some programs be disastrous. Oh, what to do? There will be no clear answer in these pages. The evaluator needs to understand that regardless of what the contract says, there will be several roles for the evaluation in the minds of administrators and stakeholders. We evaluators tend to think of evaluation as information producing, but social or political standing may be the larger effect.

ROCKY TOP

Wish that I was on Ole Rocky Top
Down in the Tennessee Hills

Ain't no smoggy smoke on Rocky Top
Ain't no telephone bills

Rocky Top, you'll always be
Home, sweet home to me

Good Ole Rocky Top
Rocky Top, Tennessee

SOURCE: From the state song of Tennessee. "Rocky Top" written by Boudleaux Bryant and Felice Bryant. Reprinted with permission of The House of Bryant, Publications.

SUMMARY OF ROLES

The six roles discussed above are important because they expand the functions of evaluation beyond those that most clients and audiences, and many evaluators, have in mind when they contemplate program evaluation. Clearly, it would be a mistake to try to engage in all roles in any one study, but there are features of each role that can enhance any one design.

These roles, as stated, belong to you and me. Other authors, even your instructor (if you have one), have other ways of classifying evaluation approaches. One of the most respected textbooks on evaluation theory has been *Foundations of Program Evaluation* by William Shadish, Thomas Cook, and Laura Leviton (1991). These three authors analyzed the writings of ten theorists according to a template that focused on assistance in five functions:

1. Social programming

2. Knowledge use

3. Valuing

4. Knowledge construction

5. Evaluation practice

Another classification was presented by House in *Evaluating with Validity* (1980, p. 21). The section titles of the widely used book *Evaluation Models: Viewpoints on Educational and Human Services Evaluation* by Daniel Stufflebeam, George Madaus, and Thomas Kellaghan (2000) are another guide to how evaluation studies are classified:

1. Program Evaluation

2. Questions/Methods-Oriented Evaluation Models

3. Improvement/Accountability-Oriented Evaluation Models

4. Social Agenda-Directed (Advocacy) Models

5. Overarching Matters[9]

There have been many other sortings of evaluation approaches, and there will be many more. In fact, I have considered it a rite of passage for my own evaluation graduate students. They are moving into an evaluation theory career when they feel the need to lay out their own classification of evaluation approaches.

Narrative

Mr. Sagredo calls Phyllis to his office.

Sagredo: I looked at the examples of evaluation reports you brought in and am troubled by the variety. Isn't there a standard way to evaluate something like our Senior Mentor Training?

Phyllis: There is more similarity among evaluators than is shown in those five reports. Many evaluators would concentrate on measuring the quality of performance before and after training. Memo writing to their mentees could be a criterion performance here. I gave you those reports to show the diversity in the field and the opportunity to link this training with other changes going on in our organization. As a manager, you appreciate the fact that what is a good report in one situation will not necessarily work in another.

Sagredo: So we can have the stripped-down model or all the glitz?

Phyllis: You are teasing me. You know that for a car, anti-lock brakes are a serious choice, and for an evaluation, the attitudes of the trainees are important in interpreting the success of the training. From what

---

[9]I found it interesting that Daniel Stufflebeam placed Michael Patton's Utilization-Focused Evaluation as an "overarching matter," citing (in a private note to me in 2002) Patton's ambivalence about assessing merit and worth and his apparent higher priority on getting findings used than on getting findings right. Patton has been a leading advocate of the external evaluator's playing the role of facilitator to institutional self-evaluation.

you said earlier, I understand that, for this evaluation, you are willing to allocate 20 days of my time and to provide, say, 48 hours of trainee and other staff time. I think we would need to pay a mentoring specialist a fee for expert interpretation of our findings. Yesterday I had Sid (the training coordinator) brief me. I have read the materials and watched a training session. With a little more information, I can write a plan of work, including a description of what I expect we will learn.

Sagredo: How about giving me a peek right now? Will your report tell how the success of our mentor training compares to similar training elsewhere?

Phyllis: If that is important and I have luck with my colleagues on EVALTALK, I could give you a bit of that. However, I consider that pretty close to glitz, because training conditions elsewhere are not likely to be similar. I think you are better off trying to maximize understanding of what is happening right here. What about the need for the training? Do you feel that I should try to verify that bad mentoring is a problem?

Sagredo: Hell, no. The problem exists because the Board said we have a problem, so they told me to spend the money for the training.

Phyllis: Wouldn't it be good to examine their assumptions?

Sagredo: No. Board members have a pretty good idea about what makes this place work. I think that would be straying pretty far from what we need to know. But what you said about attitudes and about the difference between what they *can* do and what they *do* do seems important.

Phyllis: I asked Mrs. Vivani if they had a criterion test separate from the exercises they use in the training, and she said that they do not, but that a Florida Central doctoral student in Orlando developed something that might be useful. Let me get a handle on that and get back to you with a proposal.

Sagredo: It seems a little risky to me to use a test developed down there in Disney World.

Phyllis: Well, developing a really good test ourselves would cost many times more than what you are paying for the training. But I think we can come up with something. It won't be Mickey Mouse, but it won't be rocket science either. It won't be diagnostic. It won't tell us what you should do to improve the training. What we will have is a better idea of what is happening, especially as seen by the trainees. They have a pretty good sense of how much their skills are changing—not good enough, but part of what needs to be known. Okay? I could leave tomorrow if you want me to check out that test in person.

Sagredo: Well, Phyl, that part of it I may need to take care of myself.

(To be continued)

3

Standards-Based Evaluation

The truth is rarely pure, and never simple.

Oscar Wilde

This is it! What most evaluators are most proud of is their measurements. They are really happy when they do a good job of measuring the performance of the evaluand. They get numbers down on paper that show what the "program people" have done or can do. Those numbers show whether or not standards have been met. Of course, the numbers need to be analyzed and interpreted. In this chapter, we will concentrate on using instruments to obtain evidence for a study's main evaluation questions. A magnificent statistical analysis of superficial questions will not make a good study.

A criterion instrument sometimes looks like the gender-equity program questionnaire in Figure 3.1. It is a questionnaire that several of us used to evaluate progress over three years of the Sex Equity Demonstration Center in Broward County, Florida. In our executive summary, we showed (for example, regarding question number 15) that teachers well exposed to the work of the Center increased perception that girls have to overcome more social pressure than boys to enroll in advanced science and mathematics courses. Teachers in other schools in the county showed a decrease in this perception across the two-year period.

Have a good look at Figure 3.1. Figure it out. It is a questionnaire for teachers. (Some of the same items were also administered to students and administrators.) The criterial data questions begin with numbers 4 through 10, dealing with the respondent's perception of need for the program. Items 11 and 12 ask for observations of activity at the school. Items 13 through 17 inquire about changes the program may be making. The standards of success were to be met by substantial gains in awareness of inequity and support for gender-equity teaching. No effort was made in advance to enumerate how

Directions: These questions are asked as part of evaluating the Sex Equity Demonstration Project here in Broward County. Care will be taken to avoid disclosure of individual responses. Please respond frankly to each item.

1. **Your sex:**
   A. Female
   B. Male

2. **Years of teaching experience:**
   A. 0–2 years
   B. 3–5 years
   C. 6–10 years
   D. 11–20 years
   E. Over 20 years

3. **Years of administrative experience:**
   A. 0–2 years
   B. 3–5 years
   C. 6–10 years
   D. 11–20 years
   E. Over 20 years

4. **Do you feel that sex role stereotyping has been a problem at your school?**
   A. Yes, a large problem
   B. Somewhat a problem
   C. Not a problem at all

5. **Do you feel teachers here are well informed about sex discrimination practices and opportunities for diminishing them?**
   A. Keeping themselves well informed
   B. Needing more opportunity for getting informed
   C. Other

6–10. In the schools of this district—as you see it—how much are each of the following interfering with youngsters' getting a good education? (Questions 6–10)

6. Racial discrimination:	A. A lot	B. A little bit	C. Not at all	D. No opinion
7. Sex discrimination:	A. A lot	B. A little bit	C. Not at all	D. No opinion
8. Bilingualism:	A. A lot	B. A little bit	C. Not at all	D. No opinion
9. Overemphasis on testing:	A. A lot	B. A little bit	C. Not at all	D. No opinion
10. Ineffective teaching:	A. A lot	B. A little bit	C. Not at all	D. No opinion

(Continued)

11. **As you see it, what are your school's teachers and administrators doing about sex equity? (Check the *one* that says it best).**
    A. Most are not concerned about this issue.
    B. Most watch for problems but seldom get involved.
    C. Most try to eliminate sex role stereotyping.
    D. Most believe boys and girls should be treated differently.

12. **As you see it, approximately what percentage of students in your school notice instances of sex role stereotyping in curricular materials?**
    A. 5% or less
    B. 5% to 25%
    C. 25% to 50%
    D. 50% to 75%
    E. 75% or more

13. **Which one of the following best expresses your feelings about what your school's teachers and administrators should do?**
    A. They should try to eliminate sex role stereotyping.
    B. They should watch for problems due to stereotyping.
    C. They should teach the ways boys and girls should be different.
    D. They have more important things to do than worry about this.

14. **Compared to a year ago, are you now more aware of sex discrimination occurring in school?**
    A. No, I am not aware of sex discrimination here.
    B. Yes, I am more aware of it now.
    C. No, I was very much aware of it a year ago.

15. **Do you feel that girls have to overcome more social pressures than boys to enroll in advanced science and math courses?**
    A. Yes
    B. No

16. **Compared to a year ago, are you now more aware that some people feel there is sex discrimination in schools and want to do something to stop it?**
    A. No, I am not aware of such people.
    B. Yes, I am becoming more aware of such people.
    C. No, I was very much aware of such people a year ago.

17. **Are most students in your school aware of situations where discrimination according to sex occurs?**
    A. Yes, they are very alert to sex discrimination.
    B. Yes, but it is a matter of little importance to them.
    C. No, they are not aware of such situations.

Figure 3.1   Perceptions of Sex Equity in Schools: Scale QC Spring 1983

much gain it would take to be "substantial." (Is there an anomaly here in that the more effective this program was, even if greatly increased time was spent treating inequities, the expectation was that people would find more and more to be troubled by and might become more dissatisfied with their schools?) But returning to concern about standards-based evaluation: Perhaps the most important question for you to ask is, "Would these questions focus on the most important goals and criteria of the program?"

This questionnaire was also formatted as a machine-scored, optically scanned instrument. The first three questions permit comparisons as to gender and experience of respondents. All seventeen questions require categorical choices rather than open-ended responses. Potentially useful information was lost by not asking the respondents to compose their own responses, but time of scoring those responses is too great for many evaluation situations. I prefer to include at least one open-ended response to get nuances and quotables that these items do not get. A more open-ended questionnaire for that program is shown as Figure 4.1 in the next chapter.

More often than not, several criterion instruments will be used in a single study. Still another example of a criterion instrument is the telephone interview protocol for veterans shown in Figure 2.1. It is a protocol, or rough outline, for conducting interviews by telephone for an evaluation study of the letter-writing training program described in the previous chapter. The evaluator doing the phoning was given reminders in parentheses of the seven criteria most emphasized in the training of Veterans Benefits Administration staff members, plus a list of other criteria for good letter writing. The questions in bold type were asked in a standardized way for all respondents. The numbered items were probes to be asked if the respondent did not cover them in her or his answer.

Back in Chapter 1 we considered two ways of thinking about evaluation, criterial and interpretive. The criterial way emphasizes the objective use of scales and formal measurements. In contrast, the interpretive way emphasizes successive refinements of personal acquaintance with the evaluand. Measurement and personal experience will be important in many evaluation studies, but final decisions about the quality of the evaluand will be made differently in criterial and interpretive approaches.

Standards-Based

We will use the label *standards-based* to identify a large group of evaluation methods that rely heavily on criterial thinking. Standards-based evaluation calls for a strong effort to be explicit about the criteria, the standards,[1] and other factors of evaluation. It has the criterial orientation of the National Institute of Standards and Technology (www.nist.gov). Being explicit, declaring your procedures and value commitments, is very important in criterial thinking. Interpretive evaluation depends on value standards too, but in contrast, the standards there are usually more implicit, less verbalized, and not strongly identified in the design and final report. Standards-based evaluation is a highly rational approach, not a highly intuitive approach, toward perceiving and representing program quality.

Statements of standards and other factors of evaluation are never perfect. Many of the statements will only provide approximations, simplifications, and correlates of the real criteria. Often, resources do not allow thorough study of the real criteria. Needs and goals, for example, are often taken from program specifications rather than independently researched. Orienting to standards is not just following a checklist to get everything specified but an aim to be as explicit as circumstances will allow.

Standards-based evaluation seems natural especially when the role for evaluation is assessing goal attainment. The evaluator needs to get the goals explicated and to find criteria and standards most appropriate for assessing performance. But the same kind of thinking is useful for assessing activities and contexts, for aiding organizational development, and for studying policy and facilitating social action. The various roles of evaluation can all be served well by a standards-based approach.

Anne McKee of Kings College, London, evaluated regional support for staff development in a sample of small medical clinics in Northwest England. She identified criteria of support from two regional authorities. One authority emphasized the need for alignment with central government regulations. The second one encouraged the staff to assess their own needs and plan the training accordingly. Later, McKee analyzed the training that actually

(Continued)

---

[1]It will be a bit of a struggle to keep all the standards straight. The standards in standards-based evaluation are the factors or ingredients for carrying out an evaluation. Some of those factors or ingredients are the value standards people use to judge the quality of the evaluand. The standards may be written or unwritten, but they are conscious standards. Beyond that, the process of formal evaluation is judged by professional standards, such as the *Joint Standards* (Joint Committee, 1994) or AEA's *Guiding Principles* (Shadish et al., 1995).

occurred and found that communication and organizational compliance were more frequently studied in the clinics urged to align with central regulations. The clinics more engaged in self-assessment scheduled training more frequently on medical and health care issues. That was the outcome performance to which McKee was paying attention. She used explicit criteria of agency facilitation and identified the training targets. Although highly rational in her approach, she left staff needs, standards, and weights implicit; yet she provided data for evaluating the two methods of supporting staff development. (McKee & Watts, 2000)

Rational thinking is said to contrast with intuitive thinking. Being rational in evaluation work is attractive to many clients in academics, business, and government. Most evaluators take pride in their rationality and in their ability to spell out the steps they are following in their evaluations. It is not only a matter of market value and pride; it is also a matter of controlling the subjectivity and bias in this complex work of determining merit and shortcoming.

Bias

Becoming a professional evaluator, or a professional of any kind with expertise in evaluation, is partly a matter of learning how to deal with bias. Expert evaluators have biases, as do all people, but most work hard to recognize and constrain their biases. They discipline themselves, they set up traps to catch their biases, and the best evaluators indicate to their clients and readers that since not all biases will be eliminated, they too must watch for them. Bias is endemic. Someone might wonder, "At what age does a Scottish child learn to say 'aye' instead of 'yes'?" That question suggests a bias, a false expectation: seeing things through English-seeing eyes. Representation of student views of management as essentially conspiratorial is a bias. Failing to recognize racial discrimination is a more pertinent example of evaluator bias. Good evaluators try to screen their questions for bias and to use screening procedures for recognizing the effects of bias that did not get screened earlier.

In his paper at my retirement symposium, Michael Scriven said, "Bias, the lack of objectivity, is by definition a predisposition to error. . . . It would be hard to think of a more significant reason, a better reason, for wishing to improve our qualifications [as evaluators] in the objectivity dimensions"

(Scriven, 1998, p. 15). But denial of subjectivity is a step toward oversimplification. Bias is a complex and critical matter. We will examine the concepts of bias and objectivity in Chapters 6 and 9.

The professional evaluator tries to recognize and constrain his or her own biases, then checks subsequent work with validation and review procedures, and counts on colleagues and readers to point out work that emerges still biased. One initial strategy for dealing with bias is explication—that is, making everything as explicit as possible. That means getting it down on paper or up on the screen so it can be circulated, scrutinized, and wrung out. It means taking great care to define terms and operations. It means to try out data gathering in advance and to open the use of instruments and protocols to critical review. It means to be objective, allowing the least influence of personal preference. It also means allotting a large part of the budget to planning, standardization, question development, data presentation formats, and trial runs. And strategically, it means formalizing the process of comparing measured performance to explicit standards.

Factors[2]

It is often useful to think of standards-based evaluation as occurring in phases. Proposal phase, preparatory phase, and reporting phase are examples of phases. We sometimes talk about it as a linear process even though it is cyclical and self-correcting. These phases help to operationalize (put into operation) the factors of criterial evaluation. The factors of standards-based evaluation are:

1. Recipient needs

2. Program goals

3. Evaluation criteria

4. Evaluation standards

5. Synthesis weights

6. Staff and participant/recipient performances

7. Program costs

These factors are defined in Figure 3.2.

---

[2]I call them factors because they are more than parts or components. They are forces or determinants. The term *factor* reflects some of their dynamic character. They should not be confused with factor analytic factors derived from the intercorrelation of variables.

Recipient Needs. Most of the programs we evaluate provide a service to people, such as patients, park users, trainees, or students. These people are prospective or actual beneficiaries. Other people benefit less directly, and we call them stakeholders. The services are designed to meet some of the needs of the prospective recipients. The program designers decide which needs to work on. They try to address only a few of the many needs and may fail to target the most important ones. The evaluator evaluates the choice of needs addressed and not addressed. Needs assessment may be formal or informal.

Program Goals. The goals are objects or aims the program strives to attain or others want it to attain. Reference to program goals is usually to the goals that have been stated, usually in formal language. The entire scope of goals, stated and unstated, conscious and unconscious, includes not just the goals of the sponsors and program staff but of participants and stakeholders, even including patrons, taxpayers, competitors, and opponents. Even under strict contract or assignment, the evaluator needs to decide how much attention is to be given to each of the goals.

Evaluation Criteria. A criterion (defined in the previous chapter) is an attribute of an object or activity used to acknowledge its merit and short-coming. It can be a trait or ingredient seen to be essential. It becomes a basis for judgment or action when a standard is set. Some evaluators treat criterial thinking as the only defensible process of evaluating, requiring the formal expression of goals and performance in terms of generic descriptors, such as measured gain in performance, productivity, or reduction of cost.

Evaluation Standards. A standard (defined in the previous chapter) is an amount or level or manifestation of a criterion differentiating between one level of merit and another. It is a cut-score, such as differentiation between passing and failing, but also between any other conditions of merit. A particular performance or a set of exemplars can be used as standards, but usually the standard is part of criterial thinking rather than categorizations by exemplars. Standards are implicit in the cases used to illustrate commendable performance by evaluators, lawyers, and waste management programs.

Synthesis Weights. Synthesis is the process of putting all the information together to arrive at a summary judgment of quality. The relative importance of each piece of evidence in deciding that quality is the weight given it. The weight can be statistical or impressionistic. It is not common practice to indicate in reports any precise values given the weights.

Staff and Participant Performances. The performance of the evaluand is usually taken to mean the performance of the program staff and participants. Performance includes program processes as well as products. The

(Continued)

performance may be measured by some kind of test indicating change in proficiency or some kind of inventory indicating amount accomplished. For standards-based evaluation, the evaluator compares such performance to standards to determine program merit.

Program Costs. Program costs are the funds used to staff, equip, and operate the program but also the in-kind costs of facilities, assistance, hospitality, and risk control. Opportunity costs, what was foregone because the resources were used this way, are program costs as well. Measurement of simple costs is difficult enough, and other costs can only be estimated.

Figure 3.2   Definition of the Factors of Standards-Based Evaluation

The evaluator tries to recognize, explicate, and measure these factors for the particular evaluand in the given situation. All the factors are considered in each phase of an evaluation study. We sometimes will call the phases: planning, data gathering, analysis, and interpretation. A typical sequence is illustrated in Figure 3.3 as a framework for the Quality of Life Project—a framework devised by the project staff but useful as a conceptual structure for evaluation data gathering as well.[3]

Thinking of phases here reinforces the idea that most evaluators hope that the factors will remain largely unchanged during the study. For the integrity of the evaluation, perceptions of recipient needs should not change. Goals should remain pretty much the same. Measurements especially should remain fixed because performance assessment usually depends on careful selection and representation of criteria, involving costly development of instruments and protocols. The standards-based evaluator follows the practice of the social scientist who says, "If new ideas occur during the study, start a new study to run alongside this one; don't try to change the research question, the criteria, and the data gathering in midstream."

It is important for evaluation planning to anticipate the work needed within phases. Each of the factors requires special evaluator skills, as will be more apparent when they are discussed one by one below. The individual evaluator needs to prepare for identifying and making explicit the factors. The organizer of an evaluation team needs to assure that the team members collectively have the skills. Making a critique of an evaluation study requires a sense of how evaluators grasp the meaning of the factors.

What are the criteria for good evaluation studies? They should follow accepted standards of practice (Joint Committee, 1994), describe the program

---

[3]I would like to credit Figure 3.3 to its authors but I failed to find its origins. Apologies.

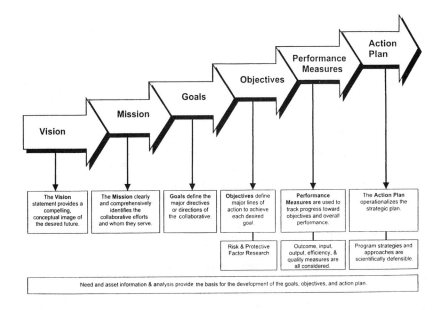

Figure 3.3   The Quality of Life Project: Strategic Planning and Performance-Based Measurement Framework

well, and get the value picture straight. But there are also the criteria of use. Tom Cook (1993) said, "Though many other criteria can be advanced, it seems that the degree of success in utilization, knowledge-building, and institutionalization should be considered among the criteria by which evaluation research is evaluated" (p. 61). With help from colleagues William Shadish and Laura Leviton (Shadish et al., 1991), Cook's evaluative criteria turned into the five functions mentioned in the previous chapter:

1. *Social programming.* Helping social programs and policies develop, improve, and change, especially in regard to social problems.

2. *Knowledge construction.* Informing people about social action.

3. *Valuing.* Attaching value to programs.

4. *Knowledge use.* Increasing the use of evaluative information to modify programs and policies.

5. *Evaluation practice.* Assisting others to use good evaluative tactics and strategies.

Cook and his colleagues were working on the dimensions of meta-evaluation (the evaluation of an evaluation; see Chapter 6), emphasizing a particular point of view, that of the large program administrator and policy developer. They did not choose to say that evaluation work should conform to the *Joint Standards* or that the evaluator should represent program quality accurately, presuming those to be understood. As we noted in the previous chapter, one of the roles of evaluators is to facilitate program development, and many evaluators (for example, Lee Cronbach, Jack Easley) emphasize this formative evaluation role above that of describing and judging the program.

In schools and agencies, program development is more of an unending process than is supposed in discussions of formative and summative evaluation. In the case of an evaluation of state learning standards, DeStefano (2001) recognized that the Illinois Standards were no longer being worked on. They had been completed once before and, in some form or another, would be worked on in the future. So the evaluation of current implementation was summative in a sense and formative in another sense.

In a four-year study, a team of evaluators led by Lizanne DeStefano evaluated implementation of the State of Illinois Learning Standards. They created five criterial levels of implementation, running from resistance to the state's intent by school staff to high consideration of the state standards (for use when teachers are choosing materials and developing local assessments). In Year 3 they surveyed 2,422 teachers in 71 schools to determine the extent to which they were implementing the standards. Principals were also surveyed. Items were categorized as pertinent to staff attitudes, community and stakeholder support, curriculum, infrastructure, professional development, and student learning and assessment. Teacher changes were noted primarily in efforts to align the curriculum to the standards, with increasing attention to after-school tutoring. Gradual increase in school implementation across the years was found. (DeStefano, 2001)

As you can see, not all seven factors were seen as needing study. Data gathering was apparently not aimed at needs, costs, and setting weights. What was delivered in the successive year reports was closely aligned with the state of Illinois Request for Proposals, the University's proposal, and the contract.

Criteria and Standards for Comparisons

Most evaluands are "good" in several ways, even in dozens of ways (and potentially "bad" in other ways). An army recruiter can win an award for enlisting large numbers of potential soldiers, but is "good" also for recognizing volunteers who are immature and those having a physical handicap. Of course, the army has criteria for the recruiter to follow, and it takes ability to apply the criteria. The army tries to be fully explicit in its eligibility standards, but the induction center doctors will make evaluative judgments in matters such as visual acuity and dental occlusion.

The subjectivity in most uses of criteria and standards cannot be entirely eliminated, and in many complex decisions, such as who will be the Boot Camp company commander, intuitive judgment plays a large part. My company commander was a lanky, big-voiced, good-looking fellow named Rogge, who liked to listen to the drill sergeant's stories. How big-voiced did he need to be? In other words, what was the vocal standard for company commanders? I don't know. It could have been that the drill sergeant would just select the loudest of us, but other criteria probably came first. Somehow the criteria were weighted, probably intuitively, and the selection was made. It was a decision easy to unmake.

Criteria tell us which characteristics to pay attention to. We use criteria in order to facilitate making good selections. When we go to the store to buy a coat, we may not be aware that we have criteria, expecting to choose the right one when we see it. But we expedite the selection and probably avoid some bad selections by conceiving criteria ahead of time. From what weather will the coat give us protection? Will it look good with a favorite cap? Is there a pocket for cigarettes? Some criteria are unrealized until a hidden standard is violated. Oh, that black one was too itchy.[4]

Standards-based evaluators try to make the criterion picture clear in advance. They do ask staff people and other stakeholders, sometimes participants and recipients, for help in identifying criteria. They do not want to be surprised by the sudden appearance of new criteria or disappearance of ones that they have counted on for making value statements. Sometimes the evaluators are in a position to know better than anyone else the relevant criteria, but often others nearby, with acuity and legitimacy, are better at clarifying the standards in use.

Multiple criteria often need attention, even if the correlation among them runs high. A recital performance needs attention not only to the quality of music but to the presentation, the match of musical selection to performance style, and to the readiness of the audience. And quality of music has its several dimensions. Music critics use a number of standards, often sorting performances into categories such as "in the manner of Aaron Copeland" or "early Bob Dylan." These categories act as both criteria and standards. By recognizing them as of a genre, the critic is speaking also of their merit, augmenting it with

---

[4]We call it "specification error" when the wrong criteria are used to answer a question. Is this the same as a "stimulus error"?

comments of falling short or sailing beyond. An effort to summarize the quality of performance of any evaluand on a single criterion is likely to over-simplify the evaluation. It is not enough to be explicit about one criterion, but all the criteria that matter.

Different criteria will be held by different stakeholder groups. Take, for example, the Basmati Indian Restaurant. Local patrons and non-Indians like the curry and other spices and rate the restaurant high. Indians tend to avoid the restaurant, finding the food unlike theirs at home.

For training and operation of the schools, and especially during a period of school reform, many efforts are made to be explicit about learning standards. What should a student know? How well should he or she have to perform? These are difficult questions, but many states within the United States have mobilized teachers and other stakeholders to identify the standards in each subject matter at each grade level. A sample of such standards developed for the public schools of the state of New York is shown in Figure 3.4. The evaluator of a program using these standards should study them thoroughly and critically. Teachers will do quite different things to meet the standards, and even when their students earn similar mean scores, the actual learning may differ considerably. Such standards do not necessarily standardize instruction or equate educational opportunity.

It was acknowledged in the previous chapter that quantitative standards can seldom be identified in advance so that one can get a simple comparison of performance to them. Using experts or stakeholders as judges, performances often are compared—after the fact—to implicit standards. Or the performances are compared to reference group performances as the indication of attainment. None of these satisfies all that the evaluation community would like as indication of quality. But if we can do some, our clients, the stakeholders, and many sectors of the public are satisfied with our work.

Needs Assessment

For a program evaluator, the evaluand is usually a functioning program. It does something for recipients: it trains them, it feeds them, it heals them, it saves their lives. The patrons and staffs who create and operate the program establish purposes for it, what they want it to accomplish. They are responding to what they see as recipient needs. In stating their goals, they indicate that they have already assessed the needs of potential recipients and are intent upon alleviating those needs.

It may be important for the evaluator to make an independent assessment of needs, partly when they are not agreed upon, or inadequately assessed, or just because the evaluator sees a need to do so. This assessment may be formal

(Text continued on page 70)

Learning Standards for Mathematics, Science, and Technology at Three Levels

Standard 1:   Students will use mathematical analysis, scientific inquiry, and engineering design, as appropriate, to pose questions, seek answers, and develop solutions.

Standard 2:   Students will access, generate, process, and transfer information using appropriate technologies.

Standard 3:   Students will understand mathematics and become mathematically confident by communicating and reasoning mathematically, by applying mathematics in real-world settings, and by solving problems through the integrated study of number systems, geometry, algebra, data analysis, probability, and trigonometry.

Standard 4:   Students will understand and apply scientific concepts, principles, and theories pertaining to the physical setting and living environment and recognize the historical development of ideas in science.

Standard 5:   Students will apply technological knowledge and skills to design, construct, use, and evaluate products and systems to satisfy human and environmental needs.

Standard 6:   Students will understand the relationships and common themes that connect mathematics, science, and technology and apply the themes to these and other areas of learning.

Standard 7:   Students will apply the knowledge and thinking skills of mathematics, science, and technology to address real-life problems and make informed decisions.

Standard 3: Mathematics

Mathematical Reasoning

Number and Numeration

1. Students use mathematical reasoning to analyze mathematical situations, make conjectures, gather evidence, and construct an argument.

Students:
- use models, facts, and relationships to draw conclusions about mathematics and explain their thinking.
- use patterns and relationships to analyze mathematical situations.
- justify their answers and solution processes.

2. Students use number sense and numeration to develop an understanding of the multiple uses of numbers in the real world, the use of numbers to communicate mathematically, and the use of numbers in the development of mathematical ideas.

Students:
- use whole numbers and fractions to identify locations, quantify groups of objects, and measure distances.

(Continued)

- use logical reasoning to reach simple conclusions.

This is evident, for example, when students:
▲ build geometric figures out of straws.
▲ find patterns in sequences of numbers, such as the triangular numbers 1, 3, 6, 10, ...
▲ explore number relationships with a calculator (e.g., 12 + 6 = 18, 11 + 7 = 18, etc.) and draw conclusions.

- use concrete materials to model numbers and number relationships for whole numbers and common fractions, including decimal fractions.
- relate counting to grouping and to place value.
- recognize the order of whole numbers and commonly used fractions and decimals.
- demonstrate the concept of percent through problems related to actual situations.

This is evident, for example, when students:
▲ count out 15 small cubes and exchange 10 of the cubes for a rod 10 cubes long.
▲ use the number line to show the position of 1/4.
▲ figure the tax on $4.00 knowing that taxes are 7 cents per $1.00.

Sample Problems

Marlene is designing a uniform for her soccer team. She can choose from 2 different shirts and 3 different pairs of shorts. How many different uniforms can she make if she uses all the shirts and all the shorts?

Answer _____

Explain how you got your answer with a picture or diagram.

Ms. Rivera's class must collect 180 soda cans to win the recycling contest. The chart below shows how the class is doing. How many cans must they collect in the fourth week to reach the goal of 180?

Week	Cans
1	42
2	74
3	18
4	____
Goal	180

Answer _____

(Continued)

Students will understand mathematics and become mathematically confident by communicating and reasoning mathematically, by applying mathematics in real-world settings, and by solving problems through the integrated study of number systems, geometry, algebra, data analysis, probability, and trigonometry.

Operations

Modeling/Multiple Representation

3. Students use mathematical operations and relationships among them to understand mathematics.

Students:

- add, subtract, multiply, and divide whole numbers.
- develop strategies for selecting the appropriate computational and operational method in problem-solving solutions.
- know single digit addition, subtraction, multiplication, and division facts.
- understand the commutative and associative properties.

This is evident, for example, when students:

▲ use the fact that multiplication is commutative (e.g., $2 \times 7 = 7 \times 2$), to assist them with their memorizing of the basic facts.

▲ solve multiple-step problems that require at least two different operations.

▲ progress from base ten blocks to concrete models and then to paper and pencil algorithms.

4. Students use mathematical modeling/multiple representation to provide a means of presenting, interpreting, communicating, and connecting mathematical information and relationships.

Students:

- use concrete materials to model spatial relationships.
- construct tables, charts, and graphs to display and analyze real-world data.
- use multiple representations (simulations, manipulative materials, pictures, and diagrams) as tools to explain the operation of everyday procedures.
- use variables such as height, weight, and hand size to predict changes over time.
- use physical materials, pictures, and diagrams to explain mathematical ideas and processes and to demonstrate geometric concepts.

This is evident, for example, when students:

▲ build a $3 \times 3 \times 3$ cube out of blocks.

▲ use square tiles to model various rectangles with an area of 24 square units.

▲ read a bar graph of population trends and write an explanation of the information it contains.

(Continued)

Sample Problems

Shanelle earns $3.50 per hour for babysitting. Each week she babysits for 4 hours.

   A. How much money does she earn in 1 week?

     Answer _____

   B. How much money does she earn in 4 weeks?

     Answer _____

Bobbie's family bought a pizza. Her mother and sister together ate ½ of the pizza. Bobbie ate ½ of what was left. Use the circle to draw a picture that shows how much of the pizza Bobbie ate.

What fraction of the whole pizza did Bobbie eat?

Answer _____

Figure 3.4   Learning Standards for Mathematics, Science, and Technology at Three Levels for the State of New York

NOTES: Key ideas are identified by numbers (1).
Performance indicators are identified by bullets (•).
Sample tasks are identified by triangles (▲).

or informal, with most people expecting that formal assessments will be more accurate, useful, and credible. The evaluator may survey people having the needs (e.g., library users) or may survey the caretakers of those having needs (e.g., mothers). Surveying people having different perceptions of the needs can increase the validity of the assessment.

A need is the absence of something essential for satisfactory functioning.[5] People have countless needs, for food and air, for livers and lovers, for privacy and educational opportunity. People also *want* such things, but they want some

_____

[5]Problems with needs assessment are nicely raised in Michael Scriven's *Evaluation Thesaurus* (1991, p. 240).

things they do not need (e.g., thrills) and fail to want some things they need (e.g., compassion). It is important for an evaluator to know what people want as well as what they need, and sometimes why. When assessing needs, it is difficult to stick to needs and not to include a lot of wants, but it is also difficult to decide what is "satisfactory functioning" in the definition above.

For evaluative work, the needs that need to be specified are those closely related to the operation of the evaluand. To evaluate a reading program, we won't give much attention to health needs, at least until we encounter reason to believe that health needs are interfering with reading. We will grant that all people need to read, even as we recognize that not all people can hope to (Who would that be?). We will want to be very careful about specifying a level at which all people should read, even as we feel political pressure to declare rock-bottom minimum levels. Human beings are resourceful and can compensate for many weaknesses, so that unconditional needs are hard to find. This is not to diminish obligations for public schools to provide good reading programs but to point out that many statements of need are political rhetoric more than careful assessment of what will be debilitating if unattained. Rather than a rigorous specification of what is needed, evaluators will often be wise to describe existing conditions of poor functioning. This represents one of the many choices for the evaluator. Full specification of factors and implications is more than can be attained. Some matters will remain unexamined and unsaid.

Goals

The goals of a program are, of course, whatever is intended of it, formally or informally, targeted outcomes—but not just outcomes. Suitable preparatory conditions and hoped-for operations are goals as well. Often there will be a statement of official goals prepared by program sponsors or staff. These usually concentrate on intended benefits, particularly the alleviation of deficits and needs. It will be argued by some that the merit of a program has to be in its outcomes, but often major efforts are made just to create and sustain a program. Intermediate or "capacity-building" goals need to be included within any evaluator's perception of goals. The goals for a youth, or a church, or a standing army may include outcomes long in coming and hidden from view. Even with a goal-based evaluation approach, the aim of evaluation is seldom best limited to stated goals. A full array of staff and stakeholder goals needs to be considered, even if the clients calling for the evaluation are requiring only that attainment of their own goals be studied.

Goal-based evaluation usually uses the stated goals put forward by sponsors or staff as the main *conceptual organizers* for the study. See, for example, the goals for the United Kingdom's National Development Programme (CET) in Computer Assisted Learning (Hooper, 1975), a higher-education research and development project.

AIMS OF THE CET PROGRAMME

- To develop and secure the assimilation of computer-assisted and computer-managed learning on a regular institutional basis at reasonable cost; and
- To make recommendations to appropriate agencies in the public and private sector (for example, DES, UGC, Computer Board, LEA's, Ministry of Defense, computer manufacturers) concerning possible future levels and types of investment in computer-assisted and computer-managed learning in education and training.

Barry MacDonald's evaluation report of CET, "The Programme at Two," was published in 1975 by the Centre for Applied Research in Education. Again look at the student performance standards for the state of New York in Figure 3.4. The standards look like goals. Sometimes a program's goals appear identical to its standards. Goals are supposed to be targets to shoot at. According to the dictionary, performance standards should be cut-scores for judging the performance. Goals should be higher than cut-scores. But the terms are used interchangeably.

More in the past than now, some authorities have required program goals to be stated as *behavioral objectives,* indicating how well the recipients of instruction should be able to perform after completing the program. In Figure 3.5 are shown some behavioral objectives drawn from what was once the Instructional Information Exchange run by James Popham. The difference between behavioral and nonbehavioral objectives is well worth an hour or two of contemplation—if one has thought little about them before. The implications for teaching become apparent. It is an error to suppose that the teaching will always improve if the instructor aims more at behavioral objectives.

Conceptual organizers are themes, major questions, or needed statements of quality that an evaluator uses to shape his or her thinking about organizing data gathering and laying out a plan for reporting.[6] It means that these goals

---

[6]Social scientists often use research questions or null hypotheses as their conceptual organizers. Theirs is the search for theory-building generalizations (e.g., Do teachers concentrate on students at the top of the bottom quarter for pacing their teaching?) more than understanding merit and worth of an evaluand (e.g., Has this teacher adapted the pace of her teaching to fit her students?).

Major Category

Our Colonial Heritage

Objective 5: Types of Colonies

Given a description of a situation that depicts some aspect of colonial life or an actual political event in a colony, the student will indicate the type of colony to which the situation applies: Proprietary Colony, Royal Colony, or Charter Colony.

Sample Items

Directions: Read the short description of some aspect of colonial life given below. Then, in the blank preceding the description, write the letter of the type of colony to which the situation applies.

The three types of colonies are:
A. Proprietary Colony
B. Royal Colony
C. Charter Colony

—— 1. Today is an important day in this colony. It has been one year since the last elections were held, so today is the day for all the freemen of the colony to elect their governor. Even though theoretically their choice for governor must be approved by the king of England, it has been many years since the king has bothered to object to a new governor. So, with little concern for what the king might think, the freemen gather at the town hall for the election.

—— 2. Today there is much unrest in this colony. News has just arrived that the king has appointed the new members of the upper house of the legislature and has also chosen a new governor. From past experience, the colonists know that the appointees of the king are usually unconcerned about the problems of the colony. The governor is usually nothing less than a tyrant who accepts the office of governor to further his own career.

—— 3. A huge tract of land was given to Mr. X by the king in return for outstanding service to the crown. Mr. X, desiring colonists to settle the land, begins offering parcels of land at such low prices that he soon has thousands of inhabitants on his land. Seeing the need for some type of government organization, he appoints a governor, sets up a court system, and announces open elections to fill the local government posts.

(Continued)

——— 4. The government of this colony, acting under orders from the crown, has just imposed a 7:00 curfew on the inhabitants. The colonists are very indignant about this but their voices are powerless against the governor. They decide to write a petition to the king, imploring him to instruct the governor to remove the curfew.

——— 5. The council and assembly of this colony were just elected in the last annual elections, held about a month ago. Last week they passed a measure that is certain to be unpopular with the king once he hears of it. The townspeople, however, are not worried about the king's reaction because he has no power to veto the decisions of the government of this colony.

——— 6. Now that independence has been attained, the former colonies are busy writing new state constitutions to replace the old colonial charters. In this particular colony, the colonial constitution is considered to be so liberal and so well suited for self-government that the leaders decide to use it as the basis for the new state constitution.

Answers:

1. C
2. B
3. A
4. B
5. C
6. C

Figure 3.5   Sample Behavioral Objectives

SOURCE: Copyright Instructional Objectives Exchange. Reprinted with permission.

are examined carefully by the evaluator to identify criteria, standards, weights, and needs, as well as opportunities to measure performance and goal attainment.

Although Ralph Tyler devoted more of his writing to instructional process and curriculum development than to evaluation, many consider him the father of professional evaluation in education. Some have attributed the goal-based approach to him. Joe O'Shea (1974) described the contributions of Tyler in his dissertation, "An Inquiry Into the Development of the University of Chicago Evaluation Movement." Tyler's student, Lee Cronbach, epitomized program evaluation as the improvement of large-scale instructional policy. With help from a consortium of Stanford colleagues, Cronbach (1982) developed a generalization-seeking version of standards-based evaluation, UTOS. It called for rigorous sampling of a population of users, treatments, observations, and specifics of time and culture (more on UTOS in Chapter 9).[7] Cronbach used a Central America nutrition study as one illustration of his system, as paraphrased:

> The nutrition study was directed by Robert Klein of the Institute for Nutrition of Central America and Panama (INCAP). It sought to test whether providing a protein supplement to expectant mothers and young children would improve the children's intellectual performance as they grew. The group comparisons were carried out in stages, with the design reconsidered at each. They assigned units randomly between two treatments, yet the questions that were of interest ranged far beyond the experimental contrast. In fact, the variables most discussed in the published papers were not those the experimenter controlled.
>
> To supply the food under conditions that would permit an exact record of who took what amount of it, a public health station was staffed at each of four small isolated villages. Medical services and social stimulation were recognized as potentially confounding, so control villages were used without the protein supplement. The experimental treatment consisted of setting up the center, offering gruel (with protein) or a sweet drink (without). Subsequent analyses showed many alternative explanations for differences in the children studied, but the lack of data supporting protein supplementation was considered important. (pp. 46–57)

Cronbach's eleven-page description of the INCAP evaluation is indicative of the far-ranging and perplexing thinking required by a complex evaluand. Part of it is the diversity of goals. The evaluator recognizes that stakeholders have goals for the program too, some of which will be different from those of the program people. The goal picture can be problematic. Long ago, when educational technology was an emerging field, a cartoon was widely circulated to show the misrepresentation potential in goal statements. That cartoon is shown here in Figure 3.6.

Stakeholders are any people who have something to gain or lose, depending on how successful the program is. This includes not just students and trainees but parents, program opponents, taxpayers, and politicians as well. Just how much to weight the goals of stakeholder groups, as well as different groups within the staff and sponsors, is a challenge to the evaluator. No goals should be completely ignored, but dividing up a limited budget among all possible advocacy groups is difficult.

---

[7]Similarly, psychologist Don Campbell of Northwestern University has been a major influence in program evaluation, especially for large federal programs. More than Cronbach, he urged the use of social science research designs with random assignment of treatment to groups. Robert Baruch, Tom Cook, Charles Reichardt, William Shadish, and Carol Weiss are among those carrying on the Campbell tradition.

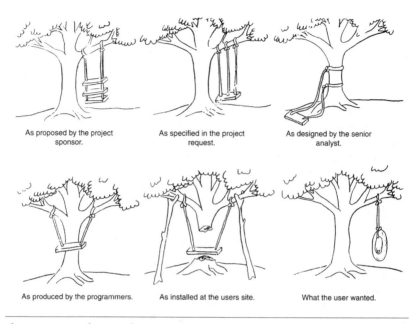

As proposed by the project sponsor.	As specified in the project request.	As designed by the senior analyst.
As produced by the programmers.	As installed at the users site.	What the user wanted.

Figure 3.6   The Transformation of Specifications

Goal-free evaluation was invented by Michael Scriven (1973) partly to protest the intent of managers and patrons to limit evaluation to what they want evaluated, but also to clarify the obligation of the evaluator to decide what attention should be paid to different goals.

Costs

Knowledge of the quality of a program is usually of limited use without some knowledge of its costs. The standards-based evaluator tries to be explicit about program costs, not only monetary costs but "in-kind," psychological, and opportunity costs as well. Sometimes the program resources noted are only the customary things, things largely known to stakeholders. But the costing out of a new or alternative program is important and often very difficult, often requiring more budget and talent than the evaluator has at hand. Even in the best standards-based studies, the costs may be merely alluded to, and may be only about expenditures. Strictly speaking, cost is not a determination of quality, but it is part of the full description needed for understanding program quality.

How can the price of paper clips or anything else be an aspect of quality? It is not, until the user sees the evaluand to be of different quality after the paper clip change. All this does not mean that customer satisfaction and quality are the same thing. The customer can perceive the quality high and the purchase poor. If the successful program is found to burn out its staff, the stakeholder's perception of the quality may change. Sometimes a free program is valued less than a high-cost program. Costs may regularly temper the sense of goodness. The evaluator does not need to know the formula—or to validate it. In tune with their personal lives, stakeholders form ideas of merit including, consciously and unconsciously, whatever ingredients experience and reason teach them. Quality is a construction of the stakeholder and, some of the time, needs to be treated that way.

Sometimes it is useful to examine estimates of resources allocated to different goals for the program. In 1969, we in CIRCE had a contract to develop evaluation methods for local school activity and materials for the Illinois Gifted Student Program. In the report at the end of the first year, we estimated the division of work and costs as shown in Figure 7.3 of Chapter 7.

Cost analysis and cost-benefit studies are held in high regard in policy evaluation. There the long-range attention is not on the single evaluand but on a larger evaluand collectively made up of many cases using the same operational approach or facilities. It is sometimes proposed that comparisons between alternatives can best be made if a cost-benefit ratio is calculated for each. In the case of the Indiana statewide Gifted and Talented Education Program (see box below), the estimated costs favored the enrichment approach over the acceleration approach, but estimated student benefits favored the acceleration approach. A quantitative ratio for objective comparison of the two was not obtained because the scaling of benefits and the scaling of costs were so hypothetical. Factors influencing costs and benefits were presented to the Indiana Department of Education, but not explicit ratios for comparison.

The schools participating in the State of Indiana Gifted and Talented Education Program in 1985 had a choice as to curricular strategy. The State Superintendent's policy supported either development and use of

(Continued)

> (Continued)
>
> - Enrichment, with special courses and activities minimally connected with the general curriculum; or
> - Acceleration, with special courses and activities for advanced work in main academic courses.
>
> Under the latter policy, a huge cost was found to be associated with additional accelerated courses needed for gifted and talented students in subsequent years. (Stake, Raths, Denny, Stenzel, & Hoke, 1986)

The data for analyzing these costs were obtained from a survey sent to all participating school corporations (districts). The survey form is shown in Figure 3.7.

The analysis of program costs is difficult and, depending on assumptions made, can be quite misleading. A search for assistance in the professional literature can start with Mun C. Tsang (1997). A cost-benefit approach in education and social programming owes much to the thinking of Henry Levin (see Levin & McEwan, 2001). A look at the state of the art of cost-benefit and cost-effectiveness analyses in education has been published by Barbara Hummel-Rossi and Jane Ashdown (2002).

Representations of Performance

Suppose the president calls you asking for an evaluation of the American Red Cross, and he wants it in an hour. Of course you would do it. And your mother wants the lowdown on the Golden Skies Nursing Home. And your bishop would like an evaluation of the Winter Retreat. Of course, not all in the same hour. What you would do in an hour is pretty much what you would do in a week or a year. You would learn as much as you can about the factors and the performance and prepare an increasingly time-tested report. What would increase greatly with more time is your confidence in what you will tell the president and those other two.

One of your first realizations would be that there are people out there who know more about this than you do. So you go on the Internet to Google for leads. Needing documents to cite, you get on the phone and ask for advice about existing reports and data sources. You have little time to read. That takes too long. You have to rely on others who know. You cannot hope to learn more

School Costs for Gifted Education
Note: Answer all questions in this section for 1985–86 only.

1. How much money did your Corporation receive in 1985–86 from the Indiana Office of Gifted and Talented to support your IDE G/T project? (IDE = Indiana Department of Education)	1. $ _____
2. How many students (if any) were immediate beneficiaries of the services and resources purchased with the IDE grant? (Note: The number here should match the totals to be reported in Sections IV and VI.)	2. N = _____
3. How many teachers participated in staff development or inservice provided from these IDE funds?	3. N = _____

4. To give us a perspective we greatly need, please identify the additional costs (projected to the end of the year) of conducting the IDE G/T project. Include budget-line items as well as hidden and shared costs, possibly Chapter 2 money or other grants or donations, whatever costs of conducting the project that were not covered by the IDE G/T grant. Estimate the amount spent for each of the several purposes below:

(We recognize we are asking for information not readily available. Please make realistic estimates.)

Additional costs for staff development, including travel and per diem	4a. $ _____
Additional costs for teacher stipends for curriculum development	4b. $ _____
Additional (outside the grant) project costs for substitute teachers	4c. $ _____
Additional costs for consultants	4d. $ _____
Additional costs for administrative salaries	4e. $ _____
Additional costs for project teacher salaries not covered by IDE G/T	4f. $ _____
Additional costs for clerical personnel and office expenses	4g. $ _____
Additional costs for materials, books, equipment, etc.	4h. $ _____
Additional costs for testing and test scoring service	4i. $ _____
Other additional costs (please specify)	4j. $ _____
Total ADDITIONAL costs to conduct IDE G/T project	4k. $ _____
	(Continued)

Now let's shift gears! There is an important distinction between the Corporation's sum-total Program for the gifted/talented AND its Project funded by IDE G/T. Often the Corporation's total program has many parts, a longer history, and is more extensive. Included in this program, in addition to the IDE project, are activities like A/P classes, college credit courses, science fairs, brain games, clubs, etc. The next few questions are about these other local efforts.

5. How much 1985–86 appropriation money was explicitly budgeted (line item) for G/T activities within your Corporation? (Do not include the IDE G/T grant and expenses above.)

5. $ _____

6. How many students (if any) were direct beneficiaries of services purchased with this money?

6. N = _____

7. What was the annual per pupil expenditure for all schooling for your Corporation in 1985–86?

7. N = _____

Now for some difficult but serious estimates of total costs. . . .

8. Relevant to whatever working definition of "gifted and talented" you want to use, please make a rough estimate of the proportion of the grand total expenditure for education in your Corporation being spent for the regular and special education of G/T youngsters.

8. _____%

9. Now whatever that amount might be, please estimate the portion of it being spent in 1985–86 to give G/T youngsters special classes or exclusive "learning experiences" not available to other youngsters.

9. _____%

10. Please add any comments to help us understand how monies were spent for G/T activities in 1985–86.

_____

_____

_____

_____

Figure 3.7   Estimating Costs of Indiana Gifted/Talented Program to the Local Schools

than a tiny part of what the Red Cross does, or what they do at Golden Skies or the Winter Retreat. You need a formal or even informal statement of program, activities, and goals, possibly in a report on the Web. Don't forget the reference librarian at the nearest big library. Perhaps someone would fax you a few pages. Needs will be implied in the report if not mentioned directly. You may want to spend a few minutes thinking of who else is providing these services or what would happen if that evaluand disappeared. What else would you do? You have to rely on other people. I'm sure I'd call Rita. You'd call your Rita.

Reporting back, you would want to say a lot about performance. That's a good topic to ask the reference librarian. In the short time, you just have to find someone with expertise who has written about this matter already, better if with long study and objectivity. Of course, it is presumptuous to ask. But you do. What are the issues of quality of service? Are there different advocacy groups with different standards and views of performance? What is the biggest disappointment?

For the Red Cross, what you will probably care most about is getting good information about performance. If you were working for the U.S. General Accounting Office (GAO) under Eleanor Chelimsky and had a year to study the Red Cross, you would interview people working at the headquarters and a few from the resource teams. Then you would read lots of existing documents. You might survey beneficiaries if a particular disaster warranted it, but a broad survey of beneficiaries would probably not provide the kind of criterial information that you need. Evaluating the nursing home or the retreat would almost certainly need the views of beneficiaries.

Some hard thinking needs to go into the question of what really is the performance of the evaluand. Can it be recognized by the beneficiaries? Do staff members have a sense of the evaluand as a whole? The more complex the operation, the more you need to deal with managers with broad perspectives and researchers doing critical studies. One of the things you say on the phone is, "I have a couple of questions I need to ask your supervisor."

Okay, you are not going to call the director of the Red Cross, or Senator Elizabeth Dole, the former director. You don't give up when three people hang up on you. The point is that you need ingenuity and perseverance to come to understand the scope of the evaluand, its positive and negative images, and its activities. You are looking for its quality, and you may be able to get better data than anyone else has, but you should not presume that only the performance data you gather yourself are worth including in the study.

The best evidence of quality, or productivity, or gain, or program effectiveness is likely to be in measurements of performance. It can be recipient performance, staff performance, stakeholder perception of benefit, or all of these. That evidence may show improvement, a gain from Time 1 to Time 2, or a drop in performance. You will directly ask people how much better (or worse) things have become.

When you ask simple questions, you usually need to ask lots of people the same questions for the findings to be credible. We aggregate these data and calculate the descriptive statistics, sometimes regression analysis or linear modeling. Statistical inference—drawing inferences to a real or hypothetical larger population—may or may not make sense. (Why not?) Note that these statistical procedures imply that the truth about the program is to be found in large aggregations of measurements, something that cannot be directly seen by individual staff members, stakeholders, or evaluators. The alternative to *aggregative analysis* is *interpretive analysis,* where truth about the program is found in what certain individuals can see for themselves. Most good evaluations include both, even when the aggregative and interpretive data lead to different conclusions.

You may think that you only can call yourself an evaluator if you aggregate a lot of observations or responses and do the statistical analysis. A standards-based evaluation of a large program will usually include a lot of statistical information, but the essence of the responsibility is to come to the best possible conclusions about program quality. It is not assured by asking a large number of people, especially about the quality of decisions in which they have little involvement.

To evaluate performance, you need to gather repeated observations of each of the several important performances. To evaluate the Winter Retreat, it is important to get data on the planning of activities as well as on participation in them. There is no need to summarize performance in a single judgment. The small, group sessions may be of a different quality than the plenary sessions. We may call it "descriptive analysis." It is up to you to think through, specify, describe, and get judgment data on the various performances.

What Goes Wrong

There is never enough time. The president wanted you to call back in an hour. The Veterans Benefits Administration wanted our evaluation of Reader Focused Writing in three months. Phyllis has twenty days. Your supervisor wants you to finish your part of another evaluation study this month—and you have all those other assignments too. When you do your dissertation, you may think that at least then you will have the time you need, but there is never enough time. You want to schedule three successive trial runs of your main instrument, but you are squeezed even to make a single one.

And validity. Probably the greatest weakness of professional evaluation work is the limited validation of interpretations. Evaluators do not obtain adequate assurance of the validity of representations of needs and performances. It is widely believed that if you get expert help, from people such as kinesiologists or choreographers or lead teachers, you do not have to check the correlation of scores with independent measures of the factor. But validity requires it. There is never enough time and funding, even in the most prestigious studies, to validate the measurements. It is important for every evaluator to recognize the risk of using unvalidated data-gathering procedures and to caution report readers appropriately.

> Jack Easley was the formative evaluator for Max Beberman's mathematics curriculum development project. The lesson writers would create lessons, and Jack would have teachers try them out in math classes in a small number of schools. He managed to get the procedure so routinized that he could get teacher and student responses, with commentary, back to the writers in two weeks. But by that time, they had usually already decided to change the explanation or to insert additional problems for the students' assignments.

One of the most discouraging aspects of evaluative studies is lack of cooperation from respondents and other data providers. Many providers are not persuaded that evaluation is worth knowing about or participating in. Some think evaluation is more likely to increase the risk to their standing than improve it. And most are too busy already. Getting a respectable return rate on the questionnaires or voluntary testing is often difficult. People are inclined to help you out as a personal favor more than to help create technical information for improved management. It takes a lot of persuasion to complete many an evaluation study. It sometimes helps to have in hand a successful, nonthreatening earlier study report to show what can be produced.

> Charles Murray had contracts with participating schools to send him student data for his evaluation of Cities-in-Schools, a well-financed, high-priority federal program to provide family services through social workers based in schools. The data never arrived. (Stake, 1986)

Narrative

Mr. Sagredo and Phyllis are having soup and sandwiches in the cafeteria. They ask Mr. Ferdy, a thirty-year veteran staff member, to join them.

Phyllis: Ferdy, how do you compare this Senior Mentor Training course to how mentors used to get trained?

Ferdy: Well, for a long time, we had no rules on how to be a mentor. We just asked the new people if they needed anything. When we didn't help them, most said nothing, not believing they could ask for help.

Sagredo: But about ten years ago we started having mentors make a quarterly report, using a checklist.

Ferdy: Right. That reminded us of some things we needed to be talking about.

Sagredo: And people started noticing Celeste. She was especially sensitive to how the younger people did or didn't fit in.

Ferdy: She became sort of a mentor to the other mentors.

Phyllis: Did the checklist change the idea of mentoring?

Ferdy: Are you asking about the goals of the training?

Phyllis: In a way.

Ferdy: Some goals now are stated on the cover of the training packet.

Phyllis: But it was probably the Davis situation that caused the Board to reorganize the training.

Ferdy: We don't want that to happen again.

Phyllis: Mr. Ferdy, do you think it would be good to have a half dozen people who have been through the training talk about the needs for mentoring and whether this particular training is right for our situation?

Ferdy: Celeste would like that.

Sagredo: Phyl, you said that we needed to compare the performance of the trainers and trainees to standards. What would those standards be?

Phyllis: We need to use standards to evaluate the trainers and additional standards to evaluate the trainees. They are related, but different, and only a part of the standards we will use to evaluate the course. These standards don't exist in writing anywhere, so they will have to be in the minds of those who help do the final synthesis. That mostly would be me, with help possibly from Mrs. Vivani and an outside expert.

   Mrs. Vivani talks about the ideal mentor, and we will find out as much as we can about the actual training, thus giving us some trainee criteria. For trainer performance criteria, I will ask all the current mentors to keep a copy of their memos and record their contacts for a month. I will get feedback from those who have completed the program. I will gather data on each of the criteria, then with help from others, decide what is poor, good, and excellent performance. So, the standards are internalized in my thinking, and reinforced by others reviewing my calculations. I will have a hard look at all the data, not just the trainer and trainee performances. Then I will draft statements summarizing the quality of the training, and modify them as further review and reflection guide me.

Ferdy: And that would be your report?

Phyllis: No, the report would also describe the training, the need for it, the criteria and standards, and the outcomes and my interpretations. I would go back to a few of the people who have given me information and hear their reactions to my interpretations. That would give me new information. And I would ask someone with mentor training experience—like a friend of mine in Navy Personnel—to talk me through the revised draft. What do you think?

Sagredo: Sounds to me more like opinions than standards. Isn't there something we can do to make it less personal?

Phyllis: Well, the obvious thing is to have the trainees take a performance test. We can use the test from Orlando, but it hasn't been validated, and it has nothing in the way of tables indicating what scores mean as to competence in mentoring. We still have to interpret the scores ourselves. We could compare scores from people who have had training with some who have not, but I don't feel that the two groups would be comparable on other criteria, such as longevity here and interpersonal skills. Still, I would like to try the test out on a few trainees and then we could decide where to go from there.

Sagredo: OK. Let's not take people away from their work any more than we have to.

(To be continued)

4

Responsive Evaluation

Don't judge any man until you have walked two moons in his moccasins.

Native American proverb

Responsive evaluation is a general perspective in the search for quality and the representation of quality in a program. It is an attitude more than a model or recipe. No matter what the role or design for evaluation, it can be made more responsive or less. Being responsive means orienting to the experience of personally being there, feeling the activity, the tension, knowing the people and their values. It relies heavily on personal interpretation. It gets acquainted with the concerns of stakeholders by giving extra attention to program action, to program uniqueness, and to the cultural plurality of the people. Its design usually develops slowly, with continuing adaptation of evaluation purpose and data gathering in pace with the evaluators' becoming well acquainted with the program and its contexts. Some of this same experiential predisposition, determination to find "what's out there," can be built into any evaluation.

SEÑOR PRETELIN'S CLASS

The temperature will climb into the 70s today, but now it is chilly in this white tile and terrazzo classroom. Eleven students (of 29 still on the roster) are here, each in a jacket or sweater. No doubt it was cooler when they left home. The instructor, Señor Pretelin, reminds them of the topic, The Origins of Capitalism, and selects a question for which they have prepared answers. An answer from the back

(Continued)

---

row is ventured. Two more students arrive—it is ten past the hour—now four more. Sr. Pretelin undertakes correction of the answer, but asks for still more of an answer. His style is casual. He draws long on a cigarette. His audience is alert. Marx is a presence, spoken in name, and looming from the cover of the textbook. Two books only are in sight. Several students have photocopies of the chapter assigned. The chalkboard remains filled with last class's logic symbols, now unnoticed. Some students read through their answers, most concentrate on what Pretelin says about answers that are offered. The first answers had been volunteered by males, now one from a female. The instructor draws her out, more of her idea, then improves upon the explanation himself.

The coolness of the space is warmed by the exchanges. Outside a power mower sputters, struggling with a thickness of grass for which it probably was not designed. It is 20 past the hour. Another student arrives. Most are around 20, all have black hair. These are incoming freshmen in the social studies and humanities program, enrolled in a sociology course on political doctrines. Still another arrives. She pushes the door closed, and jams it with a chair, to thwart the breeze from the squared-out plaza. Sr. Pretelin is expanding an answer at length. He then turns to another question, lights another cigarette while awaiting a volunteer—again he asks for improvement, gets a couple of tries, then answers the question to his satisfaction. Another question. He patiently awaits student initiative. The students appear to think or read to themselves what they had written earlier.

The haze of Mexico City shrouds the city center several miles to the southeast. Yesterday's downpour did not long cleanse the sky. Quiet again while awaiting a volunteer. The first young woman offers her answer. She is the only female of the seven or so students who have ventured forth. Heads nod to her reference to the camposinos. If capitalistic advocacy exists in this classroom, it does not speak out. A half hour has passed. The recital continues. Only a few students are correcting their notes (or creating them belatedly), most try to read or listen. Minds are mobilized, not idling. Finally a small wedge of humor.

The air may relax a bit. Four observers are dispersed about the room, little noticed even as they write. The instructor maintains his task, not ever stopping to take roll. Pretelin is a slight man, perhaps 40. He wears a smart jacket, a dark shirt buttoned high, a gold

(Continued)

neck-chain. His fingers are long and expressive. For several minutes, the dragging of heavy objects outside the room interferes. For a last time the students are sent to their answers, even asked to look further. Few have books. Then the students are invited to pose questions. The exchange becomes more good-natured, but businesslike still. The engagement goes on, minds "full on," provoked sociably, heads nodding agreement. More immediate camposinos, now drawn 17 million strong to the streets below, make the noises of the city. A poster admonishes: "Adman. Vota. Platestda." Near the door the graffiti begins "La ignorancia mata . . ." The hour draws to a close, a final cigarette, a summary, a warm smile.

The portrayal of Señor Pretelin's class was part of an informal responsive evaluation of instruction at the Universidad Autonoma Metropolitana of Mexico City. It was observed and reported so as to give the reader an experience of what it was like to be in the classroom and a sensitivity to what is weak and strong about the instruction. It shows this instructor's strong personal caring but, even when added to other portrayals, provides but a small sample of instruction in the hundreds of other classrooms.

A responsive predisposition has important consequences. The evaluation work changes as the program changes, thus making some *initial* decisions about instruments, data sources, and standards less relevant. With some changes in program and evaluation responsive to those changes comes less opportunity to aggregate banks of quantitative data and to seek statistical significance. The evaluation gets closer to people, and so raises the risk of getting emotionally involved with certain groups or positions. The evaluation hears subtle differences in language; initial designs featuring rough categories and correlations may be found less useful. And through all of this, if interpretation becomes more important than criterial measurement, it becomes not just a difference in focus of attention but a difference in what is considered *meaning* and *evidence*.

Following social science standards, most evaluators try to represent the many aspects of the evaluand with high-fidelity description. In some parts of their evaluation studies, they try to get information from all participants or a careful representation of those participants. (More about sampling in Chapter 9.) But they also look for one-of-a-kind insights, such as the trainee who says "I think this is blackmail" or the city that gives its control group extra payment because it didn't get the experimental treatment. The question is not "How representative is this?" but "Does it happen even once?" Finding a single occurrence may change perceptions of the program. Responsive evaluation is particularly alert to episodes that, however unrepresentative, add to understanding the complexity of the evaluand.

Responsive evaluation is a search for and documentation of program quality. It uses both criterial measurement and interpretation. The essential feature of the approach is responsiveness to key issues or problems, especially those experienced by people at the sites. It is not particularly responsive to program theory or stated goals; it is responsive to stakeholder concerns. The

> **issue** *n* A question, point, or concern to be disputed or decided; a main matter of contention; a sticking point or grievance; a belief at variance

understanding of goodness rather than the creation of goodness is its aim. Users may go on to alleviate or remediate or develop or aspire, but the purpose of this evaluation is mainly to understand.[1]

Issues as Conceptual Structure

Issues are often chosen as the "conceptual organizers" for responsive evaluation studies. Issues are preferred over the structuring given by goals, needs, chronology, hypotheses, input-output flowcharts, or social and economic equations.

Issues are tensions, problems, organizational perplexities, unscheduled costs, or hidden side effects—things that go wrong with programmatic effort. The term *issue* draws thinking toward the immediacy, interactivity, particularity, and subjective valuing, especially those awarenesses already felt by persons associated with the program.

EXAMPLES OF ISSUE QUESTIONS

- Does personalistic pedagogy here on campus too greatly preclude other theoretical views?
- Are the criteria for eligibility for receiving fire protection at odds with needs in this area?
- Do these simulation exercises confuse the nurses about sources of vital information?
- Does this training perpetuate an ethic of remediation rather than of lifelong learning?

---

[1]The concept of responsive evaluation belongs not only to me (whether or not I was first to attach it to program evaluation; Stake, 1974/1980) but to all those who use it. So the definition changes and diffuses as other people and I use it differently. Even those who do not call their work "responsive evaluation" participate in the continuing definition as they use the term. Thus, an official definition as represented by this book is not to be taken too seriously, and the reader should expect continuing transformation.

People involved in the program are concerned about one thing and another (or are likely to become concerned or should become concerned). The evaluators inquire, negotiate, and select a few issues around which to organize the study. They do not replace the goal of finding the merit of the evaluand, but they do influence the meaning we are giving to merit in that situation.

Evaluators being "responsive" sometimes are said to use the "power of negative thinking." They look for pitfalls and problems, partly for understanding the program's obstacles and partly so that they can examine coping behavior. To become acquainted with a program's problems, responsiveness usually calls for observing its activities, interviewing those who have some role or stake in the program, and examining relevant documents. These are not necessarily the data-gathering methods for informing the interpretation of issues, but they are needed for the initial planning and "progressive focusing" of the study. And even later, management of the study as a whole usually remains flexible—whether quantitative or qualitative data are being gathered.

Observations and Judgments

As said in Chapter 1, we see—at one and the same time—the nature and the merit of the program's activities, personnel, and spaces. Understanding is mixed with judgment. Perhaps the most controversial idea in responsive evaluation is that program merit is discerned from observations and judgments that occur simultaneously. In Chapter 1, we differentiated between *criterial* and *interpretive* thinking. Usually, responsive evaluation is largely interpretive,[2] relying on the human observer, the portrayer of human experience, to give meaning and value to the evaluation. Being responsive, the evaluator may use criteria in a strong sense or merely as part of the description of episodes and comparisons, but the determination of merit and worth is usually made by successive refinements of judgment, not by numerically comparing a performance indicator to a standard. In the eyes of many, that removes it from the territory of social science.

---

[2]Responsive evaluation is both criterial and interpretive, usually with more attention to interpretive observation than to criterial measurement. Standards-based evaluation is both criterial and interpretive, usually with more attention to measurement than interpretive data gathering. In most studies, there will be both responsive and standards-based evaluation, and both criterial measurement and interpretive acquaintance with the evaluand.

A REVIEWER'S COMMENT[3]

The difficulty I see with Responsive Evaluation is that it departs too far from the scientific evaluation model. Scientific evaluation focuses on the counter-factual—what would have happened in the absence of the program?—and works very hard to get a comparison group or other methods so as to estimate true program effects. There is thus a lot of emphasis upon the best estimate of program effect, and we learn something new about it. By contrast, responsive evaluation appears to be more a "talking process" in which, while a lot of stakeholders may express opinions, we are still not sure what we've learned, or what the magnitude of program effect, if any, was.

Anonymous reviewer

The criticism is to be taken seriously. Program evaluation is usually a clear departure from building scientific theory. The question of science may be "Do programs of this kind succeed?" But the question of evaluation is "Is this particular program succeeding?" The evaluand is particular, not general. And the question is not about tendency to succeed, but succeeding here and now. The scientific question is an important question, but it is usually not the evaluation question.[4]

But why not compare to a control group? Wouldn't responsive evaluation be better if it gave its promised attention to activity, personnel, and spaces, but compared the evaluand to a control group? Almost never. The strategic obstacle is that we are not interested in knowing whether or not the evaluand outperforms a program that may or may not represent our standards. And to find whether or not another program meets our standards would be a costly distraction from finding if our own evaluand meets our standards.

The practical problem is that, as indicated in Chapter 1, in human services evaluation, almost never is a satisfactory control group found or created. According to experimental methodology, both groups need to be essentially the same except that one gets the program being studied. We seldom can get a good match. The social science researcher can divide the cases randomly into two

---

[3]This comment was in a blind review of a manuscript I submitted to the *American Journal of Evaluation* for publication.
[4]For more on the difference between science and evaluation, see Chapter 9.

groups and operate the program in one of them. But an evaluator usually starts with the evaluand already formed, often even having completed its run.

In my work, I have found a comparison group almost never a satisfactory standard against which to evaluate a program in which we have intrinsic interest.[5] It sometimes is useful to do some comparing with last year's group or a neighboring group, but for good comparisons, a large part of the budget is needed to maintain controls, treatment, and assessment activities at the other sites. The responsive evaluation approach calls for spending most of the evaluation budget on additional multiple observations of the evaluand.

Perceptions

From the beginning of the study to the end, the responsive-leaning evaluator comes to understand with increasing precision and confidence what is happening and what is the goodness of it. First impressions are a starting point. Corrections and refinements occur because the evaluator is repeatedly checking out those impressions, challenging what only appears to be, seeking alternative views and grounds for conditional or locally separate findings. Observation is the *modus operandi* for responsiveness, although occasionally using more impersonal measurements. Impersonal measurements will often help show how early impressions are crude or even mistaken, but then new interpretations, new impressions, replace the old, taking the measurements into account, and the disciplining of perception rolls on.

Perception of the program's activity is at the heart of responsive evaluation. Instead of hoping to perceive the critical merit in some outcome or impact, the evaluator concentrates on what is good and bad about what the program's staff and participants are doing. Here is a faith in education, in nurturing. If good processes are taking place, the enhancement of the participants will be realized later on. Sometimes trainers need to train people in exact responses; often they need to give them background experiences that can be adapted. More distant program effects, such as competence, readiness, and productivity, need to be looked at too, but it is the most immediate effects that directly reflect the program's contribution to beneficiary well-being.

---

[5]In policy evaluation (see Chapter 9), we expect to have an intrinsic interest in a policy, not in the sites in which the policy is to be studied. There control groups may be valuable. See Don Campbell (1982), Tom Cook (1993), and Robert Boruch (1997).

ANOTHER REVIEWER'S COMMENT ON RESPONSIVE
EVALUATION

Responsiveness is first and foremost the virtue of being oriented or
attentive to praxis (practice). It is to recognize that one is dealing
with situations that are lived, embodied experiences, and
performed. Stake has expressed this characteristic orientation of
responsiveness in evaluation by claiming that evaluation means
attending to human practices like teaching or providing social
services as contextual experiences—"concernful dealings" of
particular kinds that practitioners "undergo" with one another.

Directed toward discovery of merit and shortcoming in the program,
responsive evaluations recognize multiple sources of valuing as well as multiple
grounds for valuing. We sometimes speak of *multiple realities*—differences in
perception so robust that they influence the recognition of meaning, propriety,
and worth. Older staff members often see things differently from younger.
Nurses see things differently from doctors. My son Jacob, the theater carpenter,
sees things differently from the theater painter. Evaluators recognize that different people have different obstacles to contend with, different burdens to bear.
The question often is not how to resolve those differences but how to examine
them, to relate them to evaluating merit and worth. There is diversity in every
group. Evaluating responsively is particularly respectful of multiple standards,
sometimes contradictory standards, standards held by different individuals and
groups, or even standards held by the same individual that change over time.

Ultimately, the evaluators describe the program activity, give interpretation to its issues, and prepare summary statements of program quality. But
first, they feed back descriptive data and interpretations to data givers, surrogate readers, and other evaluation specialists to diminish misunderstanding and misrepresentation. In their reports, they provide more than
abbreviated description of activities over time and personal viewing—so
that, with the reservations and best judgments of the evaluators before them,
the readers of the report can make up their own minds about program quality. With visualizations of space, empathy for people, narratives and
vignettes, the responsive evaluator provides the reader with a *vicarious experience,* some sense that each reader was there in person. The evaluator does
not duck the responsibility for completing the study with value judgments of
his or her own, but adds value statements and vicarious experience to a
reader's existing experience.

Combining Responsive and Standards-Based Evaluation

There is a common misunderstanding that responsive evaluation requires naturalistic inquiry, case study, or qualitative methods. Not so. With the program staff, with evaluation sponsors and others, responsive-leaning evaluators discuss alternative methods of inquiry. Often the clients will want more emphasis on outcomes, whereas responsive advocates press for more attention to the quality of processes. They negotiate. Knowing what different methods can accomplish, and what methods this evaluation "team" can handle well, and being the ones to carry them out, the evaluators ultimately directly or indirectly decide what the methods will be. Preliminary emphasis is often on becoming acquainted with activity, especially for external evaluators, but also acquaintance with the history and social context of the program. The program philosophy may be anything—phenomenological, participatory, instrumental, perhaps the pursuit of accountability. Evaluation method depends largely on the situation. For it to be a good responsive evaluation, the methods need to accommodate to the "here and now," serving the evaluation needs of the stakeholders at hand.

What works, here and now, usually is a combination of responsive and standards-based, with one of them taking the lead, the other filling in and rounding out. Criterial and interpretive thinking do not blend seamlessly; they seldom confirm each other. They maintain their separate concentrations, one on descriptors, the other on episodic descriptions. In a way, this is good because they press for deeper thinking, providing something I will call, in Chapter 9, a "dialectic." Many would like everything to merge into a single picture, without contradiction, but in comprehensive studies, it seldom does. Our combination designs are often called "mixed methods." Jennifer Greene, Yvonna Lincoln, Sandra Mathison, Donna Mertens, and Katherine Ryan (1998) have persuasively made the case for mixed methods. (See also Reichardt & Rallis, 1994, and Greene & Caracelli, 1997.)

Even with this expectation of choosing from many methodological alternatives, it has been *uncommon* for a responsive evaluation study to concentrate on standardized testing of students, large-scale surveys, or other standardized databases. This is because such instrumentation has so often been found simplistic and inattentive to local works and circumstances. At least that is what advocates of responsive evaluation are inclined to think. They see contemporary standardized criterion indicators seldom providing comprehensive measures of the outcomes intended, even when stakeholders have grown used to using them. And even when possible, developing new tests and really good questionnaires is very expensive. For good evaluation, test results have too often been disappointing—with educators, for example (often justifiably), believing that students learned more than showed on the tests. With the responsive approach, tests often are used but in a subordinate role. They are needed when it is clear that they can actually serve to inform people about the quality of the program.

In most responsive evaluations, people are used more as informants than as subjects. To emphasize program description, they are asked more of what they saw than what they felt. Participants are questioned not so much to see how they have changed but to indicate the changes they have seen. They can tell both, but often they are poor witnesses to their own changes as well as to program activity. We don't begin the study with the presumption that a survey of beneficiaries is essential.

Experience as Knowledge

When I first started working as a program evaluator in the 1960s, my thoughts were rooted in empirical social science and psychometrics. There, depersonal-ization and objectivity were esteemed. As I have described elsewhere (Stake, 1998), in my efforts to evaluate curriculum reform efforts back then, I quickly found that neither those designs nor tests were producing data that answered enough of the important questions. Responsive evaluation has been my slowly developing response to *pre-ordinate evaluation.*[6] Pre-ordinate evaluation is *a priori* selection and final measurement of a few outcome criteria. Over the years, I realized that disciplining our impressions and personal experience often led to better understanding of merit and worth than measuring gains or com-paring groups (Stake, Migotsky, et al., 1997).

Gradually, enticed by the work of Alan Peshkin (1978) and Louis Smith (Smith & Geoffrey, 1968) and others, I found ethnography a good aid to eval-uation. It focused on activity and culture—good—but not much on educa-tion—bad (for me). Does it really make a difference what students study? I think so. But I mainly held back from full immersion in ethnography because however long they committed themselves to the particular community or tra-dition, ultimately ethnographers wanted to relate their findings to generaliza-tions about the human condition. I wanted to stick with the particular community or program, less to generalize to others. So I observed activities and recorded interviews to further understanding of the particular evaluand. The reports became portrayals of the evaluand.

---

[6]Pre-ordinate evaluation is the opposite of responsive, with a design based on prespecified goals and criteria often based on little knowledge of or concern for the larger and more subtle issues of program quality.

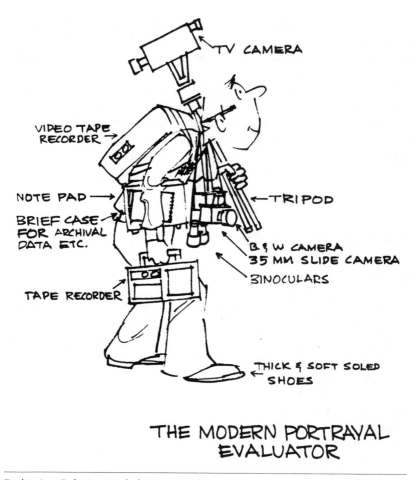

THE MODERN PORTRAYAL EVALUATOR

Evaluation Coloring Book, by Ernest Olson

Reprinted with permission of the artist.

Case study, with the evaluand as the case and the description of experience as the process, became my preferred way of portraying the activity, the issues, the personal relationships and performances that reveal program quality. Not all who have a predilection for responsive evaluation use a case study format. Many evaluators do their work responsively without calling it that. And some who call their work responsive are not responsive in the same ways I am. I do not own the approach. There is no single meaning to the approach. But the ideas of this chapter are common to much of the work that is called *responsive evaluation*.

Many who object to the responsive approach, like the anonymous reviewer in the previous section, do so on the ground that too much attention

Dear Participant,

You have participated in one or more of the workshops that are a part of the National Sex Equity Demonstration Project in Broward County. In order to more fully understand how teachers and administrators in the County were helped or hindered and how they feel about such efforts, we ask that you spend a few minutes commenting upon your workshop experience.

Please describe classroom situations and relate sex equity anecdotes to show examples of sex equity. Your help is invaluable to the understanding of this national endeavor. Use the following questions as a guide in relating your experience. Brief answers are fine. Use the back of this sheet if needed. Thanks very much.

Laura Morgan & Bernadine Stake, Project Evaluation Staff

1. How many of each of the following conducted by sex equity project staff have you attended?
   ___ Materials Review Workshops
   ___ In-Service Workshops
   ___ Sex Equity Awareness Training Workshops
   ___ Visitations
   ___ Summer Writing Teams

2. How many of each of the following conducted by outside consultants have you attended?
   ___ Materials Review Workshops
   ___ In-Service Workshops
   ___ Sex Equity Awareness Training Workshops

3. The workshop(s) was(were)
   ___ very worthwhile
   ___ somewhat worthwhile
   ___ not worthwhile

4. Did your participation in the workshops result in changes in your classroom or school? If so, tell something of the nature of the change.
   _____
   _____
   _____

5. Please recall the Action Plans drawn up at the workshops. How did your plan work out?
   ___ very well
   ___ okay
   ___ not well
   ___ not applicable

(Continued)

6. In what ways have you shared materials with other teachers/administrators? What was their reaction?

_____

_____

_____

7. What do you see as the successes and failures of the Sex Equity Project in Broward County Schools at this time?

_____

_____

_____

8. What further assistance or training would you like in order to implement the ideas of sex equity?

_____

_____

_____

Your position: ___ Administrator, ___ Teacher, or _____

Grade level: ___ Primary, ___ Middle, ___ High

Years experience: ___ 0–2, ___ 3–5, ___ 6–10, ___ 11–20, ___ over 20 years

Sex: ___ Male ___ Female

Date: _____

Return to Laura Morgan, Nova High School.

Figure 4.1   National Sex Equity Project Participant Questionnaire

is given to subjective data—the testimony of participants and the judgments of witnesses. That reviewer characterized the method as a talking process and the data as opinions. Many responsive evaluations involve quite a bit of interviewing, but—for me—the preferred data are observations. Responsive evaluation is empirical study of human activity. When the evaluators are not there to see the activity for themselves, they have to ask those who did see them; see, for example, the open-ended questionnaire in Figure 4.1. The major questions are not questions of opinion or feeling, but what was the sensory experience. And the answers come back, of course, with description, interpretation, opinion, and feeling all mixed together. An evaluator being responsive follows disciplined practices of analysis and triangulation to tease out what is dependable description and interpretation from what is opinion and personal preference.

There is nothing unusual about this questionnaire. But look at it closely. It asks for information, some of it from a personal perspective. In a sense, the participating teacher is part of the evaluation team. For description of what is happening, evaluators try (through triangulation and review panels) to show the credibility of observations and soundness of interpretations. Part of the program description, of course, especially that about the worth of the program, is revealed in how people subjectively perceive what is going on. Placing value on the program is not seen as an act separate from experiencing it.

The researchers' own perceptions too are recognized as subjective, in choosing what to observe, in observing, and in reporting the observations. One tries in responsive evaluation to make those value commitments more recognizable. An evaluator may include in the report, "In a previous study interviewing members of the clergy, I came to appreciate the service ethic." Issues such as the importance of professional development should not be avoided because they are inextricably subjective. When reporting, care is taken to illuminate the subjectivity of data and interpretation.

Objection to a responsive approach is also expressed in the belief that a single authority—the program staff, the funding agency, or the research community—should specify the key questions. Those questions are often worthy of study, but in program evaluation for public use, never exclusively. There is a general expectation that if a program is evaluated, a wide array of important concerns will be considered. Embezzlement, racial discrimination, inconsistency in philosophy, and thwarting of creativity may be unmentioned in the contract and not topics in the evaluator's expertise, but some sensitivity to all such shortcomings belongs within the evaluation expectation, and the professional evaluator at least tries not to be blind to them.

Further, it is recognized that evaluation studies are administratively prescribed, not only to gain understanding and to inform decision making but also to legitimize and protect administrative and program operations from criticism, especially during the evaluation period. And still further, evaluation requirements are sometimes made more for the purpose of promulgating hoped-for standards than for seeing if they are being attained. Evaluators expect to be working in political, competitive, and management self-serving situations. The better studies expose the meanness, as well as the goodness, they find.

By seeking out stakeholder issues, evaluators respond to political and commercial campaigns, recognizing ideological influence on education and social service. Most are not automatically in favor of activism and reform efforts, but many include the issues that reformers raise. Responsive evaluation was not conceived as an instrument of reform. Some activists find it democratic; other writers have found it conservative.[7] It has been used to serve the diverse people

---

[7]In their insightful comparison of evaluation theorists, Shadish, Cook, and Leviton (1991) found my responsive evaluation ideas provincial and unsympathetic to national programs, or any programs so large that they could not be comprehended by a single evaluator alone.

most affected personally and culturally by the program at hand—though it regularly produces some findings each side does not like.

Organizing and Reporting

Program evaluation is a big job for an individual person, and a much larger job for a team. The work can be divided into parts, but the synthesis of information and the search for a balanced expression of merit requires a lot of reflection and communication. It is important for at least one person to try to comprehend the many facets of the evaluand, the issues, and the evidence. Others may write some of the reports, but one person should digest all that others write. All those who write, and others as well, should participate in the weighing of evidence, purging of misunderstanding, and recognition of weaknesses in presentation. Critical friends, review panels, and meta-evaluators should be included as part of the routine. Perhaps a sixth of the work remains when the final report's first draft is in the hard drive.

The work may be organized in a criterial or interpretive coding system. Some kind of coding is essential. An interpretive coding system is merely sorting incoming data by time and topic and source—for workable storage and retrieval. Often a log entry or observed dialogue or e-mail message will need to be coded several ways, and stored in several files. Often both paper files and electronic files are needed, especially to accommodate graphics and artifacts. Each member of a team should have his or her own filing system and should assist the person mainly in charge of the files. One of the most elegant systems I have seen was developed for a national urban school research project that was never completed because the filing of the data was too complex and stored too deep in the computer.[8]

A strong coding system is needed when many of the data are aggregative data. With instruments based on the issues and other information needs, the codings will come from the items of standardized observation checkoffs and surveys. In those cases, statistical distribution and correlation of the data are expected to provide major findings. Chi-square hypothesis testing may be invoked to indicate non-chance distribution of responses. More of this will be discussed in Chapter 6.

The feedback from responsive evaluation studies is expected to be—in format and language—attractive and comprehensible to the various groups, responsive to their needs. Thus, even at the risk of catering,[9] different

---

[8]The Urban School Problem Solving project described by Louis Smith and David Dwyer (1979).
[9]"Kowtowing" they call it in the movies. It means showing extra favor to some groups, such as the group being addressed at the moment. See fairness as an issue to study in Chapter 8 and as an ethical standard in Chapter 10.

reports or presentations may be prepared for different groups. Narrative portrayals, storytelling, and verbatim testimony will be appropriate for some, data banks and regression analyses for others. Obviously the budget will not allow everything, so alternative formats should be considered early in the work.

Responsive evaluation is not *participatory* evaluation (where the evaluation is run cooperatively by the staff or other stakeholders at large; see Chapter 7), but a participatory evaluation can emphasize responsiveness. To be responsive, the study is organized partly around stakeholder concerns. It is common for experiential input from staff and stakeholders to come in early and throughout the evaluation period. Representatives of prospective audiences of readers should have directly or indirectly helped shape the short list of issues to be pursued. Along the way, the responsive evaluator may ask "Is this pertinent?" and "And is this evidence of success?" and might, based on the answer, change the priorities of inquiry.

Responsive evaluation has been useful during formative evaluation when the staff needs more formal ways of monitoring the program, when no one is sure what the next problems will be. It has been useful in summative evaluation when audiences want an understanding of a program's activities, its strengths and shortcomings, and when the evaluators feel that it is their responsibility to provide a vicarious experience. Such experience is seen as important so that the readers of the report can relate the findings to their own sense of program worth.

Responsive evaluation will sometimes be found "intuitive," or indeed subjective, closer to literary criticism (Smith, 1981b) and Elliot Eisner's connoisseurship (1979), or even to Michael Scriven's *modus operandi* evaluation (1976), than to the more traditional social science designs. When the public is seen as the client, responsive evaluation may be seen as "client centered," as once did Daniel Stufflebeam and Anthony Shinkfield (1985, p. 290). But usually it differs from those approaches in the most essential feature, that of responding to the issues, language, contexts, and standards of an array of stakeholder groups (Greene & Abma, 2001).

When I proposed this "responsive evaluation" approach at an evaluation conference at the Pedagogical Institute in Göteborg, Sweden, in 1974, I drew particularly upon the writings of Mike Atkin (1963), Lee Cronbach (1963), Jack Easley (1966), Stephen Kemmis (1976), Barry MacDonald (1976), and Malcolm Parlett and David Hamilton (1977). They spoke of the necessity of organizing the evaluation of programs around what was happening in classrooms, drawing more attention to what educators were doing and less attention to what students were doing. Later I reworked my ideas as I read Ernest House (1980), Egon Guba and Yvonna Lincoln (1989), Tom Schwandt (1989), and Linda Mabry (1990). Of course, I was influenced by many who preferred other ways of evaluating programs.[10]

It is difficult to tell from an evaluation report how "responsive" the study was. A final report seldom reveals how issues were negotiated and how audiences were served. Examples of studies that were intentionally responsive are those by Barry MacDonald and Saville Kushner (1982), Saville Kushner (1992), Tineke Abma (1999), Anne McKee and Michael Watts (2000), Lou Smith and Paul Pohland (1974), and Robert Stake and Jack Easley (1979). My meta-evaluation, *Quieting Reform* (1986), also took a responsive approach.

In Chapter 7, we will go further into reporting to clients, stakeholders, and other readers. In Chapter 9, I will tell you about one of my better inventions, the concept of *naturalistic generalization*. One task for the evaluator is to describe and interpret the evaluand so effectively that the reader will know not only the experience of being there but the experience of being there interactively with the evaluator. The evaluator's interpretations should enhance the experience.

Procedures

Issue statements usually are not broad questions calling for research generalizations, such as "What are the best ways of getting staff members to take responsibility for their own professional development?" or "How do youth form gangs?" or "In what situations is it ethical to break a promise of confidentiality?" These questions, important as they are, give too little guidance in data gathering and analysis. And issue statements usually are not simply information questions such as "What experience has the director had with conflict resolution?" or "What are the criteria for evaluating a PowerPoint presentation?" These may be important questions, but not as a conceptual strategy for a responsive evaluation study.

From the beginning of formal-program-evaluation time, there has been an overly narrow selection of data sources and data types. The complexity of many program calls for a broad perspective on program operation. Multiple sources of information are necessary to minimize what psychologists call "stimulus error," misperceiving what others see the program to be. (You remember the swing-building project, Figure 3.7, in the previous chapter.) Working with more than a few criteria and issues enhances the view of the program, but tends to spread the evaluation resources thin. Efforts to triangulate

---

[10]Two who later became my friends, Ference Marton of Sweden and Michael Huberman of Switzerland, cautioned me in the 1970s that my endorsement of subjectivity was equivalent to "inviting educational researchers to commit suicide."

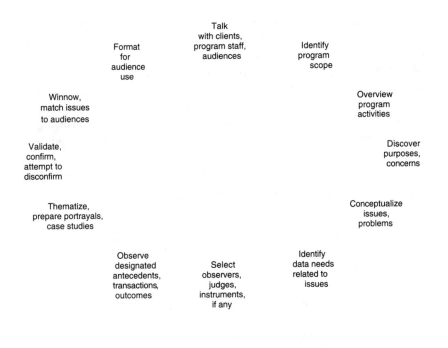

Figure 4.2   The Responsive Clock: Prominent Events in a Responsive
Evaluation

SOURCE: Stake, 1974/1980

key observations and interpretations increase the validity of the data, but risk giving too much attention to too small a view.

From 1967 to 1973, having found little success with standards-based evaluation within the contexts of curriculum development and professional training, I carefully studied the question of evaluation methods. I became even more persuaded that it was necessary to get deeply acquainted with the actual operations of the program, to collect both qualitative and quantitative data, to rely on personal interpretation of quality, and to report in ways that engage the experience and values of the readers. I summarized the steps in a graphic called the Responsive Clock, shown here as Figure 4.2. Quoting from the 1974 paper (p. 12), "I know that some of you would remind me that a clock moves clockwise, so I hurry to say that this clock moves clockwise and counter-clockwise and cross-clockwise." In other words, any event can follow any event. Furthermore, many events occur simultaneously, and the evaluator returns to many events many times before the evaluation ends.

Evaluation is facilitated and debilitated by language. We are too quick to find precedents, classifications, labels for things—in fact, we sometimes falsely believe that labeling is our assignment. The Swedish botanist Carolus Linnaeus was one of the founders of science because he classified flora systematically and meticulously. Plants were seen differently after that, just because of his classifications.[11] It was an enormous scientific step forward, a replacement of old knowledge with new. Our evaluation business is not one of categorizing things, but finding the worth of the special thing we have before us. Thus, many of us move less toward classification and more toward experiential understanding.

THE LOVE SONG OF J. ALFRED PRUFROCK

> Let us go then, you and I,
> When the evening is spread out against the sky
> Like a patient etherized upon a table;
> Let us go, through certain half-deserted streets,
> The muttering retreats
> Of restless nights in one-night cheap hotels
> And sawdust restaurants with oyster-shells:
> Streets that follow like a tedious argument
> Of insidious intent
> To lead you to an overwhelming question . . .
> Oh, do not ask, "What is it?"
> Let us go and make our visit . . .
>
> T. S. Eliot

What Goes Wrong

T. S. Eliot calls us to seek personal experience of the evaluand. In urging us not to ask "What is it?" he cautions against premature substitution of words for empirical knowledge. It can be good to make no immediate effort to capture the evaluand in words. But empirical knowing includes language. Almost simultaneously we experience and we categorize and explain—and we judge. We cannot just feel. Almost immediately, we have to describe, first maybe in some primitive language to ourselves. (See how James Reston opens Chapter 7.)

---

[11]It was another instance of research practice having a reactive effect on the meaning of criteria.

Knowing something means making images of it, some of them verbal images. Ultimately, our readers need to know *what* we think we have been evaluating.[12] Things go wrong when we rely heavily on existing or premature descriptions. But they also go wrong when we rely only on stories, impressions, and narratives to represent the fullness of the evaluand. Readers flounder without hard description.

To convey a vicarious experience to our readers, we look for experiences that we (or some stakeholders) have. We look for their stories. Although it is rather easy to find interesting stories pertinent to the evaluand, it is much harder to find stories that develop an issue. The justification for responsive evaluation, which includes personalistic, impressionistic, and subjective data gathering, is in its deeper probing of issues and meanings of quality. Critics of qualitative studies are often quieted when they recognize the complexity and contextuality of the evaluand revealed by the data and embodied in the assertions of the report. And the importance of the work is easily dismissed if important issues are not developed. In standards-based evaluation there is a pride in the instruments developed, and in responsive evaluation there is pride in the meanings found in program activity.

At the end of a study, evaluators make assertions about the process and contexts of the evaluand, and especially about its merit and shortcomings. The evaluator may hope to encourage readers to use their own experience to expand upon or counter his or her professional judgments, doing so by including additional descriptive and judgmental data. In any case, the evaluator should try to indicate the evidence favoring each assertion, and the evidence against it. It would be a violation of professional standards to base an assertion on a large presentation of statistical data not relevant to the assertion—or on irrelevant experiential data, however interesting. Most evaluators feel it appropriate to summarize their final insights, going beyond their best data to make a lengthy interpretive summary of the quality of the evaluand. But the speculative thinking should be apparent in the way the statements are made.

Narrative

Sagredo: Can you think of an example of a one-time happening that might influence judgment of the quality of our mentor training?

Phyllis: A trainee overtly harasses a subordinate.

Sagredo: And another example?

---

[12]We need to avoid the *stimulus error*, the error of presuming that we all are talking about the same thing when we are not.

Phyllis: Well, I was watching the training the other day and Sid (the Senior Mentor Training coordinator) said, "Do a good job on the quiz. My job depends on it, you know." I don't know if that was a bad thing for him to say, but it is something I will keep in mind when I think about why trainees are taking the course.

Sagredo: Yes, I did tell Sid that we need to show that training is making a difference. I didn't expect him to repeat it. I figured we would be able to show that better memos indicate that training has improved.

Phyllis: I guess there's nothing simple about evaluation. We need to think about a lot of things, Mr. Sagredo, even while we compare pretraining and posttraining memos.

Sagredo: Do you have some kind of rubric for the comparison?

Phyllis: Yes. I didn't figure you were interested in that much detail. It has five criteria, similar to those used to grade essays in school.

Sagredo: Did you have the trainees write a memo to a mentee prior to training, for the comparison?

Phyllis: No, I thought it would be artificial. I think we should compare real memos we have in e-mail files.

Sagredo: Will we know who actually wrote them?

Phyllis: Not always. But that will be true of the posttraining memos as well.

Sagredo: It could be that the writer wasn't in the training group.

Phyllis: That's true, but those numbers will be small. It won't make a difference.

Sagredo: Does the training include anything about abusive or threatening language?

Phyllis: Yes, briefly.

Sagredo: Marina (the receptionist) thinks we should instruct our people to notify my office when they are mistreated by someone.

Phyllis: So that you could alert others to the possibility of further confrontation?

Sagredo: Right.

Phyllis: Well, that's not part of the training now, but it is the sort of thing that often comes up in an evaluation. If you have an idea how you want it to work, I could ask Sid to consider including it in the training. It might be better if you asked him.

Sagredo: I would prefer that you think it through it and give me your advice, Phyllis.

Phyllis: I presume that we will not have a Senior Mentor Training course very often. What we learn now may not generalize to subsequent offerings. We will be learning something in general about professional training of our people, but it won't be a simple generalization. What we are doing is teaching ourselves a little more about training and perhaps about ongoing support of mentoring. Again, sort of a one-time happening.

Sagredo: I guess we found an example. Threatening language is an experience that can change what we think about training and evaluation.

Phyllis: And the Davis episode, of course.

(To be continued)

5

Data Gathering

There is no single best plan for an evaluation, not even for an inquiry into a particular program, at a particular time, with a particular budget.

Lee Cronbach, 1982, p. 321

Criterial data gathering is different from interpretive data gathering. For criterial data gathering, we identify a number of criteria on which we want data—criteria such as trainee performance, program support at the field sites, perceptions of accountability, or employer needs. We aggregate these data to get statistical summaries. Using enumerations, means, correlates, and graphs, we gain key information from aggregates that we cannot get from individual observations.

Seeking interpretative data, we make individual observations or find episodes giving insight into our main issues—issues such as language problems for some trainees, program support at the field sites, implied redefinition of "full service" in the accountability mandates, and employer needs. Interpretive data are sometimes reported in narratives, snapshots, and videotapes. They give us key information from individual observations.

With criterial data we hope to get statistical distributions of data that lead to assertions of success or failure. From interpretive data we hope to get unique perceptions of success or failure made possible by specially placed observers. For almost every evaluation study we will gather both criterial and interpretive data, doing both aggregative and interpretive analysis. As it works out in any given study, however, usually one kind is relied on much more than the other.

The search is for quality. Quality. I was long persuaded that quality was the target of evaluation, but as a young evaluator, I was reluctant to say so. I thought it sounded soft and gushy, too subjective. I read Robert Persig's *Zen and the Art of Motorcycle Maintenance* (1974) and knew how unattainable was

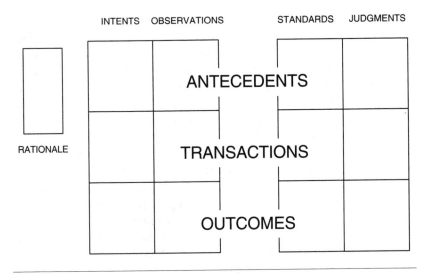

	INTENTS	OBSERVATIONS		STANDARDS	JUDGMENTS
RATIONALE		ANTECEDENTS			
		TRANSACTIONS			
		OUTCOMES			

Figure 5.1   The Countenance Matrix: Each Cell Is a Collection of Data Eligible for the Evaluation of a Program

the definition of quality, but I knew also that that was just what evaluation was all about. Clearly, it is easier to say that we are looking for goal attainment, or for improvement in production, or for program effectiveness, or testing a hypothesis. Many evaluators continue to use those terms for their conceptual organizers, rather than the more qualitative concepts of merit and shortfall and goodness and worth. (How about you? What do you want to call it?)

Well, please be forgiving and allow me to continue to talk about the quality of the evaluand. Actually, I want to talk about a number of aspects of the evaluand that can be strong or weak. When I wrote my first paper about evaluation (Stake, 1967), I was making the claim that many kinds of collectable data are suitable for use in evaluation, and that most evaluators were collecting too few kinds. In addition to outcome data, I drew attention to the eligibility of—often the need for—antecedent and transaction data (see Figure 5.1).

For operating the program, there will be many provisions or conditions or contexts, each capable of being judged as to quality. I called these background conditions and inputs *antecedents*. Some are antecedents for which the program staff is responsible, some not. In many evaluation studies, we should gather data about the intentions, the actuality, and the perceived quality of some of those antecedents.

We should gather similar data about program activities, operations, functions, processes. I called these the *transactions*. Sometimes the best data we can find are the data about the process, the activities. Sometimes we contract to carry out a "process evaluation." It may happen because the report is due before outcome data will be available, or because it is unlikely that we can get good outcome data. Or it may be because the important thing for staff and stakeholders to be told is that the program intended was not the program delivered. People may not want to know the volume or quality of the outcomes of an *unintended* program. (Can you conceive of that happening?)

In the real world, the program delivered is not exactly the one promised. It had to be changed, and the changes may make it much better. We should evaluate the program that the organization now has in place, its quality to be discovered. The usual interest is in what it has accomplished, its impact, its *outcomes*. And usually we will think of investing the greater share of the evaluation budget in gathering outcome data. But often we will obtain many antecedent, transaction, and outcome data all at the same time, sometimes with the same survey instruments or interview protocols. It would be a mistake to think of an instrument as useful only for gathering one kind of data. But it is also a mistake to think that a single instrument can get us information for all our issues.

In Figure 5.1, each of those row categories of potentially usable data has been divided into Intents, Observations, Standards, and Judgments. An evaluator may choose to gather data from each of the thirteen cells. Usually the design will emphasize data from a few cells, almost never all thirteen. Explicit standards for antecedents, transactions, and outcomes have been so difficult to find that, perhaps after a question or two, most evaluators just rely on implicit standards.

Like Klondike gold miners, we dream of discovering "the nuggets"—those rich and telling data, the observations that tell us just what we want to know. The nuggets may tell us convincingly, for example, that the trainees are now fully understanding and capable. Or that the park program activities are avoided by Latinos and Latinas almost entirely because the park director was such a vocal advocate of English as the official language. The report of the evaluation study will usually leave several issues unresolved and perceptions of accomplishment debated. Even so, hopefully, some items on our questionnaire will lead to a statistical chart having lots of punch. And a vignette about the choices faced by an ombudsperson will reveal the deep complexity of the program. We dream of those nuggets.

Choosing Data Sources

When you start asking evaluation questions, you figure the answers are going to come from other people. You don't figure the answers are going to come out of your own head. But in fact, you have to put the data together to make answers. Sometimes, if you do the job right, you get so familiar with the program, you've shared experiences with so many others, that some of the answers *are* coming out of your head. Findings of program quality are interpretations, and those interpretations are not delivered cold from analysis. It is not "Elementary, Watson," as Sherlock said. It is complicated.

Other people know important things about the program, and they have made judgments about various aspects of it. And they or others have been affected by the program, so you measure those effects as best you can to form further judgments of program quality. But sometimes, especially with a large, complex program, essentially no one knows much about the whole of it. Then the evaluator has to create the big picture. And often the effects of the program elude capture in a big picture. They may be subtle, obscured by other dynamics, slow in materializing, so that outcome measures don't tell us much. Still, we need to look for effects. And we want to capture perceptions of effect as well as actual measurement of effects. Choosing the right persons to ask is one of the first steps.

One needs to learn as much as possible from those who know most. The fact that they may also be the most misinformed and most misinforming does not rule them out. Managers and practitioners have to be asked, partly about what is working well, but mostly as to what is happening. They need to provide us with descriptions of the program. We need to learn their perceptions of need, goal, process, context, problem, and accomplishment. We will need to find other data to verify those perceptions, but we will often start there. Sometimes in their reports, they have already described much of the program, but many interconnections still need to be teased out. For example, why are there so many fewer male participants than there used to be? Or why did they change the name of the program if that might devalue the investment of those who completed it? Does someone already know? Or what does someone know that will help you figure it out? There's a lot of Sherlocking to do. Who all to ask?

And a couple other things to think about in selecting data sources: There will not be enough time to get everything done, so one should choose data sources partly on the basis of high likelihood of cooperation. Further, when you select a data-providing group, such as consultants or ministers or fast-food managers, try to get at least brief responses from every member of the group. A few of them can be selected for extra questioning, but the insight and credibility of the group is greater if everyone has an independent opportunity to respond. Costs will argue otherwise. But don't expect one or a sample to speak effectively for the rest. Time and money can be saved by developing the data sources carefully.

Instrumentation

As I said to get us started in Chapter 3, for many evaluators, instrumentation is "where it's at." It is a joy to set up a situation, hypothetical or real, where large numbers of people, responding to the same items, provide measurements that show what the program is doing. They may use a number of personal observations or small-group interviews to help with the interpretation, but for them, it is the large-scale comparisons between groups or the correlations that tell the story. So they invest a lot in good instrumentation.[1] Some of the variables they call *indicators*.

In a fine sourcebook for indicator variables (edited by Shavelson, McDonnell, & Oakes, 1989), the indicator variables for teacher qualification (secondary school mathematics and science) selected by Linda Darling-Hammond and Lisa Hudson are as follows: college major and minor; college/university attended; undergraduate grade point average; number of course hours in mathematics, life and physical science, computer science, and pedagogical course (specifically mathematics and science education courses); postsecondary degrees and coursework (types and numbers of courses, whether mandated or voluntary, recency of educational training/enrichment); and certifications status (areas of certification).

As indicators, the economic world has the Gross National Product (GNP) and the Dow Jones Industrial Average (DJA) to indicate the vitality of business and industry. Baseball teams have runs batted in (RBI) and earned run averages (ERA) as indicators of offensive and defensive prowess. The popularity of books is indicated by number of weeks on the *New York Times* best-seller list. There are problems with these indicators as summaries of robustness and goodness, but they are widely recognized by experts and the public. Indicator variables can mislead us, as they misled President Lyndon Johnson and his military team in waging war in Vietnam (see Halberstam, 1972). Unemployment rates only weakly indicate the plight of minority youth. Still, we are incapable of managing large-scale social systems without indicator variables.

---

[1]Tom Schwandt (2003) lamented the fixation of evaluators on instrumentation, instead urging dialogue and self-study of practical activities.

An indicator variable can be valid for one purpose but invalid for another. The validity depends on what we are using it to indicate. Scores on the SAT are usually valid for indicating which students on the average will be more successful in college. But the SAT is not a valid indicator of the quality of teaching received by the students in a particular school district. The validity of an indicator needs to be established by research for each of the different uses made of it. The fact of the matter is that many criteria are not validated adequately.[2] But they are used anyway, and it is expected that with sufficient use, people will come to understand for what they can be relied on.

The same is true with indicator variables used in evaluation studies. For Charles Murray's (1981) evaluation of Cities in Schools, the well-being of urban youth was considered adequately represented by grades and absenteeism from school and staying out of trouble with the police. It seemed reasonable, but no research indicated the suitability of these criterion variables for that program (see Stake, 1986). The clients, the public, and the profession are often overly generous in accepting unvalidated indicator variables as criteria in evaluation studies. Our budgets do not allow much validation, but we can be suitably cautious in interpreting the results.

Concerns about the validity of the use of scores from instruments are not a matter only for large-scale studies. Each data-gathering effort, even your own best-thought-out question to interviewees, needs to be treated with caution. It may not mean what it appears to mean. For some instrumentation, we will want to get formal indication of the validity of use. For others, we will look to see that the findings drawn from them are consistent with findings from other data. We will reflect deeply about what other meanings might be drawn. And we will subject our findings to various forms of meta-evaluation to satisfy ourselves and to help our readers understand the confidence they can place in the findings. (Is it too much to expect? But then, is it too much to expect a granddaughter to buckle up?)

Recipient Responses

What can be learned about program quality from those who received the services—for example, the patients, the students, the trainees? Perhaps the most common program evaluation instrument is the conference feedback evaluation sheet. You have seen them lots of places. It is often a single page, acknowledging the presence of the respondent and obtaining a few likes and dislikes.

---

[2]Technical standards for evaluating tests are found in the American Psychological Association's *Standards for Educational and Psychological Testing* (1999).

Most are of questionable validity for indicating program effectiveness, usually reporting general feelings of the participants, including appreciation, camaraderie, and peace of mind. Alan Knox once demonstrated that conference evaluation sheets scored higher if you improved the friendliness of the lunchroom waitresses. Respondents often have something they want to say, and often, whatever you ask them, they will first give you those somethings. The trick is to write the items that get the particular information you need.

> Prior to the 1967 meeting of the American Educational Research Association (AERA), a five-day Presession was organized by Gene Glass, Ken Hopkins, and Jason Millman (1967) on the topic Design of Comparative Experiments. It was held at a Pocono Mountains resort outside New York City. Of the 140 applying, 68 were accepted and attended. Staff assistants were Tom Maguire, Andy Porter, and Lou Pingel. Choosing a Presession location at a resort away from the main meeting was a major issue. For formative evaluation, on the third day a fourteen-item Likert scale was administered. During the week, a postlecture mastery quiz (formative, anonymous) was administered for each lecture. On the final day, a semantic differential for fourteen main concepts for the week and a participant critique (Figure 5.2) were administered. This evaluation sheet has been squeezed here to save space; the actual sheet invited and left room for comments. Each of the six staff members also filled out a critique of his own. Adding all this to comments heard during discussions—plenary and personal— during and after the week, the staff felt it knew as much about the Presession as could be known.

For that AERA Presession, participant information was available in advance. It is often necessary to get demographic and personal history from the instrument, particularly if there is interest in subgroup answers to questions such as "Did the newcomers like it?" and "Did it satisfy the participants whose jobs are threatened?" The twenty-one questions of the questionnaire shown in Figure 5.2 were what staff members wanted to know about their sessions, hoping that some of it could be scored there at the resort while some sessions remained. They solicited simple answers, having little time to read the comments of a large audience. Note the content of the first items—highly technical, sensitive to the comfort and motivation of the participants. Look at the items again. What is missing?

1a. Did the unavailability of books and journals interfere with attempts to master the content of the Presession? ___ Yes ___ No

1b. Did reproduced material handed out by the staff help you? ___ Yes ___ No

2a. Did you lack a place to work? ___ Yes ___ No

2b. Was your room satisfactory? ___ Yes ___ No

3a. Which features of the meeting rooms were inadequate?
___ ventilation
___ acoustics
___ too large & spread out
___ overhead, mike

3b. Which features facilitated learning?
___ space to spread out materials
___ ice water
___ public address system
___ isolation from competing attractions
___ swimming pools and steam baths
___ chalkboards
___ raised platform for lecturers

4a. Was 5 days too long? ___ Yes ___ No

4b. Was 5 days too short? ___ Yes ___ No

5a. Did you have enough time for your own activities? ___ Yes ___ No

5b. Would you have preferred *not* to meet in the evening? ___ Yes ___ No

5c. Would two meetings per day have been preferable? ___ Yes ___ No

5d. Would you have preferred more meetings per day than there were? ___ Yes ___ No

6a. Were lectures too long? ___ Yes ___ No

6b. Were they well scheduled? ___ Yes ___ No

7. Did you have sufficient opportunity to interact with colleagues? ___ Yes ___ No

8a. Were the instructors too unapproachable or inaccessible? ___ Yes ___ No

8b. Were graduate student assistants helpful in solving individual research problems? ___ Yes ___ No

9a. Did the evaluation interfere with your work? ___ Yes ___ No

9b. Do you object to spending time on evaluation? ___ Yes ___ No

(Continued)

10. Was the Presession well organized? ___ Yes ___ No

11a. Did the content of the lectures presuppose
more training in mathematics
and statistics than you had? ___ Yes ___ Slightly more ___ No

11b. Should less, or more, training be
presupposed? ___ Less ___ More ___ About right

12. To what extent was the content
relevant to what you hoped to
accomplish? ___ Relevant ___ Not too relevant

13a. Were the lecturers stimulating and interesting? ___ Yes ___ No

13b. Were the discussions successful? ___ Yes ___ No

13c. Were the lecturers competent to speak on
their topics? ___ Yes ___ No

13d. Were the lecturers well prepared? ___ Yes ___ No

14. Were you disappointed in any way
with the participants? ___ Yes ___ No

15. If you had to do it over again would you
apply for this Presession? ___ Yes ___ No

16. If a Presession such as this is held again would
you recommend to others like you that they attend? ___ Yes ___ No

17. Do you anticipate maintaining some sort of
contact with at least one member of the
Presession staff? ___ Yes ___ No

18. Do you feel that your understanding of
research design and/or statistical analysis has
been considerably enriched in these five days? ___ Yes ___ No

19. Do you feel that AERA is making an important
contribution to education by sponsoring
Presessions such as this one? ___ Yes ___ No

20. Do you feel that anything has happened
during these five days to make it more likely
that you will leave your present position
of employment? ___ Yes ___ No

21. Is it likely that you will collaborate in
research with someone else attending this
session (other than those you already would
collaborate with)? ___ Yes ___ No ___ Doubtful

Figure 5.2   Participant Critique: Presession on Design of Comparative
Experiments

Reprinted with permission from Gene Glass.

In this otherwise excellent questionnaire (Figure 5.2), the participants were not asked to say much about the content of the lectures. Experimental design, threats to validity, sampling—important topics for a researcher in 1967. It apparently was not seen as useful to offer participants the opportunity to challenge or substantively endorse the presession curriculum. Was it, and the contemporary AERA endorsement of experimentalism, so persuasive (or intimidating) that qualitative studies of education were discouraged for another ten or fifteen years? Can an evaluator be satisfied with a summary of participant test answers and questionnaire comments, or should the merit of the topics of training be scrutinized?

The questionnaire in Figure 5.3 was devised by Penha Tres in an evaluation of the Rochester Institute of Technology training program for teachers of deaf students (Stake, Michael, Tres, Lichtenstein, & Kennedy, 1985). An evaluation was required in the federal contract. Particular issues were the sensitivity of the program to the actual reading ability and maturity of the students, and the pros and cons of mainstreaming deaf children. Classrooms were observed. Primary data sources were recent graduates and their employers and RIT faculty members. Twenty-eight of the thirty-one graduates responded.

If you have time, give Figure 5.3 a careful read. You probably cannot guess how the responses will distribute, but you can think how you might present the results. Should you use raw tallies or percentages? Percentages are easier to read, but the term "percentages" means parts of 100. Raw numbers can be less misleading if totals are also presented. How would you present the responses to Item 15? Would it be useful to calculate a median? The response distribution is probably more informative than central tendency. What is missing? Little opportunity was taken to ask the respondents about what they observed in their many months in the program. Is it important for the evaluator to try to obtain experiential impressions of being a student at this RIT program? Why or why not?

Often when I create an evaluation form, I try hard to get it on a single page so people can see all of it at once. The idea is to inform them as to size of their task but also to lower concerns as to how much needs to be written. Also, a quick scan identifies key words that hopefully orient the respondent to the task. What does a quick glance tell you about Figure 5.3? Here colleague Tres expected glancers to see that we wanted to know quite a bit about them, that there was a lot of rating of quality expected, and that the issue of mainstreaming was important. One troublesome issue was less apparent: the claim of insufficiency of involvement of RIT course instructors in the program as a whole.

I regularly use short questionnaires for getting aggregative data from a large data source such as beneficiaries. For more in-depth questioning or observation of performance, I select a small number of those surveyed—in

1. Name _____ (optional)

2. Year graduated _____

3. Specialization _____

4. Are you presently employed in the field of Education? _____

5. Title of your position _____

6. _____ Part-time _____ Full-time

7. Type of Institution: _____ Private _____ Public

8. Level of teaching: _____ Postsecondary _____ Secondary _____
    Primary
    _____ Other (specify) _____

9. Type of classroom(s): _____ Deaf _____ Hearing _____ Mixed

10. Number of students and average time/week with them: _____
    students; averaging _____ hrs/wk each

11. Do you use sign language now?
    _____ None
    _____ A little
    _____ A lot

12. Overall, rate the preparation that the program gave you for this
    position:
    _____ Excellent
    _____ Good
    _____ Fair
    _____ Not adequate
    _____ Poor

13. How could it have been better?
    _____
    _____

14. Do you serve in any of the following functions related to deaf
    education?
    _____ resource person
    _____ advocate
    _____ supervisor of other teachers
    _____ workshop presenter
    _____ member of local committee or organization
    _____ contributor to publication(s) (please specify) _____
    _____ member of professional organization (please specify)
    _____ other (please specify) _____

(Continued)

15. Please estimate the chances that you will devote the rest of your professional life to work in deaf education: _____ 0% _____ 20% _____ 50% _____ 80% _____ 100%

16. Please check to indicate your sign language skills at the following three points in time.

	nil	basic	intermediate	advanced
On entering the JESP program	_____	_____	_____	_____
On leaving the JESP program	_____	_____	_____	_____
Currently	_____	_____	_____	_____

Please answer Questions 17–19 using this scale:
> Excellent = 5
> Good = 4
> Fair = 3
> Not adequate = 2
> Poor = 1

17. What was the quality of the coursework as preparation for the program's practicum? _____

18. Rate the practicum as to strengthening the knowledge you gained from coursework. _____

19. Rate the course sequencing as it served to prepare you for your practicum. _____

20. Please make suggestions for improving sequencing of courses and experiences.

    _____
    _____
    _____
    _____

21. Please make suggestions for improving other aspects of the program.

    _____
    _____
    _____
    _____

22. Should more of the practicum be held in less ideal teaching conditions than are in the schools near RIT?   _____Yes _____ No

(Continued)

23. What do you consider to be the most striking feature of the program?

    _____
    _____
    _____
    _____

24. Were there difficulties for you because the program was based in the two institutions?

    _____
    _____
    _____
    _____

25. Given the present national interest in *mainstreaming,* with relatively few program for training secondary teachers of the deaf, do you feel that these programs should give greater emphasis to
    X–teaching skills needed for direct instruction of deaf children, or
    Y–consultative skills to help regular teachers with deaf children mainstreamed into their classes

    Check one:
    _____ The highest possible emphasis should be given to **X.**
    _____ More emphasis generally should be given to **X** but some programs should be for **Y.**
    _____ Equal emphasis should be given to **X** and **Y.**
    _____ More emphasis generally should be given to **Y** but some programs should be for **X.**
    _____ The highest possible emphasis should be given to **Y.**

Figure 5.3   Survey of Graduates of the Joint Specialist Program (deaf education)

this RIT case, eight graduates. In Figure 5.4 is Mellen Kennedy's write-up of Mary Hayes. Notice how much and how little the reader can learn about the quality of the JESP practicum experience from reading one mini case study. Notice how much more of a vicarious experience the reader can get from Kennedy's case report. But of course, we don't know how typical Mary is. Is that important?

When there are more questions to be asked of participants than will fit into a short questionnaire and a large respondent group is available, it can be a good idea to use *item sampling.* Divide the question pool and the respondent pool into subgroups so that, for example, each third of the respondents gets a

Mary Hayes is an '83 graduate of the program with a specialization area in English. She is the only teacher of the deaf at Day Junior High School in Newton, MA, where I visited her in late May.

I interviewed Ed Mulligan, her supervisor, first. "I can't say enough good things about Mary's skills and what she has brought to the program," he emphasizes. He describes her as adaptable, confident, and energetic.

As I observe Mary, his words seem true. From the front of the room she conducts a self-contained social studies class of five deaf students. Their desks are arranged in a semi-circle. Mary involves them in today's lesson on the Vietnam War. Signing and speaking through the assignment, which is displayed on an overhead projector, she encourages and coaxes them, praising their efforts. Her classroom reflects her concern with her students and with deaf education. The calendar from Gallaudet College honors "Great Deaf Americans." One bulletin board display entitled "A Deaf World" includes the following: "President Reagan has a hearing loss. He wears an in-the-ear hearing aid." Another board shows the work of students including this poem:

Jean,
Independent, Deaf
Filming, editing, directing,
Happy, tired, excited, nervous.
Jean

We move on to an integrated social studies class of 17 students including Terry who is deaf. Mary works with Joe, the "regular" teacher. Since social studies is not her area of specialization, she is less involved in planning this class. Primarily she works with Terry.

Today Joe is showing a movie on China. Mary sits on a stool next to the screen. She interprets the film as it is being projected. Terry sits in the front row and watches the movie and Mary's signing. The other students do not seem to notice Mary's presence.

In addition to these classes, Mary teaches English and math. She grapples with the conflict between her English specialization area training and the reality of her job, which demands that she teach in content areas other than English. She recognizes that it contradicts the Joint Specialists Program philosophy. However, she feels that "realistically, there are very few programs which would allow you to teach full-time English. That restricts you solely to programs completely for the deaf." Her job also requires that she is interpreter part of the time, as in Joe's social studies class. "I have very little desire to be an interpreter. But I do it every day . . . it's teaching that I'm here for." Her training also did not specially prepare her to work with junior high students. She has adjusted to and enjoyed this challenge,

(Continued)

but expects that she will move on and return to working with older students at some point, which will enable her to use more of her knowledge of English.

Reflecting on her training from the program, her assessment is basically positive. "There is a certain lack of preparation for the real world. . . ." She acknowledges though that "I don't quite know how to deal with that because everybody's real world is different." However, provision for acquiring sign language skills in the program is one change that she feels should be made.

Mary feels that the program has a lot going for it. She is impressed with the faculty and is glad to have worked with some of "the tops in the field." Her practicum experiences were stressful, yet in retrospect, she feels that she got a lot out of them.

Mary sees herself very likely to continue being involved in deaf education and, if not actually teaching, then administering a program, writing materials, or doing something related. Beyond the classroom she is active in advocacy for her students, and serves as a resource person for parents and other teachers. Ed Mulligan refers to her as being committed to going beyond what is required in her job. He also pointed out that she is currently enrolled in a class in ESL. Reflecting on his years in deaf education, Ed exclaims that a person like Mary "doesn't come along very often!" (Mellen Kennedy, 1985, p. 48)

Figure 5.4   Mary Hayes, Graduate of the RIT Program

Reprinted with permission from Mellen Kennedy.

third of the items. Group A could get the first third of the items, B the second third, and C the remaining items.[3]

When Craig Gjerde and I (Stake & Gjerde, 1974) evaluated a six-week on-campus summer camp, The Twin City Institute for Talented Youth, we were particularly interested in changes over time. We had a dozen questions for which we wanted responses each week. We printed the questions on IBM tab cards (these historical artifacts are shown in Figure 5.5). We had the teacher at the first morning class each Wednesday hand out cards at random. Thus, we obtained responses on twelve items, week after week, each obtained from more than 150 students in a spiraling fashion. We could trace, for example, whether or not the participants felt they were "learning a lot at this

---

[3]Item sampling prevents some correlational analysis because not all pairs of items are answered by a respondent group. See Jaeger, *Complementary Methods* (1997).

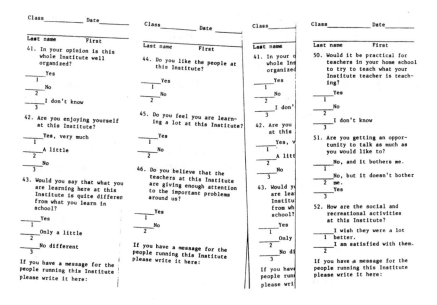

Figure 5.5   Weekly Feedback Card Used With 650 High School Students
Attending TCITY, Minneapolis, Summer 1970

Institute." A graphic representation can be impressive, but note that it shifts attention away from "level of learning" to "change in level of learning." That is worth some pondering. The evaluator has to decide which questions are most worth answering.

Staff and Management Responses

Directors are a problem. Most are interesting people, often very nice. Even if they are new to the job, they know so much that we want to know. We try to be even nicer than they are so we will get lots of information, including a few things not for the record. Consequently, we ask too few tough, potentially embarrassing questions. We won't completely believe everything they tell us, but a lot of it we'll be able to corroborate. In the end, directors often provide us with some of the best content for our report.

That happens too with the staff, and it happens with the people in the community, and with the director's enemies as well. We hang around, sometimes acting like one of the staff ourselves, and pretty soon, as the ethnographers say, we've "gone native." That is, we start to think like the people with whom we are spending the most time. We appreciate what a difficult job they have and how little their efforts get rewarded, and we start composing apologies for them.

Michael Scriven's answer to this, an extension of his idea of goal-free evaluation (see Chapter 2), has been to keep more distance between us evaluators and program administrators and other advocates (1995). That sometimes is good advice. I don't follow it as closely as I should. The evaluand is complicated, and the contexts are in some ways unfamiliar. I try to gain proximity to make reality checks and challenge mainline thinking, discrepancies that will help me to a better understanding. But maybe too often I end up reporting quite a bit about how the director and staff are trying to do the right thing.

One thing really nice about most managers and staff members is that they verbalize. They write some of it down, which, up to a point, makes the evaluator's job easier. They don't write all of it in places to which we have access, and they usually write it down in a way that reflects favorably on them. But it is easier for me to think critically about what is being said when I can read it at my own speed. It is time well spent. Carlyle (1828) said, "In every man's writings, the character of the writer must lie recorded." Is that true of programs as well as persons?

I get the bulk of my information from managers and program operators from interviews, often just informal conversations. Seldom am I asking them the carefully honed questions that will be asked identically of a big respondent group, to aggregate and analyze the data statistically. But they are carefully anticipated, topical questions that follow the issue structure. They probe and corroborate (or do not) what I have learned earlier. Sometimes I make provocative comments, such as "It's hard to believe you told your auditor." I try to root many of my questions in action I have observed or have read about. I need to get my descriptions of staff action straight, and I need to learn the reasons it occurred. So I am forever refining the interpretations of what is going on, including the merit and the flaws in it all.

I want to give every staff member an opportunity to put something in the evaluation record, either to answer my questions or to register what he or she has to volunteer. This involves announcing an availability to meet, to listen, or at least to include messages or artifacts in the data files. But more than that, I often need to use a brief survey instrument to solicit responses from every member of the staff. Since I almost never work with hundreds and hundreds, I want to take at least a brief look at every survey sheet or e-mail returned. I often get someone else to tally the returns, but I want to see the marginalia[4] and some of the open-ended writing myself.

---

[4]Especially in anonymous survey returns, there will be marginalia. Respondents are irritated by the irrelevance, insensitivity, and uselessness of our questions. Survey authors should be thick-skinned and should expect that some abusive comments are insightful and worth heeding.

Here is an example of a quantitative effort to get a quick but complex answer from a large number of teachers. We asked a group of teachers to inform us about the effects of current standardized achievement testing practices in their schools.[5] From earlier interviews with many teachers, I had recorded many statements of changes in schools, including effects from increased testing. To get a statistical record, I developed the form shown in Figure 5.6. You see there a list of thirty-four teacher comments about classroom effects of testing. Paul Theobald and I (Stake & Theobald, 1991) asked 271 teachers to comment on recent changes in emphasis in testing and then to circle each statement that applied to their own school.

For presentation in our report (presented as shown in Figure 5.6), I crossed off all statements circled by less than two-thirds of the teachers, an arbitrary cutoff. I found it hard to get the teachers to take the time to participate. I was happy finding so many issues that teachers said they cared about. We concluded that they were not voicing as much criticism of the testing as the interviewed teachers had. The following are the statements reported to best tell the effects of standardized achievement testing in their schools:

- Teachers are increasingly required to pursue stated goals.
- Generally, there is a broadening of the curriculum.
- We are seeing a gain in emphasis on problem solving and critical thinking.
- Teachers increasingly watch for "teachable moments."
- Attention is increasingly given to differences in individual students.

Theobald and I interpreted the responses from teachers as seeing the schools as positively affected by the increased emphasis on testing. I raised the possibility that they might be showing their "coping mechanisms." Although many teachers spoke about negative effects, the majority of the teachers may have felt a need to emphasize the positive. The issue was complex, but each teacher in the school had an opportunity to participate.

Generally speaking, staff members, directors, and everyone else will respond more seriously to questions that deal with the specific problems they face than they will to generic issues, such as the quality of community support or the competence of staff development consultants. Some evaluators worry that specific problems do not represent problems in general—better to stick with the global and generic. (Do you comprehend the issue? What do you think?)

---

[5]Evaluation of program management should draw from the field of organizational research and from school leadership. Heck and Hallinger's chapter in the *Handbook of Research on Educational Administration* (1999) is one source. A leading journal is *Organization: The Interdisciplinary Journal of Organization, Theory, and Society.*

SURVEY ON SCHOOL TESTING

Studies of Assessment Policy >>>>>>>>>>> CIRCE <<<<<<<<<<< University of Illinois

N= 271 teachers in MD, NC, MN, SD + IL

This section is for teachers. Within the classrooms of any school district different kinds of tests are used. Some are quizzes and examination authored by a teacher or group of teachers. Some are aptitude tests not intended to indicate understanding of subject matter but to predict how well students will do in later coursework. Standardized achievement tests are different from all of these. They are tests developed at the state or national level to indicate how well students have achieved basic skills or obtained course-related knowledge. These standardized achievement tests are the only tests we are talking about in this questionnaire.

First it is important for us to get your observation of the present level of standardized testing in the schools. For each of the items below please make TWO check marks:

1. In U.S. education generally, the present emphasis on testing is	2. In you own district the present emphasis on testing is	3. In your own school the present emphasis on standardized testing is
138 strong and/but 161 getting stronger	123 strong and/but 123 getting stronger	100 strong and/but 108 getting stronger
123 moderate " 91 holding steady	137 moderate " 132 holding steady	156 moderate " 147 holding steady
6 weak " 9 getting weaker.	6 weak " 5 getting weaker.	12 weak " 6 getting weaker.
4 omit	5 omit	3 omit 10 omit
	11 omit	

4. Next we want to identify the statements below which describe what is happening at your school. This part is like a True-False test. CIRCLE the letter in front of each statement which describes conditions which have been changing in your school during the last year or two. Your circle means the statement describes your school.

CHANGING CONDITIONS IN YOUR SCHOOL IN THE LAST YEAR OR TWO

216 A. Teachers are increasingly required to pursue stated goals.
67 B. Teachers are increasingly free to pursue unstated goals.
85 C. Generally there is a narrowing of the curriculum.
192 D. Generally there is a broadening of the curriculum.
163 E. Attention to the education of gifted children is increasing.
56 F. Attention to the education of gifted children is decreasing.
177 G. We are giving increasing time to teaching the basic skills.
83 H. We are diminishing the time given to teaching the basic skills.
173 I. Teachers are greatly encouraged to enrich the basic syllabus.
47 J. Teachers are discouraged from going beyond the basic syllabus.
176 K. Increasingly teachers draw interpretation from their own experience.
66 L. Decreasingly teachers draw interpretation from their own experience.
87 M. It is becoming easier to find grounds for rejecting contract offers.
81 N. It is becoming harder to find grounds for demanding better contracts.
62 O. We are seeing a drop in emphasis on problem solving & critical thinking.
205 P. We are seeing a gain in emphasis on problem solving & critical thinking.
125 Q. Trivial classroom activities are being eliminated.
87 R. Trivial classroom activities are becoming more common.
176 S. Homework and class time spent preparing for tests is on the rise.
59 T. Homework and class time spent preparing for tests is on the wane.
149 U. The marginal learner has become the norm for setting what to teach.
76 V. The marginal learner certainly is not the norm for setting what to teach.
192 W. Teachers increasingly watch for "teachable moments."
48 X. Teachers less frequently watch for "teachable moments."
67 Y. The hopes for all children getting a broad education are diminishing.
169 Z. The hopes for all children getting a broad education are increasing.
86 a. The image of the teacher as an effective person is improving.
94 b. The image of the teacher as an effective person is getting worse.
193 c. Attention is increasingly given to differences in individual students.
51 d. Attention is decreasingly given to differences in individual students.
48 e. There is more pressure to get everything taught.
2 f. There is less pressure to get things taught.
42 g. There is diminishing time for individual help and student interests.
9 h. There is increasing time for individual help and student interests.

Only 51 teachers got these four items

$\frac{2}{8} = 37$

Figure 5.6   Survey on School Testing

NOTE: Statements not crossed off were circled by 179 (2/3) or more teachers.

Stakeholder and Public Responses

To get responses from a large number of stakeholders or the general public, some instrumentation is required. The people usually are not in the same location, and many have little acquaintance with the program being evaluated. The evaluator may need to provide information about the evaluand.

Working for a private sector provider, Les McLean (2000) evaluated a six-month pilot program of Youth Network News, a telecast link between a Montreal station and Canadian secondary schools. In the five schools of his study, daily programming for 10–12 minutes was received in every classroom, including 2.5 minutes of commercial advertising or "social advocacy messages." The station provided wall TV screens and, as payment, a state-of-the-art computer laboratory, maintained without charge to the school. Strong public opposition to the proposed telecasting had been voiced. Among the issues were the educational value, the political orientation of the social advocacy pieces, ethnic orientation, the obligation to watch, and the incursion into instructional time. At each school, McLean surveyed 100 parents (using the questionnaire shown in Figure 5.7), obtained a secret vote of the teachers, observed the students during telecasts, and interviewed the principal, teacher groups, and student groups. He found attitudes more positive than negative, that special social topics increasingly replaced news and commercials on the telecasts, and that there was little connection between the telecast content and ordinary coursework. The computers were much needed in two schools, not in the other three. The programming was seen as highly situational, easily subject to change toward more useful or toward more offensive programming. (http://www. oise.utoronto.ca/-oiseynn/oiseynn/cgi)

One of the points illustrated in Figure 5.7 is that some very complex issues can be examined with a relatively simple data-gathering plan, but the quality of the report depends on using good issues, good items, and interpreting them carefully. (Were good issues raised in the parent survey?) McLean's report implied that the interviews dug into the issues.

When a program becomes a matter of public concern, or is attacked or aggressively advocated by a stakeholder group, then outside group opinions become much more important and it is even more important to do a good job of data gathering. It might be found that the students gained important social

How did you learn about the YNN Project? (Please check all that apply.)

O This is the first I've heard of it!
O Attended a meeting at the school.
O Read about it in the newspaper.
O Heard about it on the radio.
O From a student at the school.
O Read a notice sent out by the school.
O I am involved with the YNN project at the school.
O Other

What was your *first* reaction, on learning of the project?
(Please choose one.)

O It is a good idea.
O I decided to wait and see.
O I was opposed to it.

What do you think now? (Please choose all that apply. May use reverse side.)

O The same as before.
O I want more information.
O It is too soon for me to tell.
O It is a good/bad idea (circle one), because

What advice do you have for the school?

O Make more use of the YNN programs.
O Keep doing what you are doing now.
O Stop showing the YNN programs.
O Make more use of the computers.
O Keep using the computers as you are now.
O Give back the computers.
O Use the TV system more for teaching.
O Use the TV system for teaching as you are now.
O Use the TV system less for teaching.
O Make a better deal with YNN (specify below).
O Enter into a 5-year contract with YNN.
O Do not enter into a 5-year contract with YNN.

Anything to add?

Figure 5.7   Youth News Network (Canada) Parent and Trustee Questionnaire

perspectives from the YNN television, but the issue was not heavily weighted in the assessment. It might be found that the students paid little attention to the commercials, much as they do on home television, but the threat of subtle influence was the issue. Our program evaluation methods are seldom precise enough to show that there are subtle educational effects. When the issues are contentious, we will be able to show some of the complexity and gross differences in popularity, but often that is all that program evaluation can be expected to do. There is an expertise of public polling that few of us evaluators have. We can learn more of it from the pollsters.

To get a measure of an important concern, such as commercial television in the classroom, most research and evaluation data gatherers expect to put together multiple pieces of information. For example, to evaluate a car, *Consumer Reports* would have us consider:

Engine	Cooling	Fuel	Ignition
Transmission	Electrical	Air conditioning	Suspension
Brakes	Exhaust	Body rust	Paint/trim
	Integrity	Hardware	

And there may be several questions for each component or vulnerability. Similarly with asking questions about public perception of the city planning commission. One question is not enough. Whether we summarize it into a single rating or descriptive term or describe it multidimensionally, we are going to need to ask several questions. That is partly because the evaluand is complex and partly because we do not have a perfect way to ask the question, even with simple evaluands. And the more important the consideration, the more we need multiple questions to stabilize the informational feedback.

Data Coding and Records Processing

It is time to recall the difference between aggregative and interpretive data. It may be useful to read Representations of Performance in Chapter 3 again. Evaluators need to sort a lot of things. Let's consider the example of troubleshooting logs of repairmen.

John Seely Brown (1995) did exemplary research on the training of Xerox photocopier repairmen. For some of his data he reviewed the troubleshooting records they kept. When new models came out, many repairmen would continue the procedures for older machines, finding the new procedures by trial and error. Rather than read the new manuals, they (like us) would ask others who might know. They sought non-documentary ways of getting maintenance information, so Brown looked for more personal ways of getting it to them. (Brown & Duguid, 2000)

Following the design of Brown's study, program evaluators might recognize that relevant information on the effectiveness of the evaluand was available from troubleshooting logs that the diagnosticians kept. Variables of interest were the completeness of description of the problem, correctness of diagnosis, time on task, and legibility of information for the supervisor. Diagnostic style was of interest. Frequencies of strategies were recorded. The evaluators compared the totals and correlated frequencies with type and amount of training received. The evaluators coded and aggregated.

> **coding** *n* 2. a process of categorizing and labeling data or artifacts for sorting, storing, or statistical analysis

Coding is a technical name for sorting or grading data to be aggregated or filed. Everything can be coded. Doing nothing can be a classification. Another example is the uses made of personal retirement accounts. Another example would be ways autistic children modify unsuccessful requests. (Can you identify some coding you might need to do?)

Some standards-based evaluation requires collecting cases and coding them. While designing the study and gathering these data, the evaluator postpones most of the interpretation until he or she has completed the aggregating. Individual logs might be interesting, but the primary meaningfulness is expected to come from the analysis of the aggregation of log material. We will be able to speak about the quality of the evaluand when we understand its performance, which we will understand in terms of the comparisons and intercorrelations of the aggregated data. For example, the copy machine troubleshooters trained with a new program may have kept better logs than those trained earlier. We are able to make sense of things partly because we have done a good job of coding them.

Responsive evaluation goes more deeply into interpretation *along the way.* Then, coding can be the procedure that pulls the story together. The interpretations of each observation or interview reside both in coded information and in records describing particulars unique to each case. An interview with a repairman might code him as having a Type B approach but also note that he was an early user of a cell phone to keep in touch with a coworker. The evaluator might subsequently give special attention to use of cell phones.

Qualitative study of large numbers of cases usually relies on elaborate categories of coded observation. Matthew Miles and Michael Huberman (1984) specialized in carefully thought-out coding lists such as the one in Figure 5.8, this one for a study of the development of the National Council of Teachers of Mathematics (NCTM) Standards (McLeod, Stake, Schappelle, Mellissinos, & Gierl, 1997). The code name INHST-CHRON, for example, was to be assigned to any notes or materials regarding "adoption" of the NCTM standards, with a tally in the master file. Tallies there may or may not get large enough for statistical analysis. From time to time the evaluator reviews the master file and decides what more data are needed. The coding scheme serves as something like a

Topic	Code for Observation, Interview, Paper Trail
1. Background and History	
1.1 Circumstances under which NCTM Standards were developed? The chronicle? Were adopted? The chronicle?	INHST-CHRON = Chronicle of adoption
1.2 Prime "advocates"? Roles of admin, tchr, etc.	INHST-ADV + Activities, moves of advocates
1.3 Roles played by NCTM in state & local adoption?	
1.4 Context at the time? Social, econ, polit, etc. Context now? Ditto	INHST-CON = Contextual factors
Characteristics of school, dist, neighborhood	INHST-CON = Contextual factors
Innovation history of the school	INHST-CON = Contextual factors
2. Process of Assessment and Development	
2.1 Motivations and incentives	TAD-MOT = Motivations, incentives to adopt
Were decisions pragmatic (to do it better)? Were decisions strategic (to gain advantages)? Were decisions inherent (an obvious next step)? Were decisions pedagogical (to improve learning)?	INHST-TRAJ = Career trajectory of advocates
2.2 Were Standards seen as solution to a problem? What were initial perceptions of the Standards?	TAD-NEED = Need to which Stds were solution
What expectations were raised?	INHST-PERC = Initial perceptions, expectations
2.3 Characteristics, orientation of users?	TAD-STAT = Status of adopters
Pedagogical stance of users? Constructivist, etc.	TAD-STAT = Status of adopters
Age, experience, background, tech soph. of advocates?	TAD-STAT = Status of adopters

(Continued)

	Age, experience, background, tech soph. of opponents?	TAD-STAT = Status of adopters
2.4	Initial perceptions of:	TAD-MOD = Initial understanding of how to use
	How Standards were to be used in classroom: Level of complexity of the Standards: Demandingness on teacher skills and capacities: Clarity of the Standards: Fit with existing teacher styles, pupil readiness:	TAD-MOD = Initial understanding of how to use
2.5	Financial issues in development, adoption. Are cost, availability of materials problematic?	
3.	**Developers' Perspectives and Production**	
3.1	NCTM orientation to math education?	
3.2	Key components of the innovation? NCTM demand for "faithful implementation"?	
3.3	How does NCTM regard this site? Is it similar to other pilot or observation sites?	INHST-USE = Number of schools also using
3.4	What connection between NCTM and site? Are there interactions btw the two at this time? Organization fit?	INHST-DEV = Role of developer in adoption INHST-DEV = Role of developer in adoption
4.1	Do Standards fit into grand plan for improvement?	
4.2	Do Standards nest well into other workings?	
4.3	Do Standards fit with existing math, science curriculum? Do Standards fit with policy and vision?	

Figure 5.8   First Pages of Research Questions and Examples of Coding from the Case Study of NCTM Standards, Coordinated with Michael Huberman's Network Research Questions (4/6/93)

traffic control center as well as an information locator, increasing the likelihood that similar instances will be kept in mind when preparing reports.

Evaluation project logs are another kind of traffic control for the procedures of the evaluator. Keeping a project log is surprisingly important and surprisingly difficult. Keeping it neat and legible is not so important. Having names of contacts, starting dates, meeting notes, and negotiation points—and especially the procedural decisions and reasons for making them—is terribly important when it comes time to write up the report and complete the meta-evaluation. Early drafts should be saved. Just throwing copies of e-mails and memos into a monthly envelope is a start. We need more reminders than we have. Computers should make it easy to keep daily notes as to happenings—but somehow don't for everybody.

A log is a chronological record, a powerful ordering of memory. A coding system provides another mnemonic: people, places, quotations, photos. For frequency statistics, an entry must only count once, but for aiding a search, an entry needs to be duplicated and stored in several places. Please read the field notes presented in Figure 7.1 (Chapter 7). As to coding, we would store a copy in the Advisory Board file, another by date, another in the ethics file, and possibly another in the Kansas City file. (Where else might a copy go?)

With the Figure 7.1 notes in hand, we were able to discuss the problem with our total evaluation team of ten. We perhaps had been rude in Chicago, but the main problem, as we saw it, was carrying out an evaluation of their program without respecting their emerging definition of the evaluation. We had started to raise questions about an authoritarian relationship between the Board and the local Directors, as reflected also in organizational style at the local sites. We had started to see the Board as acting beyond the eye and rules of the sponsor, the NCAA. Before we had a plan of response, we were notified in writing that the project would not be funded a second and third year. We finished our work of the first year and published a report (available now on the Web at http://www.ed.uiuc.edu/CIRCE/NYSP/Index.html) saying that the NYSP projects varied in approach from campus to campus, but as a whole, the program was quite successful. We said it had perhaps one management problem that we had only incompletely investigated. We provided several hundred copies to NCAA. Our bills for the year were paid, but we received no acknowledgment of our report or work. (For more on relationships with clients, see Chapter 7.) During the session in Kansas City, in spite of the tension, we jotted a few notes. Shortly thereafter, the session was logged in the form shown in Figure 7.1. We sent it to Bill for a member check, but he did not reply.

Note taking for observations and interviews is an important skill, not left to chance, developed with practice and collaboration with mentors and team members. The pros and cons of note taking were used in his teaching by Barry MacDonald (see Figure 5.9).

(Text continued on page 137)

Data Generation	Characteristics	Strengths	Weaknesses
Effectiveness	Structured roles. Working relationship. Question/Answer style. Episodic discourse. Interviewer as informed questioner and ethnographer of communication.	Only what is 'finished' and valued is recorded, so interviewee's stumbles, confusions, incoherences, irrelevancies are weeded out or improved and polished. Professional control of the record. Penetrative of meaning and salience. Parsimonious.	Reductionist. Interviewee deference to recording task constrains natural discourse, invites closure and conservatism and resultant lack of penetration. Reduced nonverbal contact.
Fairness	Private except for what is noted—and remains so. Open notebook offers interviewee cumulative evidence of data value. (Even closed notes indicate selection criteria.) Time out to write and check entries enhances interviewee control of testimony.	Low-risk testimony the norm. Affords the security of the conventional recording medium. Emphasis on role performance rather than role experience protects the person.	No chance to reconsider testimony or its representation. Tendency for interviewer's structures to organize the data. Reliance upon interviewer's skill with shorthand/encoding.
Validity	Emphasis on public outcomes minimizes lazy, careless, or unsupportable testimony. But, no objective record; limited verbatim data.	Nonverbal as well as verbal components of communication taken into account. Interviewer uses knowledge and skills to cross-check, represent other viewpoints, challenge testimony.	Little raw data survives. Most data have been treated at source in some way. Difficult to respect informal, nonpropositional forms of knowledge and understanding.
Data Processing	Characteristics	Strengths	Weaknesses
Effectiveness	Negotiation of noted summary in biographic form for improvement	Summaries facilitate faster data negotiation and clearance.	Difficult to use data except in individual interview packages.

(Continued)

Data Processing	Characteristics	Strengths	Weaknesses
	and release. Interviewee invited to: a) authorize the representation, b) rewrite, c) add.	Economical in time and cost. Clearance facilitated as summary approximates to recall of event.	Paucity of raw data. Understandings of data prematurely fixed. No re-selection of raw data possible.
Fairness	Absence of high risk data reduces need for confidentiality. Joint arbitration of processed accounts. Interviewee can totally reject the account as inconsistent with his recall of event.	Nature of summary affords less threatening accounts. Summaries evidence evaluator's style and likely use of data—signals that inform and 'arm' respondent against later abuse. Economical, intelligible forms facilitate interviewee task in negotiating clearance.	Packaged nature of summaries deters from deleting/adding to accounts. Respondents' private interests underrepresented. Empathy/sympathy with interviewee at mercy of writer's skill. Lack of independent record may lead a) strong interviewees to disclaim account b) weak interviewees to accept account.
Validity	High premium places upon interviewer's skill and integrity in selection, analysis, and synthesis of data. Accounts of particular testimony structured in terms of their contribution to generalized validity of program overview.	Rich data on context of response. Interviewer's skill, interests, and overall knowledge enable valuation, validation, and rationalization of data.	Interviewer error/bias in generation compounded at advanced processing stage. Lack of objective evidence to substantiate analysis. Vulnerable to facile causal inference. Autobiography treated as biography
Data Reporting	Characteristics	Strengths	Weaknesses
Effectiveness	Biographical portrayal or narrative account of the program experience,	Condensed and susceptible to summary. Complex features noted	Individuals submerged in overview or lost in 'group'

(Continued)

Data Reporting	Characteristics	Strengths	Weaknesses
	with individual cameos. Thematic or issues organization. Interviews treated piecemeal or as epitomes of the program story.	but integrated. Commonalities emphasized. Parsimonious use of raw data to support or illustrate. Offers a synthesis of 'understandings.'	perspectives. An outsider's account of insiders.
Fairness	De-emphasis on individual testimony. Opportunities to comment, adverse comments noted and reported, usually as addenda.	Individuals protected because their testimonies are subsumed in framework of understanding.	Interviewees dependent on sympathetic evaluator as spokesperson for their realities. Importance of individuals as actors diminished. Interviewees deskilled as critics by literary construction and by lack of source data record.
Validity	Emphasis on contextualization, coherence, contingency. Inherent logical forms in summarizing afford critique. Constructs explicit.	Interviewer, with skills, interest, and knowledge, is the most qualified to judge authenticity, relatedness, and resulting hierarchies of data importance. Interviewer's commitment is to the "greater truth." Interviewer accountable to academic peers.	Loss of individual voices. Final reports are summaries of summaries—high possibility of gross reductionism, compounded error and heavy skewing. Reliance on interviewer as storyteller increases systematic bias. No objective raw data to support the account.

Figure 5.9 Note Taking, by Barry MacDonald

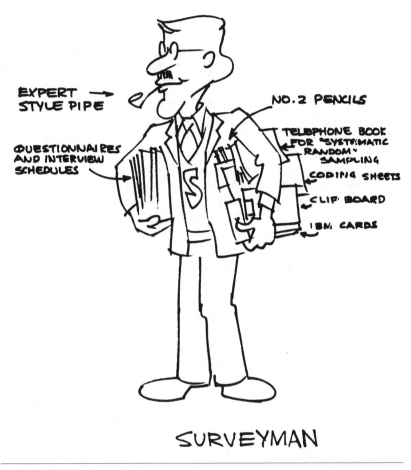

EXPERT →
STYLE PIPE

NO. 2 PENCILS

QUESTIONNAIRES
AND INTERVIEW
SCHEDULES

TELEPHONE BOOK
FOR "SYSTEMATIC
RANDOM"
SAMPLING

CODING SHEETS

CLIP BOARD

IBM CARDS

SURVEYMAN

Evaluation Coloring Book, by Ernest Olson

Reprinted with permission of the artist.

Surveys

Technically speaking, surveys are any formalized questioning of data source people for information, including informal oral interviews—but the term *survey* is usually used to mean a written questionnaire. When developed by a major professional opinion sampling organization such as the Gallup Poll or National Opinion Research Center, item content is worked and reworked to minimize errors and waste of time. Survey development is important business for any organization whose workers' views are needed. Some see it as too costly. One hundred workers taking a one-hour survey means, in the eyes of some managers, 100 hours of productivity lost.

The expectation of a neophyte survey author is usually that getting participation is a matter of persuading people that the information will be useful. Many people presume it a waste of time. Those willing to help do so perhaps because they too have had to solicit help, money, or information, and they want to be of assistance. Even when the respondents stand to gain something, such as support of their own programs or protests, the *return rate* is likely to be disappointing. Even when the survey is literate, right-minded, timely, and brief, a 40 percent return can be cause for celebration. With two repeat requests, it might climb to 50 percent. If their boss requires it, and the law as well, it might climb to 70 percent. As you know or can guess, there are lots of factors—age, gender, employment, and political affiliation—that influence return rate. Lots of research literature has been devoted to these influences. The world does not a survey love. And unsolicited marginal commentaries regularly assure authors that they are illiterate and imbecilic.

Be that as it may, surveys are important data-gathering procedures for program evaluation. It is important to get responses from many staffers, beneficiaries, and stakeholders, if for no other reason than to attest that the evaluation exists. Most of the vicious comments will be unwarranted, but a few will point to an evaluand asset or failing that was about to be overlooked. It pays to keep the survey short and to item sample. Questions should be included only if, after careful study, it is clear that the information, even if quite unsurprising, will be used, will be useful, and will not waste the respondents' time.

Should survey responses be heeded at all if the return rate is under 66 percent? It depends partly on the readers of the report. What is credible to them? It depends partly on whether the purpose is to establish a fact, such as length of employment or country of origin. The sample of returns is not a very good sample of the people solicited, and that sample is an imperfect sample of some greater population. When a true descriptor of the population is important, a 66 percent return will seldom provide a worthwhile estimate. When it is felt that any sample of returns may provide information worth pondering, especially without interest in describing another sample or population, then a 40 percent sample may be quite useful. One can come to understand a social phenomenon better by examining a single case, a sample of one, however nonrepresentative that case may be. Certainly a phenomenon can become more understandable if a dozen or more persons respond thoughtfully to several important questions. The smaller the response rate, the greater the caution in treating the information as descriptive of other cases not responding.

Another big problem is that a short survey with simple, straightforward questions will seldom penetrate the complexity of important issues. If there is a question as to effects of the admission policies of the evaluand, how can it be asked simply? If there is contention as to disposition of pension funds, how can those who are not aware of the contention provide their views unless the issues are explained? Even if you ask something as simple as length of the respondent's previous training, the definition of training may call for careful explanation and troublesome subcategories. It takes writing and rewriting, trial runs, analysis, and synthesis.

In 1976, officials of the National Science Foundation wanted to evaluate the status of science education in the public schools of the country. An official decided to use a discrepancy evaluation approach: to identify the present status of science education, independently identify the standard (the desired status of science education), and make policy on the basis of the discrepancy.

At that time, the National Science Foundation was under vigorous attack by a few conservative Congressmen who were distraught by portrayal of diverse styles of family living in distant cultures in the NSF-funded social studies curriculum, *Man: A Course of Study.* Charged with failing to understand the propriety of classrooms in American schools, NSF initiated three national studies of the status of these schools, one of them using case study methods. We in CIRCE got that contract, but only after assuring the review panel that we would add a national survey to confirm the case findings. As expected, the CSSE case findings were dynamic, situational, and contextual. They were difficult to represent in standardized survey questions. Our effort to present in questionnaire form something of the experiential meaning of current science teaching and learning in American schools is sampled in Figure 5.11. These particular items were among those administered to high school seniors and School District Superintendents. (Stake & Easley, 1979)

Please note, in the Case Studies in Science Education (CSSE) questionnaire shown in Figure 5.10, the long narrative description of a teacher's efforts to teach scientific analysis of social problems, followed by seven multiple-choice machine-scorable questions and opportunity for open-ended addenda. The usual time to complete these eight questions exceeded two minutes per question, providing considerably less data per minute than is usually expected from surveys. Eight of these issues-based narrative item clusters got us interesting data, but we did not conclude that the survey responses *confirmed* the case study findings. The quantitative and qualitative data were complementary but not confirmative. Perhaps a study's particularistic, contextual findings and criterial, generalization findings *cannot* converge to a single meaning. (What do you think?)

Please consider the following situation:

At Metro High School, Mr. Robinson's American History Class is studying immigration and the settlement of America, noting particularly how immigrants have influenced the growth of their city. Here is dialogue midway through Monday's class:

Mr. Robinson: After the Irish immigration of the 1840s and after the importation of Chinese laborers, what other waves of immigration occurred? Sally?

Sally: Europeans around 1890 and then again after World War I.

Mr. Robinson: Good. I guess that's when we got our Polish jokes, right? (no one laughs) Well, let's see. What sort of longtime trend are we studying?

Sherman: People coming to America.

Mr. Robinson: Why did they come, Tammie?

Tammie: To come to a country with freedom.

Doug: (sarcastically) Like freedom to pick cotton.

Mr. Robinson: Well, let's think about that. Some of the early colonists were seeking freedom. Were the Chinese who came after the Civil War seeking freedom? (no answer) What were they looking for? (no answer) What were the Irish looking for?

Wendy: Food!

Mr. Robinson: Food more than freedom? Let's make a list of possible reasons for immigrating, then consider each one.

Eric: My dad says we should be studying how to send them back where they came from rather than how they got here.

Mr. Robinson: Okay, that's an idea. After we make our list of reasons for immigration, let's figure out who wanted the immigrants here and who didn't want them. And then let's decide whether I should be sent back to Africa or Europe.

---

1. Mr. Robinson is asking questions about history and joking about it. What is your reaction to his teaching style?
   _____ It is fine for some teachers to teach this way. It gets their attention.
   _____ I find it offensive.
   _____ I don't mind, but he is not likely to get the job done.
   _____ Other: (please indicate) _____

_____

2. Do teachers and students talk like this in your school(s)?
   _____ Yes, lots do.
   _____ Yes, a few do.
   _____ No

3. How common is it for teachers in your school(s) to try to teach the scientific analysis of social problems? (Please comment as you see fit.)
   _____
   _____
   _____
   _____

(Continued)

4. Mr. Robinson seems reluctant to accept the idea that most immigrants came to America seeking freedom. Let us suppose that this is a bias of his. How important is it for social studies teachers to keep their biases to themselves?

_____ They should recognize their biases and keep them to themselves.

_____ They should speak honestly as to how they feel on matters.

_____ They should tell how they feel, but present alternative views too.

_____ Other: _____

5. Suppose Mr. Robinson was leading up to a critical analysis of the free enterprise system. Suppose he intended to say that the system was dishonest, that it was cruel in the way it imported cheap labor from foreign lands to work in this country. Do you feel that it would be inappropriate for Mr. Robinson to acquaint the students with his conclusions about the free enterprise system in early America?

_____ It would be right, in fact it is his responsibility to be frank.

_____ It would be all right as long as he indicated his value-orientation.

_____ It is ethically proper, but he would be foolish to do so.

_____ It is wrong for him to use his position for teaching those things.

_____ Other: (Please explain) _____

6. Some parents believe that certain topics should be left out of science and social studies courses, topics such as evolution of the species, human reproduction, and family attitudes and customs. Some parents want such things taught, and of course, want them taught well. We need to find out how you feel about *using federal funds* for development of teaching materials that include such controversial topics.

_____ Federal funds should never be spent on such development.

_____ It is all right to spend federal funds this way if it will not cause trouble.

_____ It is important to provide federal support for such development.

_____ Other: _____

7. In what ways have budget cuts in your district seriously affected the social studies curriculum? (Check one or more.)

_____ We have not had budget cuts recently.

_____ The social studies curriculum has not been seriously affected in any way.

_____ Classes have been made larger in size.

_____ Needed and highly qualified teachers have been "let go" and not replaced.

_____ We have more teaching from textbooks, less with materials or in the field.

_____ No longer can we provide a textbook for each student individually.

_____ The inservice training program has been cut back substantially.

_____ Other: (please indicate) _____

(Continued)

8. As you look at social studies courses in your high school and elsewhere, you probably see things that concern you. Please check those things below that you consider to be major problems. (Check as many as you wish.)

_____ Too much emphasis on facts, not enough on concepts
_____ Too much emphasis on concepts, not enough on facts
_____ Too much emphasis on teaching about personal values
_____ Not enough emphasis on teaching about personal values
_____ Not enough qualified teachers
_____ Belief that teachers teaching the same course should teach the same things

Figure 5.10   A Situational Questionnaire Used in CSSE

artifact *n* an object made by human work, often an object from another culture

Consider this type of item writing as one approach to interviews and questionnaires. You provide respondents with something to examine—an artifact or representation, a quote, a newspaper article, something about which they may have special views. The object may be closely related to a special evaluation issue. The issue might be, as in Figure 5.10, reasons for immigration or, more generally, the social conditions under which a nation develops. You may wonder if the history and social studies curricula follow a traditionalist line, a progressive line, or some other. You devise some questions to discover the interpretations of the respondents. You may ask if they have observed such discourse where they live or work. You may want to find if their views are correlated with age, gender, school experience, or other demographic or educational characteristics. Notice that items 5 and 6 almost directly refer to the political issue in which NSF was engaged, even though there was nothing in the contract that referred to this issue.

Item 8 allows the respondent to make multiple checks. Thus, the item becomes a set of binary items, checked or not checked. It is not the flip of a coin—for most people, the tendency to leave a line unchecked is stronger than to check it. (How would you present tallies for #8?)

Observation Schedules

The more that similar scenes need repeated observation, and the more the data need criterial thinking, the more the need for a formal observational checklist.

Student Talk		Teacher Talk	
		Direct Influence	Indirect Influence
Student Talk-Response: talk	Silence or Confusion:	Lecturing: giving facts or opinions about content or procedure; expressing his own ideas, asking rhetorical questions.	Accepts Feelings: accepts and clarifies the feeling tone of the students in a nonthreatening manner. Feelings may be positive or negative. Predicting or recalling feelings are included.
	ds s ɔn not ıe	Giving Directions: directions, commands, or orders with which a student is expected to comply.	Praises or Encourages: praises or encourages student action or behavior. Jokes that release tension, not at the expense of another individual, nodding head or saying, "um hm?" or "go on" are included.
		Criticizing or Justifying Authority: statements intended to change student behavior from nonacceptable to acceptable pattern; bawling someone out; stating why the teacher is doing what he is doing; extreme self-reference.	Accepts or Uses Ideas of Student: clarifying, building, or developing ideas suggested by a student. As teacher brings more of his own ideas into play, shift to Category 5.
			Asks Questions: asking a question about content or procedure with the intent that a student answer.

Figure 8.1.   Data Categories for Flanders Interaction Analyses

SOURCE: Adapted from Modley and Mitzel's (1963) Adaptation of Flanders (1960, Appendix F, p. 5).

As with all instruments, observation protocols are difficult to compose and field test. Sometimes one may find something useful already available in the research literature. The best known has been the *Flanders Interaction Analyses* for recording dialogue between a teacher and the students in a classroom. Hundreds of research papers have been written with Flanders data, but the protocol has not been used much in evaluation, probably because it pays no attention to what is being taught. Still, many evaluation studies get deeply into the social processes of the classroom. The Flanders has been useful in pointing out how dominating the teacher can be in the intellectual exchange in classrooms.

The Flanders categories are shown in Figure 5.11. A simple tally is made by the observer every minute or so, coding the communication with a single mark. No note is made of what they are talking about or the manner in which it is said. Teachers, classrooms, programs, and evaluands can be compared wherever a sequence of instructional question-and-answering is of importance. Other classroom observation schedules can be found in the educational research literature, but the chance of finding one that beautifully fits your evaluation criterion or issue is not high.[6] One can build one's own observation schedule using an existing model.

Site visit teams can be aided by the use of checklists and observation schedules, both to assure key scenes will be reached and to remind about issues to be noted there. They also serve as a record of where the observers have been. When individual observers visit many sites, some mechanisms such as observation schedules or structured diaries are essential for keeping recall of the sites from morphing into one another. It should be recognized that write-up time needs to be available during and immediately following the observation.

In the late 1960s, the Illinois Gifted Education Program was riding high and being evaluated with a four-year external study headed by Ernest House (House, Steele, & Kerins, 1971). That team used some Flanders data. The state director, Bob Hardy, was proud of his program but distressed that even though required by their contracts, the projects at all the several hundred schools failed to submit a required annual evaluation report. Hardy contracted with CIRCE to devise something that would get site managers to report. With Gordon Hoke, Steve LaPan, and Terry Denny, I created the *Classroom Observation Report,* consisting of one, two, or three preprinted sheets of nice paper, folding to 5 1/2 x 8 1/2. The contract could be satisfied merely by identifying the program's participating children and teachers on the first sheet and submitting it to the State Department of Education. On sheets 2 and 3, folding to be pages 3–10, the local director could provide brief descriptive and evaluative information, and use it also as promotional materials

(Continued)

---

[6]Some evaluators sometimes modify their research questions to fit the instruments available. Is this okay?

(Continued)

locally. The information solicited on two of the pages is included as Figure 5.12. The opportunity and obligation continued to be ignored, partly because it was well known that the Chicago Schools treated the funding as an entitlement, not requiring an evaluative report. And why should the others evaluate if Chicago did not?

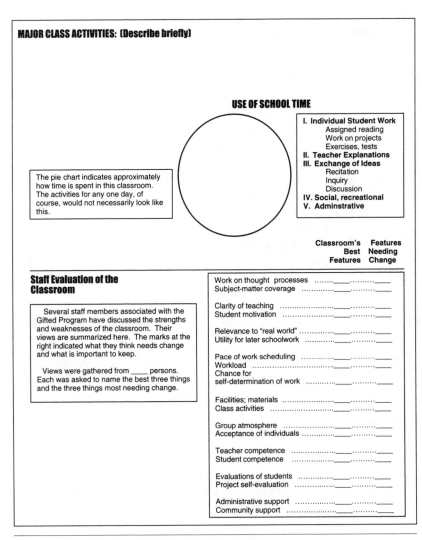

Figure 5.12   Illinois Gifted Preprinted Evaluation Form

Figure 5.13 is a summary of the site visit team protocol organized by Nanette Keiser and Frances Lawrenz to observe local technology modernization courses at community colleges across the United States. It was part of their evaluation of the Advanced Technological Education (Gullickson, Lawrenz, & Keiser, 2002) (ATE; http://www. wmich.edu/evalctr/ate/ate.html) program organized by the National Science Foundation. The attention of the visitors was primarily on educational development, and the checklists helped them take note of many important elements, leaving them more or less breathless, with perhaps too little time for intellectual targets of opportunity, the more or less unusual encounters with complexities of campus or technology.[7]

TO LOOK AT ANY THING

> To look at any thing,
> If you would know that thing,
> You must look at it long:
> To look at this green and say,
> "I have seen spring in these
> Woods" will not do—you must
> Be the thing you see:
> You must be the dark snakes of
> Stems and ferny plumes of leaves.
> You must enter in
> To the small silences between
> The leaves.
> You must take your time
> And touch the very peace
> They issue from.

John Moffitt

SOURCE: From "The Living Seed" by John Moffitt, copyright 1962. Reprinted with permission from Harcourt, Inc.

Interviewing

I think of three important uses of interviews: to learn what people have experienced, to learn how best to describe things, and to obtain their evaluation of something. Newcomers to the evaluation field tend to emphasize the latter,

---

[7]The records of this large-scale program evaluation study are available on the Web at www.wmich.edu/evalctr/ate/. Our CIRCE meta-evaluation of ATE site visiting is at www.wmich.edu/evalctr/ate/sitevisitmeta.final.pdf.

1. Site and Team Description and Schedule

2. Helpful Hints, e.g., Ask the project staff to leave the room while you're interviewing students, collaborators, faculty, etc.

3. Terminology

4. Drivers (Principal criteria of ATE for supporting redevelopment of courses)
   a. Collaboration of projects with businesses, industries, and other organizations
   b. Standards alignment between courses and workforce guidelines
   c. Course, curriculum and materials preparation, adaptation and testing out
   d. Professional development efforts to improve instruction and support
   e. Program improvement, courses, field experiences leading to degree or certification
   f. Recruitment of new students, including underrepresented students
   g. Student services enabling students in the program to be successful
   h. Sustainability, transportability, dissemination leading to broader use of courses

5. Critical questions for preparation of site visit report
   a. What do you consider to be the most important goals and outcomes of your project? What evidence do you have for this?
   b. What are your project's strongest components/outcomes? What evidence?
   c. What are the areas of your program that need improvement?
   d. What has been the role of the grant in your program? Where would it be without it?
   e. Project yourself into the future. What will happen to your project?
   f. What things are now in place that will support that vision?
   g. What barriers are there?
   h. How has the project addressed workforce needs?
   i. What role does evaluation play in your project?
   j. What else should I know or learn about your project?

6. Statement of purpose of site visit

7. Key points for site visitors, e.g., The audience for the site visit report is the site itself and the evaluators at Western Michigan. NSF will receive aggregate information across sites only.

8. General site visit plan, e.g., The team leader will be responsible for coordinating the site visit activities, ensuring that all activities are conducted by someone from the team with the appropriate expertise, and for finalizing and submitting the site visit report.

9. Site visit activities: Field notes, Planning meeting, Site presentation, Interviews/Observations, Debriefing, Report

(Continued)

10. Data collection

11. Site visit report

12. Payment

13. Site visit report outline

14. Interview protocols: Industry collaborator, Student or faculty focus group, Principal investigator, Faculty person, Administrator

15. Field Notes format

16. Classroom observation protocol, including description of the quality of the lesson

More detail on this site visit protocol is available at http://www.wmich.edu/evalctr/ate/sitevisitguide.html.

Figure 5.13   Summary of Site Visit Team Protocol for ATE Evaluation

but the best interviews for evaluations, I think, are those that get at the description of experience. The best interviews are face-to-face where people honor each other with patience and consideration. But telephone and e-mail interviews are useful too, and much less work.

One often learns a lot in casual conversation—but to structure the interview around what needs to be known about the evaluand, planning pays off. The interviewee should be given opportunity to raise other matters, but large amounts of interview time can be wasted as the interviewee talks about what is important to him or her and the interviewer lacks the skill to get back "on target." For the deadline-facing interviewer, these can be painful times.

In my first large interview experience, I was a graduate assistant formally interviewing Nebraskans about the control of wages earned by a "child" age 17 or 18. Round and round, a respondent would say, "No, the parent should not be allowed to take their earnings" and "No, there should be no law to protect the child; that is a family matter." I still can hear the husband in the other room, pacing, waiting for dinner to be prepared, and his thoughtful wife continuing past the third hour, telling me how older children should be handled.

It was a long, aggregative survey on "Sociology and the Law." The interview questions were asked verbatim, and the data were coded to generate frequencies and correlations. That is, verbatim to start, but the rule was to probe further intuitively to find perceived responsibilities of the state. We were crossing intellectual/legal territory not yet settled. When using a more interpretive interview, the questions follow the interviewee's experience or judgments more individualistically, but the responsibility remains to get responses tailored to the evaluand.

Quotations in the body of the final report will usually be few in number, but the evaluator wants to get the quote properly worded. That means he or she will edit it, usually eliminating bad grammar and finishing unfinished sentences where the meaning is clear, avoiding making the interviewee appear bumbling. It should be member checked—that is, sending a written copy of the quote to the interviewee for approval. Working with quotations is more accurate, of course, if the interviews are tape-recorded. If transcripts are made of all the interviews, the cost is very high (see other characteristics of tape-recording in Figure 5.14). I seldom tape; rather, I make notes during the interview and write up the interview immediately afterwards. If I do that, I almost never have a "member check" in which the interviewee says he or she didn't say what I have quoted. Many newcomers to evaluation are uncomfortable without the tape recorder, and they should use one for a while, but they should experiment with reconstructing responses. Transcripts can be the tail that wags the dog. Even with evaluation reports that will include a large sample of comments made by interviewees, the need for exact language is small. Especially when a quote is critical to a judgment being made, it should be member checked.

Interviewing is a high-level skill, begging for practice, flowering with experience. One needs to listen sharply, plying the knots of meaning, interjecting the occasional "You don't mean that." The interviewer shows disappointment when not enough is being told, pleasure that the tale is informative. Gordon Hoke was a master at keeping the telephone interview personal, yet sticking to the protocol. Terry Denny used to tell me that only after he had already listened to the tape a couple of times did he start to hear some of the subtle meaning. Terry would also hear subtleties during the interview, make ingenious probes, and get more out of the respondent. He and Bob Wolf once worked through these ideas with writer-interviewer Studs Terkel (see his *Working*, 1972) for examples of responses elegantly teased out), seeking to upgrade their interviewing skills. Two media interviewers I admire are Charlie Rose of Public Broadcasting Service (www.charlierose.com/biography.shtm) and Terry Gross, National Public Radio (www.whyy.org/freshair), selecting topics, probing, facilitating the telling of stories.

My interviewing isn't good; it's too wordy; but it's not unproductive. One spring I was studying a fourth-grade class in California for the National Arts Education Research Center, looking particularly at how teachers untrained in teaching the arts taught art. Classroom arts and music were required, even though California education budget cuts had "riffed" many specialist teachers. We wanted to know if classroom teachers taught some of their own avocations, such as folk dancing, choir, photography (more on this California fieldwork

(Text continued on page 153)

Data Generation	Characteristics	Strengths	Weaknesses
Effectiveness	Personalized relationship. Conversational style. Continuous discourse. Sustained multisensory communication. Interviewer as listener.	Naturalistic. Prolific. Penetrative of experience. Tolerant of ambiguity, anecdotalism, inconclusiveness.	Selective but mindless record. Data overload. Favors the articulate. Machine-phobia. Visible data lost.
Fairness	Confidential but on-the-record. Interviewee control emphasized, but hazards unknown, and minimal indication of the value or likely use of the data.	Testimony as "draft." Authority vested in objective record. Emphasis on generation maximizes opportunity to testify.	High risk testimony encouraged. Consequences of disclosure difficult to estimate. Over-reliant on interviewer integrity and interviewee judgment.
Validity	Insulated from consequences. Structured by the truth-holder. Told to a person.	Raw data preserved in verifiable form. Stimulus as well as response recorded. Time to search for truths. Freedom to tell. Safe responses quickly exhausted and superseded. Dissimulation hard to sustain under continuous observation.	Off-the-cuff data. Freedom to lie. Pressure on interviewee to be "interesting." Machine-phobia. Over-reliant on interviewee self-knowledge.
Data Processing	Characteristics	Strengths	Weaknesses
Effectiveness	Record transcribed. Transcript sent to interviewee for improvement and release. Interviewee invited to: a) amend or delete, b) extend, develop, c) prioritize, indicate high-risk data.	Data retain much of their original form. Considered testimony. Inaccuracies corrected. Additional data obtained. More clues to interviewee's values and	Costly. Time-consuming. Obsolescent. Loss of valuable data. Inadequacy of verbal record.

(Continued)

Data Processing	Characteristics	Strengths	Weaknesses
	Uncontentious data may be summarized. Deadline for return stipulated.	valuables, a guide to negotiable reporting. Interviewee's responsibility for the product is explicit.	
Fairness	Negotiation confidential. Interviewee the arbiter. Access to record. Governed by agreed rules. But "release" can be seen as a "chicken run" test for the foolhardy.	Interviewee rights respected. Time and opportunity given to change testimony, to calculate risks and benefits. Interviewee free to consult others, to take advice. Possession of transcript and agreement constitute insurance against abuse.	Interviewee asked to release not knowing: a) how the data will be reported, b) norms of disclosure. Interviewee may be poor judge of own interests. Transcripts lower self-esteem.
Validity	Characterized by set sequence of moves open to scrutiny. Based on objective record.	Depends on the argument that given the power and the responsibility for making known their own truths, interviewees will make more effort to do so.	No data on the context of response. Relies overmuch on the interviewee's belief in and commitment to the research mission.
Data Reporting	Characteristics	Strengths	Weaknesses
Effectiveness	Aspires to theatrical form of oral history. Interviews provide subscripts in program drama, interwoven in chronological, scene-by-scene construction. Draft showing data in	Naturalistic autobiographical data have inherent dramatic form. Rashomon effect—multiple perspectives. Dramatic imperative overrides interviewee's	Slow delivery. Lacking in scientific respectability. Inconclusiveness. Over-lengthy due to irreducible obligations to individuals. Costly to produce and disseminate.

(Continued)

Data Reporting	Characteristics	Strengths	Weaknesses
	context negotiated simultaneously with interviewees. Draft rewritten in response to respondent critiques. Final report public.	discretionary impulse. Surrogate experience for the reader. Yields better understandings of what has happened, challenges social beliefs underlying program policy and action.	
Fairness	Draft report confidential to interviewee group. Rewritten to satisfy interviewee criticism. But in negotiation, the researcher presses: a) audience concerns and needs and b) dramatic values.	Interviewee participation. Form of the report foreshadowed by the form of the interview. Individual testimony highly valued. Natural language maximizes accessibility to non-specialist readers and to subjects.	Researcher allocates 'star' and 'support' status. Researcher alone has all the data. Interviewee cannot retract released data.
Validity	Individual bias, censorship, inaccuracy subject to correction through consultation with knowledgeable and multi-variate constituency. Account open to external challenge based on cited testimony or back-up tapes.	"Pluralist" endorsement of account as accurate, relevant, balanced. Triangulation of oral histories. Autobiographical emphasis. Appeals to readers' own experience.	Context of generation disappears. Role and influence of evaluator under-emphasized. Formal imperatives override substantive. Genre makes he account dismissable as factoid.

Figure 5.14   Taping, by Barry MacDonald

1. What about the schools here today is different from when you went to school? . . . particularly about fourth grade?

2. Is everything else pretty much the same?

3. What about fourth-grade art and music? (How has it changed? What do you see the children learning today in art and music?)

4. How do you feel about the emphasis, or lack of emphasis, on art and music?

5. Would you like to see more attention to drama and dance in elementary school?

6. What interest does your child have in any of the arts? Crafts? Private lessons?

7. What happens to art things he/she makes?

8. Can you describe a particular project?

9. What is your impression of Mr. Free as a teacher?

10. How much emphasis does Mr. Free give the arts? (Artistry in teaching?) Do you know a teacher who does?

11. Do you know any topic or subject matter that Mr. Free treats as extra important?

12. Does your child talk about the wild animal project they presently are working on?

Figure 5.15   Interview Questions for Parents About Art Teachers

late in the next chapter and again in Chapter 10 under Human Subjects Protection). We were interested also in what the parents thought the teachers should do. I put together the following interview, field-tested it, and asked parents of students in one fourth-grade classroom I had observed for several days.[8] To make my parent-child comparisons, I limited the group to those parents who had grown up in the community.

Look at how specific some of the questions are in Figure 5.15. You need to make some of yours that specific. Immediately after interviewing one father, I went to my car and wrote up the report shown in Figure 5.16.

---

[8]The write-up of this report is on pages 235–262 of Stake (1991).

The dad graduated from a nearby high school in 1969. His elementary and junior high years were spent here. There's been a long time family presence in the community as *his* mother received all of her schooling here as well.

Says the schools are considerably different today than when he attended. Teachers and principals are less responsible for children receiving an education in basic academic subjects. Now, the responsibility has shifted more to parents to ensure that children complete assignments at home. There's a "huge stack" of materials that have come home unfinished. Not required to be returned to the school. No school notice is paid to this, and there is no communication with parents on the matter.

The way of thinking today is different from the '60s. Learning materials and methods presently used in schools are adequate for these times. Concerned that materials used are outdated (publish date of 1961 for history book) and in poor physical condition. There is more coddling in teacher's approach today, not demanding enough. If financially possible, he would send son to private school.

Is dissatisfied with policy that promotes children on the basis of age rather than achievement. Had asked for son to be retained in earlier years due to poor performance.

Didn't really notice the lack of an arts program when he was a child. Remembers that there was a band, but he didn't get involved and wondered at the time how children were selected for it and how instruments were allocated.

Personally feels that there should be more arts education. Although he is not a craftsman himself, his family background includes a father who was a music teacher and his mother was a commercial artist. Plays a little piano himself. Other boy shows much talent as an artist. Son has an accordion and plays their piano. He is not forced to practice as they are pushing him on everything else he studies. Bought him a trombone for the instrument program at school. A lost music book was replaced but he has to pay his parents. To teach him that Mom and Dad are not made of money. Parents care about his music. He has to have an outlet. If there were performing arts class, would enroll him.

The son wants to be part of the adult world. He's interested in electronics. Bought him a kit and he made many of the projects himself. Has explaining skills and always wants to explain it to everyone, especially his mother who isn't as smart in these matters. Tried to get him in to the GATE program but he didn't do well on the test.

There is not nearly enough emphasis on the arts. They're needed for a "rounding" in an education. Mentions doctors as an example (Dad is a nurse). Some are prima donnas in academic terms but are lacking in life skills due to sole emphasis on academics. Arts are needed for self-esteem, personal satisfaction. Son is an example. Not successful in other areas but considerable parental encouragement in music offsets an otherwise negative situation.

(Continued)

> (Continued)
>
> The son has an allergy to sugar, recently discovered. Is willing to take responsibility for his diet but this is sometimes difficult when eating with 200 other kids who are willing to give him sugar. This allergy has affected his school performance in past, but parents know he's smart. Some psychological testing and speech therapy has been done.
>
> Mr. Free is the best teacher son has had. He's the first teacher to really take an interest. Parents feel comfortable with him. Notes are written and there is lots of time for personal conferences. These are usually parent initiated, and the teacher responds. But there are too many kids in there to watch just one. He'll figure past what you're doing. Mr. Free just doesn't have the time.

Figure 5.16   Immediate Rough Write-Up of One Parent's Responses

In the composite final report, shown in Figure 5.17, I first commented on the son (anonymizing him as Andy Norman), then added a few sentences from the interview with his father.

It is not uncommon to use so few words from a total interview. You are influenced by it further in how you handle various issues. Although much of the description of Andy is not about the main issue, it is useful in providing a vicarious experience for the reader, giving the reader an opportunity to relate this situation to ones already known about other families.

Interviews provide important data in many evaluation studies. Sometimes it is important to base judgments of program quality partly on interviewee perceptions, but interviewees contribute much also to understanding what the evaluand is and how it is perceived. Focus groups[9] are sometimes useful. Good interviewing helps to minimize the stimulus error.

Part of the interviewing is with program sponsors and administrators. Although Mr. Sacredo is asking more questions than Phyllis, she is learning his issues and values in these conversations. (Perhaps you should read her many words again, thinking what you might have said.)

Histories and Artifacts

Evaluation studies can usually be enhanced by an issue-oriented presentation of the immediate history of the program. It is especially useful in responsive evaluation to provide something of the experience as it was before the program and during its implementation. Much historical information can come from

---

[9]Group interviews, called focus groups, allow respondents to draw each other out, although some individuals may be reluctant to speak (Morgan, 1998).

When I first spoke to Andy, he immediately wanted to show me the classroom computer. We waited until recess and he happily explained how it worked. He was disappointed that there was little software but was attentive to each option available. In class, Andy was one of the last to engage and one of the first to disengage. His description of himself was brief:

I am nine years old. My favorite color is orange. My favorite sport is baseball. I have brown hair. My favorite number is 10 and I have two cats and a dog and a catipillar.

His father, Fred Norman, was a nurse at nearby Valley Hospital. He and Andy's mother monitored Andy's progress carefully. Fred told me:

There's not nearly enough emphasis on the arts. They're needed for a rounded education. Doctors are an example. Some are prima donnas in academic terms but, due to a sole emphasis on academics, are lacking in life skills. The arts are needed for self-esteem, personal satisfaction. Andy is an example. He's not successful in other areas but the encouragement he gets in music offsets an otherwise negative situation.

Figure 5.17   The Description of Andy in the Final Report, Using Data From His Dad

formal and casual interviewing of administrators and the staff, but the search should also be made for documents. Promotional materials, minutes of meetings, memoranda, e-mail correspondence, regulations, job descriptions, apologies, dedications, photographs, tapes, and receipts are among the documentary resources establishing the history. Many of these are not immediately accessible and come at a certain cost but improve the accounts of oral history. When documents are critical in establishing the chain of events, efforts should be made to obtain and preserve copies.

Particularly in responsive evaluation, there is emphasis on describing the activity and the contexts of the program. The meaning of success and failure is tempered by the times, by the conditions. It is not primarily the evaluator who decides the standards of success, but they exist within the program, constituencies, and society. There will be competing standards. The program may have official designations of success, but people will disagree, and some practices will be incompatible with those standards. Many readers of evaluation reports expect the evaluator to resolve these complexities, but he or she cannot. The complexities are part of the contemporary scene and the social condition. The evaluator studies them, sometimes deeply developing an issue or two (as described in Chapter 8), and leaves the reader with the opportunity to understand program merit and shortcoming better, but without making it deceptively simple.

Descriptions of contemporary activity and promises of the future are enhanced with historic record and artifacts. Drawing upon the expertise of ethnographers and cultural anthropologists can be empowering (Hodder, 2000). It is important early in the design of the study to anticipate what kinds of evidence can be presented. Will there be an opportunity to present an exhibit? Can photographs, videotapes, or voice and music recordings be used? Much of the experience of being there can be captured by narratives and vignettes.

The program evaluator is something of a cultural anthropologist and something of a theater director. It is important to tease out the events and activities of the program, to organize and develop them around themes and issues, and to present them in such a way that the accomplishments and values are understood by audiences. Often those audiences include the managers, staff, beneficiaries, and other stakeholders, most of whom already knew quite a bit about merit and shortcomings but become more keenly aware of program complexity as the story is more fully told.

Narrative

Phyllis's phone rings.

Sagredo: I'm driving to the office and realize that I don't have a good idea of what good mentoring is. What do you think?

Phyllis: Well, you caught me off-guard. By the time you get to the office, I should have something for you.

(Later)

Sagredo: I have only a few minutes before my meeting, but I would like to know what good mentoring is.

Phyllis: We have two things to know. We need to know what good mentoring is, and we need to know what good training is for mentors. They should be related—but being a good mentor or knowing what good mentoring is does not assure good training. A mother who is a linguist isn't necessarily going to help her children be wonderful speakers.

Sagredo: I appreciate the point. But what is a good mentor?

Phyllis: The best two authors on mentoring I have found are Laurent Daloz and John Seely Brown. They point out that mentoring is highly situational. It depends on the mentees. Yes, that's what they call them: mentees.

Segredo: And if they are not very bright, dementees?

Phyllis: Anyway, it depends on the mentees, the relationship, the organization, and certainly on the competence and personality of the
mentor.

Segredo: If it is always different, how can there be training?

Phyllis: It is like counseling, or mothering, or managing. There are things to
know. There are skills to be developed. Even though you have to
work in different situations in different ways, there are experiences
to gain, hazards to avoid, and ways to evaluate yourself.

Segredo: I don't know if I know any more than I did on the way to work.

Phyllis: Well, mentoring is helping people understand their work, their
assets and shortcomings, their resources, opportunities. These vary
from person to person. Not much of the learning can be standardized, and it doesn't look like we could use a standardized test to see
how much the trainees have learned.

Segredo: Surely we could test them on the basics.

Phyllis: I haven't found any test I would use. To know the quality of the
training, I think we have to understand the experience of being a
trainee. Not just is it good or bad, but how did it engage the trainee's
background, competencies, personality, ethics, career plans.

Segredo: But everyone is different.

Phyllis: That's true. And the success of the training will vary from person to
person, and from situation to situation. Good evaluation shows that
distribution across different contexts. The evaluator needs to
observe the training, get into the mindset of the trainer, thoroughly
understand the experience of a few participants, and learn how they
use the experience back at the job.

Segredo: We don't have the budget for all that. And even so, it is just too
subjective.

Phyllis: Suppose that we were able to identify five really important things a
mentor needs to know. And suppose that we could test to see if all
the mentor trainees learned them. We could say that that would be
evidence of program success. But if we really care about the training's contribution to their effectiveness as mentors, don't we want
to know about change in practices? Yes, but we can't monitor their
practices. So we have to ask them, ask them in different clever ways,
to see that they are able to help their coworkers with greater understanding, humanity, and tenacity than they had before. It is subjective. And what we are looking for is a depth of knowledge that
actually cannot be known objectively.

Segredo: I'm late to my meeting. I'll have to think about it.

(To be continued)

6

Analysis, Synthesis, and Meta-evaluation

A century ago the Swiss historian Jacob Burckhardt foresaw that ours would be the age of "the great simplifiers," and that the essence of tyranny was the denial of complexity. He was right. This is the single greatest temptation of the time. It is the great corrupter, and must be resisted with purpose and with energy.

Daniel Patrick Moynihan

W ere design and data gathering perfect, then the analysis and reporting might be easy. In the real world, the design falls short, the data are puzzling, the analysis turns out to be lots of work, and the reporting calls for all our brainpower to carry beyond the simple. It's tough sledding. And yet for most of us it is fun[1] and, some of the time, a beauty to behold.

> **analysis** *n* *pl*–analyses Separation of anything into constituent parts or elements; also, an examination of anything to distinguish its component parts, separately, or in their relation to the whole

To most people, the evaluand is not simple, and their perceptions of quality differ. One can squeeze the summary of program quality into a single rating or descriptor, such as A- or Barely Acceptable or Smashing, but to ignore

---

[1] Some clients are not amused if we evaluators appear to enjoy our work. We avoid writing playful reports. An exception once was Ernest House, who distributed an executive summary of evaluation of the Illinois Gifted Education Program as a child-size jigsaw puzzle.

the complexity of the evaluand's activity and merit is to misrepresent the truth and to shortchange the audiences. Even if the contract simply calls for a declaration as to which operation is best, the answer is not likely to be simple.

You may be disappointed with this chapter and this book for providing so little technique, so few detailed procedures to follow. My intent has been to present the major responsibility in data gathering and analysis as conceptual, not technical. Much of the doing of professional evaluation is using good common sense, then adding a discipline that comes with care and experience. The technical steps are important but seldom different from other research. It is the purpose—determining merit and shortcoming—that makes evaluation different.

Analysis

As the dictionary says, *analysis* means breaking the total into its parts to get a better understanding. For the evaluator, it means having a hard look at the pertinent factors of the program, some or all of those identified in Chapter 3:

1. Beneficiary needs
2. Program goals
3. Evaluation criteria
4. Evaluation standards
5. Synthesis weights
6. Staff and beneficiary performances
7. Program costs

For many people, analysis also means putting the pieces back together again, to get the fullest possible meaning. We often call that putting-together process the *synthesis*. During the study, we do analysis and synthesis more or less simultaneously and repeatedly, taking things apart and putting them back together again, looking for patterns and nuggets, working toward descriptions and interpretations. After most of the data have been gathered and before the final organization of the report, we may dignify a period of time by calling it "the analysis," to be followed by a period of time we will call "the synthesis." But these phases overlap and repeat themselves.

During analysis, as standards-based evaluators, we take our numerical data and make statistical distributions, comparisons, and correlations. We test hypotheses. Following the procedures identified in the design, we produce the indicators and graphics that answer our research questions. For example, for the county, we report that 22 of the 24 foster families studied while providing the services required. Similarly, as responsive evaluators, we reexamine narratives and quotations and

Figure 6.1   Metaphoric Representation of Program Value in Two Dimensions

triangulate interpretations. We finish the analysis phase finding illuminative support for assertions of program quality, including a long narrative between the parents and a social worker. The procedure is to use the summaries of data as evidence to answer the questions around which the study was organized.

The true value of a program is not something that can be reduced to a table of specifications. Not everything can be specified. Just as smog exists as an amorphous thing, so also can value. It sometimes exists only indistinct in form. We may discern some of the value there but not all. The value of some programs is ill formed, nebulous, not just poorly seen, not just obscured, but without body. How should an evaluator represent that value? Suppose the best possible representation of that value would be quite nebulous, as is the shape at the left in Figure 6.1. Assume that blob on the left is the true picture of the program's value. By brute force, we might use our techniques to give the value shape so that it is seen as more vivid, as shown at the right.

It can be argued that by making it clearer to behold, we have *lost* validity in the representation. (Does that make sense to you?)

When I first reread those last two paragraphs, I worried that it was too much of a downer. How could we be enthused about doing analyses if we even have to worry about value being stated more clearly than it really is?[2] Implied precision and validity cause some people to shudder, yet we make it as clear as we can. Even if the truth is difficult to grasp, we find approximations and summations that satisfy the needs of clients and stakeholders. An evaluand is weak and strong in various ways, and we can see enough of each, and spell it out in our reports.

---

[2]Some people see *value* as a human construction rather than as an intrinsic property of the evaluand. The substance and clarity of value (for them) derive from people's perceptions of value. Value would not be unclear if everyone concerned had a clear idea of the merit and shortcoming. (We call people *realists* who take as real the things that only seem to be. The people who treat the real as hypothetical, we call *constructivists*.) According to Lewis Carroll (*Alice's Adventures in Wonderland*, 1865),

> Alice laughed: "There's no use trying," she said; "one can't believe impossible things." "I daresay you haven't had much practice," said the Queen. "When I was younger, I always did it for half an hour a day. Why, sometimes I've believed as many as six impossible things before breakfast."

Reference Work	Issues	Patterns		
Tracy Kidder, *Among Schoolchildren* (1989), p. 46	Insularity of the teacher. Depersonalization of teaching.	Al says "which is fine" over and over, maybe indicating reluctance to face facts. No notes coming from parents.		
Jacquetta Hill, *Archipolis* (1978), pp. 9–14	Nonconforming behavior of students obstructing instruction.	Tardy arrival of students in class. Stealing pennies. Damage to microscopes.		
Day, Eisner, Stake, Wilson, & Wilson (1984): Larry Ecker vignette, pp. 4–32	Student disbelief in importance of instruction, low work ethic. Work ethic contingency with teacher treatment of students.	Slow engagement in lessons. Student appetite for socializing.		
		Students Are:	*Teacher Encourages*	*Teacher Discourages*
		Avoiding Work		
		Engaging Work		
Bob Stake, *Quieting Reform* (1986): Bill Milliken, p. 100	Use of evaluation reports.	Interest in evaluation coinciding with promotion of Cities in Schools program.		

Figure 6.2   Issues and Patterns in Four Reference Works

The analysis of an observation or interview identifies components that draw us to think about how usual it is or to what it is related. We look for *patterns*. Patterns are consistencies, repetitious happenings, contingencies or covariation, occasionally cause-and-effect relationships. We may use statistics to indicate the strength or nonrandomness of the pattern. Patterns are important in all kinds of analyses. Recognition of patterns is facilitated by categorizing the data, by coding it. Note in Figure 6.2 the observations from four reference works, a couple of issues for each, and the patterns the evaluator found in each data source.[3]

How do we do it in the simplest evaluation studies? How do we analyze? We observe patterns of performance of the staff or the newly achieved performance

---

[3]In the Patterns cell for the Larry Ecker vignette is a typical fourfold contingency table, in which frequencies of responses are accumulated in each subcell, a contingency coefficient of pattern strength is calculated, and possibly a chi-square statistical test is applied for checking the strength of the pattern.

of the beneficiaries, concentrating on the main criteria of intended success. For standards, we draw upon perceptions of merit from those around the program, from our colleagues and advisers, and possibly, what it says about performance and merit in both professional and popular journals. We add those to our own growing conviction about program quality. We reflect on needs, goals, costs, and issues, noting what can be considered *evidentiary* and which is mere conjecture. Sometimes we modify and remodify our summarization of program quality. We study criterial comparisons among subgroups or across time. We think carefully about the strengths and weaknesses of our instruments and procedures. All the while we are drafting bits and pieces for the final report, a table here and a quotation there. It is a thought process. And that is our analysis. It is followed by synthesis, the main effort to bring it all together.

In larger studies, the activities are much the same, but larger and more diversified. Efforts are made to gather a variety of evidence on each aspect of performance. Triangulation, meta-evaluation, or critical review procedures start earlier, last longer, and are more demanding, formally and informally increasing the certainty that meanings and assertions are trustworthy. Among the concerns within analysis and synthesis in some studies are the attribution of evidence of outcome to the evaluand and generalization of the findings about the operations observed, within this evaluand and to programs elsewhere. We will look further into attribution and generalization in Chapter 9.

Some large evaluation studies concentrate on a single performance criterion. Almost unbounded is the optimism of some clients that one instrument can measure effectiveness. Such was once the case with the evaluation of literacy of Texas teachers:

> In the mid-eighties, under contract with the State of Texas, James Popham evaluated the English language literacy of all public school teachers in the state. State officials recognized that all teachers did not have equal need for language skills but had decided there was a minimum competency below which teachers should not be allowed to teach. Popham provided a standardized literacy test and protocol for a writing sample. A minimum qualification standard of 75% correct was set in advance. A distressingly large portion of teachers scored below the standard. The standard was revised so that only the 5000 lowest scoring teachers would have their certificates taken away. One observer claimed that these teachers were disproportionately in special education and the practical arts, and teachers of children whose home language was Spanish. These were pedagogies of high need and low supply. The state did not authorize a validity study to determine the number of effective teachers decertified and the number of truly illiterate teachers not so identified by the testing.[4] (Popham, 1989)

---

[4]Errors in such a sorting are sometimes called *false negatives*, the number of qualified people failing, and *false positives*, the number of unqualified people slipping by.

Note that although the testing was highly objective, the cutting score was set arbitrarily (subjectively), then set again. Was a single criterion adequate? According to the standards for accountability systems put forward by Eva Baker (Baker, Linn, Herman, & Koretz, 2002), Bob Linn (Linn, Baker, & Betebenner, 2002), and their CRESST associates, any criterion (including teacher literacy) should be evaluated using different types of data from multiple sources.

Most evaluators want to get started on the statistical analysis as soon as the numbers are in. They usually have set up the coding and want to compare group performances. Many have correlated first-half-of-the-test scores with second-half-of-the-test scores to estimate test reliability. Many have combined weighted parts for a composite measure. Strict use of statistical inference requires deciding about what will constitute evidence of program success before looking at the data. Most evaluators do not set such standards in advance.

Perhaps because one can see its progress faster, the standards-based analysis is likely to move ahead even in studies that are primarily responsive evaluation. It is also true that the preliminary findings from criterial thinking are likely to be useful in organizing the qualitative analysis. But as I said earlier, work on the two sides of the study overlap, with crescendos and diminuendos from day to day. The key interviews are constructed, transcribed, and coded. The staff memos are examined for verification of patterns discerned earlier.

Obviously, the evaluator and other principal investigators have to be familiar with a range of research methods, better still, have long experience with them. But each study is a new experience for everybody in many ways. Even when the internal evaluator is carrying out what was planned as repetitious quality-control evaluation, the organization changes, the instruments are revised, new statistical software is installed, and much has to be learned over again. Even when it can be routinized, our curiosities resist letting it be.

We have to have routines. Without routines, without plans, outlines, models, checklists, flowcharts, whether mental or in print, our work cannot proceed. As a graduate assistant, I helped with a psychology project studying effects of putting young adult men into strict sensory deprivation for a week, blindfolded, hands in tubes, in a soundproof room. We got volunteers (for $75) partly with the deception that they would be able to plan further work on their dissertations undisturbed. None of them made any progress at all during sensory deprivation, perhaps because to organize their thoughts they needed to write things down, and couldn't.

We need conceptual structures from which we can keep on track, or away from which we can soar, but few of us, if any, have the mental discipline to organize things entirely in our heads. The business of science and humanistic inquiry is partly the provision of routines. Knowing when to stay on and when to get off the routines is partly what you are learning. Consider this description of the work of one of the greatest scientists of all time. The following paragraph is from Lou Smith's "Charles Darwin, a Biographical Portrait":

> But even in his mode of thinking and methods of inquiry controversy exists. At one extreme is the Baconian view of making many observations and slowly and inductively coming to a theoretical position. At times, Darwin himself indicated this was his approach. At the other extreme is the evidence from his journals and notebooks that what he did was very different. Gruber, a recent analyst, commented about "The pandemonium of Darwin's notebooks and his actual way of working, in which many different processes tumble over each other in untidy sequence—theorizing, experimenting, casual observing, cagey questioning, reading, etc." (Gruber, 1969, p. 123). Pat formulas for scientific inquiry fall apart in the Darwin story. (Smith, 2000, p. 8)

Sometimes the analysis workload is so heavy that the evaluator's attention is drawn away from the issue questions to the methodological questions. That is such a common problem that mechanisms should be created (memos should be sent to one's self, tickler files should be set up, etc.) so that, every so often, implications of new data for the issue questions are raised again. Every Thursday at four, maybe, the evaluator meets with several "critical friends." It could be with a colleague, a program person, and a surrogate for a stakeholder. The question is asked, "Now what does this one mean?" or "Perhaps we were too hasty last week in concluding that the organization was overly attentive to its personnel policies. Let's see if we can think of the arguments against that assertion." Maybe at three would be better. The project log should be examined.

Oh, did I fail to tell you about logs? No, it is in the previous chapter under "Coding." You need to keep a project log. Very few evaluators do, but those who do do 15 percent better work than those who do not. Or was it 35 percent? In Figure 6.3 is a Site Manager's Diary that I developed to provide the manager with a running record of events. It was also to provide me, the evaluator, with data from distant sites that I could not get to myself. Note that it is oriented to change, helping to keep track of when things started or stopped. Note that it implies that goals, activities, personnel, outside support, and context are the most important things to be watching. You might substitute some other things. The idea is not to keep a complete record, just a reminder of how things were changing and not changing at various times. We think we won't forget, but we do. This diary could be modified to be the evaluator's own diary. It would be an additional place, perhaps a better record of dates, names, changes in plans, and so on. Yes, most evaluators don't keep a diary or a project log, but they should.

Even with good records, analysis takes a lot of remembering. "Now what do these photos mean?" "Does this vignette change the sense of quality for this evaluand?" Part of the thinking goes immediately into draft write-up.

Monthly Observations of Project Change

Month Covered: _____	Entry Date: _____	Observer: _____
Main Events for the Project This Month: _____ _____	Describe What Is Happening In and Around: _____ _____ _____	
What changes in GOALS this month? Major: _____ _____ Minor: _____ _____	Causing what problems? _____ _____ _____ _____	Bringing what opportunities? _____ _____ _____ _____
What changes in ACTIVITIES this month? Major: _____ _____ Minor: _____ _____	Causing what problems? _____ _____ _____ _____	Bringing what opportunities? _____ _____ _____ _____
What changes in PERSONNEL OR CLIENTELE this month? Major: _____ _____ Minor: _____ _____	Causing what problems? _____ _____ _____ _____	Bringing what opportunities? _____ _____ _____ _____
What changes in INTERAGENCY SUPPORT this month? Major: _____ _____ Minor: _____ _____	Causing what problems? _____ _____ _____ _____	Bringing what opportunities? _____ _____ _____ _____
What changes in PROJECT CONTEXT this month? Major: _____ _____ Minor: _____ _____	Causing what problems? _____ _____ _____ _____	Bringing what opportunities? _____ _____ _____ _____

Is the formal evaluation plan needing change? _____Yes _____ No
Should the project office be called?
For which problems is additional information needed? Who can obtain it?
Which of these changes need further staff discussion? And with whom else?
What comment or incident should be remembered to stimulate discussion?

Figure 6.3   Project Management/Evaluation Diary

Explanation of each table should get several times as much page space as the table itself. It takes practice, including study of the reports of other evaluators.

Suppose you are evaluating a staff development project aimed at improving communication between teachers and headmasters. You have made observations of teachers. Suppose one of the observations was more or less the same as the Figure 6.4 excerpt from Muriel Spark's *The Prime of Miss Jean Brodie*. (Don't think now about how the observer obtained a record of what Sandy was thinking.) There are two main issues here. (What are they?)

Would this be a good vignette to illustrate the communication issue? Can you conclude that you know what Miss Mackay's position is from what Miss Brodie says? During the analysis, we increasingly figure out the meanings of our data. The vignette of Miss Brodie might be considered a single datum, but you may take a number of meanings from it. The evaluator jots down each meaning, files it, perhaps immediately writes about it.

Have you had a hard look at the vignette? I would say the first issue here has to do with children's readiness to learn what the teacher is ready to teach. And as a corollary, it is about students learning other things while the teacher is teaching, for Sandy is stretching her vicarious experiences (moving beyond the action of the novel *Kidnapped*) as well as beyond her previous comprehension of personal affection. Does that relate to the intended issue of staff communication? Or does it get in the way of evaluating the progress of the school's efforts at improving communication?

How many detailed observations do we have to make to feel that we understand a teacher's teaching? How many vignettes do we need to include in the report? From just this one vignette of Jean Brodie, do you see a couple of paragraphs forming in your head about whether or not the school is making headway with staff relations? No, of course you cannot draw a conclusion yet about the effectiveness of this school's continuing professional education, but yes, you may probably contemplate the complexity of the problem better than you would have before you read the vignette. And your readers may as well.

I am not irritated because we evaluators find many notions of what good teaching is. Complex representations we can handle. I *am* irritated because so often we fail to see that the whole is greatly different from the sum of the parts. For Olympic diving, the aggregate of perpendicular entry and small splash poorly tell the quality of the dive. For creative writing, grammar, sequentiality, illustration, and closure fail to tell the quality of the essay. And description and judgment of antecedents, transactions, and outcomes do not encompass the quality of the evaluand. When are partial representations good enough?

We can take little solace in the fact that most of the world does not want to know more about diving, essays, or complex operations of the evaluand. There is a large market for the simple.

Their walk had brought them into broad Chambers Street. The group had changed its order, and was now walking three abreast, with Miss Brodie in front between Sandy and Rose. "I am summoned to see the headmistress at morning break on Monday," said Miss Brodie. "I have no doubt Miss Mackay wishes to question my methods of instruction. It has happened before. It will happen again. Meanwhile, I follow my principles of education and give of my best in my prime. The word 'education' comes from the root e from ex, out, and duco, I lead. It means a leading out. To me education is a leading out of what is already there in the pupil's soul. To Miss Mackay it is a putting in of something that is not there, and that is not what I call education, I call it intrusion, from the Latin root prefix in meaning in and the stem trudo, I thrust. Miss Mackay's method is to thrust a lot of information into the pupil's head; mine is a leading out of knowledge, and this true education as is proved by the root meaning. Now Miss Mackay has accused me of putting ideas into my girls' heads, but in fact that is her practice and mine is quite the opposite. Never let it be said that I put ideas into your heads. What is the meaning of education, Sandy?"

"To lead out," said Sandy who was composing a formal invitation to Alan Breck, a year and a day after their breath-taking flight through the heather.

Miss Sandy Stranger requests the pleasure of Mr. Alan Breck's company at dinner Tuesday the 6th of January at 8 o'clock.

"That would surprise the hero of Kidnapped coming unexpectedly from Sandy's new address in the lonely harbour house of the coast of Fife—described in a novel by the daughter of John Buchan—of which Sandy had now by dubious means become the mistress. Alan Breck would arrive in full Highland dress. Supposing that passion struck upon them in the course of the evening and they were swept away into sexual intercourse? She saw the picture of it happening in her mind, and Sandy could not stand for this spoiling. She argued with herself, surely people have time to think, they have to stop to think while they are taking their clothes off, and if they stop to think, how can they be swept away?"

"That is a Citroen," said Rose Stanley about a motor car that had passed by. "They are French."

"Sandy, dear, don't rush. Take my hand," said Miss Brodie. "Rose, your mind is full of motor cars. There is nothing wrong with motor cars, of course, but there are higher things. I'm sure Sandy's mind is not on motor cars, she is paying attention to my conversation like a well-mannered girl."

"And if people take their clothes off in front of each other, thought Sandy, it is so rude, they are bound to be put off their passion for a moment. And if they are put off just for a single moment, how can they be swept away in the urge? If it all happens in a flash . . ."

Miss Brodie said, "So I intend to point out to Miss Mackay that there is a radical difference in our principles of education. Radical is a word pertaining to roots—Latin radix, a root. We differ at root, the headmistress and I, upon the question whether we are employed to educate the minds of girls or to intrude upon them. We have had this argument before, but Miss Mackay is not, I must say, an outstanding logician. A logician is one skilled in logic. Logic is the art of reasoning. What is logic, Rose?"

Figure 6.4   From *The Prime of Miss Jean Brodie* by Muriel Spark (1962)

Reprinted by permission of HarperCollins Publishers, Inc.

Reprinted with permission of Tribune Media Services.

Thirty years later, we marvel still at exit polling, at the Dow Jones average, at the vignette, the sound bite, at countless simplistic representations. All representations are misrepresentations to some degree, but worse than mis-informing, many of them numb the curiosity for knowing the real meanings of the matter. Even the best of our representations encourage people to falsely presume that a no-holds-barred evaluation has been done. The truth is that we have only looked at selected parts.

We should not be satisfied that the quality of training is captured by trainee ratings, or by performance scores, or by peer reviews, or by trainer-of-the-year awards. Training, counseling, and leadership are situationally respon-sive acts, each role a hundred times more complicated than the best checklist or set of standards. Meaning and quality of each role are constructed by the folks closely involved every bit as much as the meaning of a child's story is constructed by the children read to. The value is embed-ded in the situation, only in small part accessible to evalua-tors, supervisors, or other pro-fessionals. The best analysis cannot make patchy measures

> **synthesis** *n* the act of putting together, assembling the parts; making sense of complex issues

into whole cloth. Half a story may be good enough, but it should come labeled with that warning. Good evaluators tell their readers something of what they are not including.

Synthesis

This is another time and place to work through the practical difference between criterial and interpretive thinking, as introduced in Chapter 1. At the same time, we should review the differences between standards-based evalua-tion and responsive evaluation, as described in Chapters 3 and 4. You may want to scan those chapters before going on.

Deborah Fournier (1995, p. 16) has written that the general logic of evaluators is:

1. *Establishing criteria of merit.* On what dimensions must the evaluand do well?

2. *Constructing standards.* How well should the evaluand perform?

3. *Measuring performance and comparing with standards.* How well did the evaluand perform?

4. *Synthesizing and integrating data into a judgment of merit or worth.* What is the merit or worth of the evaluand?

This can be a useful heuristic and it is the way that Consumers Union tests many products, but as Fournier and Nick Smith (1993) say, it is not the way that most program evaluators actually work. Many try first to learn a great deal of program detail and background for use—along the way and at the time of the syntheses. Many try to capture something of the experience of being a staff member or beneficiary of the program. Only a few program evaluators set standards of performance in advance. When they do, it is often because a contracting agency has required it. When it is done, often everyone is embarrassed by setting the standards too high and thus making competent people appear incompetent. Unless they know the instruments and performers extremely well, evaluators should not set explicit standards in advance. They should and do look for standards that already exist—but they find few. They carefully try to understand what is the nature of quality in the situation, and they may end up being explicit about how they classify performance as to merit and

> **epistemology** *n* The study of the nature of knowledge. The aim of epistemology is the justification of knowledge claims.

worth. But it is a back-and-forth process involving revision of criteria, rethinking performance, and reflecting on standards. Even with the most psychometric standards-based evaluation, the conceptualization of standards of quality requires lots of negotiated thought and only a little explication.

The way you do your evaluating will be indicative of and conditioned by your epistemology of goodness.[5] What do you know "quality" to be? Think about it. Where is the quality to be found? According to your knowledge of things, does the evaluand itself have intrinsic value? It may help to think this way: Is a strawberry itself good? Does the strawberry have a goodness

---

[5]Knowing goodness in a rational, analytic way is so, so difficult. One might call it *goodness grief.* Knowing goodness intuitively is so much easier.

independent of people's opinions of it? Does a spring rain that nourishes the deepest forest have an intrinsic goodness? Does the policy of requiring community service of those found guilty of certain misdemeanors have an intrinsic merit, independent of human valuing? Is goodness a property of the evaluand, or is it something entirely determined by people? Or can it be both? Can it be an excellent program regardless of what people think of it? Or is its value entirely a human construction? Or do we evaluate best by examining both views? There's no right answer. Your evaluating will have its own answer.

We should speak of goodness and worth not only in terms of criteria and standards, but also as perceptions of performance? The views of people should not be ignored. We often want to speak of a program's having a quality of its own, at least partially independent of the opinions that people have of it. If we say that the effects of a program have an intrinsic merit regardless of what people think, then it makes sense to try to discover that merit in impersonal ways. Perhaps a small amount of opinion could be included. That, more or less, is the standards-based strategy.

If you are inclined to think that the value of an evaluand is more or less entirely constructed by people through their perceptions, choices, and judgments, your synthesis strategy is likely to be different. Even if you are inclined to think the program has an intrinsic value but find it too difficult to discover, then it may make sense to attend to criterial performance less and concentrate more on the people having useful perceptions, choices, and judgments.

That difference in epistemology partly determines the design of your evaluation, including the instrumentation, observation, analysis, and synthesis. The standards-based strategy calls for measurements for which good performance is more or less self-evident. Suppose that in one program, the community health students all graduate, get good jobs, and are retained and promoted at their workplaces. An evaluator without any particular competence to assess community health skills could conclude that the program is meritorious. Of course, the instructors, recruiters, and supervisors are making evaluative decisions, and perhaps are elated or disappointed, but on the face of it, the training program is a success. While taking a standards-based tack, evaluators look for signals that indicate good performance on criteria widely accepted as relevant. They may study the tests, performance arrangements, and grading scheme at length, but that is done so that they can feel confident in their least personal, least judgmental process.

Minimizing personalization and judgment in the evaluation situation minimizes the bias of participants and observers. Biased assessments can distort the evaluation and even be harmful. According to Michael Scriven (1998), "Job 1 [for evaluators] is getting the bias out of action and practice." We will pursue bias control later in this chapter and even more in Chapter 9. Ingenuity in recognizing standards and devising data gathering so as to minimize human subjectivity is the trademark of good standards-based evaluation.

But the nature of many a program makes it very difficult to identify standards and to gather data that should be considered objective evidence of quality. The evaluator may be faced with the choice between measuring weak correlates of criterion performance and relying on people to testify as to the quality of the program. In their testimony, people may provide descriptions of program performance independent of their judgments of quality, but usually it is expected that bias for or against the program will at least partly invalidate their descriptions and judgments.

ALTERNATIVE TEACHER EDUCATION

Unable to attract enough applicants for teaching vacancies in 1998, the Milwaukee Public Schools undertook an alternative teacher training program. It was devised by Martin Haberman, long an advocate of special training for urban teachers. They recruited people with baccalaureate degrees having several years of non-teaching work experience from business, farming, and industry. They screened them carefully, gave them a few weeks of summer orientation, then assigned each their own elementary classroom. The inservice support during the following year included an evening a week of group work and a highly experienced mentor shared with ten others. CIRCE was engaged to evaluate the program. We observed many teachers in their classrooms and the orientation and inservice activities. The mentoring faculty worked hard at formalizing standards for the teachers as well as for the program, yet they were not an objective base for deciding whether teacher performances were above or below standard. (Chandler et al., 2000)

In the CIRCE evaluation of the Milwaukee alternative teacher training program, an internal evaluator was assigned by program managers to observe the teaching of each trainee using a mentors' checklist. The effort to be standardized and fair was strong, but it was not as objective as sponsors wanted. Do you see alternative criteria? The National Board for Professional Teaching Standards (Ingvarson, 1998) has a much better procedure for assessing teacher competence with highly trained assessors—but it is much more expensive and time-consuming.

When evaluators use a responsive strategy, they choose to attend to the special circumstances of individual persons, settings, and operating styles.

Context is expected to amplify the meaning of program operations and the range of real but problematic outcomes. Personalized data gathering is expected to yield insight into the experience of providing and receiving services that is not available to evaluators concentrating on standardized measures and group comparisons. But it lacks the credibility of criterion measurements.

As I have said over and over, most evaluators try to be both criterial and interpretive. Still, their epistemological convictions, the political environment, and the press to get the work done cause them to center their syntheses on standards-based data or responsive data, one or the other, seldom both in equal helpings. The syntheses depend on standards. The standards tell how well the evaluand should perform. But who is to say? Lots of people. And lots of precedents exist. Many expectations can be seen as standards. The evaluator holds up the performance observed against standards obscurely held in his or her own mind and in the minds of many others. It's very difficult, but with good data, hard thinking, and reworking the ideas with others, evaluators do the job.

A program can be thought of as a case to be studied. The case is the evaluand. Midway through my career, partly from listening to Lee Cronbach, I realized that almost all program evaluations are studies of a case. Sometimes the case has lots of sites, lots of service providers, and lots of functions, such as the ATE community colleges Arlen Gullickson was evaluating (Migotsky & Stake, 2001), but the conclusions are about the collection as an entity, a case. Sometimes the evaluand is a single program, a single case. We should draw upon the various methods of case study (Stake, 1995; Yin, 1994) in addition to the more traditional research methods of the social sciences.

I have spent more than twenty years developing skills as a case researcher, concentrating more on the particularity of the case than on its generalizability. It is not so much "a case of something general," but a case of particular interest. As I told you in the previous chapter, with Jack Easley and others, I directed a large national study called *Case Studies in Science Education* (1979). There the reference population was all the public schools in the United States. We actually made observations of just eleven cases (communities), each a high school with its feeder elementary schools. We needed to draw conclusions about the quality of teaching science in American schools. There was no stated standard, no consensus of what constituted good science education. Even if we had found a wonderful measure of the quality of teaching in those schools, we had no explicit standards to evaluate them. And even if we could compare them to how good they were ten years earlier or how good science teaching was at the same time in other countries, we still did not have the answer as to how good it was. The difference could have measured out at 10,000 points, but there was no basis for saying whether that difference was an important difference. The only standards we had, and usually have, are perceptions of quality held by people, people such as the sponsors, the staff, the beneficiaries, the public, the experts, and the evaluators.

Connoisseurship evaluation (Eisner, 1979) solves the standards problem by saying that whatever respected experts perceive to be of quality is the standard. To evaluate, you carefully expose experts to the performance, and they will indicate the quality. They may pay attention to the other factors (beneficiary needs, program goals, evaluation criteria, and program costs), and they may make reference to a genre of performances (citing specific benchmark performances such as Tom Stoppard as a playwright or the architecture of Frank Lloyd Wright). But their report will state or imply the quality of the evaluand drawn from their inside-the-head understandings of quality.[6]

The work of the evaluator culminates in representations of quality. Having made all the comparisons of data, working through triangulation and meta-evaluation, reexamining issue by issue, the evaluator makes assertions of merit and shortcoming. He or she may state it boldly or indirectly (by implication). It may need to be presented as an array of goodnesses. It may be pointed out how the quality varies with the situation. But the culmination of the evaluation study is the expression of merit and weakness. Recommendations may be made, but recommending can be thought of as something beyond evaluation. There may be steps toward remediation, but that too can be separate from evaluation. Evaluation fundamentally ends with the realization of evaluation quality.

Finalizing the realization of quality is the synthesis. The aim is usually to report that program outcomes have attained some level of merit. It may be in an assertion that the outcomes are more valuable than outcomes from other programs, or better than earlier. It is also the aim to say that the transactions were carried out with fidelity to the plan and drawing admiration (or not) from relevant managers, staff members, and beneficiaries. And those antecedent conditions provided by the program should be seen as deserving of evaluation judgment as well. Psychometrician Sam Messick (1970) once commented that the person who wraps butter at the dairy

> **naturalistic generalization** *n* the act of drawing broad conclusions primarily from personal or vicarious experience, rather than from formal knowledge, however obtained

should not be commended for extraordinary productivity if he licks his thumb to pick up a wrapper. How the different aspects of quality fit together is part of

---

[6]Most evaluators believe that expert (blue ribbon) panels do better work when all panel members work from a common guideline. It is clear that panel members can then be brought to a more common response (with higher interrater reliability), but perceptions of quality vary, and evaluations are not necessarily better if fixed upon stated goals or standardized criteria. Sometimes it is better for the panel to resist a common guideline, retaining multiple ideas of merit and shortcoming.

the synthesis. Sometimes (following the "compensatory" approach) it can be done by weighting factors; sometimes (following the "multiple cutoff" approach) a single low performance is seen as cause for failure.

Experiential and Probative Inferences

Not only the evaluators but members of their audiences are synthesizing meanings and values. No matter how technical, corporate, or bureaucratic the situation, people rely on what they infer from their experiences. They take not only the data provided them by the evaluators but much also from their own experience and reading. Their experience is limited and sometimes biased, but it is the experience they will be relying on in many of their decisions. The evaluator plays a teaching role (Cronbach et al. 1980), providing information and *vicarious experience,* adding to existing information and experience.

When the grounds for action that people take are primarily from experience, I call the synthesis *naturalistic generalization.* If Bernadine takes an umbrella on her January trip to Seattle to see our grandchildren, not because the family advised it or she sees a warning on The Weather Channel but because she has been drenched there before, the action is based on naturalistic generalization. We make many of our decisions based both on the generalizations coming from treating formal information logically and from the naturalistic generalizations of personal experience.[7] It is the responsibility of the program evaluator to provide formal generalizations (conclusions, assertions), but additionally useful to provide ingredients for readers to make up their own minds about program quality. Among those ingredients are vicarious experiences drawn from narratives, stories, and vignettes. Vicarious experiences drawn from evaluators' reports are enhanced by vivid portrayals of persons, places, and events. This is not to advocate that the evaluator should defer to forthcoming conclusions of merit made by audiences. The evaluator should speak summarily in one way or another about the program merit perceived. But audiences will do their own thinking, and the evaluator should help them do it well.

In his paper "The Final Synthesis," Michael Scriven (1994b) advocated the least possible reliance on judgment. He expressed high concern for the influence of bias on perceptions of quality—bias that showed up not merely in consistently incorrect answers but in the disposition to depart from what are

---

[7]There is more on naturalistic generalization in the section on Petite and Grand Generalizations in Chapter 9.

logically considered the pertinent criteria. His urging was for the evaluator to use *probative inference* to identify performance that is objectively classifiable as meritorious or not. Scriven described that inference this way:

> [Probative inference] is inference that makes a *prima facie* case for a conclusion: . . . inference that is heavily contextual. It is the "logic of considerations" . . . It will rely on a complex missing premise of roughly the form: "If the performance of X on criteria A, B, and C, etc., is high (these being the leading criteria), and there is no evidence of Q, R, or S (these being all of the serious threats to the inference) . . . then one may conclude that the evaluand is a *prima facie* good (better, best, competent, etc.) wrist watch (judge, clinic, school, analgesic, etc.). (p. 371)

It is then such a strong criterial performance that one doesn't have to "judge" its quality. On one or more criteria, the quality is self-evident. Other observers would come to the same conclusion. It is simply apparent the performance does (or does not) meet the standard. Most of the examples Scriven gave are examples of product evaluation, such as the accuracy of a watch or the acceleration of a car, but we can imagine performance in letter writing or community service as well. An example of a *prima facie* case would be an orientation program that leaves all participants clearly better able to function in the organization. Or if it is understood that an effective program will not leave "beneficiaries" hurt, and some are unequivocally hurt, then it is a *prima facie* case of program shortcoming. The standard could have been defined as no more than a single instance of hurt, or at another level, such as seriously hurting 1 percent of the beneficiaries. I argue instead for judgment, disciplined judgment.

Making it vivid does not itself eliminate the need for judgment. Defining hurt is a matter of judgment. Defining effectiveness, productivity, or social benefit is regularly a matter of judgment, not a *prima facie* matter. Selecting criteria is a matter of judgment. Changing from the judgments of direct observers to the use of criterion performance changes the locus of judgment. Judgment still is needed. Inside-the-head criteria and standards are problematic, but so are inside-the-head choices of performances to observe and the definitions of wristwatch accuracy and trainee injury. What is tolerable to one user may be intolerable to another. These are choices the evaluator has to make, not alone in contemplation, but drawing on critical resources and trying, as Scriven says, to be as explicit as practicable. For setting least subjective standards, evaluators may find help in the professional literature or among stakeholders and colleagues. But ultimately, in practice, it is the evaluator who must decide to use a particular standard or not. Standards set by client definition or public law are not to be ignored, but the evaluator must decide whether or not those will be the main and only standards.

Most evaluators are strong believers in explication. They are effective explicators; that is, they can effectively describe program intentions, activity, and accomplishments. And clearly, their job is made easier when the evaluand has effective writers and conversationalists. In my view, evaluators have a disposition to favor programs that strive for good explication.

This can be a problem. Explications, like all descriptions, can be invalid and misleading. Even people describing their own programs and standards sometimes explicate them poorly. Sometimes they do not know what the staff is actually doing. Explication needs the evaluator's critical scrutiny.[8] Existing program specifications are seldom a rock on which to build an evaluation design. It is the program in actuality that is to be evaluated.[9] Observed performance always will be the result of program transactions and natural changes in beneficiaries and outside influences, not the result of what anyone claims the program is.[10] More on attribution later.

All statements of specification have faults. We cannot count on explication to fully capture reality. The description of a program can exhibit greater complexity than the program really has, but usually it is the other way around. A complex program, such as the operations of the Los Angeles Public Schools or the Roman Catholic Church, especially one that operates differently in different locations and situations, is likely to be represented overly simply by its own spokespersons and by evaluators.

So we see a trade-off. The greater the emphasis on explication, the more that oversimplification can be expected. To avoid oversimplification, the evaluator has to get closer to the antecedents, transactions, and outcomes. That means getting closer to the *experience* of the program. It also means making a closer examination of records, if good records can be found. It also means getting perceptions from others who have experienced the program. So this book's grand trade-off for the evaluator is getting better explication and variable

---

[8]In the Dan Stufflebeam–Egon Guba CIPP model (Stufflebeam, Madaus, & Kellaghan, 2000, p. 279), with attention to Context, Inputs, Process, and Product, the Context section urges an evaluation of the program's goals, decisions, obstacles, and standards. Guba brought an instructional research orientation to the model (hypotheses to be tested), and Stufflebeam a management orientation (future decisions to be made). The model is heavily standards-based but gives responsive attention to departmental and media discourse. The model is widely used around the world, although its users often do not give much attention to the evaluation of program goals and standards.

[9]This was the point Michael Scriven (1973) was making in introducing "goal-free evaluation."

[10]Still it is very important to honor the program for what it is trying to be rather than what outsiders, including external evaluators, would like it to be. One of the best things about traditional accreditation evaluation was that, even though set up by centralized committees of organizations or governments, it traditionally oriented to the stated goals of the local unit. At the same time, it imposed certain common standards, such as minimal requirements for staff training or financial audit. Whether local or central standards, they were explicated more than derived from action. Accreditation continued over the years as a protective device for program operations as much as an evaluative device, yet it gave managers the opportunity to raise the standards of the local units and organization as a whole.

selection or getting more intimate knowledge of the program. Increasing the use of responsive evaluation promises better acquaintance with what is going on. Increasing the use of standards-based evaluation promises more exact description of criteria and performances. Neither one is a guarantee that standards will be handled well in the synthesis.

The evaluator makes key choices early in the study. A responsive emphasis puts more energy into personal acquaintance with the program. A standards-based emphasis gives more attention to identifying criteria and building data-gathering instruments. Every evaluator gets early impressions of program quality. Talking and reading and looking around, exercising inside-the-head standards, he or she gets a feeling of strengths and weaknesses of the program. Are those impressions an asset or an obstacle? The synthesis theory inside responsive evaluation treats them as an asset, working with those early impressions, adding to them, challenging them, correcting them, refining them. The work is subjective and evolutionary.

The synthesis theory inside standards-based evaluation treats personal impressions and opinions as biased. It seeks to *replace* casual data with formal data, personal data with impersonal data. It sets out to get statistical data— evidence in the form of group means, standard deviations, and correlation coefficients. It works to avoid the subjective contours of performance and values obtained from informal observation and interview. Measurement of performance, explication of the factors, and probative reasoning are made technical and rigorous, with stress on methodological quality control. Standards-based evaluation does not dismiss experiential records and expert testimony but treats them more as background than as ingredients for the calculation of program merit and shortcoming. Meta-evaluation is called for. Deliberate efforts are made not to rely on personal interpretations until analyses have been completed. The work is objective and dedicated to that final comparison of performance to standards.

Yes, you've noticed. My presentation here is pretty esoteric. These ideas about synthesis theory and the epistemology of evaluation do not loom large in the consciousness of the typical program evaluator. When getting into a new contract, he or she quickly gets busy with the information needs of the assignment. Later, if there is time, concerns theoretical and epistemological come to mind, particularly when the program has weak claims to success, and when the evaluator wonders how to resolve conflicting information. Luckily, unless the evaluator has promised to deliver a summary judgment, he or she can identify and discuss the pros and cons of the program without having to recommend action. What looks to some like equivocation may be the evaluator indirectly admitting the irresolution of key program factors. As I see it, the task for the evaluator is not to have the last word, but to describe effectively and usefully the diverse aspects of quality in the program.

Analysis and synthesis have a *reactive effect* on our perceptions of the evaluand. As evaluation happens, we start to see the evaluand differently. We see not only its quality differently, but also the criteria and performance by which it is being evaluated. To some extent, there is a change in our definition of goodness. The experience of evaluating includes a maturation, perhaps sometimes a deterioration, in our powers to see merit and worth. Measurement affects the performance and the performance affects measurement. We affect the performance and the performance affects us.

Now, here's a secret peek at the metaphors of evaluation synthesis. Nobody will know this except you and me. Standards-based synthesis is a metamorphosis. The butterfly of "value realization" emerges predictably yet magically from the chrysalis of analysis. For the foreseeable future, synthesis cannot be done by computer. It needs human thinking to weight the factors, to replay the situation, and to spot inconsistencies and omissions. The realization of merit and worth is a part of everyone's thinking, but the radiance of realization from measurement and logic, with refined insight and skepticism, is a beauty to behold. And there it is, right on the cover of your book.

Synthesis from responsive evaluation is equally chromatic, but evolutionary more than suddenly transformative. From the very beginning, shimmers of program value are apparent to almost everyone. Value accompanies meaning. The accomplished evaluator increases the illumination, sees more, and finds meaning that many others do not see. He or she relates these meanings and hues of quality to the important questions around which the evaluation is structured. With greater familiarity with the crystal, the spectrum of values becomes more vivid, yet increasingly ranging across different cultural perspectives and realities. The responsive synthesis has its moments of emergence and transformation, but most of the process is experiential and evolutionary, from initial impressions to the final realization of quality. The two syntheses are represented there on the front and back of this book.

An individual evaluator and evaluation teams use both standards-based and responsive evaluation, both probative and experiential inference. And thus, they use both the butterfly and the description-judgment spectrum. There are moments of synthesis all during the evaluation study, and there is the final synthesis near the end. Value has been perceived along the way and is still being transformed while the final report is being written. It might be better if there were a long impersonal process with judgment held back until a final and unchangeable stamp of quality was affixed, but it doesn't happen that way. No matter how much the aim is to be objective and standards-based, the evaluation will be a developmental process. And no matter how much the aim is to be responsive and conditional, the values will be determined by certain evidence more than other. And yet determined in personal and idiosyncratic and multisplendored ways. You don't have to keep it secret.

Meta-evaluation

One of the marks of science has been the desire to be explicit about the confidence that can be placed in measurements and conclusions. When predictions of elections are made using science-based sampling polls, the information will include a margin of error, or some other sense of the range in which the actual voting for candidates might fall. Statistical analysis is elegant in its effort to show how much the data differ from random

> **meta-evaluation** *n* evaluation of the quality of an evaluation; a determination of the strengths and weaknesses of a study of program quality. It can be formal or informal; it can be done by the evaluators themselves, by coworkers, and by outsiders

(meaningless) data. Qualitative inquiry has not developed such systematic ways of expressing levels of confidence. But all inquiry has ways of improving confidence. In evaluation, we call them *meta-evaluation*.

Just as one can give more or less attention to the transactions (processes) of the evaluand or its outcomes (products), meta- evaluation can give more attention to how the evaluation was conducted or to what it produced. The meta-evaluation can be more heavily standards-based or more heavily responsive.

One form of standards-based meta-evaluation, following the lead of Daniel Stufflebeam (Stufflebeam et al., 2000), checks[11] the various activities of the evaluator to see that process standards have been heeded. The most common source of these process standards is the *Joint Standards* (Joint Committee, 1980). For example, Standard A3 says:

> Information collected should be of such scope and selected in such ways as to address pertinent questions about the object of the evaluation and be responsive to the needs and interests of specified audiences.

And the meta-evaluator can inquire about transactions to see how well that standard is being or has been met. The four subdivisions of the *Joint Standards*—Fidelity, Feasibility, Propriety, and Accuracy—are quite appropriate to the business of meta-evaluation.

Another form of standards-based meta-evaluation, following the lead of Michael Scriven (1969), gathers or reanalyzes a small amount of key outcome data independently, to see if similar conclusions or statements of merit and shortcoming are found. This form of meta-evaluation most closely follows the psychometric

---

[11]Other checklists collected and made available by Stufflebeam are at www.wmich.edu/evalctr/checklists.

procedures for estimating test *validity*. The classical form of psychometric validation is to compare what is learned from a small amount of criterial data to what can be learned by much more intensive study of those same cases.[12]

For example, to validate a performance test for a training program, the evaluator can take the results of, say, thirty trainees and compare those scores to the proficiency of the same trainees when put through longer and much more extensive performance routines. That is a more powerful standard than to calculate the results of the trainees twice (test, retest with same test) and see if the two sets of scores are highly correlated.[13] That standard, as you probably know, is called *reliability*. Of course, it is important that our evaluation instruments are reliable, but it is much more important to assure that their results are valid. Data reliability and validity are major components of meta-evaluation efforts, whether done psychometrically or otherwise.

Meta-evaluation along responsive evaluation lines does what you would expect. Its protagonist becomes familiar with the activities of the evaluators, trying to understand them and capture the merit and shortcoming as experienced in previous work. It relies on direct personal acquaintance with the people, evaluation events, and judgments the people make. One of my own examples was the meta-evaluation of Charles Murray's evaluation of Cities in Schools (CIS, mentioned at the end of Chapter 3), which I published as a book, *Quieting Reform* (1986).

In 1983, the National Institute of Education funded Murray's stakeholder-oriented evaluation and invited us at CIRCE to do a stakeholder-oriented meta-evaluation. I visited the projects in Atlanta, New York City, and Indianapolis, making my own assessments of the quality of work but paid closest attention to what Murray's small team was doing. I looked closely at the interaction between the evaluators and stakeholders, particularly the staffs of host schools providing social services to the families of participating students. I had help from the CIS internal evaluator Joyce McWilliams. I saw Murray becoming increasingly skeptical that the federal government could and should provide such services. I described his inability to carry out a carefully planned evaluation design, a step toward his 1984 book, *Losing Ground*.

---

[12]This way of validating a test—or more particularly, the use of results from that test—is too expensive for most test developers. Evaluators too, for the most part, cannot afford the assurance that the instruments and procedures they use provide approximately the same information that a much more intensive study would.

[13]Procedures for estimating psychometric validity and reliability of testing are found in Mehrens and Lehmann (1984) and Payne (2003).

The issues for this responsive meta-evaluation were issues identified by the evaluators and the CIS stakeholders. Many urban parents saw the school efforts as sound educationally, valuable for its ethic of concern for family services, but actually not better than conventional delivery of social services. Murray (the evaluator) did not fulfill contract obligations, having failed to obtain promised student and family data from schools. The synthesis for this meta-evaluation conclusion was portrayed through the experience of stakeholders more than in the indicators of productivity or contractual fulfillment. The story was a story of evolving realization of good intentions and *prima facie* shortcoming.

In most of our CIRCE evaluation projects since 1990, we have included a brief but formal meta-evaluation step. Upon nearing the preparation of the final report, we have paid a colleague not working on the project to study critically the work we have completed. In various ways, they have come to CIRCE and talked with us, read our drafts, spoken with some of our data sources, and challenged us with their questions. We chose colleagues familiar with our working styles and previous studies, people we thought we could count on to be tough with us, ask us at least a few nasty questions. Actually, they have not been critical enough. Each meta-evaluator has written a report. One example appears in the Web appendix to this book. It is Jennifer Greene's meta-evaluation of our evaluation of VBA training on the rating of veterans' claims.

A pair of more external meta-evaluation reports was published in the *American Journal of Evaluation* (1999). First came a description by Rita Davis and myself (Stake & Davis, 1999) summarizing our CIRCE evaluation of Veterans Benefits Administration training in Reader Focused Writing for the improvement of writing letters to veterans. After an explanation by *AJE* editor Blaine Worthen, two professional evaluators, Lois-ellin Datta (1999) and Patrick Grasso (1999), presented their meta-evaluations. In our regular work, we include the statement written by the meta-evaluator in our own final report, although we had created it more to stimulate further thinking on our part as we worked through our synthesis efforts. Figure 6.5 suggests some focus questions to guide the meta-evaluation of an evaluation.

For standards-based and responsive evaluation alike, the meta-evaluation strives to provide confirmation of what was being found in the evaluation. Some of the more qualitative evaluators use the term *triangulation* to indicate their efforts to clarify meanings and to substantiate assertions. As postmodern thinking became increasingly visible in program evaluation (Mabry, 1997; Flick, 2002; Schwandt, 2002), the importance of confirming a single sense of program value diminished somewhat and the importance of showing cultural differences and situation dependencies of value increased. Thus, triangulation

To design the meta-evaluation study, one may focus on:	Process: How well did the evaluator examine it?	Product: What verification of findings can be found?
Program Quality		
Program Operation		
Substance/Issues		
Program Context		
Program Impact		
For presentation in a meta-evaluation report, one may focus on:	What key data are there on . . . ?	What conclusions should have been made about . . . ?
Evaluation Study Quality		
Its Rationale; Bias		
Evaluation Study Operation		
Evaluation Study Issues		
Evaluation Study Utility		
Its Generalizability		

Figure 6.5   Questions to Guide Program Meta-evaluation Emphasizing Evaluation Processes and Evaluation Products

and meta-evaluation extended the search for additional complications,[14] contributing sometimes to confirmation and other times to further differentiation. For example, it may have been the evaluator's intent to conclude that the reengineering was increasingly opposed by the elder staff members, but the meta-evaluator pointed to important subdivisions even among the elders, and that further teasing out of opposition to reengineering was needed. Or, to take another example, meta-evaluation may argue that differences between rural and urban social workers were being ignored in the study. Triangulation can be

---

[14]Evaluators are not very good about providing descriptions of their triangulation, and it can be pretty boring reading, but it is useful for readers to know how much confidence can be attached to the findings.

worth its weight in gold, whether it confirms the emerging assertions or causes them to be rethought.

In *The Research Act,* Norman Denzin (1970) spoke of ways of triangulating observations. Triangulating findings would follow the same outline. I have reformatted Denzin's outline in Figure 6.6.

The questions in Figure 6.6 are to be used with both confirmation of data observed and substantiation of an interpretation. Some would call it "ruling out rival hypotheses." As meanings increasingly remain the same, the confidence grows that a good interpretation is being made. Let's consider some examples of simple data statements that could be triangulated:

1. The headmaster sat in the auditorium, in the front row on the aisle.

2. Academic students sat in the front rows, technical students in the rows behind.

3. Some technical students taunted the headmaster.

The first statement is almost uncontestable. Almost no reader would doubt this observation, and it needs little triangulation. The evaluator could be wrong, but it probably would make little difference. The second statement needs a little more checking. If the two groups were completely separated, even if not by far, it makes a difference in meaning as to how differentiated the groups were. The third statement needs triangulation. Was the headmaster the victim? Were they taunting or kidding around? Were only technical students taunting? The assertions about tensions in the school depend on careful triangulation of these simple data.

Next are some examples of interpretation statements that, if important, may need triangulation:

1. The headmaster was anxious.

2. Seating assignments reflected an institutional/societal view that academic study is superior to technical study.

3. Unstructured public ceremonies make headmasters anxious.

4. Graduation marks the shift of dependence on family and teacher to dependence on peers and the social system.

As a complex descriptive statement, Number 1 needs triangulation. Is there evidence to confirm the anxiety? Did senior teachers agree that the headmaster was feeling anxious? Number 2 implies agreement at the school and broadly across society of a difference in respect given the two curricular paths. Is it warranted? The evaluator should assure himself/herself. Number 3 is almost a gratuitous stereotyping of headmasters, difficult to document, difficult to cite supporting literature. Number 4 is likely to be seen by readers as a

---

DATA CAN BE TRIANGULATED
WITH REGARD TO EACH OF SIX THINGS:

1. Time. (Does the meaning of the observation remain the same at different times of the day, week, year?)

2. Space. (Does the meaning of the observation remain the same from one place to another?)

3. Persons. (Does the meaning of the observation remain the same with different groupings observed?)

Differences in persons can be considered at three levels

    a. Across persons. (Do interpretations change from one lone person to another?)
    b. Across interactive persons. (Do meanings change from one family or group to another?)
    c. Across larger collectivities. (Do meanings change from one large organization to another?)

4. Investigators. (Does the meaning of the observation remain the same with different investigators?)

5. Theories. (Does the meaning of the observation remain the same when studied against different theoretical perspectives, such as Special Education versus Disabilities points of view?)

6. Methods. (Does the meaning of the observation remain the same when obtained with different data-gathering methods, such as observation and interview?)

Figure 6.6   Six Meta-evaluation Questions for Clarifying the Meaning of Observations

generalization authored by the evaluator. The evidence should have been shown earlier in the report, but we usually grant the author of a thorough evaluation study the privilege of going a bit out on a limb. If the statement is clearly presented as assertion or speculation created by the writer, then little triangulation is required. Not everything needs to be triangulated, but key pieces of information and summaries of issues need careful triangulation, particularly if they run counter to the expectations of the audiences.

Increasingly, triangulation has come to mean not just confirmation but also the search for alternative meanings. The disapproval of a larger group may mask the approval of a subgroup. Good evaluation is partly the search for particularity and uniqueness. Triangulation is a search engine. It is a win-win inquiry because if it finds confirmation, more confidence can be placed in the interpretation, and if it finds disconfirmation, that may increase the recognition of diversities and multiple realities. Triangulation is one of the most important processes of program evaluation.

An Ethic of Continuous Self-Challenge

Perhaps the most important aspect of meta-evaluation is a day-by-day reflection on the part of the evaluator as to what he or she is doing. No matter what the function—stating goals, writing a contract, forming a team, assessing needs, constructing instruments, redefining issues, interviewing, analysis, synthesis, or writing the report—high-quality evaluation depends on its own *quality control* mechanisms. Don Schön wrote about it in *The Reflective Practitioner* (1983) as *reflection,* a role to which we should all aspire.

> **quality assurance** *n* the effort to monitor and correct ordinary operations so that a high level of effectiveness is attained and maintained

If you choose to be a professional evaluator, it is important for you to make specially scheduled checks on how well the evaluation is going, particularly as to how you are doing your job. Such intermittent quality control checks were mentioned a few paragraphs back and will be again, under Skepticism, in Chapter 9. It is important that the functions are carried out reflectively.

Ordinary behavior is monitored, and it could be monitored more deliberately, more meaningfully.[15] You should ask, "Is this really what I should be doing?" The large part of these checks will be self-challenges: "Are my pencils sharpened?" "Is the interviewee answering the question I asked?" "Am I revealing too much about the director's intentions?" We don't have to learn this strategy, because each of us has it already. But we do need to extend it to questions that do not come intuitively. We need to review our efforts to review our work. Sometimes we need to organize a bit of self-study *action research,* as described in the opening to Chapter 2. An evaluator without self-evaluation is a wedding without the bride.

---

[15]Of course, too much attention can be given to reflection, so that it interferes with the doing. Here is a bit of doggerel that long ago helped create some of my first doubts: "A centipede was happy once / Until a frog in fun / Said, 'Pray, Madam, which / Leg comes after which?' / She lay distracted in the ditch / Deciding how to run."

Almost always, one should draw others into the quality control effort, including your data resource people. Once again, the jargon term is *member check*. When the evaluator drafts a description of a person or quotes someone, if practical, the passage should be "member checked." The evaluator should provide the description or quote to that person, sensitively requesting correction and possible objection. Often what the person was doing or saying seems ambiguous, and even if not, evaluators need their own interpretations checked. Often the feedback amplification is more valuable than the original version. Furthermore, the evaluator is not fully aware of implications being generated. You may think you are favorably describing the industriousness of a staff member, but to him, your portrayal shows him to be "curve pushing" or "sucking up." Member checking gives the data resource person an opportunity to object to misrepresentation. Of course, there are instances when a negative portrayal that the evaluator is making offends the staff member. It is especially a problem if the evaluator has enjoyed generous hospitality and cooperation.

Such was the case for me in 1990. Late in the previous chapter, I spoke about interviewing parents of children in Mr. Free's class. In 1990 in California, with deep school budget cuts brought about by "Proposition 3," including a thinning out of teachers of art and music in the elementary schools, I was seeking to understand how classroom teachers were carrying out the continuing state requirement for art and music instruction. I chose not to tell this purpose to Mr. Free, a very able fourth-grade teacher who energetically supported my observations in his classroom for a week. I feared that my aim, if disclosed, would unduly increase his attention to the arts and crafts while I was there. When he read my draft "member check," he was distraught, saying it showed him and his colleagues in a poor light. He would not identify offensive passages. I rewrote the paragraphs that I could see possibly troubling. Still remaining was my observation that although he was an avid horticulturist, square dancer, vintage car keeper, and collector of patriotic materials, he did not choose to use those or his students' hobby collections and avocations as illustrative of a form of art, aesthetics, and cherishings. I did not intend to indicate that he *should have* seized those opportunities. He would not discuss the problem with me. He asked me not to publish the account. I had not promised that I would make changes to suit him and, feeling guilty, published (with an extra layer of anonymity) the evaluative case study (Stake, 1991).

The evaluator may be reluctant to ask for further feedback but usually owes that staff member the courtesy of letting him see how he is described before others do. (I will raise the ethics questions again in Chapter 9.)

Program quality control is the manager's responsibility and everyone's responsibility. An evaluator also plays that role for a program, pointing out strengths and weaknesses, sometimes providing corrective feedback information. If neither the manager nor the evaluator nor the stakeholders are sensitive to dangers, the program may be lost.

The evaluator senses a program's well-being, but intuition will not be sufficient. An internal evaluator should have a set of checks and balances to ascertain when the program is veering off course. The question "What may be going wrong?" needs raising again and again. Neither internal nor external evaluators can rely on their own sensitivities alone, nor on the trustworthiness of others. The evaluator needs to set up review mechanisms to validate observations, to reanalyze data, to challenge interpretations. This is what we call *meta-evaluation,* the evaluation of evaluation. It has its special procedures, but mostly it is an ethic of continuous review, continuous self-challenge. It is an obligation to speculate as to what may be going wrong and what may be falling short.

Narrative

Phyllis:	We've concentrated our data gathering on four criteria: observations of trainer engagement with trainees, feedback from trainee interviews, memo comparisons, and feedback from mentee interviews. And we haven't forgotten that people don't always perform as well as they know how.
Sagredo:	I'm still not clear as to what we will consider a gain in performance in memo writing. I am troubled about what you said about standards for all the criteria.
Phyllis:	Some evaluators have opportunities to work with explicit standards, but most do not. If a decision will be made on the basis of the results, then it is sometimes a good idea to set a cut-score in advance. Usually we just look at all the data, then the evaluators and other people decide for themselves. There is no official threshold of merit for training programs. People have to decide each time what action, if any, should be taken. This is as true of the development of pharmaceuticals as it is for training mentors.
Sagredo:	When you compare posttraining memos to pretraining memos, will you use a statistical test?
Phyllis:	I will probably calculate the statistical significance of the gain (or loss), but I wouldn't recommend using that as our standard.
Sagredo:	Why not?
Phyllis:	Statistical inference testing is for making decisions about large populations from which samples have been randomly drawn. Even if we selected memos randomly, our interest is in the size of the improvement, not whether it is a nonzero difference in some

hypothetical population. We will look at a sample of current memos and a sample of earlier memos and the average difference as we decide what to conclude about the quality of the Senior Mentor Training.

Sagredo: I guess you are saying that we aren't trying to decide whether mentoring training generally is good but whether or not this particular training is good for us.

Phyllis: That's right. Statistical significance doesn't tell us whether or not the difference is important for this organization.

Sagredo: Doesn't this leave too much to personal preference? It sounds pretty weak to me, Phyl.

Phyllis: Program evaluation depends on personal choices, including what standards to use. We can make it less dependent on a single person's views by getting a panel of people we respect to interpret our measurements of changes in memo writing. Having reviewers and a dialogue about the comparisons and standards is a basic part of professional evaluation.

Sagredo: What about the observations of training? Do we have standards there?

Phyllis: Well, mentors, trainers, and others do have standards as to what is a good training session. Remember that consultant who advised you on changing the retirement benefits plan? You wrote in the Newsletter that he really made the options clear. You drew this somehow from your experience of clarity and other standards as well. Those standards were never put into writing, but you were using them.

Sagredo: I'd like it better if we could make this evaluation less intuitive.

Phyllis: These decisions are much the same as you and other people make to run this place. Sometimes options and implications are clear. Often they are not. What you get from evaluation is not accuracy and objectivity and absence of risk, but more information about what is happening and a sense of how good it is. Hopefully, the analysis will be so well done that you will have confidence in the assertions in the evaluation report.

(To be continued)

7

Clients, Stakeholders, Beneficiaries, and Readers

How can I know what I think until I read what I write?

James Reston, *New York Times*

L ike most professions, professional evaluation has a service ethic. It is the
obligation of evaluators to help clients, beneficiaries, and audiences obtain
the information they need. It is sometimes tempting to be "of service" by avoiding looking at anything that might be negative. Most programs have a political
side, with adversaries, sometimes with respectful contesting, sometimes with
hostile confrontation. Information that one side may want reported, another
side wants left undisclosed. This creates an ethical dilemma for the evaluator—
one to be treated in Chapter 9. The point here is that different people want
different help. The help offered (the roles played) by professional evaluators is
of many different kinds. More than in chapters past, in this chapter we will
examine the help offered by evaluation report writers.

The client sets forth a definition of the evaluand, speaks of targets for investigation, and sometimes, if only by omission, identifies matters not to be investigated. As providers of the funds for the evaluation, clients often figure that
they have the final say as to what will be studied. There should be a negotiation,
with the evaluator having considerable say about what is needed for a good
study and what can be accomplished. Client and evaluator should recognize
that "social contracts" already exist, written and unwritten, between agencies
and the citizenry, between producers and consumers. The services of the client
are sought and allowed by the social system because the services contribute to
the general welfare. Especially if funds are from tax monies or publicly certified
foundations, the public has a certain right to know the workings of the program,

its merit and major shortcomings. Thus, the scope of work and distribution of findings need to be negotiated, by client and evaluator, sometimes with others represented, sometimes in public session. It's not a contract to paint the garage. (More about negotiating contracts and disclosure later in this chapter.)

Throughout the conduct of an evaluation, the well-being of the client, the staff, the beneficiaries, and the public needs to be kept in mind. Much of the obligation to them is fulfilled by good communication, some by "indicators." In the abstract of a paper, "Technical and Ethical Issues in Indicators Systems: Doing Things Right and Doing Wrong Things," Carol Fitz-Gibbon and Peter Tymms (2002) say:

> These (data collection) systems would not have grown had they not been cost-effective for schools. This demanded the technical excellence that makes possible the provision of one hundred percent accurate data in a very timely fashion. An infrastructure of powerful hardware and ever-improving software is needed, along with extensive programming to provide carefully chosen graphical and tabular presentations of data, giving at-a-glance comparative information. Highly skilled staff, always learning new techniques, have been essential, especially as we move into computer-based data collection. It has been important to adopt transparent, readily understood methods of data analysis where we are satisfied that these are accurate, and to model the processes that produce the data. This can mean, for example, modelling separate regression lines for 85 different examination syllabuses for one age group, because any aggregation can be shown to represent unfair comparisons. Ethical issues are surprisingly often lurking in technical decisions. For example, reporting outcomes from a continuous measure in terms of the percent of students who surpassed a certain level, produces unethical behavior: a concentration of teaching on borderline students. Distortion of behavior and data corruption are ever-present concerns in indicator systems. (p. 1)

There is much to commend in that summary by Fitz-Gibbon and Tymms, school indicator specialists from Great Britain. They promote interactive data systems that provide information important to stakeholders as well as to managers. But look at the paragraph's lack of "reader friendliness" and "user perspective."

- It is difficult to read.
- It overpromises data accuracy.
- It invites expectation that understanding of problems is possible at a glance.
- It implies transparent data analysis is a virtue.

Misrepresentation as to what evaluation can accomplish can obfuscate as much as incomprehensible language.

Most program evaluators want their data systems and their reports to be reader-friendly, not simply by being transparent but also by being relevant.

Relevancy and comprehensibility sometimes conflict. Our clients sometimes want everything said in an executive summary, but condensation obscures important issues and complex relationships. Our clients sometimes want no mention made of quality of management. Compromises are needed—in content, rhetoric, and style—compromises between what the reader wants to read and what the evaluator feels should be said.

Many years ago, a Columbus, Indiana, project named "Corporate Responsibility" requested funding from the Irwin-Sweeny-Miller Foundation, its patron, to challenge corporate practices least considerate of public well-being. Among the initiatives, the staff sought ways to get corporations to appoint people representing the public, especially nonbusiness people and people of minorities, to their Boards of Trustees. The project staff identified General Motors as a principal target for this initiative. Officers of the Foundation opposed it, saying that since much of the funding had come as profits of the Cummins Engine Company and that since General Motors was its principal competitor, it would be seen as a competitive rather than a philanthropic effort. Many an evaluator would feel that this issue[1] should be examined as part of an evaluation of the Corporate Responsibility project.

This incident and the words of Fitz-Gibbon and Tymms remind us of more than a rhetorical discrepancy. What a client wants in the way of an evaluation that facilitates management of the program is not usually sufficient to serve the needs of others as to the quality of the program. It is a difference between what Jürgen Habermas (1984, 1987) identified as *system* and *lifeworld*. I read him to mean that system is the way that global markets, central governments, and media management work. Lifeworld is typically the way that students, families, scientists working alone, and artists work. Evaluator Stephen Kemmis (2002), in speaking of the lifeworld side and the system side of organization and community, suggested that the lifeworld aspect of social interactivity encompasses the processes by which people

- Relate to each other as persons, not just in terms of roles (as found in the systems view)
- Aim to achieve intersubjective understanding, mutual agreement, and consensus about what to do, not just meet specific objectives (as found in the systems view)

---

[1]The technical term *issue* was defined in Chapter 4.

- Secure a shared culture, social network, and sense of identity, not just their place as role incumbents in an organization with particular functions to discharge (as found in the systems view)

Most of us in professional evaluation define our work primarily in the systems view, orienting primarily to a client who heads an agency, institution, or organization and identifying an evaluand that is a formal activity of that agency, institution, or organization. In our formal writings and informal conversations, we speak of the staff and the beneficiaries and other stakeholders as groups, rather than as individual human beings. On many of our pages, we write for individuals to read, but the report is also an institutional document. Kemmis (2002) contends that system and the lifeworld require not only different words and formats but different value orientations and standards. Both are important, yet in tension, often so different that they cannot be brought into a single focus. Kemmis speaks of our views of them as *stereoscopic,* with an eye to lifeworld and an eye to system, not just from the lifeworld or system side alone. As evaluators give greater attention to clients, stakeholders, beneficiaries, and readers as persons, their approaches, designs, and writing often move toward the lifeworld and toward *participatory evaluation.*

Participatory Evaluation

Managers and field representatives, doctors and nurses, and other principal actors of the evaluand have important information for the evaluation, not just as data sources but as interpreters of merit and shortcoming. As suppliers, they are participants in the evaluation. With help, such stakeholders could also organize the evaluation and make the key decisions about issues and reporting. Then they would be more than collaborators; they together would be owners of it. The evaluation could properly be described as *participatory evaluation.*[2]

One of the most important choices of evaluation strategy is between independent, external evaluation and self-study. Both can be dedicated to the production of a report of program quality. Both can be a part of organizational development and institutional renewal. Independent, external evaluation, crafted by professional evaluators, lays claim to freedom from client and participant self-interests. It may be in the best interests of the participants to call for external evaluation, but if the study is done according to American Evaluation Association *Guiding Principles* (Shadish, Newman, Scheirer, & Wye, 1995), it will find balance among the interests of insiders and outsiders.

---

[2]It could be called action research or self-study, but usually participatory evaluation has an evaluation specialist and action research does not.

Participatory evaluation lays claim to maximizing the organizational benefits from carrying out an evaluation. Extra benefits may accrue because more of the right issues are identified, because the findings are more closely linked to remediation and organizational development, and because the participants become more adept in carrying out day-to-day monitoring and the resolution of newly emerging problems. Self-study is expected to be self-critical but also self-serving. It is not a search for the unvarnished truth (Nyberg, 1993). A single evaluation study cannot really be expected to be both objectively credible and "building the capacity" of the organization—a little of both sometimes, but not maximal for either.

Jean King and three University of Minnesota doctoral students agreed to assist a community social services agency with its contract-required evaluation. The agency had several sites dedicated to "help individuals and families . . . to strengthen their abilities, expand their opportunities, and change the conditions that limit their choices for the future." The agency director and a few colleagues were predisposed to do action research, but needed professional help. An Action Research Facilitation Committee was formed, then expanded to include all site managers. The evaluators and the committee created two documents, (1) an introductory handout for new employees introducing them to the process and (2) a notebook outlining how to conduct an evaluation and providing materials and directions for a self-conducted workshop. Evaluation at the sites continued to be carried out locally but increasingly in tune with the notebook. At end of the year, the committee held a staff workshop on ways of doing action research.

The participatory evaluation got off to a bad start because the action researchers did not have the support of the site managers. But because they too found the ongoing evaluation requirements overly demanding and of too little value, they joined the action research committee. Concerns about intrusion and extension of central authority were reduced and evaluation efforts were turned toward making things work better within the agency. (King, 1998)

That Minnesota evaluation was a self-study in that the program people were evaluating their own program. It was action research in that they chose issues that were likely to facilitate taking action to change their functioning (or to protect threatened functioning). It was participatory evaluation because staff members were called upon to do most of the work, but it did not include beneficiaries, funders, competitors for turf, and other possible stakeholders.

Participatory evaluation usually can obtain (and tolerate) the work of only a limited number of possible participants. These are technicalities. Participatory evaluation can be the best way of gaining understanding of strengths and weaknesses and moving on toward improvement. A facilitator trained in evaluation is almost a necessity to keep the focus on issues of program quality.

There are so many ways an evaluation can be made more "participatory." Remember that in Chapter 3 we identified seven factors for an evaluation study. Each of them could be based increasingly on the perceptions of stakeholders; each of them could be responsibilities of the stakeholders. In other words, participants could:

- Determine beneficiary needs
- Define program goals and problem areas
- Set evaluation criteria
- Set evaluation standards
- Determine the synthesis weights
- Gather data and interpret the quality of staff and participant performances
- Examine, evaluate, and redirect program costs

Usually, participants have limited time to work on the evaluation, but they may take part or all of the responsibility for managing the study. These roles and functions are usually decided at the time of contracting, but for various reasons, they may be changed along the way. And with those changes probably come changes in the authenticity and relevance of the study. The role of the evaluator changes too, following the concepts noted in Chapter 2. As stakeholders gain responsibility for the conduct of the study, the professional evaluator becomes more of a consultant and facilitator of organizational development (Bickman & Rog, 1998; also see http://www.nisod.org/).

The arguments in favor of participatory evaluation aim to make the evaluation less intrusive, more relevant, and more useful. Professional evaluators usually have greater technical skills, knowledge of strategy and tactics, and better reporting competence, but clients, the staff, and other stakeholders have insights into the program that the outside evaluator will never attain. Not only relevant but usable. A feeling of ownership of the evaluation is expected to draw attention to the findings and to increase the chances that future operations will be thus guided.

Stakeholding

Stakeholders are all the people who have a stake in the program, certainly the beneficiaries and injured parties, but also those who suffer lost opportunity because something else was not carried out. For any evaluand, it is a heterogeneous group, so no one policy or set of criteria serves stakeholders generally.

The *audience* of an evaluation study is made up of those who will pay attention to the evaluators' findings—also a heterogeneous group, usually a small group, including program managers and sponsors and other evaluators. Many members of the potential audience will be stakeholders in the program.

When being particularly responsive, evaluators pay high attention to both stakeholders and audiences. Responsive evaluation does not directly try to serve these groups and subgroups other than to help them become better acquainted with the quality of the program. As a side benefit, responsive evaluation helps the audiences become acquainted with the plight of various stakeholder groups.

In responsive and standards-based evaluation, as you know, an issue structure or some other conceptual design is devised by the evaluators, perhaps with some negotiation with stakeholders or audience members. However much the input from stakeholders, it is the evaluators' design, chosen to best inquire into the quality of the program. Meanings are negotiated; the design may be negotiated a little but is ultimately the choice of the evaluators. Responsive evaluation design changes as the study progresses. The work of designing and conducting the study may be congenial, the assistance of many people is needed, but it is not partnered. Harmony is attainable, but it would be misleading to equate responsive with participatory.

Any evaluation team of mine will give special attention to educational issues chosen mainly to dig into the deeper questions of social philosophy and valuing in schools and communities. These questions contribute to the understanding of the program so that what is being evaluated is better realized. We emphasize educational issues because education is what my teams know most about. We pay attention to the interests of sponsors, program administrators, the educational practitioners, the students, and community members, but the issues are not chosen mainly to further their interests. The focus is not on being useful to stakeholders but on helping them understand what is good and bad about the program. Remedy of problems will come into consideration, but it is not simultaneously pursued. Helping educators gather better data, keep better records, be more rational, be more ethical, these sometimes happen, but they are not the purpose of evaluation, as I practice it.

It is important to give special consideration to stakeholders who have little opportunity to voice their concerns, not because evaluation is much of an opportunity to right the wrongs of the political system, but because the quality of the program will not be adequately recognized if those concerns do not contribute to issue selection and data gathering. Much of my observation will be of teaching and administration because those are the responsibilities of educators, and failure to live up to responsibility is always a potential issue. It is not that educators regularly want such scrutiny—most feel they can monitor themselves—but we take pride in finding aspects of quality to which they have not been paying much attention.

Through detailed description of the program and interpretation of its quality, constructively and dialectally seen, I believe that stakeholder groups—some, not all—will be served. Their concerns are acknowledged, their problems told, but program improvement or restructuring power is not part of my evaluation contracts. There is nothing better that we can do than serve the people, and the special way for evaluators, as I see it, is the identification of program quality.

Utilization

Among the evaluators claiming that "participation promotes use" is Michael Patton (1997), whose meticulously developed ideas continue to gather under the banner of *utilization-focused evaluation*. As have many others,[3] Patton's criterion for good evaluation has been whether or not the findings are used. (Do you agree?)

Patton's strategy for program evaluation is shaped less by the idea of determining the quality of a prespecified evaluand, more by the idea of making what happens during and after the study enhance the functioning of the evaluand, particularly as to prespecified uses by prespecified users. He has the outside evaluator, if there is one, assume the role of facilitator. Inside persons closely related to the program assume the roles of investigator. It is a form of inquiry that he has made popular in schools, foundations, and businesses. Although most of us think we can specify an evaluand and its criteria, Patton recognizes the inexactitude and often unimportance of the evaluand as an entity. He draws our attention away from program quality toward program well-being, by treating particular users in an especially personal way. What are their decisions? What are their needs? There are such *facilitation* roles in many evaluation studies, but in this participatory approach, facilitation becomes the major role. The evaluator borrows from the counselor the skills of listening, respecting, noting options and resources, and supporting newfound action. In this sense, utilization-focused evaluation is oriented to the lifeworld side as well as the system side of community and organization. Standards-based and responsive evaluation stick with the idea of coming to know the merit and worth of the evaluand, for whatever uses people may have. Utilization-focused evaluation does not. Of course, different people will do it different ways in different contexts. The followers of Michael Patton are no less adaptive than the rest of us.

Several other forward-looking evaluation theorists, particularly Jennifer Greene (1996), Hannele Niemi and Stephen Kemmis (1999), and Jean King (1998) have pressed the field of evaluation toward participatory designs. Their writings will be essential reading for many of you becoming professional evaluators. As mentioned above, Kemmis and Niemi have drawn on the theories of Olafur Proppé (1980) and Jurgen Habermas to urge a conceptualization of

---

[3]Bhola (1988); Braskamp, Brown, and Newman (1978); Weiss (1995).

evaluation as communication. The utilization they have in mind has to do with groups and societies being able to share meanings and understand critical differences in policy and practice.

Not all evaluation writers concerned about the use made of evaluation studies have taken up advocacy of participatory evaluation. Tom Hastings, a student of Ralph Tyler and founder of CIRCE,[4] was one of the first to write that finding merit and shortcoming contributed too little to improvement and that, for effective use, the evaluation study should be designed to examine "the whys of the outcomes" (1966). A similar line is followed by those promoting *theory-based evaluation*, taking a social science orientation toward generalization seeking more than determination of merit in the particular evaluand. Utilization, then, is up to researchers and practitioners who work with other programs more than with those being evaluated. Lee Cronbach (1963), Carol Weiss (1977), Patricia Rogers (2000), and Harvey Chen (1990) have been among the advocates of investing more in studying how programs and policies work rather than whether or not they worked.[5]

A special kind of participatory evaluation is *institutional accreditation*. Its history has been the banding together of schools or colleges themselves to promote their own standards and to ward off evaluation by government. As part of the regulatory and accountability movements, government offices have increasingly developed their own accreditation requirements. In any case, it is predominantly standards-based evaluation.

Traditionally, accreditation was based on an institution's own goals and extended faculty self-study. Structured by guidelines (see National Study of School Evaluation at its website, www.nsse.org), the self-study report was subsequently confirmed by a site visit team of peers from sister institutions.[6] These visitors usually followed a more responsive approach, relying on professional experience and a spirit of camaraderie, but also a tradition of avoiding criticism of teaching and administration. Seldom was evaluation coaching provided for the site visitors. In recent years, increased attention was given to standardization of goals and to examining student performance. Critics often found this evaluation, as practiced, naïve and self-serving. Its potential for good participatory evaluation was undercut by defensive administrators, often saying "We must report what we are doing in a way that assures public respectability" rather than

---

[4]Center for Instructional Research and Curriculum Evaluation at the University of Illinois.

[5]What works? has been a slogan of the U.S. Department of Education under President Ronald Reagan and since. It intends to assure that properly evaluated programs will be adopted but silently dismisses the importance of contextuality. Programs work differently in different contexts, so it is an invitation to waste resources and frustrate people to import a program just because it showed significant benefits elsewhere.

[6]The labor-intensive costs of site visits for accreditation were made tolerable by institutions' sending their visiting team faculty members without charge.

"We have to be accredited, but let's use the opportunity to take a deep look at what we are doing." Accreditation became a matter of bolstering the façade more than reflecting on purpose and practice.

Another special kind of academic participatory evaluation is called *school-based evaluation*. It has faculty members, sometimes students and other stakeholders, pay balanced attention to pedagogy, curriculum, ambiance, opportunity to learn, and student achievement. Good information on this approach has been provided by David Nevo (2002).[7]

Democratic Evaluation

Taking the concern for beneficiaries and stakeholders a step further, we raise the question of how program evaluation is contributing to everyone, to the integrity of our society. The most relevant movement in the contemporary political world has been the accountability movement, an effort (primarily by conservative politicians including former president Jimmy Carter) to assure that public monies are spent according to plan. It is a goal that everyone can support, except when the plans are poor—and they often are, from inadequate statements of what needs to be cared for to authorization of inequitable distribution of resources. Some people use demands for accountability to support their opposition to paying fully for social services. To be sure, there are slippages in social programs and all the programs we evaluate, and the evaluator should be a watchdog for accountability. Personal accountability also is a matter of keeping one's promises.

Dedicating formal evaluation to the cause of democracy began in Britain and the United States in the 1960s. Ernest House (1993) characterized that decade as the "unravelling of consensus." In many parts of the world, the decade was a time of antiwar protest and rethinking civil rights, a time of advocacy for women, blacks, and homosexuals. It was a time of civil disobedience and resistance to the war in Vietnam. These challenges to the *status quo* invited a review of the principles and practices of democracy, a rethinking of the legitimacy of authority, and greater inclusiveness of minorities. As House observed, both theory and practice of evaluation were influenced by these forces. In the Western world, the "hippie movement" grew out of an antiestablishment mood. Some evaluations showed that educational and social service programs were not achieving their aims (Sarason, 1990; McLaughlin, 1975). Dissatisfaction with the traditional role of the evaluator as measurement expert emerged. House argued that qualitative research, particularly with its emphasis on gathering the views of participants

---

[7]Also see Simons (1987) and Alvik, Indrebo, and Monsen (1992).

and outsiders, gained popularity. One definition of democracy in evaluation means honoring the issues, experiences, and values of people, especially the poor and minorities and those remote from the centers of power.

In 1971, Barry MacDonald (1971) sought a different way to evaluate Lawrence Stenhouse's radical Humanities Curriculum Project (HCP):

> The HCP evaluation was determined by the fact that there were no specified objectives (for student learning) and there were no tests for the aims of the programme because they were of a kind that could not readily be subjected to testing. Case study [evaluation] was a response to the fact that clearly nobody had sufficient understanding of what was happening in schools and why it was happening that way and why it was difficult for schools to do new things.[8]

Stenhouse and MacDonald saw that they needed to examine the experience of individuals—students, teachers, and others. Ultimately, they related personal experience to democratic principles, but at first they just sought to understand individuals. Later, Robert Yin (1994) and others adapted case study for scrutinizing program activity.[9] Case study is the pursuit of the uniqueness of individual cases more than their commonality.[10] The studies can be done in many different ways, but using interpretative methods, one seeks representations of personal experience, the complexity of problems, and situational constraints. Case study became recognized as a method for democratic evaluation—not because it is structured on democratic principles, but because its attention to lived experience documents the dynamics of individual human action over time. That documentation includes portrayal of intention, interpretation of experiences, and discussion of implications for social well-being.

Case study, a medical tradition and a method of instruction in law and business, became a method of program evaluation. Traditional aspirations for evaluation were challenged at a small gathering of evaluators at Cambridge University in 1972. A "manifesto" was drawn up to legitimize a form of evaluation study based on case portrayal of human experience (Hamilton, Jenkins, King, MacDonald, & Parlett, 1977; Simons, 1987, pp. 57–58). This Cambridge manifesto was a precursor to democratic evaluation. It spoke of both a personal and public

---

[8]Personal communication between Barry MacDonald and Anne McKee, 2000. An extension of these views is found in McKee and Stake (2001).

[9]Helen Simons (1987, pp. 55–89) provided a brief history of the evolution of case methodology within evaluation. See also Ragin and Becker (1992), Mabry (1998), and my 1995 book, *The Art of Case Study Research.*

[10]Sameness, or commonality, as it is often called, is the basic building block of quantitative data analysis. What is unique to an individual usually shows up there as error variance. In case study, uniqueness of an individual that recurs consistently is not error variance but the basic building block of understanding.

service obligation. Traditional emphasis on outcome measurement was criticized for its failure to grasp the complexity of change in individual behavior resulting from programmatic action. The shortcoming was compounded by a neglect of stakeholder issues and limited accessibility to the reports. Greater focusing on processes, according to the manifesto, was the immediate purpose of evaluation. Illumination of programs and their contexts as seen by multiple audiences came into focus. The manifesto provided preconditions for informing deliberation about public interests.[11] Not surprisingly, these reformist views were rejected at the time by most evaluators, who found them impressionistic and unscientific.

In his paper "Evaluation and the Control of Education," MacDonald (1976) recognized differences in method in terms of an evaluator's "stance towards the prevailing distribution of educational power." He was thinking of the role of the evaluator in relation to who the evaluation is serving and how information is used. MacDonald (1977) identified three types of evaluation: bureaucratic, autocratic, and democratic. Put simply, bureaucratic evaluation casts the evaluator in the role of the client's "hired help," playing an instrumental role in maintaining and extending managerial power. Autocratic evaluation casts the evaluator in the role of "expert adviser," legitimizing public policy in return for the extension of academic territoriality. According to MacDonald (1999), democratic evaluation casts the evaluator in the role of "information broker," serving the public "right to know" (see also Simons, 1987).

In this early version of democratic evaluation, there is the assumption that power should be invested in "the people" and the evaluator should serve them. In bureaucratic and autocratic evaluation, the evaluator allies with those who hold office or seek academic authority over the issues. The democratic evaluator seeks to serve the public and others remote from power, not those in political, economic, and academic control. Democratic evaluation is usually allied with strategies for emancipation and decentralization. It requires independence for both the evaluation and the evaluator in serving the information and advocacy needs of the public.

Drawing upon his earlier thinking on justice in evaluation (House, 1980) and upon long conversations with MacDonald, Ernest House related the role of evaluation to societal perspectives, and particularly social class issues. Instead of starting with the program, he started with social conditions and the various constituencies and, through evaluation, tracked back to programs devised to relieve social distress and to facilitate emancipation. One of his

---

[11]Interestingly, and pertinent to current discussions of democratic evaluation, the Cambridge manifesto concealed divergent views about relationships among evaluators, the evaluated, and commissioners of evaluation. The "unraveled consensus" provided space to rethink principles and practice. It was not the time to construct a new concord. The evaluation community proved to be as pluralistic as the societies from which it is drawn.

central ideas was that "in practice, evaluation can be further democratized by extending evaluative choices to all groups and by extending public evaluation to all public choices" (House, 1980, p. 142).

Later, coauthoring with philosopher Kenneth Howe, House urged evaluators to assure deep deliberations of the interests of people outside the concentrations of power. House and Howe (1999) suggested three criteria to bring balance to evaluations in terms of values, stakeholders, and politics:

- Represent all relevant views, interests, values, and stakeholders.
- Dialogue with relevant groups so that views are properly and authentically represented.
- Create deliberation to assure arrival at proper findings and operational decisions.

Such criteria are complex and contextual, too little served by information alone, needing something to energize deliberation and informed argument. Thus, MacDonald's emphasis on "evaluator as information broker" was extended by House and Howe to "evaluator as facilitator of deliberation." The evaluator apparently was to be constrained (by all three) from participating in the deliberations among patrons, stakeholders, and the public. Still, is not detailed description with reference to value questions a participation in the deliberation? As of 2003, the lines between staying neutral, sharing, facilitating, negotiating, and deliberating continue to need clarification.

Although they supported inclusion, dialogue, and negotiation, MacDonald and House and Howe did not indicate that the evaluator should yield final say to nonevaluators on design, data gathering, or interpretation of findings to report. Like Thomas Schwandt (1997) and Jennifer Greene (1997), their advocacy was for moral sensitivity more than for shared or conjoined action. Pluralists Michael Patton (1997), Brad Cousins and Lorna Earl (1995), and David Fetterman (1994) went the extra step—described above as participatory evaluation—encouraging an assumption of the evaluative responsibility by program staff members and stakeholders, perhaps with the professional evaluator as consultant.

Experience assures us that theories and intentions are not easily converted into practice—rather like the innovations we investigate. This was recognized by House and Howe (1999), who added the following caveat to their advocacy of evaluation as a means of fostering deliberative democracy:

Evaluators conduct their work in concrete social circumstances, and we recognize that the deliberative democratic view is too idealized to be implemented straight-forwardly in the world as it exists. (p. 111)

Their work offers criteria and guidelines for a deliberative democratic approach to evaluation, rationalized within a philosophical framework and referenced to practice. They urge systematizing an approach rather than leaving fairness to chance or intuition. In their call for inclusion, dialogue, and deliberation, House and Howe offer a philosophical rationale for values, like facts, that legitimize action.

Negotiation of a Contract

A client and an evaluator discuss a contract to carry out an evaluation of a program. That discussion may have been preceded by an RFP (a formal Request for Proposals) and submission of proposals by evaluators bidding for the contract. Somehow, one bidder is found to be best qualified, or possibly to have submitted the low bid, and the discussion occurs. The scope of work in the RFP and the work proposed will not be identical, so the discussants work out the differences and the proposal is modified. Still, the actual work will be much more complicated than is covered by the details of the contract, so many differences may remain after the discussion.

The two parties need to get better acquainted. Even if the client has examined the vita of the evaluator and several previous evaluation reports, he or she needs to know more—something about other work coming up, personal interest in the program, availability of assistance, access to data-processing resources. The prospective evaluator needs to know more about why the evaluation was called for, whether other evaluations are also happening, what will be the reception of program people to data gathering, and how this client and others on-site have handled evaluation reports in the past.

The two parties need to state and restate what the evaluand is, probing to find areas about which there might be misunderstanding. They should perhaps look at previous evaluation studies, especially earlier ones on the same evaluand. Whose program is it? What is the setting? What is its history? They are beginning to put together a description of the program for the final report.

Even with an elaborate proposal, the evaluator should talk casually about working style. What participation is described, allowed, even required by staff members or recipients of services? And motivation. Why is this a desirable study for the evaluator? Who else would the client like to have helping with the work?

The proposal will say, but they need to talk further about, what is to be delivered. On what schedule? Are there only written reports, or will there be oral briefings? What reporting is expected with regard to authoritative judgments, recommendations, causal determinants, cost-benefit ratios, and points of view? What will be the dissemination and circulation of the reports? What audiences? Who will own the reports? Is anyone to be authorized to publish the findings in a research journal?

They need to discuss the roles of the evaluator (as described in Chapter 2). They need to consider how this role might change during the work and how they would come to agree to such changes. Is the evaluator expected to participate or to be barred from participating in program developments called for in the evaluation findings?

They need to consider, in addition to the questions raised in the proposal, what persons closely involved perceive to be major issues or problems. Are these the same problems faced by other organizations? Are program operations perceived to be related to major social, political, or economic movements?

They should talk about what can go wrong. What will they do if the program changes in a large way? What if a key member of the evaluation staff is lost? What are the mechanisms for conflict resolution?

Not all these things will be discussed. The client often is not interested in the operations of the evaluation. The evaluator will not seek knowledge about some things that might possibly go wrong because he or she does not want to raise apprehensions. But even if they wanted to, they cannot anticipate all matters of mutual interest. There are many ways the evaluation can go wrong. The more those possibilities are enumerated, the more the client or evaluator is tempted to set up barriers that keep things from going wrong. Many things have to remain unsaid. Meetings between client and evaluator during the study should lower the possibility that things that can go wrong will.

There is also the problem that clients and evaluators change. What was written down fails to mean the same thing to the next ones. And what was only spoken between them may be lost forever. There is safety in elaboration of what is being done by e-mail or project log, but such communications do not have the authority of a formal agreement. One story of what goes wrong appears in Figure 7.1. It happened in the National Youth Sports Program (NYSP) project evaluation by Stake, DeStefano, Harnisch, Sloane, and Davis (1997).

Shortly after the Kansas City meeting, we were notified by NYSP officials that at the end of the first year, our contract would not be renewed. We finished the work for Year I and submitted a supportive report, but included some criticism of authoritarianism in the organization. (The report is accessible to you on the Web.) We decided that the main problem was that we had negotiated the contract with the NCAA's research office, with almost no participation of the NYSP Office or Advisory Committee.[12] We should have gone down the chain of command more carefully. And of course they were right: We should have trained ourselves better.

Any contract is as much a business document as a guide to inquiry, even with the renegotiated proposal included within the contract. Many contracts are created by legal departments, and they are written first to protect the client,

---

[12]The National College Athletic Association (NCAA) created and sponsored NYSP.

We were meeting at an elegant Kansas City hotel. The three of us from CIRCE introduced ourselves individually to the Advisory Board members we didn't know. It was a cordial moment before we took our chairs away from the table and sat against the wall. It was our first opportunity to observe one of their Advisory Board meetings.

We had the agenda on our laps and were surprised when the Youth Programs Director opened the meeting with a request to the senior *internal* evaluation person to describe the progress of the *external* evaluation project, now five months old. We were unaware that our work would be discussed and we were unprepared to assist.

Let's call him Bill. Bill said, "The researchers from CIRCE visited 20 of our 170 campuses last summer, surveying the students, interviewing the coaches, counselors, administration, and campus officials. They had some serious data gathering problems." This was news to the three of us.

Bill was the liaison between the Advisory Board and the CIRCE team and had participated in access arrangements and some summer feedback. We had talked with him frequently but had not learned someone had spotted serious flaws in our work.

The National Director and Bill and the three of us were white. The Board and the 10–15-year-olds at the sports camps were predominantly African American. One Board member, Austin, asked Bill, "Were the problems a matter of insensitivity to Black children and their parents?" Bill said, "That seemed to be part of the problem."

Austin turned to us and said, "Did you ask our children racist questions? Did you invade their privacy?" I tried to think what he could be talking about. In a whisper, I asked Kathryn and Rita if they knew. "No." "No," I said. "Most of our questions were drawn from surveys of children used before in research projects. They were piloted at trial sites." I could have said, "We sent the surveys to project headquarters here for review."

Austin said, "But you asked them what their mothers thought, not their fathers. Why not? You asked children when they had last smoked a cigarette." "That's true. Part of your program is on drug and tobacco education. We needed to know something about the frequency of smoking of the youth. According to the Center for Alcohol and Drug Abuse, proper training depends on knowing it."

Max said, "I wasn't aware that this was information we wanted. Don't you find out what it is your employers want to know?" He went on to elaborate as to how things worked in the business world and drew supporting comments from other Board members.

I said, "As you know, we have a contract to evaluate this program. This first year we are concentrating on the children. Next year, the staffs on campus. And in Year III, the national organization. The contract was based on our proposal, which outlined the data we would gather but did not detail the instruments and observations we would use. You on the Board reviewed and approved that contract."

(Continued)

"You may have signed a contract," Max said, "but you apparently don't realize you work for us. Now if you are expecting to continue this research next year, you'll be asking what *we* want to know." The exchange went on partly relating to how contracts should be negotiated, then returned to our fieldwork.

Austin said, "Apparently one of your people insulted our students, claiming that they couldn't read. What kind of training do you give your people?" "I'm sorry. I don't know what your are talking about. Bill, do you know?" "Yes, it's true," he said.

The National Director said, "I'm afraid we've run out of time. We need to go out to my office. The photographer is waiting to take our annual picture."

We sat stunned while they filed out. I asked Rita, "Could this have something to do with Chicago?" She said, "I think there was some problem there. Harriet arrived with the wrong answer sheets, ones with names of the Notre Dame kids. Same questions, of course, but the wrong names. The Project Director (who seemed surprised we had come that day) said, 'Oh, we can just have the kids write their own names at the top.' And Harriet said, 'No, we need to be completely sure they are legible. Some kids don't write very clearly.' And the Director said, 'So you think our kids can't read! It's insulting for you to come in here and confront us this way.'"

Figure 7.1   Notes of a Disagreement Leading to a Contract Termination

to reduce risks of loss and lawsuit. If those people had their say, most studies would be reduced to simple tasks. Good clients and evaluators keep the level of complexity compatible with the program.

The contract needs also to be compatible with the ethical standards of professional evaluation organizations. Protecting program participants and data sources from exposure and other risks often requires strong rules of confidentiality. Discussion of this important contracting issue is postponed until Chapter 10. In Figure 7.2 is a selection of Evaluation Standards seen by the *Joint Standards* authors as most pertinent to the preparation of contracts. Read those 14 standards and identify the ones most important to you in a contract negotiation. It should be remembered that just meeting formal codes of ethics may not be enough. Each evaluation is a particular situation. Individual evaluators have to decide on additional protections for that situation.

Writing Reports

You have done all that work. Now it is time to write it up. If you have been tidying up the various pieces of work along the way, you have tables and quotations and

Standards for Evaluations of
Educational Programs, Projects, and Materials

STANDARDS MOST RELEVANT
FOR CONTRACTING EVALUATIONS

A1.   Audiences involved in or affected by the evaluation should be identified, so that their needs can be addressed.

A2.   The persons conducting the evaluation should be both trustworthy and competent to perform the evaluation, so that the findings achieve maximum credibility and acceptance.

A3.   Information collected should be of such scope and selected in such ways as to address pertinent questions about the object of the evaluation and be responsive to the needs and interests of specified audiences.

A6.   Evaluation findings should be disseminated to clients and other right-to-know audiences, so that they can assess and use the findings.

A7.   Release of reports should be timely, so that audiences can best use the reported information.

B2.   The evaluation procedures should be practical, so that disruption is kept to a minimum, and that needed information can be obtained.

C1.   Obligations of the formal parties to an evaluation (what is to be done, how, by whom, when) should be agreed to in writing, so that these parties are obligated to adhere to all conditions of the agreement or formally to renegotiate it.

C2.   Conflict of interest, frequently unavoidable, should be dealt with openly and honestly, so that it does not compromise the evaluation processes and results.

C3.   Oral and written evaluation reports should be open, direct, and honest in their disclosure of pertinent findings, including the limitations of the evaluation.

C4.   The formal parties to an evaluation should respect and assure the public's right to know, within the limits of other related principles and statutes, such as those dealing with public safety and the right to privacy.

C5.   Evaluations should be designed and conducted, so that the rights and welfare of the human subjects are respected and protected.

C8.   The evaluator's allocation and expenditure of resources should reflect sound accountability procedures and otherwise be prudent and ethically responsible.

D1.   The object of the evaluation (program, project, material) should be sufficiently examined, so that the form(s) of the object being considered in the evaluation can be clearly identified.

D3.   The purposes and procedures of the evaluation should be monitored and described in enough detail, so that they can be identified and assessed.

Figure 7.2   Standards Relevant to Contracting

SOURCE: The Joint Committee on Standards for Educational Evaluations (1981)

written interpretations to slip right in. But these nuggets are not the crown. You have a complex message to communicate. How good was the program? How well did it perform? Did it meet standards? You should not leave it to the reader to draw the conclusions about quality from a simple presentation of data. Readers will draw their own conclusions, and you should help them. But the report should be a collection of inferences about program quality, usually as seen from more than one point of view.

It cannot be presumed that the reader knows what it was that you evaluated. You have to describe the evaluand. Even the reader who created the program and considers it his or her possession needs to be told what you, the evaluator, saw to be the program. And what you saw may help all readers to see the program better. But that is not why you did the evaluation. You did it to determine and report the merit of the program.

The evaluation report usually is an official document, specified in a contract or assignment. Content and style are usually left to evaluators, but it is wise to show key audience members and collaborators a draft of the table of contents and key entries long in advance. A title should be chosen that identifies the evaluand, indicating that the study has been one of evaluation, and sometimes making reference to an outstanding constraint or issue. Quotes or allusions such as "Time Well Spent" or "Math and Aftermath" diminish the reference value of the title. The first author listed is usually the person carrying the primary responsibility for the evaluation (a person sometimes called the "principal investigator"), not necessarily the person doing the most work or the one writing the report. Author and major team member names should appear on the cover of the report; other evaluation participants and contributors should be acknowledged inside.

The purpose of the report is to indicate the findings of program quality, with ample description of the program and the evaluation method. (If you estimate final report page allocations early in the work period, it will assist the gathering of data and interpretation, helping you avoid gathering data that will not be used. You update your page estimates as the study progresses.) Some clients expect that the report will be used in promotion or fund-raising and oppose the inclusion of negative findings, but the integrity of the report depends on inclusion of all major findings.

Some clients, stakeholders, and evaluators prefer a very formal report, similar to a research report or legal document, sometimes with generic chapter titles such as Introduction, The Problem, Analysis, Findings, and Recommendations. A description of the evaluation work is common, with statements of methods. The methods used are needed for interpreting the data, but most readers will skip it. Costs incurred are often omitted, but possibly useful. Figure 7.3 shows an example of a report on costs for evaluating a Gifted Education Project, noting modifications in use of the budget and the assignment

Objective			Tasks and Results
Development of Evaluation Design			Analysis of techniques
Intended	.75 FTE	$18,000	Self-evaluation plan
Actual	.65 FTE	$13,000	DESDEG tryouts
(1970–71)	(.75 FTE)	($18,000)	Lakeview plan
Development of In-Service Training Materials			
Intended	.75 FTE	$12,000	
Actual	.00	0	
(1970–71)	(1.50 FTE)	($20,000)	
Development Selection of Instruments			Test and evaluation guide
Intended	.75 FTE	$10,000	OSOT observations
Actual	.75 FTE	$9,000	
(1970–71)	(.00 FTE)	(0)	
Research on Achievement Motivations			Experimental findings
Intended	.50 FTE	$4,000	Instrument surveys
Actual	.50 FTE	$5,000	Working Paper 5
(1970–71)	(.00 FTE)	(0)	Working Paper 6
Development of a Classroom Report Form			Forms
Intended	.00 FTE	0	Field test results
Actual	.25 FTE	$7,000	Manual
(1970–71)	(.00 FTE)	(0)	Teacher materials
Study of Educational Priorities			Working Paper 1
Intended	.00 FTE	0	Review of literature
Actual	.40 FTE	$5,000	AERA paper (7)
(1970–71)	(.75 FTE)	($8,000)	Items for survey
Organize Reference Library			Library collection
Intended	.50 FTE	$4,000	Files
Actual	.50 FTE	$4,000	Newsletter
(1970–71)	(.50 FTE)	($4,000)	
Liaison with Schools and State Office			Identification of needs
Intended	.50 FTE	$8,000	Staff-briefing notes
Actual	.70 FTE	$12,000	Working Paper 4
(1970–71)	(.25 FTE)	($5,000)	Categorical aid paper

(Continued)

Administration			Coordination
Intended	.25 FTE	$9,000	Evaluation
Actual	.25 FTE	$10,000	Final Report
(1970–71)	(.25 FTE)	($10,000)	

Figure 7.3   A Summary of the Allocation of Work and Funds for Production for Each of the Main Objectives of the CIRCE Gifted Experimental Project, 1970–71

NOTES: FTE = Full-time equivalent for academic year; faculty and graduate students not distinguished. All figures are estimates. (1970–71) = intended allocations for academic year 1970–71.

of data gathering to the nine components of the study. Detailed description of methods and data analysis should probably be placed in an appendix or addendum, possibly on a website. Except for theory-based evaluation, reviews of literature are minimalized, to the disappointment of a few readers. Demonstrating that the contract has been fulfilled can be shown by a table or format showing each evaluation objective or item of work (sometimes called a "deliverable") in this way:

Evaluation Question	Methods Used	Findings
1. Have the nursing home's services improved? 2.	a. expert observation b. patient interviews c. doctor complaint log	i. on 3 criteria, no change ii. staff objection to Plan B

Depersonalized and decontextualized findings are more common with standards-based emphases than responsive emphases. With reports including detailed observation reports and interviews, chapter titles may be more descriptive of the data gathered or of the issue pursued.

It is all for naught if only the evaluator learns how good the evaluand is. Spreading the word is an integral part of the evaluation responsibility. How widely it is spread should have been indicated in the contract, but dissemination seldom strictly follows aspiration. Promises as to confidentiality should be strictly followed. Whether or not the report should be declassified and more widely distributed requires the authorization of all who have been assured limited disclosure. Clients and other readers often will not consider themselves bound to the original expectations about circulation.

Styles of Reporting

Many evaluators like to use a distinctive style of reporting, reflecting their personal approach in evaluation or their attention to the client, stakeholders, and others. Because I like to emphasize attention to personal experience and stakeholder values, I like to use quotations and vignettes, sometimes even to open and close the report. I dislike including executive summaries and recommendations, but many of my clients have insisted on them. I feel that all too often executive summaries are simplistic, failing to deal with issues in depth, without important contextual data, and lacking the individualistic personal interaction apparent in reading the report as a whole. Often the summary encourages generalization where little is warranted.

The standards-based evaluation report usually concentrates on program performance. Several of the seven factors identified early in Chapter 3 are developed at length, sometimes all of them. The idea of comparing performance to standards, explicit or implicit, dominates the presentation and contributes to the credibility of the findings.

One of the ideas of responsive evaluation is to convey the sense of value through personal experience. The evaluator provides a vicarious experience by describing the evaluand and the data gathering vividly. Narratives and stories can be useful in portraying the character of the program. The reader gets an impression of what it was like to have been there, and draws some sense of merit and shortcoming from that vicarious experience. You may recall that I call conclusions that a person draws from personal experience *naturalistic generalization.* (More about this in Chapter 9.)

The reader recognizes links to other experiences of the past and bring those in to sensing the quality of the evaluand.

Suppose you are evaluating an international conference being held in Almuñecar, a resort town on Spain's Costa del Sol. You notice that the conference hotel, Melia Almuñecar, has been built with its big, main entrance on an alley and its "side entrance" on Paseo de San Cristobal, the grand street along the beach. You learn that hotels with addresses on the Paseo pay a much higher municipal tax than hotels on small streets. Do you mention this in your report?

Dramatization can be carried too far. The evaluator can be too much in love with himself or herself as storyteller or confidant. Writing can be

CLOSE TO HOME By John McPherson

"Look at that, everyone! Annette was able to walk right past the computer *even though she knows* there are 27 e-mails waiting for her!"

Reprinted with permission of Universal Press Syndicate.

intoxicating. The merit of the professional evaluator is not in entertainment but in the validity of the representation of strengths and weaknesses of the evaluand.

Representations of the Evaluand

Standards-based evaluation places high priority on accurate representation of program activities, staff, beneficiaries, standards, and outcomes. If a sample of participants or sites is used, care is taken to assure representation of others, often by random sampling. Responsive evaluation also values accurate description, but often selects samples or individual cases because they provide good data-gathering opportunities. For example, an unusual minister or social worker may illustrate, better than more typical ones, the depth of a certain problem. Next note the thinking about the sculpture by Giacometti shown in Figure 7.4.

Is it the complexity of the problem or the typicality of it that needs illustration? The same data do not tell both. You have to choose. How *representative* is the evidence? That is an important concern for the evaluator. The more the evaluation follows a responsive line, the more the feedback will be in forms and language attractive and comprehensible to the various stakeholder groups. Thus, even at the risk of patronizing, different reports and conversations will happen.[13] Portrayals and verbatim testimony will be appropriate for some, data banks and regression analyses for others. Obviously a budget will not allow everything, so these different communications need to be considered early in the work.

It is not uncommon for informal feedback to be given early and throughout the evaluation period, particularly as a part of refining the list of issues to be pursued. Some of the evaluator's interview questions ask for interpretations of what has just been learned elsewhere. The evaluator may ask "Is this issue relevant?" and, following progressive focusing, change the priorities of the interview or even the whole evaluation.

As analyzed by Ernest House (1980), responsive evaluation can be considered a transactional approach, depending on interactivity with stakeholders (p. 6). An essential feature is that of using issues, language, contexts, and standards of stakeholders to organize the report. The issues, language, contexts, and standards of standards-based evaluation are quite similar to those of social science research reports, even while the purpose is to understand the merit and shortcoming of the particular evaluand.

It is often difficult to tell from an evaluation report whether or not the study itself was "responsive." A final report seldom reveals how issues were negotiated and how audiences are being served.

Names and Labels

Many a sophisticated-looking report is actually quite weak as communication because it puts labels on things without explaining what the labels mean. Consider this fictitious paragraph from the evaluation report of a program of police training. Read it carefully.

---

[13]Barry MacDonald recognized that sending different reports to different groups would sometimes be unfair, often because the more empowering data are likely to be forthcoming in a report to the client. He advised one report for all and no oral debriefing (personal communication, 1973).

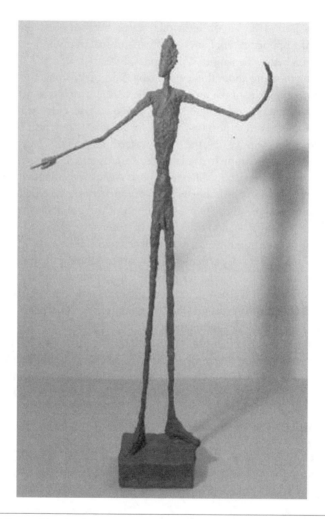

Figure 7.4   Giacometti. For centuries, some sculptors have tried to fashion, in bronze and marble, truthful representations of what human beings look like. Giacometti seems to care little for that project. His figures are all out of proportion—the heads too long, the bodies too spindly—and yet this great sculptor is just as interested in producing a truthful representation of a human being as Michelangelo. It is just that he has taken on board the central insight of modern art: that by distorting what we take to be the real appearance of something, we can often get closest to its true reality.

SOURCE: Tate Museum, London, 2000. Reprinted with permission.

Selection for admission to the training has continued to be controversial. In our interviews with precinct commanders, we identified the criteria used for selection mainly as inexperience, aptitude, deservedness, leadership potential, and power orientation. Teaming capacity at the precincts had not been assessed, and need achievement was a factor we felt greatly overlooked.

Even if the audience for the report is limited to experienced police trainers, the writer should not presume that terms like *power orientation* and *need achievement* will be understood. Such common words quickly bring images to the mind of the reader, but not necessarily the right images. Even if the readers are more familiar with the terms than the writer, the writer should explain the terms so that the readers are assured that the writer uses the same meaning they do. Here again is the problem of the stimulus error. People move ahead not realizing they are working with different definitions of terms. And there are other problems with naming things.

Naming things is always implicitly categorizing and therefore collecting them, attempting to own them, and because man is a highly acquisitive creature, brainwashed by most modern societies into believing that the act of acquisition is more enjoyable than the fact of having acquired, that getting beats having got, mere names and the objects they are tied to soon become stale. There is a constant need, or compulsion, to seek new objects and names. (John Fowles, 1979, p. 29)

There is always a problem with technical terms, especially if the researchers are making them up (examples: *evaluand, issue, achievement motivation, fudge factor, focus group, control group*). This applies not only to terms used as outcome criteria but also to those used to describe treatment, antecedents, contexts, or reference groups. Even if the label has come from a well-developed instrument or occurs frequently in the evaluation literature, some readers of the evaluation report, maybe most, will be unfamiliar with the prior meanings. When the reporting is casual, it is not a big problem for the technical meaning to differ from the vernacular. When the reporting aims at precision, then technical terms should be explained.

Programs, criteria, and standards, like babies, are usually named with care. One of the early program evaluators was Wells Hively III. Although he has done well, his mother named him to a generation, not to a destiny. It is risky to assume he was like Wells the first or Wells the second. Bernadine and I named our second son Benjamin because my father once said that there hadn't been a Benjamin Stake for a long time. Do we unconsciously expect the family to fulfill a destiny if we give our children family names? Do we expect a man named Frank to be frank?

Can one tell a book by its cover? Evaluators sometimes give names to their instruments. They may call something Evaluation Checklist or Participant

Index, but the resulting tallies may not indicate quality or participation. The items may have *face validity.* They may look like they should bring forth data on quality or participation, but sometimes they do not. Ratings of quality of a police training session may indicate more about mandatory attendance or the personality of the presenter than about anything else.

Fifty years ago, based on Karl Jung's theory of personality, Katherine Briggs and her daughter Isabel Myers created their now famous *Type Indicator* (www.personalitypathways.com). They were warmly received by Henry Chauncey, president of the Educational Testing Service (ETS), who believed that eligibility for college admission should not be rooted in verbal and numerical abilities alone (Lemann, 1999). One of the ETS staff researchers, John Hills, lost his job because he protested the lack of evidence of validity of the Type Indicator as a selection device. Whether or not its four dimensions are valid for counseling is still debated, but the instrument is widely used.

Data-gathering procedures should be critically reviewed and piloted or field-tested in advance. An evaluator should not use respondent time without confidence that the responses will be useful. It is too late to check reliability and validity after the data are collected. Part of the final meta-evaluation should be scrutiny of the selection of instrumentation. An evaluator's conclusions about program success may be of high or low validity. Such validity is not based on appearances, not assured by procedures or factors used in arriving at the conclusions. Meta-evaluation needs to look for evidence that the conclusions are actually wrong. The item below appears to be a part of an achievement test in American history or literature. What does it more likely measure?

> *Item A.* Who said, "I am fighting this war so that my son may plant grain and his son may paint pictures."
>
> 1. George Washington
> 2. John Adams
> 3. Dwight Eisenhower
> 4. Ronald Reagan

Few students would know the answer, but some would get it right. It is not something a modern president would say and it is not for which Washington was fighting. The only to get it right would be some patient reasoners (having test-taking skill) and the lucky. Knowledge of history and reasoning ability are both valued, but labeling the item a "history item" would be mislabeling. (More on student achievement testing in the Web appendix.)

Obviously, the amount of validation of data gathering should depend on the amount of use and importance of the data to the evaluation findings—their evidentiary value. Evaluation offices in large universities, consultancies, and government agencies should have empirical validation procedures they can boast about. The most important validity confirmation you may obtain

THE SPELLBINDING

Then by all means, the baker said,
Step in and help yourself. My bread?
Sea-salt and honey, flour and yeast,
Dab of shortening, cold distilled
Water, and seasonings to taste—
Not everyone's of course! He smiled
Politely, dusted floury hands,
Smooth crusts lay cooling in some pans;
Bulging from its bowl, a batch
Of dough puffed on the pilot light,
Working, alive. He let me watch
Him pummel all the yeast gas out,
Flapping and kneading, sprinkling flour—
Fingers, wrist, joy-dance of power,
Motion and form in beauty blent . . .
I bit, chewed twice: astonishment,
Shock, even rapture! Stout and proud
Then oven breathed a hot sweet cloud.
No change forever. Here I stay
Spell-bound in this bakery.
The baker, like his bread, is good:
He minds, but gives me what he can.
The staff of life! For gratitude
I strive to live by bread alone,
But every morsel touts his skill
And stupidly my weak eyes fill.
I can't break loose, or learn or quit—
Oh baker, what a fool I feel!
I've tried, it isn't possible.
I can't distinguish you from it.

Judith Moffett

may come simply by interrogating personally an advance sample of respondents about their instrument answers or procedural responses before the main data gathering.

Description is what Judith Moffett offered in her poem, above. Of the evaluand, we strive in our reports to give a full description, the measure of what has happened, a bit of cause and much of effect, the experience of the happening, the merit and worth. Still so much is not said, not known. And what is said is a mixture of standards-based performance and interpreted outcome. Some readers say, "Say it simply." And others say, "What's it mean?" We can't distinguish names from meaning, nor experience from value. We try to help the reader know what we know.

Cutting Edge

How sharp should be the evaluator's teeth? When asked about leg length, Abraham Lincoln said, "Long enough to reach the ground." Of course, it depends. In some situations the evaluator should bite hard, and in others just gnaw a little. Some say teeth are for smiling. Most of my friends say that we usually should be just a little more cutting (thought-provoking, vinegary) than the situation calls for.

I am talking about the standards of goodness and badness that we honor, but also about the questions we raise. We quickly recognize some of the vulnerable areas of the program—at least potentially vulnerable. Although the proposed evaluation contract calls for a routine set of observations, we should range further. When the evaluation sponsors want to concentrate on the vulnerable, we should range further, attending to conventional questions, attending to program strengths as well. In his novel *Where the Truth Lies* (2002), Ernest House has the protagonist evaluator, Reeder, musing,

> How positive and how negative should he be? The message was that the test score gains were non-existent. That message alone was too negative. He could balance that conclusion with an assessment of the evaluation plan the district had developed, which was not bad, and throw in a reference to Mrs. Douglas's class to provide hope that things might improve. (http://www.house.ed.asu.edu, Chapter 21, p. 1)

We should not suppose that the contract decides the degree to which weaknesses will be probed, nor should the evaluator's personality decide it. Both will influence it considerably. Yet, within limits, there remains a conscious decision on the part of the evaluator as to how tough to be.

Clearly we want to stay far from whitewashes and hatchet jobs. We want to see the bad with the good and the good with the bad. We are aware that to guarantee further employment, some evaluators will not bite the hands that feed them. And we are aware that many of our fellow evaluators admire us for our indignation. These motivations should not be prominent in what we do.

Clearly we need people of various personalities in the evaluation specialization, just as we need people with different experience and different disciplines. Internal tensions facilitate self-evaluation of the profession and stimulate creativity in method. But from the papers at our annual meetings, there appear to be persons who are so uncritical in their approach, and others so critical in their approach, that they serve the profession poorly. It is impractical, perhaps impossible, to prevent them from being program evaluators, but there should be review mechanisms by other evaluators that identify their work as having too little or too vicious a bite.

The evaluation process is less a knowledge-producing process than we would like it to be. That is what Mark Lipsey was saying in First Words at the beginning of this book. Of course, we should not abandon that intent. The evaluation process is more a social and political process than most evaluators would like it to be. I favor strong recognition of the social role of evaluation when deciding how much to probe and expose the frailty of the program, and even its iniquities, and how much to help develop rationalizations for its shortcomings. In a situation marked by complacency, self-satisfaction, and sweetness, the evaluator should, as Bernadine's uncles used to say, "raise a little hell." But in a situation marked by strife, confrontation, and bitterness, the evaluator should find words to help lower the tensions. The wisdom of the evaluator's findings will be little appreciated if couched in words that hurt too much, or hurt too little. Sometimes instructive, sometimes demanding, the evaluator should know how to bite gently.

Offering Recommendations

It is common practice for evaluators to include recommendations in their reports. For example:

- It is recommended that library users be given direct access to video storage files.

Sometimes the contract specifies provision of recommendations. Recommendations are expected to indicate action that should be taken, including "don't change anything." Recommendations sometimes are statements of advocacy, drawing little from the data gathered, such as this next one suggested by a librarian, following a practice of serving special interests, common in accreditation reports:

- It is recommended that professionally trained librarians be used in all library positions.

Or they can aim at decisions for quite specific action, such as:

- It is recommended that the library records be computerized using DESIRE Project criteria.

In such a case, the evaluator has an obligation to go beyond the determination of program merit to ascertain that the benefits of following the advice exceed the costs. Evaluation report recommendations are all too seldom empirically based, being little more than thoughtful speculation by the evaluator and resource people. Evaluators should carefully ensure that their recommendations are considerate of diverse stakeholders and possible forthcoming adverse conditions. Naturally, program clients appreciate recommendations that support management decisions already made or about to be made. Recommendations can be helpful in authenticating changes needed. They sometimes follow from data analysis, but often are expressions of need passed along in conversation between evaluators and stakeholders.

In this chapter, we have talked about recommendations and contracting and a number of technical matters. We have talked about utilization and democratic responsibilities and things that often are considered evaluation models. The idea that holds these several topics together is the idea of service to people. The evaluator serves clients, the program staff, recipients, stakeholders close by, the general public, fellow evaluators, and students studying evaluation like yourselves. The evaluator seeks and reports the quality of an evaluand, recognizing that the readers of his or her report, and the audiences beyond that, are a diverse, many-splendored lot. They have different perceptions of the program, different uses for it. Evaluators have little time to make a study of *their* potential beneficiaries. But a few hours, or at least a few minutes, should be taken to think about who they are and what they need.

Narrative

Phyllis goes to Mr. Sagredo's office to ask a question.

Phyllis: I sort of remember you telling me that the Board instructed you to change the mentor training program because there was some kind of problem. Is that correct?

Sagredo: Yes.

Phyllis: It is time for me to find out more about that problem.

Sagredo: Well, let's just say there was a problem. That's enough.

Phyllis: Are you saying that it is a personnel matter that I best not know about?

Sagredo: That's a good way to put it.

Phyllis: Perhaps I may ask if the mentors were asked their views on how to solve the problem.

Sagredo: I don't see that this is a matter for us to be talking about, Phyl.

Phyllis: Well, one of the matters for an evaluator is to see if a program instituted to clear up a problem has cleared up the problem.

Sagredo: I see your point, but all you need to find out is whether or not the quality of mentoring is better now than before the training.

Phyllis: Mr. Sagredo, I am not sure what "better" means unless I know what was "bad" about the way it was. I have talked some more with Mr. Ferdy, and he says they had a pretty good procedure for breaking in new mentors and evaluating their progress. So I think I need to find out why the new training was called for.

Sagredo: Well, we aren't going into that.

Phyllis: One of the reasons I'm asking is that I would like to advise you on the quality of arrangements for this evaluation. It is part of my idea of meta-evaluation. Increasingly, I am thinking that we could have set this up for the mentors to do a participatory evaluation.

Sagredo: What is that?

Phyllis: Sort of a self-study. With some help, the staff could have looked at the quality of the training Mrs. Vivani provides and would have seen—better than I—how it fits the mentoring here.

Sagredo: But I have more confidence in you. Your bio sheet says you studied evaluation at the university.

Phyllis: Well, I did, and I do know a few things, but I also know that the mentors consider me, shall we say, inexperienced. I think that a participatory evaluation might have contributed more than I can.

Sagredo: They already have more to do than they have time for.

Phyllis: I am sure you are right, but still I feel that I need to inquire further into the decision to contract for this training in the first place.

Sagredo: I told you it was a Board decision.

Phyllis: And Board decisions are not to be raised in an evaluation?

Sagredo: Well, not this one, anyway. That was just a simple management decision, not included in your assignment.

Phyllis: Well, that makes sense to me. I want to do a good job for you. But I am kind of stuck with some information that raises some doubts about the decision.

Sagredo: I think I know where you are going, Phyl. You have learned that Mrs. Vivani is related to one of the Board members.

Phyllis: Yes, that's true. May I ask if the Board instructed you to use Vivani Associates for the training?

Sagredo: Well, Phyl, we just are not going to talk about how this Senior Mentor Training got started. It is not relevant to the question of how good the training is.

Phyllis: Does it mean that if we find that the training is poor, the training will stop? I had anticipated that we would report on the evaluation in the Newsletter, thinking that that would be consistent with your efforts to make operational decision making more democratic here.

Sagredo: Well, Phyl, I hadn't given it much thought. I was curious, but supposed the training would be found okay and that we would use it to springboard other training opportunities around here. It is my decision as to the reporting, but I appreciate any advice you have about it. How should we report it?

Phyllis: Well, you know the four criteria of the study: trainee performance, trainee feedback, observation of training, and memo comparison. I thought we would have a section on each. I have some observations of the training that are pretty interesting, but probably will be criticized by the outside specialist I want to have review my analysis and interpretations.

Sagredo: You have a sense of what he or she will criticize?

Phyllis: Yes, he probably will say the mentoring work seems not to be adequately analyzed. Task analysis sort of thing. Too much treating mentoring as the same thing as leadership, maybe.

Sagredo: Could it be that he sees task analysis as the answer for everything?

Phyllis: I don't think so. I have a lot of respect for his background and experience. But I suppose everyone has an ax to grind.

Sagredo: What else about the report?

Phyllis: Well, I would like to portray an anonymous mentoring session that illustrates the complexity of the work.

Sagredo: It sounds like the report will be longer than our usual Newsletter.

Phyllis: Yes, I guess so.

Sagredo: And what about the summary of how good the training is?

Phyllis: Well, it won't be a simple good or bad, but it should be pretty clear to the reader whether or not the training should be continued.

Sagredo: How could a reader know that without knowing a lot more?

Phyllis: Well, that was why I was asking about the problem that needed fixing.

Sagredo: Hmm. I'll have to think about it. I appreciate your coming in, Phyl. You take care now.

(To be continued)

8

Issues Needing Interpretation

And so no force however great
Can stretch a cord however fine
Into a horizontal line
That shall be absolutely straight.

William Whewell, 1819

In this chapter, I will present three examples of the kind of perplexing issue that needs the evaluator's study and thoughtful interpretation for an evaluation report. Two additional issues (student testing and possible bias in committee work) are available for study on the website for this book. The deep thinking is needed whether the evaluation leans toward standards-based or responsive methods. As you read the three issues here, think about what kind of thinking they need. How would you get started on or continue your exploration of such an issue?

These are examples of content that an evaluator works to understand in the context of his or her evaluand. The three issues are:

- Program standardization
- Program fairness
- Staff development

These three issues may be interesting to you, or not, but that is not important here. Issue wrangling[1] is the important thing. In time, maybe already, you will develop your own set of issues—arguable topics you know a lot about, issues that pop up from time to time in program evaluation studies. These will

---

[1] Wrangling is what cowboys do, but their issues are cows that need rounding up.

be a prominent part of the substantive content of your professional career. People will see you at conventions and say, "That's Stephanie, she's the one who makes the distinction between special education and disabilities." A lot of other people make a similar distinc-

> **wrangle** *vt* to accomplish by intense, prolonged argument (here, usually with oneself)

tion, but you are one of the ones who keeps digging deeper into it.

In developing your issues, you will also improve your own version of investigative inquiry (Smith, 1992). Your version will be similar to others' but will have your own personal touches and dispositions.[2] And the point of this chapter is: These ways of wrangling will be useful in approaching a new issue that pops up in a new evaluation study. Partly consciously, partly unconsciously, you will figure out your way of doing it. The tactic here should cut down on the time you fret about it before getting started.

For getting acquainted with a new issue, you need a chart, maybe a blackboard. Here's a plan to consider. Step 1 is identifying the issue topic, such as "program standardization," then to think of a few synonyms or jargon words that mean more or less the same, such as "getting uniformity, lockstep, attaining compatibility, and dumbing down." These are keywords for coding, for entry into a storage system.

Step 2 is looking up the topic in some source books or search engines, such as Google, the *International Handbook of Educational Evaluation* (Bhola, 2003), and the *Evaluation Thesaurus* (Scriven, 1991), and the reports of previous evaluations of this or a similar evaluand. This is scanning activity more than reading. You are trying to get an idea of where the good stuff is at the right depth.

Step 3 is identifying some helpers—a colleague with a good mind willing to give you some time, the person in the evaluand closest to being its philosopher or historian, the reference librarian at the nearest big library, and members of your evaluation Advisory Committee if you have one. You are going to ask each of them what this topic means to them and how they would suggest you learn more about it. I am talking minutes, not days.

Step 4, for me, needs a large blackboard.[3] I write the topic in the upper corner and start adding spaces and items as they come to mind. It's brainstorming. It is a crude form of concept mapping.[4] Sometimes Rita or several others

---

[2]Blessed is the graduate student who gets the opportunity to watch an experienced researcher or team talk through the origin and development of a research question or project design. It usually is without step-by-step procedure, recipe, or mnemonic. Of course, they don't do it all in one session. There has been thinking earlier, and there will be revising after. It is an evolving knowledge.
[3]The advantage of a blackboard is that it is easy to erase and squeeze in on.
[4]For concept mapping, one might start with Robert Gowin (1970). For more technical concept mapping, one would go to William Trochim, http://trochim.human.cornell.edu/kb/intreval.htm.

What sources?	**Who cares?**	
What virtues?		**What methods?**
	What else?	
What problems?		**What stories?**

Figure 8.1   A Blackboard Layout for Developing an Issue

help. It sometimes works better if I work toward an outline, or start with an empty matrix or Venn diagram. These imply that some aspects of the topic are already in mind. Here is the chart I put on the board just now to sort out and draw forth some ideas about the topic "Standardization."

I started with the question *What sources?* trying to remember some really good authors or writings on the topic. Who are the experts? The question *Who cares?* was the place to note the stakeholders (generally or for this particular evaluand), the interest groups, the advocates and opponents. *What methods?* was the hardest to fill this time, hardest to make use of. I substituted *What variables?* but that didn't help. The others are obvious, I think. One recollection led to another. I went back and forth across the board.

So I chalked up the ideas that came to mind. I will show you the result when we get to the section on Standardization. What we are doing here is trying to get started thinking about matters we need to keep in mind, mostly as background, as we gather data, analyze and synthesize, and write the report. If we were to keep the graphic updated, we would probably see it change during the study, mostly getting larger, but dropping some things along the way. "Progressive focusing," Malcolm Parlett and David Hamilton (1977) called it.

Of course, there is the question of how did "standardization" become an issue in the first place. An issue usually has some policy implication, some social context, some tension. Many people find too much demand for uniformity or too little uniformity among practitioners troublesome. Standardization is a common issue. It could be identified in the rationale or problem statement of the contract. It could come from lots of places. The client, a staff member, or a stakeholder may speak of it, directly or indirectly. It may come from the research literature or from prior evaluation studies. Often it depends on the evaluator's recognizing that it is important, that more should be known about it, and that commentary on it is part of the contribution the evaluation study can make.

Good issues or research questions are critical to good evaluation studies. The National Science Foundation *User-Friendly Handbook for Project Evaluation* (2002) says, "Depending on the situation and the political context . . . a judicious mix of cross-cutting and audience-specific issues may need to be included" (p. 20). The evaluator often needs to upgrade the quality of the issue statements to assure comprehensive interpretation of the data.

Complexity

In standards-based evaluation and responsive evaluation alike, complex issues regularly appear. The evaluation of educational and social service programs occurs in widely different places and times, bringing forth issues such as equal opportunity, event sponsorship, endorsement, budget cuts, recruitment of staff, and use of performance indicators. These are among the hundreds of issues that evaluators study, briefly or at length, sometimes as background, sometimes as foreground. The likelihood that an issue will come up again next time—right or wrong—increases if the evaluator thoroughly studied it last time. It is partly a function of evaluator sensitivity. Evaluators with issue experience, with issue specializations of their own, have something extra to contribute.

Whether the evaluand is a fire drill or the training of firefighters in a forest preserve, it has its complexities. It is embedded in a social milieu. Any program has lots of ways to be made successful and lots of ways to go wrong. An evaluator needs to determine what happened and what did not happen. Considerations of quality extend to antecedents, transactions, and outcomes. The reputation of a professional evaluator is made partly by the depth of thinking given to complex problems. The organization of a good evaluation depends on the quality of its conceptual organizers. What are the important questions? In this chapter, we are examining some issues to illustrate the depth of thinking often needed in program evaluation.

On many of the issues, evaluators will not be entirely neutral. Each of us has our own views on issues such as what is good training, the ethics of equal opportunity for health care, and the importance of standardization of operating procedures. We should keep our personal standards from determining final judgments of quality, but we cannot design the study and interpret the data without some attention to heartfelt personal values. We should try to assure that points of view other than our own will be prominent in our reports, partly by doing a thorough job of meta-evaluation.

Each of the following three issues is part of a continuing program of research and critical study[5] in the academic community. Our evaluation studies usually cannot be expected to contribute much to that research. We will have

---

[5]Critical study is a social discipline (see Kinchloe & McLaren, 2000). Its scholars usually reflect a deeply developed ideological position—e.g., feminism, Marxism, libertarianism—against which to hold an object (an evaluand) up for analysis. The effort is to advance that ideological perspective as much as to recognize the value of the object.

no time or expertise for digging deeply into some issues. But we owe our readers the identification of such issues, with whatever data are pertinent and however we can use them to add to the understanding of the quality of the evaluand.

The additional issues are presented in the Web appendix, http://www.sagepub.com/stake/evaluation/webappendix. No external evaluator will be an expert in many of the issues of the evaluand. But he or she should expect to study and get assistance so that such complex topics can be effectively examined.

Program Standardization

Wanting to further develop some ideas about "standardization," I followed the steps identified at the outset of this chapter and used the outline shown in Figure 8.1. After some preliminary entries on the blackboard, I prepared the following summary of my thinking:

> Evaluators sometimes get involved with a program having a strong advocacy for standardization. Evaluators sometimes are distressed by the lack of standardization in a program and become advocates for greater standardization. Clearly there are good reasons for making practices and assessment more uniform across the organization, but standardization can be an issue to be studied in each situation. It is a mistake to take at the outset the position that greater standardization will improve every program.

In 2000, the European Union undertook to improve trade and governance of the participating countries by standardizing monetary currency. The EU authorities invented the Euro to replace the franc, the lira, the Deutschmark, and other currencies. What were the pros and cons? Business was facilitated, and travelers were convenienced; national sovereignty and pride were diminished. In another example, the National Association of Medical Colleges set a minimum credit level for graduation from U.S. medical schools. The intent was to help prevent schools from offering a degree with less integrity. Obviously, that standard provides little assurance that new doctors will be minimally qualified. More standardization might be in order, or it could be that uniformity is already a constraint not in the best interests of the public. Standards serve to protect the standing of those already established in the profession as well as to assure that the work of newcomers is of high quality.

Advocacy of standardization is sensible when conditions are similar from place to place and some nonstandard practices are hurtful. Opposition to standardization is sensible when it prevents people from fitting a simplistic solution to a problem. Often standardization is increased not because the quality of activity is enhanced, but because standardized activity is more easily monitored and controlled. Effective management is important, but greater control can constrain the productivity and creativity of the group. In the Web appendix, we will examine the use of standardized achievement test scores as a mechanism for school reform, a practice supported by the psychometric definition of program evaluation advocated in the early evaluation handbook edited by Benjamin Bloom, Thomas Hastings, and George Madaus (1971). Common standards can be good for beneficiaries, but the evaluator needs to examine the claims for standardization, avoiding being a blunt instrument in the hands of overcontrolling managers.

Under a strong standardization ethic, there may be problems with what we have called the *stimulus error*. Presuming that people are seeing one thing when they are actually seeing something else is a stimulus error. This is a general methodology problem because respondents to data-gathering instruments and procedures will sometimes interpret questions differently from what the evaluator intended. On the back cover of this book is a partially filled glass. If the evaluator expects the viewer to see it half filled but the viewer sees it half empty, it is a stimulus error. Whether that has anything to do with pessimism is a different matter—although I will admit I tend to see it as needing filling rather than as still providing. Back to the topic: When an organization is strongly committed to standardization, then there will be expectations that "everyone is on the same page," and departures from standard protocol will be treated more as infractions than clever adaptations. Standardization is a complex matter, often needing the evaluator's study.

After reflecting further, I modified the blackboard entries as shown in Figure 8.2.

My reflections on these aspects of standardization will lead to more reading, talking, and thinking about it. I will look more closely at how standardization is operating in the evaluand at hand. I will go back to my resource materials and helpers. Soon I will prepare a first draft, maybe just a few lines, that I will want to say about standardization in the final report. To and fro. I think the procedure here is pretty much a matter of common sense, but disciplined by meta-evaluation and other challenges.

Program Fairness

Please read this next section and copy off some words about program fairness that should be wrangled onto your blackboard.

An Army ROTC colonel is quoted as saying, "We don't necessarily discriminate. We simply exclude certain types of people." In social situations, most people consider discrimination to be bad. Emphasis is on the fact that equal opportunity is not available for those people. But in a measurements situation, we consider discrimination to be appropriate.[6] The emphasis is on giving special consideration to those with greater ability or experience or productivity. To measure comparatively is to discriminate between the less and the more.

Issue: Standardization

	What sources?		Who cares?
	Bureau of Standards		consumers
	Handbooks I-VI		nonconformists
	Intl Org for Standardization		managers, business officers

What virtues?		What methods?
control & efficiency		measurement
communication		comparison
lower costs		
ease of replacement		
fairness		

What else?

What problems?		What stories?
relevance		buying batteries
fairness		school biz offices 1920s
constrains creativity		the Euro
confusion with setting		Swedish chg to right lane
performance standards		Luddites

Figure 8.2   Ongoing Entries on a Blackboard for Developing an Issue

We live in a society in which it is usually not right to give special privileges to people because of their gender or social class or skin color. It is considered fair, however, to give extra privileges to those having academic ability or potential for capitalizing on their opportunities. Thus, more power is given to those already having ability and opportunity. We call such a society a *meritocracy*. It is claimed that investing more in talented people will lead to additional important accomplishments and lower risks for all of the society.

Less attention is given to the possibility that the many persons denied such opportunity will thereby be a greater burden on society. Feeling discriminated against, many people lose aspiration, care less for the general welfare, and slip into further dependency. There are costs as well as benefits to selective distribution of privilege.

MERITOCRACY

Where is the fairness in meritocracy? Meritocracy is seldom questioned by evaluators, but it is possible for a program to discriminate too much among its trainees, workers, managers, or students. When it is important to know the quality of their performance, then the agency should measure it as well as it can. Differentiated treatment becomes a problem when we cannot suitably

---

[6]Psychometricians speak of the discrimination power of test items, and statisticians have methods they call discriminant analysis. In this context, discrimination merely refers to differentiation.

measure the merit needed by the agency and when it cannot effectively justify differentiated opportunity based on levels of performance.

Sociologist Daniel Bell (1977)[7] identified three arguments against meritocracy, noting contradictions and overlap in them:

1. *Genetics and intelligence.* If one assumes that a meritocracy is purely a selection by intelligence, and that intelligence is based on inherited genetic differences, then one obtains privilege on the basis of a genetic lottery, and this is an arbitrary basis for social justice.

2. *Social class.* There can never be a pure meritocracy because, invariably, high-status parents will seek to pass on their positions either through the use of influence or simply by the cultural advantages their children would possess. Thus, after one generation, a meritocracy simply becomes an enclaved class.

3. *The role of chance.* There is considerable (upward) social mobility in the United States, but it is less related to schooling or ability or even to family background than to intangible and random factors such as luck and competence in the particular job one falls into.

In addition to these three, I have already mentioned the problem of the effects upon those not selected. These same problems occur beyond attention to intelligence and social class—for example, when graduation, promotion, or increments in pay are based on standardized performance—because measurement of quality and utility of performance is related to previous standing and opportunity. It is almost impossible to establish "a level playing field" and thereby claim fairness to all competing. Standardized tests are supposed to be fair tests of ability and achievement, but psychologist Claude Steele (2003) has demonstrated intimidation factors in these tests, especially for high-ability members of minority groups.

Lee Cronbach and Goldene Gleser (1965) made an important distinction between *selection* and *placement* decisions. When there are lots of applicants for a single position, such as in ordinary job employment or choosing the soloist for the choir performance or choosing the soldiers to lead the charge, it is a selection decision.

When everyone on the staff is participating in staff development and the decision is made as to what training each shall have next, it is a placement decision. A family makes placement decisions in assigning household chores. With placement decisions, the agency has a responsibility to see that support is distributed equitably, which does not necessarily mean that the most senior or

---

[7]Other good writings on meritocracy are Michael Young (1959), *The Rise of the Meritocracy;* David Gilborn and Deborah Youdell (2000), *Rationing Education: Policy, Practice, Reform and Equity;* Richard Teese (2000), *Academic Success and Social Power;* and Peter Sacks (1999), *Standardized Minds.*

top-rated get the best deals. The welfare of individuals, as well as the welfare of the group as a whole, needs to be taken into consideration.

Awarding or denying major opportunities to personnel is a "high-stakes" decision. It is not just a matter of being nice to high performers. It is sometimes a matter of being unfair and unwise. Rewarding repetitive good performance may reduce further striving by those rewarded as well as by those not rewarded. The effects of the policy need to be assessed. For every high-stakes discrimination among performances, there needs to be lots of experiential and psychometric validation—lots more than we usually have.

Measurement of competence and discrimination emerge as issues for program evaluators who study the policies and practices of organizations. Not all their policies can be studied, and the evaluation team often lacks the expertise to study the most troublesome policies; furthermore, the evaluation sponsor often does not want management policies studied. An example was raised in the previous chapter, the case of the National Youth Sports Program. You remember the aborted evaluation went like this:

In 1996, Lizanne DeStefano, Del Harnisch, Kathryn Sloane, Rita Davis, and I evaluated the National Youth Sports Program, a summer program mostly for urban youth. NYSP was a partnership between the National Collegiate Athletic Association, colleges and universities, and the federal government, offering underprivileged youngsters (ages 10–16) five weeks of sports, physical fitness, and educational instruction. That summer, in its twenty-seventh year, it served 66,000 boys and girls on 170 campuses. We contracted to provide in-depth evaluative description of a sample (4) of local programs, also describing the student body, relating program features to student outcomes, and examining policy issues. We found the local activities high in quality, effectively pursuing their aims. Both the issues of "standardization" and "fairness" came up, and we thought a while about them, then moved on to other issues. We found no substantial problems regarding discrimination. We anticipated intrusion by varsity coaches, found none. We did find authoritarian management and questioned its value. This evaluation was to have been a three-year study, but we were perceived as intrusive by some, especially for inquiring into administrative policies of the national coordinating committee. When we were told we were out of bounds, we said we were carrying out our contract. The NCAA did not extend it into the second and third years. (Full report available at: www.ed.uiuc.edu/CIRCE/NYSP/index.)

The evaluator has to decide, usually after consultation, whether an examination of distributions of opportunity may add to an understanding of the merit of the program.

EQUAL OPPORTUNITY FOR CHILDREN

It is part of a fairness ethic to offer each child equal educational opportunity (Segerholm, 2002). Measuring the size of opportunities is very difficult, and assuring equality for each child seems to be well beyond our capability. Yet it is within our power to strive to diminish the existing inequalities of opportunity.

Each child is different—different in the already-learned, different in readiness to learn, different in ability to use an opportunity to learn. Guaranteeing each child equal time, equally good learning space, and an equally capable teacher would be a big step forward—but misses the point that different children need to learn different things next.

The easiest way to assure equal opportunity is not acceptable: to give no opportunity, or the same minimal opportunity, to everyone. To do the best we as a people can for our children is to give them each differentially the greatest opportunity we can devise. But, paradoxically, that will increase the differences in opportunity and accomplishment.

The ordinary operations of good schooling tend to move faster those children already ahead and to move more slowly those who are furthest behind. Education is a discriminating process, increasing the kinds and sizes of difference among children, even when the teachers try hard to provide equal opportunities to learn or compensatory help to some.

An expected function of schools, as Joel Spring described in *The Sorting Machine* (1976), is to identify which of the children are becoming ready for more advanced coursework and employment. It is expected that teachers will identify and encourage those children doing their coursework well, who are usually those who have had the greatest previous opportunity to do well. Many teachers feel obligated to assure the slowest-learning students that they should expect only limited success in certain areas of intellectual development and application.[8]

Teachers deliberately do not treat everyone the same in the classroom. Of course, there are great differences in teachers too, but in some ways, they have

---

[8]Among some advocates of children, it is often said that a child should be helped *to rise to his potential*. It's a good slogan, but misleading. Children and all of us have potential for improvement, for excellence still to come. But no one has a knowable destiny or a potential in the sense of some level to which to finally rise. It is important to acknowledge that no matter how high one rises, as long as one lives, one has an enduring potential to rise further. As I write this, I have just turned 73. I resent it if anyone implies that I have reached "my potential." I may actually have been at my best years ago, but as Deborah Laughton, my editor, reminded me, I still have potential to do better. Potential is not some destiny, but a set of resources for better things still to come.

much in common. Most have an enduring commitment to doing what is best for each child—best, of course, as they see it. It is common to find in classrooms, in schools everywhere, teachers who have given lots of thought to what is best for different children. They seldom strive to give equal amounts of their time to each child; rather, they allocate time to those they see as needing it most, whether it is to guide their curricular progress or to redirect their attention to their work.

Children are different, and teachers should treat them differently, but sometimes they treat them more differently than they should. Sometimes teachers work so hard for conformity and traditional thinking that they interfere with the unique maturation of an individual child. Sometimes they concentrate on cultural differences that would better be ignored. Whether the purpose of Education is more to draw children toward a common definition of maturity or to help children build upon their individual strengths is one of the eternal questions for the philosophers and practitioners of Education.

Evaluators can inquire into grand aims with survey items such as the one in Figure 8.3. We used this long-winded item in our Case Studies in Science Education (Stake & Easley, 1979) to compare administrators, science teachers, and others as to their own grand purpose for education and to indicate how they saw the schools operating the same or differently.[9]

There is no doubt that the society cannot prosper if there is not a great deal of shared value and common perspective among its citizens. And it cannot prosper if it harnesses thinking and aspiration to that of earlier generations. Teachers seek a balance between what seems good for the child and what seems good for the rest of us.

Equal opportunity is part of a *fairness doctrine:* equal rights under the law, equal respect from those who bring order to our lives. A single curriculum and common criteria and standards of success are widely advocated as part of the fairness doctrine. Instructional goals should be the same. A grade of B should mean the same, no matter who gets it. Or so this fairness doctrine goes. Advocacy of state and district goals, standards, and mandated testing is regularly couched in terms of fairness.

Were there an ombudsman for children, he or she might urge differentiated goals, standards, and assessment. It is of some importance for children to know something of how their performance compares to that of others. It is of greater importance to know the progress of the child in his or her personal maturation. How well is the child attaining the education that will be uniquely his or her own? What is best for the child is seldom to be treated the same as

---

[9]Note that, for the sheet, each respondent would provide only six marks. How much test time per mark do you estimate that would be? What kind of evaluator might find that information worth it?

Each of the three paragraphs below has been said to be THE MAIN PURPOSE of our schools. Which do you think the schools *should* do? Please circle one letter (a, b, c, or d) below each paragraph.

The HUMAN Purpose of Education	The KNOWLEDGE Purpose of Education	The CAREER Purpose of Education
The main responsibility of the schools should be to experience what human society is—the history, human values, work and play, the arts and sciences, what men and women have accomplished, and what they have failed to accomplish. The schools should give students the opportunity to be a participant in the human experience, the aesthetic and emotional experience as well as the intellectual experience.	The main responsibility of the schools should be to help young men and women know all about the world. Each student should have maximum opportunity to study the basic facts and concepts of nature, technology, commerce, the languages, the fine arts, and practical arts. The schools should help young men and women build skills for explaining—and even discovering—new knowledge.	The main responsibility of the schools should be to prepare young people for their life-work. Though most careers require training on the job and continuing education throughout life, the schools should lay the foundation for successful work. For students who will take further training in technical school or professional college, the schools should emphasize entrance requirements and preparatory skills.
The statement directly above tells us—in my opinion— what should be	The statement directly above tells us—in my opinion—what should be	The statement directly above tells us—in my opinion— what should be
a. the *most* important task of the schools.	a. the *most* important task of the schools.	a. the *most* important task of the schools.
b. an important task, but not the most important task, of the schools.	b. an important task, but not the most important task, of the schools.	b. an important task, but not the most important task, of the schools.
c. a relatively unimportant task of the schools.	c. a relatively unimportant task of the schools.	c. a relatively unimportant task of the schools.
d. a task that the schools should *not* undertake.	d. a task that the schools should *not* undertake.	d. a task that the schools should *not* undertake.

The HUMAN purpose:	___ only a little	___ quite a bit	___ more than the other two	___ far more than the other two
The KNOWLEDGE purpose:	___ only a little	___ quite a bit	___ more than the other two	___ far more than the other two
The CAREER purpose:	___ only a little	___ quite a bit	___ more than the other two	___ far more than the other two

Figure 8.3   The Main Purpose of Education

234

others. A child needs to be treated in special ways, ways best for the individual and best for the community and society surrounding. That will mean basing instruction, grading, and guidance on where the child is intellectually, what the child is ready to learn, and which of the many next opportunities fit that child's personal, social, and community development. Should the program evaluator be attentive to such differentiation (Selden, 1999; Lemann, 1999; Steele, 2003)?

Staff Development

One issue that repeatedly comes up in the program evaluations I know about is the need for a continuing professional education ethic. Company documents and practices across the evaluand usually identify training as important, but often the expectation seems to be that workers will arrive well trained in basic skills, will get some orientation to the new position, then will self-pursue their curiosities about new techniques and problems, and—with occasional seminars and attendance at conventions—keep up-to-date. Leaving it up to the individual worker is not always in the best interests of the organization. Sometimes the pursuit of further qualification is a step toward taking a position elsewhere. A major responsibility for any organization is the recognition of how the field is changing. It is a management responsibility to assess the competence and inspiration of the staff collectively and individually. It is sometimes the responsibility of an evaluator to examine critically the vision and conduct of staff training.

The evaluators at CIRCE were invited by William Platt, a training development specialist at the Veterans Benefits Administration, to assist in the evaluation of the training of Rating Specialists. They are document reviewers, able persons who, under productivity pressures, examine veterans claims for benefits, particularly benefits due to service-related injury. Congress provides the basis for a complex guidebook of eligibility. The Rating Specialists examine medical and service records to find the proper intersection in benefits matrices and set check-writing operations into motion. They are also the people who are unable to find all the needed information and thus are in part responsible for delays in final resolution, delays for some veterans that run into several years. It is a complex and changing work, one for which various forms of training are needed and developed. Platt started us out on several years' work. The issue of training as a matter of ever-continuing professional education came up gradually and now is a part of every annual report we write for the evaluation of VBA training.

For example, in the executive summary of one report (Davis, Stake, Chandler, Heck, & Hoke, 2000, p. 5), we included these three paragraphs:

Although this called for more knowledge of operations than we have, as we saw it, the Veterans Benefits Administration needs to make a deep commitment to professional development. Both Regional Offices and the Central Office need changes in infrastructure to make in-service education part of the workday routine. Heretofore, training has been seen as adjustment to technical advances and as change in the organization to satisfy the requirements of strategic planning. We have observed a wide array of new training at the stations. Much of it was an effort to keep Rating Specialists current on changes in the law. This has updated the staffers' technical knowledge, as we showed in the Denver Training Log in Chapter 8, and that is commendable. But the expectation has not been raised in at least some Regional Offices that training also needs to be for the growth and development of each staff member toward becoming a more professional worker.

In 1997, we recommended a greater shift toward professional development and training as an organizational ethic. Evidently we paralleled some of the thinking already occurring within the Agency at that time. Shortly thereafter, a broad array of Training Modules was announced to address—in an all-encompassing manner—each primary activity of the Agency from veterans' claims to loan processing. The expectation that each station and employee would be drawn into carefully planned and expertly conducted Training Modules as a way to upgrade their work suggested pursuit of a sustainable training culture. The volume of training had been proposed, the need for standardization made clear, but the ideal ownership remained a bone of contention. We perceive that these Modules are seen by the staffers as imposed from the outside, something of an indoctrination, rather than fitted to what is needed locally. At least in part, "local ownership" of these Modules needs to be more intensely developed to promote a truer sense of professionalism in this VBA training activity.

Contemporary responsibilities for training at a Regional Office are large and increasing. The need for professionally developed, modularized training packages cannot be satisfied by even the best locally developed training. On the other hand, the need for mentoring and other locally developed training is growing as well. Training will continue to require a substantial sector of total workload time, clearly more than the current 2.5%, clearly more than an hour a week on average, for all full-time personnel. There is attitudinal endorsement of training throughout the Regional Offices but, from the Director to the lowest-ranking employee, training time is too easily given up to the press of productivity. Each Regional Office and the VBA as a whole need to become more of a "learning organization" and each Rating Specialist a career-long learner.

And in a subsequent report, we urged extending the concept of training to including maintenance and improvement of institutional climate, with a lengthy discussion of management responsibility. The section on a "fully integrated" training program included this paragraph.

So, whether calling it "training" or not, some redirection of performance is needed at the central and regional levels, as well as at the team and individual levels. A policy of institutional quality control needs mechanisms to assure that there will be collective response as well as individual response to needs and challenges. It calls for creating better conditions at the workplace, not just better employee skills. Fully integrated training is also a matter of nurturing and improving the institutional climate.

Staff development is so common an issue in program evaluation that a stock paragraph can almost be kept ready for inclusion in evaluation proposals.

THE CONTENT OF THE TRAINING

A training program evaluator has some responsibility to evaluate the substance of the training. Have the program people chosen the right things to be learned? Often the clients are satisfied that the syllabus has been prepared well and only want the training activity evaluated. And often the evaluator lacks the expertise and resources to make a careful examination of questions of training content. But it is a professional embarrassment if the evaluator finds the training effective only to have it shown by someone else that the program developer omitted critical content from the training. The content of training is the topics, subject matter, skills, and knowledge taught.

An AERA Presession for educational researchers was described in Chapter 5. The title was Design of Comparative Experiments. There were fourteen sessions, with subtopics including Principles of Design and Analysis, Experimental Design and ANOVA, Rules of Thumb for ANOVA, Analysis of Covariance, Failure to Meet Assumptions, and Multiple Comparisons. The participant critique is shown in Figure 5.2. The presession *content* was self-evaluated by the diversified staff without assistance of participants or an external research methods expert. Study that Chapter 5 evaluation again, and decide whether the issue of "continuing professional evaluation" needed to be studied by the evaluators.

Any training package developed has to satisfy various groups with different expectations and values; thus, some compromise in content is inevitable. The arguments die down, and some people would not like to see them revived by the evaluator. "Let sleeping dogs lie." Some pessimists fear the training will make things worse if the trainees question the content. Can the evaluator ignore the content questions entirely, or is at least some small mention of strength and weakness, or sides to the argument, necessary?

A common strategy of developers is to specify what should be learned in broad terms so that coverage and relevance are apparent but so that different scopes and intensities of coverage can be selected by managers or trainers. Not every task within an important category represents the category well. For example, a trainer can teach about the preferred treatment for HIV without examining risks of exposure. How should the evaluator treat the shortfall?

The particular knowledge or skills to be cultivated in a training program are a major question for many evaluators. Experts in training content and curricula such as Joseph Schwab (1965) and Basil Bernstein (2003) have written on the complexities of the syllabus. They have pointed out how the perception of what is taught by trainers is social, political, and economic. The content is seldom decided directly as to what ought to be known. It is determined by contexts as much as by needs and intentions that trainees be optimally knowledgeable. Sometimes trainers set their standards too high, aspiring to unrealistic improvement for the field, defining competence in terms of their own expertise.

There is widespread recognition that training could be and should be much better, whatever the disagreement as to how good it is. People often believe that a program organized in their community is not as faulty as one organized in a distant place. The stakeholders of a large program are hopeful that training to be offered in different places will be standardized and improved. Programs are increasingly examined by the media, regulatory bodies, and elected officials. It is not uncommon to hear that education is too important to be left to educators, and this refers to continuing professional education as well.

When training is to be redirected by outsiders, there often is pressure for simplification and standardization of the training. The primary advocates of simplification and standardization have been managers. If a manager is to be held responsible for the quality of the training, he or she prefers to understand it. For many of them, knowing what trainers and trainees are doing requires large labels. Goal statements and performance scores provide such labels.

Technologists, particularly those trained in psychology, have contributed greatly to defining instruction and to the standardization and "behaviorization" of it. Task analysis is a training specialization. Many psychologists are strong advocates of individualization of instruction, but most prefer a standardized operation. Most psychologists have been more concerned with the process of thinking than with the content of thinking. At least by inattention, they contribute to the notion that the content needs little evaluation. Nor has it mattered very much how much the trainees should be adapting the training to unique applications and circumstances. The evaluator sometimes needs to bring in a content specialist for help with the evaluation.

Driving course content unduly toward uniformity and simplicity can be the reaction of trainers when they are criticized. Some of them have promised that they can train any trainee. Seeking to survive in a sometimes hostile environment, many pace their own training specifications on the easy side. This translates into instructional contracts, formal or informal, that aim at explicit and simplistic accomplishment. This might serve the client and the trainees well, but sometimes it was done not because it had been found to be the best for them but because it was protecting the training program.

TRAINING STRATEGIES

Personnel throughout the organization may accept simplification of training partly because it fits with the way they see things: task analysis and memorization. Task analysis (Jonassen, Hannum, & Tessmer, 1999) is seen as the assurance of relevance, and direct instruction (Rosenshine, 1985) is seen to be the platform for deeper thinking later on. Such a theory has been authenticated by the "mastery learning" writings of Robert Gagné (1985). Many trainers argue that simple elements of competence need to be mastered before complex learning is undertaken. The theory helps keep complex content at the periphery even in advanced courses. That is likely to happen when the main task of a trainer is to get all the trainees to perform above the criterion on a standardized posttest.

As a primary training strategy, this elementalist theory has not been adequately confirmed in research or experience. It gets lots of opposition from educational philosophers. Some psychologists oppose it, instead promoting early use of problem solving, reflection, and critical thinking (Schön, 1989; Brown & Duguid, 2000). Yet to many administrators and mentors, memory training is "self-evident." Less apparent to them are the advantages of individualized growth through the processes of generalization, metaphoric thinking, and stochastic thinking. Such alternatives are fairly uncommon in evaluations of training programs. Evaluators may find support for either side in a large literature on adult learning and training (Knox, 2002).

The quality of the training strategy will depend greatly on instructional resources, trainee readiness, and trainer competence—that is, on local support. Where possible, the choice should include cooperative learning and inquiry methods such as those advocated by David and Roger Johnson (1998). One can imagine places where and times when individualization and abstraction are overdone. Warranted then is the call for standardized direct instruction

(Rosenshine, 1985). But in most places, weakness in instructional strategy calls for more individualization and synthesis of content.

ASSESSMENT

Most efforts to improve training are supported by a plan for assessing trainee performance. Trainers and mentors have always had informal means of assessing readiness to learn and achievement. But with the desire to tighten control on training, standardized testing has increased.

Performance testing can provide an assessment of trainee learning of skills carefully embedded in the tests. But as Walt Haney (1983) contended, the scores are seldom validated as indicators of accomplishment for the individual student, for the classroom, or for the training system. Unvalidated testing regularly fails to indicate how well trainers are doing their jobs and which ways they could do better. The tests appear to be much more than they are, particularly when the scores rank the more generally sophisticated trainees higher than the others. (What is wrong with that?) Increasing the requirements for assessment may lower the ability of managers to know that the quality of training is poor. Without validation of the testing, program evaluation becomes a source of misinformation.

Visits by evaluators and blue ribbon panels can spot many problems, and they are more likely than testing to recognize the quality of the content of training—but they have little ability to discern quality of training. There have been too few ways to observe and analyze ordinary instruction. Especially if visiting teams are to be sent to different sites to evaluate training, noting the content in particular, they should undergo carefully developed orientation sessions, even if they are highly qualified trainers and practitioners.

When problems of standardization and simplification are adequately recognized, it is reasonable to suppose that qualitative assessment techniques will be useful. These include review of the trainer's notes and cumulative files as well as more formally developed performance assessments (Berlak et al., 1992), profiles (Broadfoot, 1986), and portfolios (Mabry, 1999). School-based assessment, as portrayed by Helen Simons (1987) and David Nevo (2002), sets up site-based evaluation as a potential alternative to agency-wide assessment. The items of these methods are of limited value in comparing training from place to place but are of substantial value for improving understanding of what actually occurs in training. The evaluator uses them to peer into the complex problems of instruction. They add to the experience that training developers need for choosing one content emphasis over another.

The planning of training is incomplete without review of assessment options. Unrealistic promises for standardized testing have distorted many an

CLOSE TO HOME

**A diabolical new testing technique:
math essay questions.**

evaluation report, yet organizational pressures continue to inflate expectations. The evaluator will seldom have a budget to study deeply the quality of training but, with a thorough review of practices and trainee performances, can recognize at least the greatest merit and deepest shortcomings. The nice thing is, many trainers and trainees themselves are aware of the good and the weak, and will tell you. Of course, you have to triangulate it.

Originally I wrote still an additional fifteen pages to this chapter, but I decided it was too much. I presume you are disappointed, but the material is still available to you. It is in the Web appendix, http://www.sagepub.com/stake/evaluation/webappendix. The titles are "Issue 4. Standardized Student Achievement Testing" and "Issue 5. Possible Bias in Committee Work."

The purpose of this chapter has been to illustrate repetitive issues that need the program evaluator's interpretations (as they relate to the evaluand) and to suggest a blackboard technique for fleshing out the issue and starting to wrangle with it. Do you have a better way of getting started?

Somewhere in all this, one needs a sensitivity to evidence. While working on background for issues, one still needs to recognize connections to foreground—that is, the merit of the evaluand. What of the study of the issue may actually lead to evidence of merit or shortcoming?

Such conceptual backgrounding is to be found in most of the best reports. Phyllis should provide some good generalizations about mentoring. At first, you will not be expected to be an expert on such issues. When you write your next evaluation reports, it is unlikely you will be going into the depths of interpretation. But maybe in the third one, a little, and thereafter. I hope that you agree that it is important for the evaluator to be an interpreter of issues.

Narrative

Sagredo: Phyl, you have been talking to quite a few people around here. I would like you to tell me what you have learned about the management of this organization.

Phyllis: Sounds like a good idea. I'd like confirmation of a few things. Of course, I won't be telling who told me what.

Sagredo: I appreciate that some interviews need to be kept confidential. What did you learn about the work that Davis did?

Phyllis: You told me not to look into previous training problems, and I didn't push it, but several people wanted to tell me about it. Apparently, the contract with Davis was terminated last year not long after the mentor training began. He was a doctoral student in cultural anthropology who—unbeknown to anyone around here—was studying the culture of corporate management. He didn't mention it when interviewed for the job. He used his access to the mentors and others to study our organization climate.

Apparently, he was doing a good job with the trainees, who warmed up to him quickly. He was a good listener, treating everybody with respect, eliciting what each of them knew before launching them into training. As a good listener, he got an earful about the dynamics of leadership around here. He interpreted it as a culture of secrecy. He heard rumors that this part of the organization might be closed down, although you and others in middle management assured us that there were no known plans for change. Some continued to remain anxious about their jobs. Davis concluded that no one in this building was getting the facts from higher up.

Davis drafted a section of his dissertation describing the organization in terms of family systems theory, portraying the top people as autocratic parents in a dysfunctional family. One day you happened by Davis' desk to drop off something. Maybe you noticed your name on a printout. You read a bit and realized it could be damaging material. As I understand it, you made a copy and walked it over to the Director. It happened that the Board was meeting in executive session that week, and she brought to their attention the content of this potentially embarrassing document. They moved to dismiss Davis on grounds of contract violation. He was told that if he protested, his surreptitious spying would be studied by the legal office for possible litigation. He was told that if he kept quiet, we would keep it quiet too. He agreed not to tell others, including his adviser.

A Board member recommended that Vivani Associates continue the training, not disclosing that Mrs. Vivani was a personal friend. The mentor trainees were given some indefinite reason for the change. Two of them decided to do a little informal evaluation on their own and found that Vivani Associates was often called in to assist a corporation getting ready to merge with another. They also learned that Mrs. Vivani is a personal friend of a Board member, their families vacationing together, that sort of thing. They wondered if this was a conflict of interest, an ethical problem, then started to worry about their own job security and dropped it. So, tell me, Mr. Sagredo, do I have the story straight?

Sagredo: Well, I don't know all the story, not even all you have told me. I am not going to give you any details I do know, but I will say that what I know does not contradict what you have said. But this is what is important: As I said earlier, I do not see that this story is relevant to your report on quality of current Vivani training. Can I count on you, Phyl, in the report, to stick to the evaluation task as I have defined it?

Phyllis: I have given some thought to the responsibility of an evaluator to promote democracy by opening up problems for wider deliberation. And I hope my report will do that for our mentor training. As far as I can tell, this historical background does not deal with the need for mentor training. I see no connection between corporate merging or organizational shutdown and the current training, so at this time, I see no reason to refer to how Vivani got the job.

Sagredo: Thanks, Phyl. As you know, I am looking forward to seeing your first draft as soon as you put it together.

(To be continued)

9

Evidence-Based Evaluation

Facts are stubborn things; and what ever may be our wishes, our inclinations, or the dictates of our passions, they cannot alter the state of facts and evidence.

John Adams, 1770

Professional evaluation is a process of finding evidence of quality. Whatever methods are used, it is a search for evidence. That includes evidence of low quality. Assertions of quality are based partly on the failure to find searched-for evidence of flimsiness and dysfunction. We have to look for the good and the bad. Standards-based and responsive evaluation are both searches for evidence.

Increasingly, in the United States and Great Britain, some prominent education authorities have expressed a preference for evaluation studies said to be "evidence-based" or "science-based" (Pring & Thomas, in press). In 2002, the Council for Evidence-Based Policy set the groundwork for promoting evidence-based studies. In 2002, the National Research Council adopted the name "science-based research." It listed six principles to guide researchers toward aligning their studies with science:

- Pose significant questions that can be investigated empirically.
- Link research to relevant theory.
- Use methods that permit direct investigation of the question.
- Provide a coherent and explicit chain of reasoning.
- Replicate and generalize across studies.
- Disclose research to encourage professional scrutiny and critique.

These are important considerations for evaluation studies. Please consider each principle one at a time, noting how the principle might be slightly restated, based on the previous chapters of this book.

- Evaluations should be empirically developed around significant questions about program quality.
- Evaluation studies should be linked to three sets of theories: the formal theories of the social sciences, the systems of thinking of the humanities, and practice-based professional experience.
- Multiple methods should be used to permit direct investigation of the value questions.
- Evaluators should provide a coherent and explicit chain of their own reasoning, but include judgment data from participants whether or not their reasoning is coherent and explicit.
- Evaluators should triangulate key data, draw in other studies as relevant, and particularize or generalize as circumstances require.
- Evaluators should submit the process and findings to professional scrutiny and critique.

There are three points of difference in these two sets of principles. First is the emphasis on evaluation as a search for program quality. Second is the honoring of judgment data from participants. And third is the question of whether or not any particular evaluation should try to be scientific.

> **research** *n* 1. careful, systematic, patient study and investigation; 2. a body of evidence-based conclusions

Is Evaluation Science?

As noted in Chapter 2, *research* and *science* are common words in the languages of the world. Let us use the term *research* broadly, not limiting it to academic or scientific research. All formal evaluation studies, then—even ones that are short or misguided—are research studies. Most research studies are not evaluation studies—only the ones that have a major interest in finding the quality of an object, program, or process.

> **science** *n* systematized knowledge obtained from observation, study, and experimentation, carried on to determine the nature or principles of what is being studied

Scientific study is special because it seeks to gain deep understanding of a field, resulting in generalizations and creating new hypotheses and explanations. Some scientists choose to speak of cause and effect; others speak of functional relationships and generalizations (Glass, 1976; Cook, 1993). Evaluators speak of outcomes and impacts; even with the strongest designs, cause usually remains only inferred (Cronbach, 1982).

Science is not just a search for knowledge, but the systematic organization of that knowledge. Ideas need to fit together to explain the way the world works. No one piece of research determines anything. Researchers replicate and vary conditions to make generalizations credible. They aggregate and integrate, drawing not only from formal studies but from personal experience. Sometimes their evidence causes them to reject experience, tradition, and intuition, but their hypotheses about improving explanations often come from personal views. Science is not aimed at solving practical or technical problems, although it sometimes does. D. E. Stokes (1997) drew the distinction between Niels Bohr, a theoretical physicist with little concern about practicalities, and Thomas Edison, an inventor with little concern about theory. Somewhere between them is Louis Pasteur, a scientist committed to the control of disease.

We have the science of mathematics and the science of sociology, but we do not have the science of football or the science of Antonio Carlos Jobim. There is much to investigate about football and much complexity in the music of Tom Jobim. We have football theory, and we have hypotheses about "The Girl from Ipanema," but football and Jobim are not what we consider fields of scientific study. Language and logic and religion are fields of study too, but we consider them as disciplines, inattentive to the phenomena of nature that we associate with the sciences.

For evaluators, an important characteristic of science is that it is a search for generalizations, not particularities. It is little interested in the crash of a particular PC or the crash of a particular early retirement policy; it is interested in the lawfulness, the consistency, and the predictability of all kinds of forces crashing around. It is a search for what happens everywhere, without much interest in what happens in a particular spot at a particular time, unless those observations might contribute to a better theory.[1] Quite often, as I claimed in Chapter 8, the evaluator will need to draw upon science as background for interpreting the evidence about the value of a program. Only a few evaluators consider it foreground.

Evaluation is sometimes interested in the worth of a general policy or some generic treatment, such as teaching better letter writing in diverse settings, but it more often is interested in the worth of a particular program, possibly at many sites, possibly at various times, but still a particular program. When interested in generalizations, the generalizations tend to be petite rather than grand.

Petite and Grand Generalizations

When we summarize what we know, we also generalize, a little bit or a lot. We try to think how broadly and to what other instances these findings apply. If we

---

[1] Psychologist Silvan Tomkins asked us students, "If there were a car crash in the street, would I notify a physicist?"

put the ideas into words, they are *propositional generalizations*. If some particular knowledge is based largely on personal experience, in our minds it exists as *naturalistic generalizations* (Stake & Trumbull, 1982). But as soon as we put that knowledge into words, the statements become propositional generalizations. Naturalistic generalizations are conclusions based on experience and intuition, good and bad; I defined them in Chapter 6 in the Synthesis section. Propositional generalizations are based on reason and intuition, good and bad. We use both the propositional and the naturalistic in our thinking.

Nick Smith (1998) speaks of evaluators, when seeking explanation, as relying on *investigative reason*, trying to be driven by logic more than personal experience, but relying on intuition too. Audiences, including policy setters, managers, and other researchers, also rely on investigative reason, but often acknowledge their reliance as well on personal experience, direct and vicarious.

Standards-based evaluation, cautious about subjectivity, maximizes the role of investigative reason and minimizes the role of naturalistic generalization, for both evaluators and audiences. Responsive evaluation seeks to facilitate audience understanding with considerable reliance on naturalistic generalization powers. Narrative reports facilitate vicarious experience, without too much neglect of formal description and probative inference. The idea is that audiences are going to use the thinking powers habitual to them, so evaluators should help them.

Often some of our experiential knowledge doesn't fit with our propositional knowledge. In *Anna Karenin*, Leo Tolstoy (1876) wrote:

> Yes, what I know, I know not by my reason but because it has been given to me, revealed to me and I know it with my heart . . .
> Lying on his back, he was now gazing high up into the cloudless sky. "Do I not know that that is infinite space, and not a rounded vault? But however much I screw up my eyes and strain my sight I cannot see it except as round and circumscribed, and in spite of my knowing about infinite space I am incontestably right when I see a firm blue vault, far more right than when I strain my eyes to see beyond it." (pp. 834–835)

Part of the knowledge that evaluators deal with has been accessed using reason, and is then further processed with reason. Part of the knowledge that evaluators deal with is heartfelt, and that too is interpreted and included in the report of the quality of the evaluand.

Imagine that you are helping to fill a position. If you say, "This job application is good", you have made a descriptive statement, dealing with the particular. If you say, "These job applications are good", that is a petite generalization—a summary statement dealing only with the immediate situation, not all situations. Having certain jobs in mind, considering just these applicants, you have made a petite generalization. You compared the applications to some standard—perhaps the applications the last time applications were solicited, or perhaps just what you have come to expect applications to be. Most evaluators are interested in the particular—the particular operation of a particular program in its particular contexts. And into their reports they put both descriptive statements and petite generalizations. For example: Staff size dropped by half last year. Economic constraints are having an influence on program operations here.

Science includes the business of making grand generalizations— descriptions of what can be expected, across the population, throughout the territory. "Elementary teachers will pay more attention to boys than girls." "Immigrants will be confused by requirements for withholding taxes." These are two examples of grand generalization. The expectation is not that the generalization will hold over all teachers or all immigrants—just most of them. If the generalization is meant to hold in all cases, such as "Daylight hours are shorter in winter," then we are more likely to call it a law or a universal truth. Science seeks laws and grand generalizations, and is also interested in the exceptions, the limits of generalization. Scientists try deliberately to falsify their grand generalizations (it sometimes takes but a single negative case), thus testing the integrity of their piece of science.

The greater the territory of an administrator, the greater the interest in grand generalization. He or she is looking for a policy that works across the territory. It complicates things, sometimes is unfair, if different policies are established for different groups. When commissioning research to establish or support a policy, the administrator is likely to want studies that provide the widest generalization. What works? What always works? What works most of the time? What works at least half the time? Grand generalizations. Science-based generalizations.

The evaluations most likely to produce science-based generalizations are standards-based—particularly the randomized trial comparisons described in Chapter 3. Grover Whitehurst (2003), director of the (newly formed in 2003) federal Institute of Educational Sciences, called randomized trial comparisons the "gold standard" of evaluation designs because they were superior for establishing confidence in the merit of alternatives. He indicated that these designs would henceforth be more frequently funded and used for policy setting.[2] The 2003 U.S. Federal Education Bill used the words "scientifically based" education research more than 100 times. In 2003, program officers for many federally funded evaluation activities were pushing hard for randomized experimental designs.

Partly because randomized experiments are seen to be highly successful in the development of hybrid seeds and new pharmaceuticals, the intent of the National Research Council is to apply the same reasoning to the improvement

---

[2]Whitehurst acknowledged that experiments are not suitable for all evaluation questions and situations. He also expressed an interest in "what works" for individual children in unusual situations, a research interest of most responsive evaluators but few experimenters.

of education and social services. In the laboratory, there have been experiments on learning and motivation for almost a century. In the classroom, a few large and small experimental studies have been tried, without much success. Pleading for much greater use in policy evaluation, Thomas Cook (2002) lamented the failure of educational evaluators to respect the control of bias through randomization. After thoroughly examining a number of limitations and objections to randomized experiments, Cook concluded, "Random assignment is the best mechanism for justifying causal conclusions" (p. 195). He was talking about setting policy, not about determining present program merit.

Policy Evaluation

Advocacy for randomized experiments is based on the idea that policy should be backed by research showing the general benefit of widely used programmatic procedures.[3] It should be. Such study is a justifiable and needed role for educational research. Evaluation specialists should be helping with the questions of merit and worth. The full business of program evaluation should include *policy evaluation* and *evaluation research* that seek the "causal links" between institutional effort and accomplishment. Nonexperimental studies also contribute to good policy studies (Cook, 2002; House, in press).

Lee Cronbach (1982) strongly supported formal evaluation of large-scale government-funded programs but usually without randomized experiments. He took issue with experimentalists Donald Campbell and Julian Stanley (1963), seeing poor prospects of adequate match between policy and practice in the field. Like many scientists, he called the innovation a *treatment* and looked for ways of measuring its effects. His UTOS scheme let *O* stand for the effects, the outcomes.

In a variation of one of Cronbach's examples, the problem was violence in schools. The schools needed better procedures for handling disruptive student behavior. Experts recommended a kind of negotiation during a cooling-off period. The policy was to provide incentives and resources to schools that drew up and carried out their own project following program guidelines. The treatment (*T*)

(Continued)

---

[3]The debate over educational research aligning with science was summarized by Feuer, Towne, and Shavelson, and others, in the November 2002 issue of *Educational Researcher*.

would be the collection of activities authorized in the main policy statement. Any one school's project would focus on a particular treatment (t) that would include some activities not included in T. As a result of the evaluation, the policymakers would revise the policy to authorize a revised collection of activities (T*).

Cronbach (1982, p. 79) argued that a randomized experimental approach would not provide as good a research basis for policymakers as standards-based correlational studies that kept thorough records of the actual treatments (t) and various outcomes (o) for each participating unit (u). Any change in school violence would be better understood from the correlational analysis, he said. An experiment would work toward one big comparison on criterion O, with the treatment group compared to the nontreatment group. According to Cronbach, the experiment would provide too little needed information about the interaction of various treatment components with various situational features of the participating units. He saw it as too likely that the grand composite of activities to restrain violent students in the participating schools would poorly represent the treatment (T) as indicated in the policy statements and as needed in future policy statements (T*).

Science requires more than correlation between effort and accomplishment. It requires being able to link particular efforts with particular accomplishments. When accomplishment increases, science-based evaluation is expected to attribute the accomplishment to a particular cause. Attribution is hard to do. Experiments only account for some of the many causes of accomplishment. Good policy needs to be backed by a broad range of studies (Campbell, 1982). Certainly that includes responsive evaluation.

In recent times, there has been little government funding for large evaluation research studies in education and social service. But also, there has been little advocacy by evaluation specialists for experimental designs. Program evaluators have been giving greater priority to the search for under-

attribution *n* determination of the cause or causes that are most responsible for the effect

standing of what is happening in *particular* rather than *general* circumstances. Some have interests in causality, but few a primary interest. Contract funding had been more available to study an evaluand in its particular situation.

A potential client such as Mr. Sagredo may say, "We want an evaluation to show how good this program is." If the evaluator replies, "Do you mainly want to find out if your approach generally works well?" the client says, "Don't spend our money to find out if the approach works elsewhere." And further, if the evaluator asks, "Would we limit the measurement of effects to a single criterion?" the client may say, "One is enough if you get it right." Most evaluators think that getting it right requires attention to multiple measures.

For clients wanting evaluation of a single program, should randomized experiments be recommended? The funding is limited. A lot of it could be spent on organizing a good control group and carefully developing a criterion indicator, thus leading possibly to a strong assertion of cause and effect. Or it could be spent on coming to understand the activities, perceptions, and measurements of the program, then reporting little about cause but lots about function and quality. Or spend a little on both. What will give the clients the most for their money? What will serve the other stakeholders well? How can the evaluator best use his or her skills? The answers depend on the circumstances.

For an evaluand small enough for personal acquaintance, many evaluators will be interested in the substantive questions—questions of use of staff time, outcomes, constraints, leadership, and the like. They see the program as complex and nuanced. They want to get personally acquainted with the operations. If they have less interest in the science of these operations and more interest in experience in real circumstances, they are likely to lean toward responsive evaluation activities and petite generalizations.[4]

If the evaluand is something that can be represented in operational terms and indicator variables, such as time on task, performance ratings, need achievement, and community integration, evaluators may lean most heavily on standards-based evaluation. Many of them speak of the program as a set of functional relationships. They invest in good measurements. If they have considerable interest in these relationships as a science, they are likely to be considering the possibility of a controlled experiment, possibly even randomized selection of beneficiaries as participants and randomized assignment to treatments (Lipsey, 1993). Some of them warm to the idea of generating grand generalizations.

Some of us evaluators should work closely with social science, working toward improving the understanding of human affairs, drawing our research questions from formal theory, adding new data and interpretations. In First

---

[4]Even with small studies, evaluators and readers sometimes modify the grand generalizations they have relied on. When the new case strongly supports an existing generalization, many of us will reinforce the generalization, and vice versa for a case that goes against the generalization. Our generalizing is based not just on an immediate case but on other cases we have known, and on existing generalizations (House, 1991).

Words, the preface to this book, Mark Lipsey made a well-reasoned plea for evaluators to help cultivate the theories most useful for policy evaluation. And some of us evaluators should work closely with the practitioners of education and social service, working to understand and assist that practice, drawing from their experience and expertise, providing vicarious experience and interpretation. Also in First Words, Tom Schwandt answered Lipsey's plea with his own: that formal evaluation be more tied to the realities of practice than to the rationalities created by science.

If you haven't read that debate, this might be a good time to do it. The gap between them seems like night and day, but that shows the complexity of the world of program evaluation.

Both ways of thinking are important, and not as tied together as most scientists and policymakers think. I think we need evaluators of both persuasions—and the realization that in each of us, both realities exist, both formal and experiential knowledge. In our evaluation work, we should draw from both, knowing that there will be gaps and contradictions. We should help our readers understand the gaps and contradictions as well as the evidence of quality.

Director Whitehurst (2003) expressed the hope that an experimentalist cadre of evaluators would mobilize. In pressing for reductions in bias, his stand was similar to that of Michael Scriven (1976), both noting the greater control of bias expected in randomized experiments. Whitehurst went so far as to categorize educational studies as either "experiments" or "advocacies," failing to acknowledge that scientists are advocates too.

Bias

Just as there is evidence in all evaluations, even the bad ones, there is advocacy in all evaluations, even the good ones. Advocacy is bias. Bias weakens evidence. Distinguished philosopher of science Thomas Kuhn (1970) said that the observations of all researchers are "theory-laden," that personal and cultural values color their expectations and render them unable to be neutral interpreters of truth claims. But bias in evaluation is not always bad. In one of my papers (2003), I identified six forms of advocacy that most evaluators practice and defend:

- Advocacy for the particular evaluand, with hope that it will succeed
- Advocacy for evaluation, with hope that more of it will occur in the future
- Advocacy for rationality, with hope that management of the evaluand improves
- Advocacy for utility, with hope that our findings will be used
- Advocacy for ethical standards, with hope that fair conditions prevail
- Advocacy for democracy and support for those seldom heard

Calling them "dispositions," I spoke of additional advocacies of evaluators in Chapter 2.

Evaluators use some working time to promote these advocacies and seldom feel that without them their work would be better. They have various value commitments that can influence their perceptions and interpretations. These could cause them to make poor interpretations of the quality of the evaluand. But I believe the commitments also push evaluators to dig deeper into important issues. This is not to say that advocacies are no problem, just that we cannot keep them entirely in check, and that we should reflect on them, get help digging them up, make them more transparent to readers, and find ways of including advocacies counter to ours in our data and reporting.

The point—made beautifully by Michael Scriven (1998)—is that it is easier to control bias than to remove it. Here is what he said:

> The oft-given [example] of bias in the statistics and methods text is the thermometer that regularly reads too hot. A scientist . . . would never use that as an example of bias. He or she would simply say the instrument is inaccurate or reads high. Bias is not a systematic error. Its core meaning in common parlance is a culpable human disposition to systematic cognitive error. [For] analogy, [take] the ball used in lawn bowling. It is weighted—the term commonly used is in fact "biased"—so that it will roll in a curved path, deviating from the straight path that would be there without the bias.
>
> What is actually called the bias in the lawn bowling ball is in fact the lead weight in the ball that gives it the disposition to roll in a curved path. This case might be called the purely descriptive sense of bias. It's just a fact that the ball is biased. It's not an evaluative term because the error is only metaphorical, the factual deviation from a straight path (when launched in the conventional way). But it is clear that the property of bias in this case is a dispositional property.
>
> . . . The bias is not the deviation from the original path, but the propensity to so deviate. This distinction between bias as systematic error . . . is not a mere terminological point. It . . . makes possible remedial procedures. . . . The distinction between bias and the systematic error it tends to produce is critical in evaluation because it creates the possibility of controlling bias without having to remove it. And, with most biases, it's easier to control than remove. If bias were the actual bad result, it would often be impossible to remove. (p. 14)

For evaluators, bias is a propensity to treat what we ourselves, or our group, or our culture, value *too* favorably—more favorably or less favorably—than we should. It is favoritism not only in our interpretations of data but in the ways we design the study, in the questions we raise, in the data sources we select, and in the ways we write the report. Our conscience and ethics plead with us to be unbiased. We can reduce some of our strongest lead-weight leanings, but bias will remain—especially if observations, interpretations, and reporting are done by a single person or closely knit team. We need a diversity of views. We need a vigorous meta-evaluation mechanism, and we need a pride in presenting unconventional and unattractive (to us) points of view. These are some of the needed correctives to bias.

Skepticism as a Commitment

I have heard Barry MacDonald say that no evaluator should take a job where he or she does not support the goals of the program. Although it could be argued that even programs with questionable goals are entitled to a fair evaluation (as with a court-appointed attorney), it is not a good situation where the evaluator is not supportive of the aims. This does not mean that the evaluator should be favorably disposed toward program activities and outcomes—just, at the outset, its aims.

And yet, it is important for all evaluators to be well stocked with skepticism. In Chapter 6, I spoke about continuous self-challenge. Let's speak here of the virtues of skepticism. It is not necessary for you to broadcast skepticism of everything you encounter, but every evaluator should have doubts about everything about the evaluand as well as everything about his or her evaluation practice. In real life, it is debilitating to question everything, so we have to be selective. While the cadre of evaluators needs personalities of all kinds, the work of evaluation depends on a personality that worries about everything. It depends on a set of mechanisms that automatically raise doubts about such things as the meanings of goals, the dedication of staffs, the honesty of testimony, and the validity of inferences. Of course, you need to worry—not too much and not too little—about the integrity of your own work.

So much to manage! How can you know how much to worry? You cannot. You ask others for advice. You examine your work. You reflect. And you don't let it immobilize you. You write down key points of your operating plan but you let intuition have its sway.

Part of your skepticism ethic needs to be prominent in your meta-evaluation planning. You follow Don Schön's advice (1987) about being a *reflective practitioner*. You work with others, critical friends, who cast a critical eye on plans, choices of instruments and quotes, and the strategy of your reporting. You do "member checks," asking data sources to review your drafts of what you say they said or did. You triangulate. You bring in a meta-evaluation person as you approach the end of your analysis and begin the early drafting. All the while you are working, one part of your brain is thinking, "Is this really the way to find the quality here?"

Meta-evaluation works in two ways at the same time. By bringing in alternative voices, multiple points of view, redundant observations, it helps you converge on defensible interpretations. But it also keeps introducing new diversities, alternative interpretations, additional aspects of context that need to be acknowledged. You find, perhaps, that the married trainees see it differently. Or the Cuban Hispanics don't agree with the Mexican. The portrayals and conclusions "complexify," seldom leaving the reader with a simple understanding of merit and shortcoming.

Your gut tells you that consensus is better than diversity, that the readers of your report want straight answers, not complications. You may need to discipline your gut to appreciate here the value of diversity. As I said early in Chapter 6, it is an invalidity to portray the world as simpler than it is, but it is also an invalidity to portray it as more complex than it is.

> **dialectic** *n* a method of logic used by Hegel and Marx to analyze social and economic processes, in part using the principle that the interpretation of an idea or event may be enhanced by counterposing an opposite interpretation

Your work cannot be good if you fail to show the different interpretations of quality you encounter, adding whatever resolution you can. You may present the alternative views as a dialectic, engaging the reader in the resolution. Not only is the dialectic a representation of reality, it is a part of the ethic of skepticism. You create alternative interpretations partly to keep your mind open to still newer possibilities (Proppé, 1983).

Narrative

Sagredo: I appreciate receiving this rough draft of your executive summary, Phyl. I have some suggestions to make.

Phyllis: I am guessing that you would like a stronger statement about the success of the Senior Mentor Training.

Sagredo: That would be helpful. I think you have made a good case that success is not consistent across all criteria. And that there are some weaknesses. But you haven't really indicated that, all in all, the training is a good investment.

Phyllis: I don't know that it is. As I have said, I worry that informal mentoring around this place changed with the onset of formal training. Yes, the merit of the training is showing up in several ways. More than half the trainees are supportive.

Sagredo: This is what your survey told you.

Phyllis: There is more, as you know—a mixture of hard data and soft. We used the four main criteria: trainer engagement with trainees, satisfaction of trainees, trainee performance, and mentee views of trainee improvement. For trainee satisfaction, we used the survey. For mentee judgments, we used interviews. For trainee performance outcomes, we examined the test from Orlando, but decided it didn't fit our situation. We compared memos to mentees, pre and post, but the number of memos was too small. We took a hard look at the trainee writing assignments from Mrs. Vivani's materials. We had the trainees critique a videotaped mentoring session, and Sid and I scored them according to the Vivani approach. And Sid had given trainees ratings as to understanding and technique. That gave us some reasonably good performance measurements. And we have asked the mentees of these trainees to gather for a group interview in three months.

I observed three of Sid's training sessions and had a long, probing talk with him. He said I was trying to give him the third degree. I concluded that he followed the training protocol pretty closely and had good reasons for the assessments he made of trainee participation and comprehension. He said that at the outset, he had conceptualized what levels of assistance should be considered minimum competence for a mentor, but acknowledged that it was situational.

On five different dimensions, Sid and I compared memos from Senior Mentors written before and after training. The numbers of participating mentors was small, as was the total number of memos we were able to track down. On only one of the five dimensions, "making reference to documents," was there clear improvement in their memos to mentees. Sid emphasized that dimension a lot in the training and, sure enough, the mentors came through. I was not going to do a statistical test of significance, but I guessed that you would want one, so I did, getting a nonsignificant difference. The number of memos was too small. It's in the report.

You will recall that I e-mailed you several weeks ago asking to have an outsider, a mentoring consultant, come in for a meta-evaluation day. I didn't get a green light from you. I wrote a short section on the issues of mentoring. It would have been better had we brought in the meta-evaluator.

The training benefits were several, summarized there in the Executive Summary. There were costs as well. There were the usual costs, but also, perhaps, an oversimplification. It appears that, because of the training, mentoring has been redefined here as a six-step process, an activity much more explicit than it used to be. In a way, that's good. But I was greatly troubled by Mr. Ferdy's comments. He said senior staff members felt discouraged about giving time to what wasn't specified. And he complained that Sid called the personal relationships between mentor and mentee in the past "too sentimental."

Sagredo: Perhaps it has been.

Phyllis: Of course. But this complaint has not come from a review of mentoring here. Some mentoring may be sentimental—or frivolous, old-fashioned, paternalistic, or intimidating, or exploitive. But Daloz and the other researchers I recently read about mentoring and training of mentors did not speak of those problems. And in my brief interviews of mentees who were mentored before our training started, I failed to uncover any feeling that sentimentalism was a problem. I asked about it indirectly several ways before asking directly. I asked Sid where he got the idea. He said it was in the prologue to the training materials. It was promotional, not evidence-based. But the real question is, when mentoring is taught to be antiseptic and depersonalized, is something lost to the organization? In Mr. Ferdy's view, that may be happening here.

Sagredo: Ferdy is a fine fellow, but can your evaluation be determined by the words of one person?

Phyllis: No, you have to triangulate. I tapped into the experience of the Senior Mentors, just as Mr. Ferdy did. I examined descriptions of the training circulated in the Newsletter. And more. The evidence on depersonalization is spotty.

I believe there is a *risk* of lowering the quality of mentoring with this particular training approach. I do not have the budget, and probably not the skill, to do the research needed. But I cannot give the training a clean bill of health with such an important weight on my mind.

All in all, I tried to combine standards-based data gathering with a personal effort to get deeply acquainted with the training. I learned something about mentoring, and about the teaching of mentoring, and my experience influenced how I synthesized the information about the quality of the training.

Sagredo: But you treat your experience as important as measurement.

Phyllis: It depends. I doubt that I often weight them the same, but since I don't use numerical weights, I don't know. I reflect. I ponder what standards-based thinking and responsive thinking tell me: from hard measurements and soft; from my experience and that of others. I rethink and revise. I get others to review and challenge my thinking. The quality of the data is important, but I am seeking the meanings that will make the most sense to me, and to my audiences.

   Freaky? Not freaky at all. Professional. An aunt of mine is a doctor, internal medicine. My father is an architect. My sister works for the church. They all dig deeply to get good evidence: good measurements and good experience. They don't let it become mechanical. Their professional judgment determines how they will use the data they have.

Sagredo: Okay, I'm persuaded that you did more work than I asked you to. Good work. I'll talk with Mrs. Vivani about Ferdy's concerns about depersonalization.

10

Doing It Right

Let us so live that, if there is no heaven, we'll have been cheated.

Miguel de Unamuno

B y now you are well aware that evaluation is the discerning of good. Of course, real evaluation studies discern only some of the good. Some of the bad is missed too. Evidence of benefit and trauma is vigorously sought, but both exist in the absence of evidence.

Some good can be considered self-evident, not needing justification other than a widespread belief that it is good. Having foster homes and living by the Golden Rule are good, whether or not their good can be measured. Efforts to be fair are good. Safety is good. Artistic expression is good. An evaluator needs to keep in mind that the good of expression and the good of caring are virtues to be looked for, that need to be questioned and yet need to be granted, sometimes in the absence of evidence that they have an impact. Granting that widely felt good *is* good is part of doing the job right. I consider it unethical practice for evaluators to imply that any schooling or social service is unworthy of support because formal evaluation discerns no effects.

The good of many practices is discerned not only by their effects and the quality of their provision but, in a human society, by their existence. Firefighting. Midwifery. What about soldiering? What about running for office? Can it be said that evaluation itself is good, independent of its effects? Program evaluation has not proven itself in the ways that foster-homemaking and hospice service have. Many people are frightened by evaluators, dubious about their standards, doubtful they are sensitive enough to discern the merit of the work. Good evaluation is a societal asset. Bad evaluation is a perpetuation of wrongs. We are not good people just because we are evaluators. We have to do special things to make our evaluation good.

260

Quality Work Is Ethical Work

The good evaluator draws from the precepts of standards-based evaluation and responsive evaluation. At the same time, high-quality programs are what people define them to be—high in efficiency or sensitivity or impact—and what people experience them to be—compelling or interactive or hurtful. The program can be identified by its attributes and by its activities, and the evaluator needs to understand what is of quality. It is often hard to define quality, but with enough measures and testimonials, and skeptical interpretation, people can evaluate well.

The rationale for evaluation presumes an audience interested in information and interpretation. Sometimes key questions lead to decisions to be made; other times the key questions are more for exploratory purposes. What is the case in the following situation?

> The Director of Institutional Research and Evaluation at the County College of Morris in New Jersey—using the Noel-Levitz Student Satisfaction Inventory—collected baseline data on student opinions about the college. Two years later, after several changes in college operations, the inventory was administered again and differences noted. In several areas, particularly on the criterion of registration effectiveness, the improvement in student perception was found to be statistically significant (Charles Secolsky, personal communication, 2003).

Their key question was, "Did we make good changes?" The significant difference told them that the registration was probably improved. Not all of the changes made were endorsed by the survey respondents, but the director could take satisfaction broadly from what the students said.

Here the research assignment was to provide information about change in student perception. It was not an assignment to evaluate student services at Morris or its registration procedures. It did not have what we have called "an evaluand." Yet it contributed to the ability of the central office to evaluate some of its management. Perhaps the intent of this book to focus on the merit of an evaluand has been too narrow. When the target is an evaluand, there are issues to determine. Processes and personnel and context and history need inquiring into. Evaluation has been presented as a comprehensive activity. Sometimes the evaluator needs to concentrate on a much smaller task. Evaluators help clients and stakeholders by playing various roles, as I said in Chapter 2, large and small.

Some evaluation studies are done for information, some for understanding, some merely for show. It may be that in calling for the study, the agency or administrator seeks to reinforce the perception that the organization is prudent and accountable. Often evaluation is carried out expecting that the findings will substantiate and support action anticipated, or already taken, such as requesting further funding or other promotional efforts. Program evaluation has long been an instrument of promotion as well as an effort at understanding processes and quality.

Evaluators sometimes get irritated by clients. There was talk in the Evaluation Research Society in the late 1970s about setting standards for client conduct. Such standards were not included in its subsequent *Standards for Evaluation Practice* (Rossi, 1982), but the feeling remained. The strategy would have been to establish the expectation that evaluation is a joint endeavor, which it is, and to put both sides under ethical obligation. It was the evaluators pushing for rational program management—management that makes matters explicit and puts everything on the table. But most clients and other stakeholders are going to play it safe and keep some things under wraps, just as evaluators do. It is the standards *for evaluators* that we need to worry most about. The Golden Rule of Evaluation is not "Do unto others only as much good as they will do unto us." The rule is to do the best we can. The theory and practice of evaluation are of little good unless we can count on vigorous, principled behavior by evaluators.

Ethical behavior turns out to be not so much a matter of following rules as of balancing competing principles. The protection of personal privacy ethic bumps into the providing full disclosure ethic. At a codebook level, it is useful to have not just one but multiple codes of ethics. Circumstances vary. We hold one code up against another, not so we can rationalize whatever we care to do, but so that we can recognize different manifestations of ethical value and better deliberate their implication. Such deliberation is served by reflective recall, storytelling, and intuition and by formally comparing practice to standards. As with all good deliberation, input is needed from various points of view. But in the end, realization and resolution of ethical conflict come largely from within ourselves (Newman & Brown, 1996; Stake & Mabry, 1997).

Included in any search for quality is the obligation to challenge questionable practices. Taking part in the promotional efforts of program administrators can interfere with reporting questionable practices. In the long run, promotional activities undercut professionalism and diminish the contribution that formal evaluations make to human affairs. But full reports on program shortcomings in highly contentious situations are overly hurtful. Where will *you* draw the line?

We need an evaluation literature that includes codes and rules and principles, but we should not wholly rely on formal statements, for in one situation or another, they will translate poorly into reality. The diversity and particularity of practical issues ensure that codes of ethics will be of limited utility. In the United States, the National Council of Teachers of Mathematics (1989) provided a good example of how to treat standards more as visions than as cutting points. The standards mentioned below are part of a panoramic vision of ethics, but personal, situational interpretation is always required.

We need a professional history, the collected stories, of where evaluations coped well with adversity and where they did not. We need to collect the personal experiences of evaluators facing dilemmas. As part of the self-value-resolution process, we need to present to surrogate audiences, sometimes to specially appointed panels, cases that illustrate obstacles to honor, respect, and fairness.

As a matter of ongoing practice, it should be the responsibility of every evaluator to discuss real and potential problems with fellow professionals and thoughtful clients. As more and more contracts are offered for promotional reasons, resolution of ethical principles will be an increasing challenge.

Personal Standards

The professional literature and oral history include examples of researchers who cheated. They selectively omitted data and fabricated quotations. They drew conclusions not backed up by their data and presented someone else's ideas without acknowledgment. Not many get caught. Not many try. As you increasingly will find in examination of your coworkers, most people doing program evaluations have high personal standards. There are many opportunities to cheat. No one is closely watched, but cheating is rare. The fear of being caught probably has something to do with it, but most evaluators avoid misrepresenting program quality just because it would be wrong to do so.

Personal standards get challenged when one's job or future contracts are seriously at risk. Especially when there is little funding for evaluation work, it is not uncommon for proposal writers to claim they will do more than they or others have been able to do before. For example, they will claim to measure impact or find causes beyond what methodology has found in the past. When the evaluator sees a good program in danger, he or she feels the pressure, internally or externally, to overstate the merit and understate the shortcomings. It is a violation of personal and professional standards, but it happens.

I sent a draft copy of our next annual evaluation report to the program director. Each year we observed teachers participating in the program's staff development workshops and then again as they taught in their own urban classrooms. Our draft spoke of the program's sophisticated theories of pedagogy and curriculum. We told of teacher and student enthusiasm, sometimes high and sometimes low, for the development of experiential learning in schools pressed to improve test scores. Our draft also spoke of a weakness in the program's new training of teachers in the matter of assessment of student project work. The director said we should remove that statement because "their enemies would use it against them." I knew that the director was apprehensive about forthcoming funding and that the program was disdained by some authorities and competitors, but I doubted anyone was paying that close attention to them or to our evaluation reports. Still, I had been impressed by the director's political sensitivity. My colleagues and I considered the matter at length. We asked for and got the program staff to attend a meeting at which we presented our criticism of the grading practices. And we softened the language of the criticism in the written report.

Did I cave in? You may feel you need to know more of the situation before deciding. Did I violate professional standards? Michael Scriven (1997) says "Yes!" Standard C3 of the *Joint Standards* (Joint Committee, 1981) calls for full disclosure of strengths and weaknesses. Should we have informed others besides the staff of our evidence (several instances) of poor instruction on the topic of grading student performance? Student assessment was a very minor part of the academy curriculum, newly undertaken. If I say anything to a program representative about the quality of something, am I obligated to say it to all? What does full disclosure mean? My personal standards included a standard not included in the *Joint Standards*. It might be stated, "The evaluator shall not provide data to an audience likely to use those data in an inappropriately harmful way." Or "Beyond reporting major strengths and weaknesses, the evaluator shall not make it more difficult for the evaluand to do *its* job." What is right?

There is a generic dilemma of disclosure accompanying many evaluation contracts and assignments. Many clients and supervisors show little curiosity about our views of the workings of their programs. Many expect us to become, in person or in effect, testifiers as to the strengths of the program and discreet about the shortcomings. They know that the public concentrates on a derelict of bad, even in a sea of good. Clients seek or tolerate evaluation because they hope it will help keep the program afloat. Sooner or later, those officials point to the evaluation as evidence of program integrity or productivity or worthiness. Even beyond ethics, we have an obligation to audiences, some of whom we will never know, to represent the quality of the program as accurately as we can.

Professional Standards

It is to the AEA *Guiding Principles for Evaluators* (Shadish et al., 1995)[1] and to the *Joint Standards* (Joint Committee, 1994) that many evaluators look first for guidance in ethical matters. To me, the two documents say pretty much the same thing. There is more detail and illustration in the *Joint Standards*. The *Program Evaluation Standards* are organized into four domains, as shown below:

JOINT COMMITTEE ON STANDARDS:
PROGRAM EVALUATION STANDARDS

Utility. The utility standards are intended to ensure that an evaluation will serve the information needs of intended users.

Feasibility. The feasibility standards are intended to ensure that an evaluation will be realistic, prudent, diplomatic, and frugal.

Propriety. The propriety standards are intended to ensure that an evaluation will be conducted legally, ethically, and with due regard for the welfare of those involved in the evaluation, as well as those affected by its results.

Accuracy. The accuracy standards are intended to ensure that an evaluation will reveal and convey technically adequate information about the features that determine worth or merit of the program being evaluated.

One of the four sections of these *Joint Standards* is called Standards of Propriety.

---

[1]See also Sieber (1992), *Planning Ethically Responsible Research: A Guide for Students and Internal Review Boards.*

JOINT STANDARDS OF
PROPRIETY FOR EVALUATORS

P1. *Service organization.* Evaluations should be designed to assist organizations to address and effectively serve the needs of the full range of targeted participants.

P2. *Formal agreements.* Obligations of the formal parties to an evaluation (what is to be done, how, by whom, when) should be agreed to in writing so that these parties are obligated to adhere to all conditions of the agreement or formally to renegotiate it.

P3. *Rights of human subjects.* Evaluations should be designed and conducted to respect and protect the rights and welfare of human subjects.

P4. *Human interactions.* Evaluators should respect human dignity and worth in their interactions with other persons associated with an evaluation so that participants are not threatened or harmed.

P5. *Complete and fair assessment.* The evaluation should be complete and fair in its examination and recording of strengths and weaknesses of the program being evaluated so that strengths can be built upon and problem areas addressed.

P6. *Disclosure of findings.* The formal parties to an evaluation should ensure that the full set of evaluation findings along with pertinent limitations are made accessible to the persons affected by the evaluation and any others with express legal rights to receive the results.

P7. *Conflict of interest.* Conflict of interest should be dealt with openly and honestly, so that it does not compromise the evaluation processes and results.

P8. *Fiscal responsibility.* The evaluator's allocation and expenditure of resources should reflect sound accountability procedures and otherwise be prudent and ethically responsible so that expenditures are accounted for and appropriate.

Propriety here means caring for people, informing them, being of service. Most evaluations do these things pretty well, but a forthcoming revision of the *Standards* is expected to increase attention to cultural sensitivity.

As you read earlier, I am troubled by deliberate efforts to simplify the description of complex programs. More than with ethics, the Assessment principle, P5 above, and the Disclosure principle, P6, are concerned with utility and accessibility. So, a simplistic summary of values, even when the program is complex, gets no protest from these *Standards*. Neither do the final synthesis procedures proposed by Scriven (1994b) that—in our view—work toward a general oversimplification of program merit (Stake, Migotsky, et al., 1997).

Inadequate attention to complexity in the *Joint Standards* allows inattention to a range of ethical concerns in which evaluators find themselves. Of course, we should not object to having codes or scriptures or laws or standards just because they fail to mention all possible wrongs. But if the list of unspecified wrongs is long, then we should look beyond those standards for grounds for resolving ethical conflict. I will have more to say about what to expect from codes. Before that, I have a second example in the box below to illustrate an ethical problem resulting from weak efforts to describe in advance the evaluation work.

Human Subjects Protection

Medical, psychological, educational, and other research on human subjects can expose people to physical, social, and psychic dangers. Embarrassment is bad enough, but some injuries are traumatic and long-lasting. Because some careless researchers, some immoral ones, and some corporations and governments have at times violated the protections of individuals and groups, the U.S. government created a code of protection for human subjects. Its authors were concerned not only with violations of personal safety and sanctity but with exposing citizens to research that had little chance of advancing science or social practice. They established that parties contracting with the government would set up screening of research proposals to minimize the risk. Put at jeopardy of losing federal funding for a vast array of programs, all but a few American universities, corporations, and agencies agreed to set up Institutional Review Boards to screen proposals (see Sieber, 1992).

Such protections are essential. Many well-meaning researchers do not realize that their interviewing is intrusively personal or their confidentiality protections inadequate. Evaluators should take these procedures seriously. And they should not presume that institutional screening relieves them of extending their own protections to human subjects. One of the problems with standards is that they cannot anticipate many of the special circumstances to be found in individual studies. Another problem is that institutional standards make it too easy for individual researchers to suppose that no further protections are needed. Their emphasis on consent procedures does not assure that the appropriate monitoring will take place. It is the responsibility of every evaluator to study the access, the instruments, and personal interactions to attain a high level of sensitivity to the risks to people because of the studies. Many of an evaluators's standards should be higher than the Institutional Review Board's.

Toward the end of Chapter 6, I spoke about my study of Mr. Free's fourth-grade class in California. It turned out to be a situation needing more human subjects protection than it got from my university and from me. I started the study before there were obligations to get institutional clearance, but as a study of arts teaching in elementary schools, had I submitted a proposal, it would have been approved.

Explaining in detail the two-week field study, I obtained access and support from the district superintendent. I said I wanted to observe a good teacher but not one having a reputation for being outstanding. She helped me get Mr. Free to allow me to observe himself and his classroom. Because I was looking for easily created but relatively rare teaching moments, I explained to her that I would not tell him the entire purpose of my study. After almost two weeks of warm hospitality from teacher and students, I shared the draft of my report with Mr. Free. Perhaps offended, perhaps ashamed, perhaps injured, he withdrew his invitation and asked me not to publish it. I offered deep anonymity and other concessions, but he would not talk with me about it. I had not given him control of publication, and I included his story in our multisite report, perhaps unrecognizable even inside his community except for people who had met me there. I sent a draft to the superintendent but no printed reports into that community.

What would you have done? What should I have done when first gaining admission to his room and confidence? This was an example of a case where institutional review procedures probably would not have lowered the risk of an ethical problem. The rule has to be: Follow the IRB protections and create your own as well.

Confidentiality and Anonymity

I had not helped Mr. Free recognize his rights. In negotiating a contract and in arranging for data gathering throughout the evaluation, it is important that the persons providing data understand their rights. In a few cases, providing data to evaluators may be a requirement of their job, and they should be notified by supervising officers of their obligation again. In other cases, they give information voluntarily. They should have the right to change their minds about the use of their data, including data already given. Signatures of data release are desirable and may be required by Institutional Review Boards.

Anonymity of persons, places, and programs deprives audiences of potentially useful, legitimate information. They can expect to tie together evaluation information with that they already have. With anonymity, more of a reader's interpretation of data will draw undesirably on stereotype. But information should not be obtained at the price of personal exposure. Privacy is often more important than the additional interpretation from identities given.

In many program evaluations, persons contributing views or observed performances may be put at risk. The concentrated study of juvenile delinquency, or of teaching and learning, or of commercial sales and services may expose people to public recognition. Even in survey studies with individual responses seemingly obscured by hundreds of data gatherings, there are dangers of exposure. The evaluator should provide highly developed storage and retrieval systems, guaranteeing confidentiality to persons. Evaluators should refrain from using real or lightly camouflaged names, photographs, and other identity-revealing information. Cute pseudonyms that hint at the actor's identity should be avoided.

Even for persons observing the highest standards of moral, ethical, and legal conduct, an inquiry into personal ideas and actions can become an invasion of privacy. Subsequent publication can become stressful to relationships with family members, colleagues, students, and the general public. Ordinary living is not so open to disclosure—and ordinary safety is a standard to observe. Privacy is implied, if not guaranteed, constitutionally and culturally.

Essentially the same questions about personal background or preference can be raised outside research and evaluation with little need for formal protection. If a casual acquaintance raises such questions, the respondent should feel free to answer or avoid the question. If a personnel officer raises such questions in an employment interview, or if a teacher raises such questions during student examinations, or if a citizen raises such questions of a candidate for election, the respondent is under some obligation to answer—but with the understanding that that is part of his responsibility there and with the potentiality of personal benefit. Confidentiality is less an issue if the respondent has placed himself/herself in the review situation and has something to gain from it.

The need for confidentiality varies. It should be negotiated according to the situation. The rule I usually work toward is that people having responsibility to the public (such as elected officials, corporate officers, superintendents, directors) should not be offered confidentiality.[2] But persons who work in the

---

[2] They may be anonymized to protect others.

offices, classrooms, and field settings should be made to understand that confidentiality is standard procedure. Students, children, spouses, and parents should routinely be anonymized. Even when such persons ask to be given personal credit for their words or work products, this should be granted only if it can be assured that it will not expose others.

Names of institutions, organizations, schools, churches, and cities sometimes should not be disclosed when there is a risk of exposing participants. If a person is quoted anonymously but reveals, for example, an interracial marriage, then the identity of his/her organization may make it as obvious as giving the name. Confidentiality should be negotiated with organizations at the time of contracting, and the issue should be open for review along the way.

The Business of Evaluation

In addition to program evaluation, which this book is about, the business of evaluation includes policy evaluation (mentioned in Chapter 9), product evaluation, and personnel evaluation (to be mentioned below), and a number of other formal and informal uses to be continuously found around the world—as summarized by Michael Scriven (1994a). The common thread among them is the search for quality, for merit and shortcoming, for worth. As Scriven says, evaluation is as central to communication and advanced thinking as logic and statistics.

For criterion thinking and standards-based designs, the evaluation business relies on indicators. Jeannie Oakes (1989) described them for school mathematics and science as follows:

> Systems that monitor the nation's progress in science and mathematics education should include indicators of schooling processes. Such indicators can help policy-makers, educators, and the public better understand the conditions under which students particpate and achieve in science and mathematics. [Here we are] concerned with the school as a whole: how resources are allocated among classrooms, what general policies construct and constrain teacher behavior, and general schoolwide attitudes, values, and morale. These features of school context and organization mediate (in the broadest sense) the influence of public expectations, resources, and state and local district policies, and they shape classroom teaching and learning. (p. 40)

Most of the time we talk about program evaluation as a professional activity, but it is a business as well. We have something to sell. There are lots of offices and projects that need our services, and some with some money to spend. We prepare websites, conference presentations, and portfolios of work completed to persuade buyers to buy from us.

Most beginning evaluators looking for full-time jobs start by working for more experienced evaluators. It is unusual to get an open assignment like Phyllis had for Mr. Sagredo. Your supervisor will probably want you to do detail work for which you didn't need to read this book. But you will need to raise some of the same questions that Phyllis and Sagredo did. You will need to make suggestions that occurred to you first during some of the chapters past. In a way, you never stop selling your services to your boss and colleagues.

With a little experience, before long you may win a little independence, possibly set up your own consultancy. Or just do the occasional evaluation work as it comes along. An academic all my career, I don't know how that works. I suggest you go to EVALTALK (evaltalk@bama.ua.edu) and ask the good people there for advice. They will tell you there are new vistas opening.

NEW GLASSES

New glasses. Everything bright again. I can see
signs at the street corners and the names of buses,
and I am pleased at the richness
of the red brick of the church hall
and the white of that patch of daisies
in the rock garden
I never noticed before.

I think
I will go all over town
and look at the paint on houses
And notice the pattern
of the old-man dandelion heads

And I am surprised how pretty
the waitress in the shop is,
how becoming her green uniform,
and I think I must look again
at the faces of all my acquaintances
and the wrinkles of old women at street corners.

(Continued)

(Continued)

> Just as the moment I pity
> people with perfect vision
> who have never worried about going blind
> and who never experienced
> this joy of fresh sight
> and the marvel
> of the old world made new again
> and yet again.
>
> How many times
> since I wore my first pair of glasses
> when I was fourteen?
>
> Elizabeth Brewster

"New Glasses" by Elizabeth Brewster is reprinted by permission of Oberon Press.

Personnel Evaluation

Personnel evaluation is different in important ways from policy studies and program evaluation, particularly because of the extra need for personal fairness or due process (Joint Committee, 1988). A small negative finding can severely hurt a person being evaluated. As mentioned in the Meritocracy section in Chapter 8, the procedures of personnel evaluation fall into two common situations: (1) *selection,* when lots of candidates are competing for one or a few positions, and (2) *assignment,* when staff members or beneficiaries are being evaluated for promotion or other reassignment. These situations have been carefully worked through by Lee Cronbach and Goldene Gleser (1965).

As with the evaluation of programs taken up in this book, people can be evaluated by reference to criteria and standards, or by performance observation and interview. Standards-based evaluation has the advantage of providing common scales for comparison among people; observational techniques have a greater potential for finding subtle strengths and weaknesses in behavior. In either case, careful advance planning—identifying questions or issues and arranging for multiple raters or observers—is important.

One rule of personnel evaluation is so counterintuitive that it deserves the careful attention of every evaluator (Scriven, 1995).[3] We take it up at length here because it is related to the expectation that science-based research is a

---

[3]This issue, Using Correlates as Criteria, could have been included as an illustrative issue in Chapter 8.

dependable resource for evaluation. As is shown below, one cannot use high correlations between personal traits and performance as a basis for indicating the suitability of a candidate for hiring, firing, or reassignment.[4] Similar cases could be made for evaluating managers, the police, anesthesiologists, and cashiers, but I will use nurses in my example.

Directors of nursing in many hospitals hope to avoid giving patients full information about the day's schedule. Let's call it the "schedule silence" criterion. Nurses are not encouraged to find out when doctor visits or procedures will most likely occur because availability changes, sometimes due to crises, and patients are seen to be more upset by schedule changes than by being kept uninformed. Suppose research studies were to show a strong correlation between schedule silence and credible ratings of nursing quality. To help a nurse having difficulty with patient care, it might be appropriate to coach them on improved schedule silence. But to *evaluate* a nurse for promotion or merit pay, we cannot (without having informed her or him) use schedule silence as one of the evaluative criteria. Because some highly effective nurses do let patients know when their doctor is likely to come in, schedule silence is not an essential characteristic of effective nursing. And therefore—as long as the nurse is not told even indirectly to withhold the scheduling from patients—it would be unethical to use that as one of the criteria.

Here's an example of the same principle, but easier to figure: Suppose a large research study concludes that paralegals of Puerto Rican heritage, as a group, do poorer than average when preparing briefs. Should every Puerto Rican paralegal be automatically classified as a poor preparer of legal briefs for attorneys? Of course not. It would be unethical to evaluate individual workers by cultural background. It is not just a matter of cultural discrimination; it is also a matter of misusing correlational data. In any real-life correlation, there is some range of criterion scores for each level of inputs. Any one individual may be a person greatly different from his or her subgroup. Correlation among traits does not provide evidence for personnel evaluation.

If there is to be evaluation, the criteria by which people will be evaluated must be made known to them in advance. The criteria need to be stated or recognizable by tradition or routine. High performance in another important area is not to be added or substituted. Consider my summary of Marya Burke's (2000) case study of a Chicago grade 7–8 classroom.

> During the year, several refugee group students joined Miss Sherman's class. School rules required students participating in gym activities to wear shirts displaying the school mascot. The immigrant parents had no money for the shirts.

---

[4]The same would be true of any trait that the rater supposes is indicative of good performance, if it has not been brought to the attention of the performer.

Sherman made a deal with the supplier to provide these children shirts at no cost. Her principal expressed gratitude and mentioned it at a faculty meeting. No problem there. For the annual teacher evaluation, she wanted to add a plus to Sherman's rating of Superior, but then remembered that the rating was for teaching effectiveness, not generosity, and desisted.

When evaluating human performance for benefit or sanction, it is unethical to discriminate on any criterion not included in public, traditional, or contractual definition. Thus, for evaluating trainers, unless they were sufficiently warned by contract or rule, we should not include in the evaluative criteria any of the following:

1. Whether or not the trainer repeats the main points of lessons
2. Whether or not the trainer maintains eye contact with trainees
3. The trainer's knowledge of the Internet
4. The trainer's mumbling
5. The trainer's intimidation of students
6. The trainer's use of unfair tests
7. The trainer's humor

If there is evidence regarding the individual trainer, it is acceptable to evaluate on

1. The trainer's ability to communicate
2. The trainer's ability to discriminate between good and poor performance
3. The trainer's avoidance of sexist behavior
4. The trainer's avoidance of embezzlement

because these are matters of duty, work rule, and law.

Good research about human factors statistically or experimentally associated with good workplace performance of groups is not a proper basis, without notification, for evaluating performance of individuals. It would surprise many managers (and researchers) to learn that some checklist items they think pretty good are in fact used unethically. For nursing, paralegal work, teaching, training, and other job performance, ethical evaluation requires limiting criteria to what is defined narrowly as criterion behavior. Of course, an administrator can specify additional criteria in advance of the performance period. The ethical obligation is for early notification of the criteria to be used for evaluation. (Does the same hold for instructor evaluation of students?)

A rather different aspect of personnel evaluation has to do with the emphasis given to performance.[5] Current policy in many places has it that the merit of teaching is indicated by the performance of the teacher's students. Many schools have the obligation to enforce it, but it is problematic. There are instances of student performance that can be traced directly to what the teacher has taught, such as intriguing students with oral history or global positioning devices. But student performance on standardized achievement tests is seldom attributable primarily to teaching. Almost all people directly responsible for supervising teachers and for research on teaching know that test scores reveal little of the quality of the teaching.

Teachers teach the children assigned to them. There are great differences in children across classrooms and schools as to readiness to learn and readiness to be tested. In determining test performance, as demonstrated once again by the International Mathematics and Science Studies (Schmidt & McKnight, 1995), the biggest influence is the socioeconomic class of the children. What happens in the classroom, however important in the lives of the children, is far less a factor in their scores on tests.

Teachers do make a difference in how children become educated. And there are good ways to evaluate teaching. Principals, students, attentive parents, and other teachers close at hand can help assess the quality of work of individual teachers. Principals, supervisors, and others can develop special skills and experience for analyzing teaching and student performance.

Noting the similarity to the problem of evaluating campus instruction, Edith Cisneros-Cohernour and I (2000) urged attention to the fit of an instructor within the existing faculty group. Daniel Stufflebeam, George Madaus, and Thomas Kellaghan (2000) urged concentration on the instructor's performance of specific duties rather than on personality traits. A thorough redevelopment of teacher assessment has been completed by the National Board of Professional Teaching Standards (www.nbpts.org). But these improvements over personal impression are costly and seldom used.

Much of an educator's competence and influence on the lives of students, immediate and long-term, good and bad, remains beyond contemporary evaluation (Stake & Burke, 2000). The remedy is partly to improve procedures for evaluation, but also to back away from implying better data gathering and validity than we have. It is a management problem more than a technical problem. All

---

[5]One instance of "apparent" evaluation of personnel is the letter of recommendation. As you know, letters of recommendation usually are letters of endorsement, not letters of evaluation. Committees that ask for them know they cannot be trusted, but collect them partly to back up their decisions, if need occurs. People who get asked to write them are usually those who will write an endorsement, sweetening the shortcomings. As David Nyberg (1993) points out in *The Varnished Truth*, that isn't necessarily all bad.

this is the same for many personnel evaluation situations. As José Luis Aróstegui said (personal communication, 2003), "In personnel evaluation, we should find the balance between stated criteria to be followed and the holistic comprehension of human merit that standards matching alone cannot provide."

This brief section gives you only a glimpse at the complexity of one of the most common and important evaluation responsibilities. Other starting points can be found in American Psychological Association (1980), Braskamp and Ory (1994), Eder and Ferris (1989), Ryan (2000), Stufflebeam (2003), and Wise and Darling-Hammond (1985).

Product Evaluation

One early scale of merit was found in the 1930s catalogues of the Sears and Roebuck Mail Order Company. They would identify three versions of shovels and bonnets as Good, Better, and Best. Hypothetically, the scale would extend to Poor and Worst, but those products did not appear in the catalogue. For most product evaluation, different models or brands are compared by criteria. The criteria for competing ice creams in Chapter 1 were flavor, texture, and density. Six criteria for personal computers were, in 1991, ease of learning, ease of use, speed, power, safety, and support (see the *Evaluation Thesaurus,* Scriven, 1991).

Product evaluation differs from program evaluation and policy evaluation in at least four ways. First, there usually are a number of products to choose among. Second, comparison is against competitors more than against standards. Third, there is often a fog of advertising to discourage buyers from believing the more legitimate claims. And fourth, the choices usually involve less intense personal or political loyalties. Artistic criticism belongs in the field of product evaluation but often uses different means and metaphors (Smith, 1981a). Michael Scriven, a longtime advocate of summative evaluation and concern for consumers, created the following Key Evaluation Checklist (KEC) (1991, p. 204).

KEY EVALUATION CHECKLIST (KEC)

1. Evaluand description
2. Background and context
3. Consumer (beneficiary)
4. Resources available

(Continued)

5. Value standards

6. Process activities

7. Outcomes

8. Costs

9. Comparisons

10. Generalizability

11. Significance

12. Recommendations

13. Report

The evaluation profession has worked too little on standards for program and personnel evaluation, but little too on product evaluation standards. Many of us program evaluators think of the evaluation of products as a responsibility of consumer and regulatory agencies. Such agencies as the Underwriter Laboratories use a great many engineers and a few opinion surveyors, but few professional evaluators to study the way the products are actually used by buyers. Many of the agencies are staffed with people of competence and integrity, but many are stuffed with advocates for the industry or product they are supposed to be regulating.

Typically, these agencies use a criterial approach more than a responsive approach to evaluation. They identify characteristics of the shovels or cars or DVD players and test the alternative models, as I said before, comparing them among themselves more than against standards. The exception seems to be with safety criteria, where formal standards are set. Environmental impact is a criterion born in recent decades.

The magazine *U.S. News & World Report* uses the product evaluation approach to evaluate colleges and universities. Rather than gather performance data, they rate the schools on weighted characteristics such as incoming student aptitude test scores, student/faculty ratios, size of library, and budget per student. And they give special attention to school reputation as perceived by school administrators, faculty members, graduates, and other observers. It is not a whimsical procedure, but it badly needs meta-evaluation. What it does is sell magazines. Some of the staff refer to the annual ratings issue as the "swimsuit issue." Law professor Jeffrey Stake demonstrated that his School of Law would be rated the top law school in the nation if the criterion "number of nearby Tibetan restaurants" were heavily weighted. Other evidence-thin evaluations, in my view, are the Good Housekeeping Seal of Approval, the Best Western motel designation, the annual Oscars competition, and the electoral college. But these are not the great evils of product evaluation. What of tobacco research? Thalidomide? Chevrolet Corvair? It is important to remember that evaluation methods can be used by both crooks and whistle-blowers. If you had no other reason to go into evaluation, helping to right some of the political and cultural wrongs would be reason enough.

Political and Cultural Contexts

Lee Cronbach (1977) warned against perceiving program evaluation as a branch of social science:

> [Evaluation] is first and foremost a political activity, a function performed within a social system. The evaluation enterprise is an institution—a set of mechanisms, of roles, and of persons socialized into those roles. The person's role leads him to *want* certain things from any evaluation that impinges on his position, and to *fear* certain things. Persons holding different roles thus have discordant views of what the evaluation enterprise as a whole is to accomplish for society. (p. 1)

Ernest House points out, in his chapter in the forthcoming revision of the *Handbook of Qualitative Research* (in press), that formal evaluation became overtly political in 1965 when Senator Robert Kennedy managed to get an evaluation rider on the first Elementary and Secondary Education Act. Many who supported the amendment were confident that evaluation would show that President Lyndon Johnson's War on Poverty was wasting the taxpayers' money. In the years since then, the most common findings have been politically unclear, neither supporting change nor justifying the status quo. Typical conclusion: This federal program did not fulfill its promises, but it was not carried out as it had been designed. And the reasons they operated as they did were largely political. Often, as designed, they threatened existing power structures.

Recently, the New York Commissioner of Education appointed five specialists in psychometrics and me to evaluate the application of a consortium of thiry-five alternative high schools in and around New York City using their own long-developed performance assessment procedures in lieu of the state's Regents

(Continued)

Examinations, the standardized student achievement tests required to qualify for high school graduation. The commissioner's view was that all schools should use the Regents testing, but he set up criteria for alternative assessment procedures. The schools contended that the standardized testing would interfere with their approach to teaching the state's curricular standards, and even that some schools would be forced to close. In a year's study, the evaluators were unable to get from the schools the technical data deemed most appropriate, but came to the decision that the pedagogy and assessments used were serving the students pretty well, and said so in their report, urging at least further years of meta-evaluation. The commissioner disregarded the findings and ruled that the "high-stakes testing" would be undertaken immediately.

Local program evaluation is likely to be as political as that of state and federal programs—not Republican and Democrat political as much as change versus status quo political. Many evaluation designs are disposed to help the innovators, whose work is shown in a favorable light, but the results of the evaluation are often supportive of those already in charge. Designs that propose digging deeply into problems are less likely to be funded. The small interest shown by managers in findings that might help future operations of the program is usually disappointing to the evaluators.

Should the novice evaluator try to avoid politics in conducting evaluations? In most cases, to avoid politics is to obscure the reality of social and educational affairs. It is not better to aspire to be apolitical if it means being less relevant. Political issues are part of the evaluative inquiry, whether or not the contract identifies them. Meanings of merit and shortcoming are usually incomplete if they lack reference to political contexts. Politics can distort the findings of an evaluation study, but a study without consideration of political contexts is surely distorted. Evaluators should insist that it is their responsibility to study issues that are raised by stakeholders and political activists as well as by program sponsors and managers. Their reports should provide alternative interpretations of the data.

Of course, I take that bold stand from the security of retirement. A new evaluator must weigh carefully the political uses of negative findings. Capturing the truth can be as risky as it was for Zog and friend in the cartoon (Figure 10.1).

THE FAR SIDE® BY GARY LARSON

"Shhhh, Zog! ... Here come one now!"

Figure 10.1　The Subtle Design Problems of Participant Observation Research

Political context is one influence on program activity and the perceptions of program quality. Culture is another. And there are many other contexts: economic, educational, medical, aesthetic; local, regional, national, and international. You can name others. *Context* is an often misused word, sometimes thought to mean content. Program content is inside; program contexts are outside.

Like political contexts, cultural contexts influence the conduct and findings of evaluation. When we pay attention to culture, we see that race and ethnicity, language and custom, religion and

> **context** *n* 1. milieu, environment, background 2. something that surrounds, influences, and gives special meaning to an object or utterance

leisure activity interact with the meanings of a program, affecting perceptions of activity and worth. A view of hell is not the same in a church, a hospital, and on a football field.

Let us use the seven factors of standards-based evaluation to round out our reflections on culture in doing evaluation right. Remember, the factors are recipient needs, program goals, evaluation criteria, evaluation standards, synthesis weighting, staff and participant/recipient performances, and program costs.

Programs of many kinds are developed to serve the *needs* of the public. Even with universal human needs such as food, health, and employment, the needs are defined differently in different places and different times. A particular program is designed to attend to the needs of a particular group, but within that group, the recipients are different and are not equally served by standardized program offerings. Needs are defined partly by the culture. The evaluator cannot be satisfied with an assessment of needs that fails to draw upon the experience and values in the relevant contexts. It is not sufficient to say that everyone needs to read or to have legal aid. To treat them as real needs, one must show, in context, the high costs of not having them.

Culture needs to be taken into account in both evaluation theory building and practice. Bhola (2003, p. 391) wrote:

> Context matters both in the theory and practice of evaluation. Theory builders and model makers have to realize that their work is context-bound in several ways. First, theory often gets its color from its ideological context. Liberational evaluation, participative evaluation and now deliberative-democratic evaluation are more ideological positions than theoretical advances. More importantly, and more concretely, theory building and model making are also confined within particular politcal, economic, and cultural contexts (such as England or Indonesia) and are located in differentiated professional cultures (such as education, welfare, or business).
>
> Evaluation as practice has to resonate to a multiplicity of layered contexts: the professional culture of evaluators and the institutional culture of the place in which evaluation is commenced or commissionsed, designed, and implemented. In the process of gathering data, whether qualitative or quantitative, it will be necessary for evaluators to enter the personality and culture dialectic, including class and gender (Harding, 1987; Harris, 1998; Schudson, 1994).

Expectations are different in an upper-middle-class setting and a poverty setting. A male-dominated organization is different from an organization that has opened all the doors to women. The evaluator can err by attributing too much importance to these differences, but ignoring them is regularly a mistake. Program *goals* have different meanings in different contexts. A Nestlé Corporation aspiration to provide inexpensive baby formula to African mothers disregarded the economic context—many mothers could not continue to buy the formula after substituting it for breast-feeding. A goal to communicate better about available medical services is different for Christian Science families and for holistic medicine users. Goals need to take into account the current conditions or performance within the recipient group and the readiness of the program staff to implement the goals. These are more than cultural conditions, but cultural contexts are a necessary realization for goal setting.

Costs are an important part of evaluation, especially if the client or stakeholders want to know which program can provide targeted outcomes for less money. Many clients, however, do not expect the evaluator to take costs into account, possibly figuring that that is a matter for them to determine, not the evaluator. Obviously, under stringent economic contexts, issues of cost will be important.

The *criteria* to be attended to for evaluating a program are also influenced by contexts. What is deemed an important criterion in one setting is not in another. Nor across communities, nor across times. As we noted in Chapter 1, explicit criteria are not essential in evaluation, but almost always criteria can be deduced—as if they had been used—from thorough examination. That does not necessarily mean that it would have been a better evaluation had criteria been explicit. When criteria are not fully explicit (and are they ever?), there are more opportunities for people to misunderstand the bases and implication of the evaluation. A substance abuse program may appear to be valued if it helps victims reduce their dependencies, but the criteria most attended to by the governing board may be those of media attention to the methods being used. Increased attention to contextual influence on criteria may not always be good. Here is another hypothetical situation:

An external evaluator visits Cyprus to evaluate a loan to the Ministry of Agriculture to make its farm exports more attractive to world markets. The evaluator, an American expatriate, becomes increasingly sensitized to the centuries-old battle between Turkey and Greece involving the island. For his report, he intends to give major attention to the cultural clash to explain resistance of some farmers to changes in how they farm. The ministry liaison person says that such an emphasis will aggravate the problem rather than help. The evaluator does not know whether to draw attention to the historical context or not.

For many observers, attention to culture is attention to domination: the colonial culture, the culture of state legislatures, the culture of the family. These have been scenes of power domination by rulers, special interests, and fathers. The people empowered set the *standards;* the disempowered find those standards a perpetuation of their dependence. As a profession, program evaluation is committed to unbiased recognition of merit and shortcoming, but there is no way to remain neutral in these contexts. Ignoring the issue is an acceptance of the status quo. An evaluator either accepts the standards expected of the dominant forces or entertains (to some extent, in one way or another) the standards of subordinate stakeholders. Evaluators with a more democratic bending give focus to standards by which the subordinates might at least "hold their own." Evaluators with a "system" orientation emphasize the standards of funding agencies and administrators. *Weighting* of standards works in the same way.

The development of these six factors provides a conceptual structure for evaluating the *performance* of the evaluand. Then (or simultaneously) the performance itself needs to be observed or measured. We used Chapter 5 to talk about data gathering, much of which had to do with recipient performance. Has the patient gotten better? Has the trainee gained proficiency? Are the stakeholders satisfied with the evaluand's performance? Probably your greatest disappointment as a reader of this book has been to realize the difficulty evaluators have in getting valid and comprehensive measures of performance. Stimulus errors abound. Scores are often greatly influenced by something other than the criterion performance. Scores from a single instrument leave out much of the complexity of what the evaluand is doing. It is usually beyond the talent and resources of the evaluator to develop a battery of valid instruments, and those for sale or previously used fail to match the present target well. Performance assessment in responsive evaluation is at least as error-prone. However we do it, we do the best we can and try to be clear in stating that the scores are far from error-free.

What is the influence of culture on measuring performance? What the service provider or recipient does is partly influenced by the program, but also influenced by years of personal experience: family, friends, television, community, school, and so on. I sometimes say that the greatest influence on standardized achievement scores is the wordplay and puzzle solving of the family during the child's early years. Having a sense of what sort of answers the instrument calls for is very important. Schools try to give students practice on tests so they will develop that sense, and students do, but not enough to give everyone a level playing field. Home cultures are a huge influence on some performances, not much on others.

Culture challenges both criterial and interpretive thinking. Classifications of culture can be included as experimental and correlational variables in the standards-based evaluation study. Awareness of culture will enrich and complexify responsive evaluation. Sometimes culture is so obvious that it needs little special thinking. Sometimes it is so subtle that it escapes the best efforts at meta-evaluation. Repeatedly, evaluators need to ask themselves, What are the contexts of this evaluand? Which are most in need of inclusion in the narratives to be told? There are no codes to indicate the level of need for attention to race or nationalism or maternal care. Such need is facilitated by observing, asking, reading, and thinking. In the end, it is intuition that tells (Smith, 1992). Intuition is a large part of doing evaluation right, not so much in recognizing quality but in deciding what to pay attention to.

In all that we ponder, there will be help from criterial and interpretive thinking. In all that we evaluate, there is need for both standards-based and responsive evaluation. Together they seldom add up, but with their separate insights, together they cause us to move more sensitively, to think more deeply, to report more cautiously, and to be more committed to the representation of quality.

Last Words

I will end by summarizing what evaluation means to me. Grand summaries with which every evaluator should be familiar are Lee Cronbach's "95 Theses" (Cronbach et al., 1980) and Michael Scriven's "Hard Won Lessons" (1993). Evaluation is the recognition of quality, then reporting the evidence of that quality to others. You know the scene: There is a something to be evaluated—an entity, an evaluand, or particularly for this book, a program. In health care, it might be a program of announcements about early detection of cancer for non-English speakers. In education, it might be a lesson, an online course, an innovation, or a charter school. For social work, the evaluand might be a staffing protocol, a training session, or a child and family services agency. Study its performance, find its quality, and represent it in numbers and words and pictures.

Goals, problems, hypotheses, and issues are our "investigative structures" for studying the performances. Such structures are drawn from troubles the program is having. Evaluation questions are also found in the research literature, in the history of the program, in the coping behavior of stakeholders, and in the concerns of evaluators. And those tell some of the reasons quality is seen differently by different people. Different views give us the opportunity to extend the arguments, the imagination, and the dialectic. Were there no differences, we might need to invent them in order to tease out the complexities of program quality.

To focus on their concerns, many clients substitute other questions for the search for quality: Is the program in compliance with promises and obligations? Does the program meet the needs of beneficiaries? Is the program productive? What works? All of these questions may be important and they help move us toward interpretations of quality. Some of the questions come from professional practice and meta-analyses from the literature (see Lipsey and Schwandt in First Words). The central questions of evaluation remain: What is the quality of the evaluand? What are the many perceptions of its quality?

People may agree on criteria, or they may not. Merit and shortcoming are sometimes difficult to see and often difficult to explain. We may break it into parts, such as the merit of the outcomes, the merit of the process, the merit of the staffing, the setting, and other provisions, but the sum of the quality of the parts may not represent well the quality of the whole.

Usually, evaluation starts with getting acquainted with the evaluand, responding to its particularities, its people, its spaces, its activity, its needs, its decisions, its problems, its fears and aspirations. Its provisions and performance need to be observed in various circumstances. The evaluators' criteria, transcripts, measurements, artifacts, and stories need to be worked and reworked for evidentiary meanings. Performance is then held up to relevant standards. The standards may be explicit, right there on paper, or may be internal and difficult to explain; yet eventually explain we must, as best we can. Our analysis raises as many questions as it answers. Greatly needed is the help of colleagues, critics, and reviewers for the meta-evaluation.

Quality is seen differently by different people. It is not the job of the evaluator to find a consensus but to weigh the evidence, make judgments, and report the different ways merit and shortcoming are seen. Observations and interpretations that do not agree do not necessarily indicate a failing of evaluation but perhaps the complexity of the program and its contexts. It is problematic to assume there is a simpler world behind the world that people see.

Does quality exist only if seen, only if the lens is right? According to my criterial eyes, quality is real, independent of the viewer. According to my constructivist eyes, quality was born when it was seen. On the back cover of this book, the rainbow spectra stream from the bevels of glass, because the lens is right. The colors gradually became better as the lens became better. From the beginning we see quality, although poorly. And gradually it becomes more sharply apparent. Were the spectra there when the lenses weren't there?

Seeing quality is a human construction, whether measured or felt. Some people do not see what others see. And thus that quality—for the moment, at least—is hidden from them. Those who can see are struck by the good and the bad, the exquisite and the hurtful. They are moved by it, there in the chrysalis as well as in the butterfly.

In the text, I said that the emergent butterfly was a metaphor for standards-based evaluation and the spectrum from the crystal a metaphor for responsive-based evaluation. Maybe it should have been the other way around. You decide.

cherish *vt* 1. to protect, care for tenderly 2. to hold dear, as a memory 3. to cling to, as a hope

Probably simultaneously, a person sees something and feels something, senses and emotions together, and is moved to remark of its quality. When one sees the best, it is something to be cherished. Quality is related to cherishing, an intellectual emotion. It can be felt by groups but remains tied to personal experience.

We grandparents observe the children performing, and for those things we did not expect ours to be able to do, we marvel at the accomplishment. Nearby teachers and others of experience are likely to see this performance as pretty ordinary. For those who are moved, it is special. And for the rest, it is not. Averages are not the answer. Standardization often serves us poorly. We find life enriched by quality, however hidden it may be to everyone else. When we are forced to use inappropriate standards, quality of life is lowered, not just for a few, but for all.

References

Abma, T. A. (1999). Powerful stories: About the role of stories in sustaining and transforming professional practice within a mental hospital. In R. Josselson (Ed.), *The narrative study of lives* (Vol. 6, pp. 169–196).

Alkin, M. (in press). *Evaluation roots.* Thousand Oaks, CA: Sage.

Alvik, T., Indrebo, A., & Monsen, L. (Eds.). (1992). *The theory and practice of school-based evaluation: A research perspective (77).* Lillehammer, Norway: Oppland College.

American Psychological Association. (1980). *Principles for the validation and use of personnel selection procedures.* Washington, DC: Author.

American Psychological Association. (1999). *Standards for educational and psychological testing.* Washington, DC: Author.

Atkin, J. M. (1963). Some evaluation problems in a course content improvement project. *Journal of Research in Science Teaching, 1,* 129–132.

Baker, E. L., Linn, R. L., Herman, J. L., & Koretz, D. (2002). *Standards for educational accountability systems* (CRESST Policy Brief 5). Los Angeles: UCLA, National Center for Research on Evaluation, Standards, and Student Testing.

Bell, D. (1977). "On meritocracy and equality." In J. Karabel & A. H. Halsey (Eds.), *Power and Ideology in Education* (pp. 607–635). New York: Oxford University Press.

Beschloss, M. (2001). *Reaching for glory: Lyndon Johnson's secret White House tapes, 1964–1965.* New York: Simon & Schuster.

Berlak, H., Newmann, F. M., Adams, E., Archbald, D. A., Burgess, T., Raven, J., & Romberg, T.A. (1992). *Toward a new science of educational testing and assessment.* Albany: SUNY Press.

Bernstein, B. (2003). *The structuring of pedagogic discourse: Class, codes, and control.* New York: Routledge.

Bhola, H. S. (1988). The CLER model of innovation diffusion, planned change, and development: A conceptual update and applications. *Knowledge in Society: An International Journal of Knowledge Transfer, 1,* 56–66.

Bhola, H. S. (2003). The social and cultural contexts of educational evaluation. In T. Kellaghan & D. L. Stufflebeam (Eds.), *International handbook of educational evaluation.* Dordrecht, Netherlands: Kluwer.

Bickman, L. & Rog, D. J. (Eds.). (1998). *Handbook of applied social research methods.* Thousand Oaks, CA: Sage.

Bloom, B. S., Hastings, J. T., & Madaus, G. F. (1971). *Handbook on formative and summative evaluation of student learning.* New York: McGraw-Hill.

Boruch, R. F. (1997). *Randomized experiments for planning and evaluation: A practical guide.* Thousand Oaks, CA: Sage.

Brandt, R. (1981). *Applied strategies for curriculum evaluation.* Washington, DC: Association for Supervision and Curriculum Development.

Braskamp, L. A., Brown, R. D., & Newman, D. L. (1978). Studying evaluation utilization through simulations. *Evaluation Review, 6*(1), 114–126.

Braskamp, L. A., & Ory, J. C. (1994). Assessing faculty work. San Francisco: Jossey-Bass.

Brewster. E. (1977). New glasses (poem). *Sometimes I think of moving.* Ottawa: Oberon Press, p. 66.

Broadfoot, P. (1986). *Profiles and records of achievement.* New York: Holt, Rinehart, & Winston.

Brown, J. S. (1995, October 11). The social life of documents (Release 1.0). *Esther Dyson's Monthly Report.*

Brown, J. S., & Duguid, P. (2000). *The social life of information.* Cambridge, MA: Harvard Business School Press.

Burke, M. (2000). A teacher and her students: What they think, what they do, particularly reflecting professional development. In R. Stake & M. Burke (Eds.), *Evaluating teaching.* Urbana: University of Illinois, CIRCE.

Campbell, D. T. (1982). Experiments as arguments. In E. R. House, S. Mathison, J. A. Pearsol, & H. Preskill (Eds.), *Evaluation studies review annual* (Vol. 7, pp. 117–128). Beverly Hills, CA: Sage.

Campbell, D. T., & Stanley, J. C. (1963). *Experimental and quasi-experimental designs for research.* Chicago: Rand McNally.

Carlyle, T. (1828). Goethe. In John Barltett (Ed.), *Bartlett's Famous Quotations, 14th Edition.* New York: Little, Brown.

Carroll, L. (1865). *Alice's adventures in wonderland.*

Centre for Applied Research in Education. (1975). *The program at two: An UNCAL companion to* Two Years On. Norwich, England: University of East Anglia.

Chandler, M., Stake, R., Montavon, M., Hoke, G., Davis, R., Lee, J., & Rierson, S. (2000). *Evaluation of the MTEC alternative teacher education program.* Urbana: University of Illinois, CIRCE.

Chen, H. (1990). *Theory-driven evaluation.* Newbury Park, CA: Sage.

Cook, T. D. (1993). A quasi-sampling theory of the generalization of causal relationships. In L. B. Sechrest & A. G. Scott (Eds.), *Understanding causes and generalizing about them. New Directions for Program Evaluation,* 57, 39–82.

Cook, T. D. (2002). Randomized experiments in education: Why are they so rare? *Educational Evaluation and Policy Analysis, 24*(3), 175–200.

Cousins, J. B., & Earl, L. (1995). The case for participatory evaluation: Theory, research, practice. In J. B. Cousins & L. Earl (Eds.), *Participatory evaluation in education: Studies in evaluation use and organizational learning,* pp. 3–18. London: Falmer.

Cronbach, L. J. (1963). Course improvement through evaluation. *Teachers College Record, 64,* 672–683.

Cronbach, L. J. (1977, April). Remarks to the new society. *Evaluation Research Society, 1*(1).

Cronbach, L. J. (1982). *Designing evaluations of educational and social programs.* San Francisco: Jossey-Bass.

Cronbach, L. J., & Associates. (1980). *Toward reform of program evaluation.* San Francisco: Jossey-Bass.

Cronbach, L. J., & Gleser, G. C. (1965). *Psychological tests and personnel decisions* (2nd ed.). Urbana: University of Illinois Press.

Datta, L. (1999). CIRCE's demonstration of a close-to-ideal evaluation in a less-than-ideal world. *American Journal of Evaluation, 20*(2), 345–354.

Davis, R., Stake, R., Chandler, M., Heck, D. & Hoke, G. (2000). *Evaluation of the VBA Appeals Training Module, Phase II Report.* Urbana: University of Illinois, CIRCE.

Day, M., Eisner, E., Stake, R., Wilson, B., & Wilson, M. (1984). *Art history, art criticism, and art production: An examination of art education in selected school districts: Vol. 2. Case studies of seven selected sites.* Santa Monica, CA: Rand Corporation.

Denzin, N. (1970). *The research act.* Chicago: Aldine.

DeStefano, L. (2001). *Evaluation of the implementation of Illinois Learning Standards: Year three report* (Report to the Illinois State Board of Education). Urbana: University of Illinois.

Easley, J. A., Jr. (1966). *Evaluation problems of the UICSM curriculum project.* Paper presented at the National Seminar for Research in Vocational Education, University of Illinois, Urbana.

Eder, R. W., & Ferris, G. R. (Eds.). (1989). *The employment interview: Theory, research and practice.* Newbury Park, CA: Sage.

Eisner, E. W. (1969). Instructional and expressive educational objectives: Their formulation and use in curriculum. *AERA Monograph Series on Curriculum Evaluation* (No. 3, pp. 1–31). Chicago: Rand McNally.

Eisner, E. W. (1979). *The educational imagination: On the design and evaluation of school programs.* New York: Macmillan.

Eliot, T. S. (1915). The love song of J. Alfred Prufrock (poem). Chicago: University of Chicago Press.

Fetterman, D. M. (1994). Empowerment evaluation. *Evaluation Practice, 15,* 1–15.

Fitz-Gibbon, C. T., & Tymms, P. (2002). Technical and ethical issues in indicators systems: Doing things right and doing wrong things. *Educational Policy Analysis Archives, 10*(6), 1–19. http://epaa.asu.edu/epaa.

Flick, U. (2002). *An introduction to qualitative research.* Thousand Oaks, CA: Sage.

Fournier, D. M. (1995). Establishing evaluative conclusions: A distinction between general and working logic. In D. M. Fournier, (Ed.) *Reasoning in evaluation: Inferential links and leaps. New Directions for Evaluation, 68,* 15–32.

Fournier, D. M., & Smith, N. L. (1993). Clarifying the merits of argument in evaluation practice. *Evaluation and Program Planning, 16*(4), 315–323.

Fowles, J. (1979). *The tree.* New York: Ecco Press.

Gagné, R. (1985). *The conditions of learning and theory of instruction.* International.

Gilborn, D., & Youdell, D. (2000). *Rationing education: Policy, practice, reform and equity.* Buckingham, England: Open University Press.

Glass, G. V. (1976). Primary, secondary, and meta-analysis of research. *Educational Researcher, 5,* 3–8.

Glass, G. V., Hopkins, K, D., & Millman, J. (1967). *Report of the AERA 1967 Presession on the Design of Comparative Experiments.* Champaign: University of Illinois, CIRCE.

Gowin, D. B. (1970). The structure of knowledge. *Educational Theory, 20*(4), 319–328.

Grasso, P. G. (1999). Meta-evaluation of an evaluation of Reader Focused Writing for the Veterans Benefits Administration. *American Journal of Evaluation, 20*(2), 355–371.

Greene, J. C. (1995, November). *Evaluators as advocates.* Paper delivered at the annual meeting of the American Evaluation Association, Vancouver.

Greene, J. C. (1996). Qualitative evaluation and scientific citizenship: Reflections and refractions. *Evaluation, 2,* 277–289.

Greene, J. C. (1997). Evaluation as advocacy. *Evaluation Practice, 18.*

Greene, J. C., & Abma, T. A. (2001). Responsive evaluation. *New Directions for Evaluation, 92.*

Greene, J. C., & Caracelli, V. J. (Eds.). (1997). Advances in mixed-method evaluation: The challenges and benefits of integrating diverse paradigms. *New Directions for Evaluation, 74.*

Greene, J. C., Lincoln, Y. S., Mathison, S., Mertens, D. M., & Ryan, K. (1998). Advantages and challenges of using inclusive evaluation approaches in evaluation practice. *American Journal of Evaluation, 19*(1), 101–122.

Gruber, H. E. (1969). *Darwin on man: A psychological study of scientific creativity,* 2nd edition. Chicago: University of Chicago Press.

Grutsch, M. A., & Themessl-Huber, M. (2002). *From responsive to collaborative evaluation.* Unpublished doctoral dissertation, University of Innsbruck.

Guba, E., & Lincoln, Y. (1989). *Fourth generation evaluation.* Newbury Park, CA: Sage.

Gullickson, A., Lorenz, F., & Keiser, N. (2002). Survey 2002 report: The status of ATE projects and centers. http://www.wmich.edu/evalctr/ate/survey2002report.html

Habermas, J. (1984). *Theory of communicative action: Vol. 1. Reason and the rationalization of society* (Thomas McCarthy, Trans.). Boston: Beacon.

Habermas, J. (1987). *Theory of communicative action: Vol. 2. Lifeworld and system: A critique of functionalist reason* (Thomas McCarthy, Trans.). Boston: Beacon.

Halberstam, D. (1972). *The best and the brightest.* New York: Random House.

Hamilton, D., Jenkins, D., King, C, MacDonald, B., & Parlett, M. (Eds.). (1977). *Beyond the numbers game.* London: Macmillan.

Haney, W. (1983). Validity and competency tests. In G. F. Madaus (Ed.), *The courts, validity and minimum competency testing* (pp. 63–93). Boston: Kluwer-Nijhoff.

Harding, S. (1987). Introduction: Is there a feminist method? In S. Harding (Ed.), *Feminism and methodology: Social science issues* (pp. 1–14). Bloomington: Indiana University Press.

Harris, M. (1998). *Theories of cultures in post modern times.* Walnut Creek, CA: AltaMira.

Hastings, J. T. (1966). Curriculum evaluation: The whys of the outcomes. *Journal of Educational Measurement, 3,* 27–32.

Havel, V. (1971). Estrangement. In M. E. Solt, (Ed.), *Concrete poetry: A world view.* Bloomington: Indiana University Press (p. 149).

Heck, R. H., & Hallinger, P. (1999). Next generation methods for the study of leadership and school improvement. In J. Murphy & K. S. Louis (Eds.), *Handbook of research on educational administration.* San Francisco: Jossey-Bass.

Hill, J. (1978). Archipolis. In R. E. Stake & J. Easley (Eds.), *Case studies in science education.* Urbana: University of Illinois, CIRCE.

Hodder, I. (2000). The interpretation of documents and material culture. In N. Denzin & Y. Lincoln (Eds.), *Handbook of qualitative research* (pp. 393–402). Thousand Oaks, CA: Sage.

Hooper, R. (1975). *Two years on: The National Development Programme in Computer Assisted Learning* (Report of the Director). London: Council for Educational Technology.

House, E. R. (1980). *Evaluating with validity.* Beverly Hills, CA: Sage.

House, E. R. (1991). Realism in research. *Educational Researcher, 20*(6), 2–9.

House, E. R. (1993). *Professional evaluation: Social impact and political consequences.* Thousand Oaks, CA: Sage.

House, E. R. (2002). *Where the truth lies.* http://house.ed.asu.edu.

House, E. R. (in press). Qualitative evaluation and changing social policy. In N. K. Denzin, & Y. S. Lincoln (Eds.), *Handbook of qualitative research,* (3rd ed.). Thousand Oaks, CA: Sage.

House, E. R., & Howe, K. R. (1999). *Values in evaluation and social research.* Thousand Oaks, CA: Sage.

House, E. R., Steele, J. M., & Kerins, T. (1971). *The gifted classroom.* Urbana: University of Illinois, CIRCE.

Hummel-Rossi, B., & Ashdown, J. (2002). The state of cost-benefit and cost-effectiveness analysis in education. *Review of Educational Research, 72*(1), 1–30.

Ingvarson, L. (1998). Teaching standards: Foundations for professional development reform. In A. Hargreaves, A. Lieberman, M. Fullan, & D. Hopkins (Eds.), *International Handbook of Educational Change.* Dordrecht, Netherlands: Kluwer.

Jaeger, R. M. (1993). *Statistics: A spectator sport* (2nd ed.). Newbury Park, CA: Sage.

Jaeger, R. M. (1997). *Complementary methods* (2nd ed.). Washington, DC: American Educational Research Association.

Johnson, D., & Johnson, R. (1998). *Learning together and alone: Cooperative, competitive, and individualistic learning* (5th ed.). Boston: Allyn & Bacon.

Joint Committee on Standards for Educational Evaluation. (1981). *The program evaluation standards.* Newbury Park, CA: Sage.

Joint Committee on Standards for Educational Evaluation. (1988). *The personnel evaluation standards.* Newbury Park, CA: Sage.

Joint Committee on Standards for Educational Evaluation. (1994). *The program evaluation standards* (2nd ed.). London: Sage.

Jonassen, D. H., Tessmer, M., & Hannum, W. H. (1999). *Task analysis methods for instructional design.* Mahwah, NJ: Lawrence Erlbaum Associates.

Kemmis, S. (1976). *Evaluation and the evolution of knowledge.* Unpublished doctoral dissertation, University of Illinois, Urbana.

Kemmis, S. (2002, October 24). Private email communication to Katherine Ryan's evaluation class.

Kemmis, S., & McTaggart, R. (1992). *The action research planner* (3rd ed.). East Gelong, Victoria, Australia: Deakin University Press.

Kennedy, M. (1985). Mary Hayes, in Stake et al. (1985).

Kidder, T. (1989). *Among schoolchildren.* New York: Avon Books.

Kilpatrick, J., & Stanic, G. M. A. (1995). Paths to the present. In I. M. Carl (Ed.), *Seventy-five years of progress: Prospects for school mathematics.* Reston, VA: National Council of Teachers of Mathematics.

Kinchloe, J. L., & McLaren, P. (2000). Rethinking critical theory and qualitative research. In N. K. Denzin & Y. S. Lincoln (Eds.), *Handbook of qualitative research* (2nd ed.). Thousand Oaks, CA: Sage.

King, J., (1998). Making sense of participatory evaluation practice. In E. Whitmore (Ed.), *Understanding and practicing participatory evaluation. New Directions in Evaluation, 80,* 56–68.

Knox, A. (2002). *Evaluation for continuing education: A comprehensive guide to success.* San Francisco: Jossey-Bass.

Kuhn, T. (1970). *The structure of scientific revolutions.* Chicago: University of Chicago Press.

Kushner, S. (1992). *A musical education: Innovation in the conservatoire.* East Gelong, Victoria, Australia: Deakin University Press.

Kushner, S. (2000). *Personalizing evaluation.* London: Sage.

Laxness, H. (1968). *Under the glacier.* Reykjavik, Iceland: Vaka-Helgafel.

Lemann, N. (1999). *The big test.* New York: Farrar, Straus & Giroux.

Levin, H. M., & McEwan, P. J. (2001). *Cost-effectiveness analysis: Methods and application.* Thousand Oaks, CA: Sage.

Lipsey, M. W. (1993). Theory as method: Small theories of treatments. In L. B. Sechrest & A. G. Scott (Eds.), *Understanding causes and generalizing about them. New Directions in Evaluation, 57,* 5–38.

Lipsey, M. W. (1995). What do we learn from 400 research studies on the effectiveness of treatment with juvenile delinquents? In J. McGuire (Ed.), *What works? Reducing reoffending* (pp. 63–78). New York: Wiley.

Lipsey, M. W. (2000). Meta-analysis and the learning curve in evaluation practice: A debate with Thomas Schwandt. *American Journal of Evaluation, 21*(2), 207–212.

Little, J. W. (1993). Teachers' professional development in a climate of educational reform. *Educational Evaluation and Policy Analysis, 15*(2), 129–151.

Mabry, L. (1995). *Advocacy in evaluation: Inescapable or intolerable?* Paper at the annual meeting of the American Evaluation Association, Vancouver.

Mabry, L. (1997). Implicit and explicit advocacy in postmodern evaluation. In L. Mabry (Ed.), *Advances in program evaluation: Vol. 3. Evaluation and the postmodern dilemma.* Greenwich, CT: JAI Press.

Mabry, L. (1998). Case study methods. In H. J. Walberg & A. J. Reynolds (Eds.), *Evaluation research for educational productivity. Advances in Educational Productivity, 7,* 155–170.

Mabry, L. (1999). *Portfolios plus: A critical guide to alternative assessment.* Newbury Park, CA: Corwin Press.

MacDonald, B., (1971). *The evaluation of the Humanities Curriculum Project: A wholistic approach.* Paper presented at the AERA Annual Meeting, New York.

MacDonald, B. (1976). Evaluation and the control of education. In D. A. Tawney (Ed.), *Curriculum evaluation today: Trends and implications.* London: Macmillan.

MacDonald, B. (1977). A political classification of evaluation studies. In D. Hamilton, D. Jenkins, C. King, B. MacDonald, & M. Parlett (Eds.), *Beyond the numbers game* (pp. 224–227). London: Macmillan.

MacDonald, B. (1999, November 9). Statement on occasion of his investiture as Doctor Honoris Causa, University of Vallodolid, Spain.

MacDonald, B., & Kushner, S. (Eds.). (1982). *Bread and dreams.* Norwich, England: University of East Anglia, Center for Applied Research in Education.

McKee, A., & Stake, R. E. (2001). Making evaluation democratic in a climate of control. In L. Bresler, A. Ardichvili, & S. R. Steinberg (Eds.), *Research in international education: Experience, theory, & practice.* Peter Lang.

McKee, A., & Watts, M. (2000). *Protecting space? The case of practice and professional development plans.* Norwich, England: University of East Anglia, Centre for Applied Research in Education.

McLaughlin, M. W. (1975). *Evaluation and reform.* Cambridge: Ballinger Publ. Co.

McLean, L. (2000). Metamorphosis of YNN: An evaluation of the pilot program of the Youth Network News. Toronto: Ontario Institute for the Study of Education.

McLeod, D. B., Stake, R. E., Schappelle, B. P., Mellissinos, M., & Gierl, M. J. (1997). Setting the standards: NCTM's role in the reform of mathematics education. In S. A. Raizen & E. D. Britton (Eds.), *Case studies of U.S. innovations in mathematics.* Dordrecht, Netherlands: Kluwer.

Medley, D. M. & Mitzel, H. E. (1963). Measuring classroom behavior by systematic observation. In N. L. Gage (Ed.) *Handbook of Research on Teaching.* Chicago: Rand McNally, 247–328.

Mehrens, W. A., & Lehmann, I. J. (1984). *Measurement and evaluation in education and psychology* (3rd ed.). New York: Holt, Rinehart & Winston.

Messick, S. (1970). The criterion problem in evaluation of instruction: Assessing possible, not just probable, intended outcomes. In M. C. Wittrock & D. E. Wiley (Eds.), *The evaluation of instruction: Issues and problems.* New York: Holt, Rinehart & Winston.

Metcalf, S. (2002, January 28). Reading between the lines. *The Nation.*

Migotsky, C., & Stake, R. (2001). *An evaluation of an evaluation: CIRCE's meta-evaluation of the site visits and issue papers of the ATE program evaluation.* Urbana: University of Illinois, CIRCE.

Miles, M. B., & Huberman, A. M. (1984). *Qualitative data analysis.* Beverly Hills, CA: Sage.

Moffett, J. (1984). The spellbinding (poem). In J. Moffett, *Whinny Moor Crossing* (p. 67). Princeton, NJ: Princeton University Press.

Moynihan, D. P. (1970). Remarks at the White House on the occasion of his resignation from the President's staff, 1970.

Murray, C. (1984). *Losing ground: American social policy 1950–1980.* New York: Basic Books.

Murray, C., Bourque, B., & Mileff, S. (1981). *The national evaluation of the Cities-in-Schools program. Report No. 4: Final Report.* Washington, DC: American Institutes for Research.

National Board of Professional Teaching Standards. www.nbpts.org.

National Council of Teachers of Mathematics. (1989). *Curriculum and evaluation standards for school mathematics.* Washington, DC: Author.

National Research Council. (2002). *Scientific research in education* (R. J. Shavelson & L. Towne, Eds.). Washington, DC: National Academy Press. www7.nationalacademies.org/cfe/Scientific_Principles_in_Education_Research

National Science Foundation. (2002). *The 2002 user-friendly handbook for project evaluation.* Washington, DC: Author.

Nevo, D. (2002). *School-based evaluation: An international perspective.* Kidlington, England: Elsevier Science.

Newman, D., & Brown, R. (1996). *Applied ethics for program evaluation.* London: Sage.

Newmann, F. M., & Wehlage, G. G. (1995). *Successful school restructuring.* Madison: University of Wisconsin, Center on Organization and Restructuring of Schools.

Niemi, H., & Kemmis, S. (1999). Communicative evaluation: Evaluation at the crossroads. *Lifelong learning in Europe, 1,* 55–64.

Nyberg, D. (1993). *The varnished truth.* Chicago: University of Chicago Press.

Oakes, J. (1989). School context and organization. In R. J. Shavelson, L. M. McDonnell, & J. Oakes,(Eds.), *Indicators for monitoring mathematics and science education: A sourcebook.* Santa Monica, CA: Rand Corporation.

O'Shea, J. (1974). *An inquiry into the development of the University of Chicago evaluation movement*. Unpublished doctoral dissertation. Urbana: University of Illinois.

O'Sullivan, R. G. (in press). *Practicing evaluation: A collaborative approach*. Thousand Oaks, CA: Sage.

Page, E. B. (1979). Should educational evaluation be more objective or more subjective? More objective! (A debate with R. E. Stake). *Educational Evaluation and Policy Analysis, 1*(1), 45.

Parlett, M., & Hamilton, D. (1977). Evaluation as illumination: A new approach to the study of innovatory programmes. In D. Hamilton, D. Jenkins, C. King, B. MacDonald, & M. Parlett (Eds.), *Beyond the numbers game* (pp. 6–22). London: Macmillan.

Patton, M. Q. (1997). *Utilization-focused evaluation* (3rd ed.). Thousand Oaks, CA: Sage.

Payne, D. A. (2003). *Applied educational assessment* (2nd ed.). Belmont, CA: Wadsworth/Thomson.

Persig, R. (1974). *Zen and the art of motorcycle maintenance*. New York: William Morrow.

Peshkin, A. (1978). *Growing up American*. Chicago: University of Chicago Press.

Pring, R., & Thomas, G. (in press). *Evidence-based practice*. Buckingham, England: Open University Press.

Proppé, O. J. (1980). *Dialectical evaluation in education* (A thesis proposal). Urbana: University of Illinois, CIRCE.

Proppé, O. J. (1983). *A dialectical perspective on evaluation as evolution: A critical view of assessment in Icelandic schools*. Unpublished doctoral dissertation, University of Illinois.

Ragin, C.C. & Becker, H. S., (Eds.). (1992). *What is a case? Exploring the foundations of social inquiry*. Cambridge: Cambridge University Press.

Reichardt, C. S., & Rallis, S. F. (1994). The qualitative-quantitative debate: New perspectives. *New Directions in Program Evaluation, 61*.

Ridings, J. M. (1980). *Standard setting in accounting and auditing: Considerations for educational evaluation*. Unpublished dissertation, Western Michigan University.

Rogers, P. J. (2000). Program theory: Not whether programs work, but how they work. In D. L. Stufflebeam, G. F. Madaus, & T. Kellaghan (Eds.), *Evaluation models: Viewpoints on educational and human services evaluation* (2nd ed.). Boston: Kluwer.

Rosenshine, B. (1985). Direct instruction. *International encyclopedia of education*. Oxford, England: Pergamon Press.

Rossi, P. H. (Ed.). (1982). Standards for evaluation practice. *New Directions for Program Evaluation, 15*. San Francisco: Jossey-Bass.

Ryan, K. E. (Ed.). (2000). Evaluating teaching in higher education: A vision for the future. *New Directions for Teaching and Learning, 83*.

Sacks, P. (1999). *Standardized minds*. Cambridge, MA: Perseus Books.

Sanders, J. R. (1002). Presidential address: On mainstreaming evaluation. *American Journal of Evaluation, 27*(3), 253–259.

Sarason, S.B. (1990). *The predictable failure of educational reform*. San Francisco: Jossey-Bass.

Schmidt, W. H., & McKnight, C. C. (1995). Surveying educational opportunity in mathematics and science: An international perspective. *Educational Evaluation and Policy Analysis, 17*, 337–353.

Schön, D. A. (1983). *The reflective practitioner: How professionals think in action.* New York: Basic Books.

Schön, D.A. (1987). *Educating the reflective practitioner.* San Francisco: Jossey-Bass.

Schön, D. A. (1989). *Beyond the stable state: Public and private learning.* London: Maurice Temple Smith.

Schudson, M. (1994). Culture and the integration of national societies. *International Social Science Journal, 46,* 63–81.

Schwab, J. J. (1965). Structure of the disciplines: Meaning and significances. In G. Ford & L. Pugno (Eds.), *The structures of knowledge and the curriculum.* Chicago: Rand McNally.

Schwandt, T. A. (1989). Recapturing moral discourse in evaluation. *Educational Researcher, 18*(8), 11–16.

Schwandt, T. A. (1997). *Qualitative inquiry: A dictionary of terms.* Thousand Oaks, CA: Sage.

Schwandt, T. A. (2002). *Reconsidering evaluation practice.* New York: Peter Lang.

Schwandt, T. A. (2003). *"Back to the rough ground!" Beyond theory to practice in evaluation.* Unpublished manuscript, University of Illinois.

Scriven, M. (1967). The methodology of evaluation. In R. E. Stake (Ed.), *Perspectives of curriculum evaluation.* Chicago: Rand McNally.

Scriven, M. (1969). *An introduction to meta-evaluation* (Educational Products Report #2). New York: Educational Products Information Exchange.

Scriven, M. (1973). Goal-free evaluation. In E. R. House (Ed.), *School evaluation: The politics and process* (pp. 319–328). Berkeley, CA: McCutchan.

Scriven, M. (1976). Maximizing the power of causal investigation: The *modus operandi* method. In G. V. Glass (Ed.), *Evaluation studies review annual* (Vol. 1, pp. 120–139). Beverly Hills, CA: Sage.

Scriven, M. (1991). *Evaluation thesaurus* (4th ed.). Newbury Park, CA: Sage.

Scriven, M. (1993). Hard-won lessons in program evaluation. *New Directions for Program Evaluation, 58.* San Francisco: Jossey-Bass.

Scriven, M. (1994a). Evaluation as a discipline. *Studies in Educational Evaluation, 20,* 147–166.

Scriven, M. (1994b). The final synthesis. *Evaluation Practice, 15*(3), 367–382.

Scriven, M. (1995). *Advocacy in evaluation.* Panel on "Advocacy for our clients: The necessary evil of evaluation?" at the annual meeting of the American Evaluation Association, Vancouver.

Scriven, M. (1997). Truth and objectivity in evaluation. In E. Chelimsky & W. R. Shadish (Eds.), *Evaluation for the 21st century.* Thousand Oaks, CA: Sage.

Scriven, M. (1998). The meaning of bias. In R. Davis (Ed.), *Proceedings of the Stake Symposium on Educational Evaluation.* Urbana: University of Illinois, CIRCE.

Segerholm, C. (2002, September). *Educating democratic citizens in the Swedish school.* Paper presented at the ECER conference, Lisbon.

Selden, S. (1999). *Inheriting shame: The story of eugenics and racism in America.* New York: Teachers College Press.

Shadish W. R., Cook, T. D., & Leviton, L. C. (1991). *Foundations of program evaluation.* Newbury Park, CA: Sage.

Shadish, W. R., Newman, D. L., Scheirer, M. A., & Wye, C. (Eds.). (1995). Guiding principles for evaluators. *New Directions for Program Evaluation, 66.*

Shavelson, R. J., McDonnell, L. M., & Oakes, J. (Eds.). (1989). Indicators for monitoring mathematics and science education (R-3742-NSF/RC). Santa Monica, CA: Rand Corporation.

Sieber, J. E. (1992). *Planning ethically responsible research: A guide for students and internal review boards.* Newbury Park, CA: Sage.

Simons, H. (1987). *Getting to know school in a democracy: The politics and process of evaluation.* Lewes, England: Falmer.

Smith, L. M. (2000). Charles Darwin, a biographical portrait. In J. Palmer (Ed.), *One hundred key thinkers on education.* London: Routledge.

Smith, L. M., & Dwyer, D. C. (1979, October). *Federal policy in action: A case study of an urban education project.* Washington, DC: National Institute of Education.

Smith, L. M., & Geoffery, W. (1968). *The complexities of an urban classroom.* Austin, TX: Holt, Rinehart, & Winston.

Smith, L. M., & Pohland, P. (1974). Educational technology and the rural highlands. In R. E. Stake (Ed.), *Four examples: Economic, anthropological, narrative, and portrayal* (AERA Monograph on Curriculum Evaluation). Chicago: Rand McNally.

Smith, N. L. (1981a). New techniques for evaluation. *New Perspectives in Evaluation* (Vol. 2). Beverly Hills, CA: Sage.

Smith, N. L. (Ed.). (1981b). *Metaphors for evaluation: Sources of new methods.* Beverly Hills, CA: Sage.

Smith, N. L. (1992). Aspects of investigative inquiry in evaluation. In N. Smith (Ed.), *Varieties of investigative evaluation. New Directions for Program Evaluation, 56,* 3–13. San Francisco: Jossey-Bass.

Smith, N. L. (1998). Naturalistic generalizations as the source of investigative insight. In R. Davis (Ed.), *Proceedings of the Stake Symposium on Educational Evaluation.* Urbana: University of Illinois, CIRCE.

Sobel, D. (1999). *Galileo's daughter.* New York: Walker & Co.

Spark, M. (1962). *The prime of Miss Jean Brodie.* Philadelphia: J. B. Lippincott.

Spring, J. (1976). *The sorting machine.* New York: David McKay Company

Stake, R. E. (1967). The countenance of educational evaluation. *Teachers College Record, 68*(7), 523–540.

Stake R. E. (1980). Program evaluation, particularly responsive evaluation. In W. B. Dockrell & D. Hamilton (Eds.), *Rethinking educational research.* London: Hodder and Stoughton. (Originally published 1974)

Stake, R. E. (1986). *Quieting reform: Social science and social action in an urban youth program.* Champaign: University of Illinois Press.

Stake, R. E. (1991). Luther Burbank Elementary School, Las Lomas, Calfirnoa.

Stake, R. E. (1995). *The art of case study research.* Thousand Oaks, CA: Sage.

Stake, R. E. (1998). Hoax? In R. Davis (Ed.), *Proceedings of the Stake Symposium on Educational Evaluation* (pp. 363–374). Urbana: University of Illinois, CIRCE.

Stake, R. E. (2003, April). *How far dare an evaluator go toward saving the world?* Paper presented at the annual meeting of the American Educational Research Association, Chicago.

Stake, R. E., Bresler, L., & Mabry, L. (1991). *Custom and cherishing: The arts in elementary schools.* Urbana: University of Illinois, School of Music.

Stake, R., & Burke, M. (Eds.). (2000). *Evaluating teaching.* Urbana: University of Illinois, CIRCE.

Stake, R. E., & Cisneros-Cohernour, E. J. (2000). Situational evaluation of teaching on campus. *New Directions for Teaching and Learning, 83.*

Stake, R. E., & Davis, R. (1999). Summary of evaluation of Reader Focused Writing for the Veterans Benefits Administration. *American Journal of Evaluation, 20*(2), 323–344.

Stake, R. E., DeStefano, L., Harnisch, D., Sloane, K., & Davis, R. (1997). *Evaluation of the National Youth Sports Program.* Urbana: University of Illinois, CIRCE. http://www.ed.uiuc.edu/CIRCE/NYSP/Index.html

Stake, R. E., & Easley J. A. (Eds.). (1979). *Case studies in science education* (16 vols.). Urbana: University of Illinois, CIRCE.

Stake, R., Flores, C., Basi, M., Migotsky, C., Whiteaker, M., Soumare, A., Dunbar, T., Mabry, L., Rickman, A., & Hall, V. (1995). *Restructuring: Teacher professional development in Chicago school reform.* Urbana: University of Illinois, CIRCE.

Stake, R. E., & Gjerde, C. (1974). An evaluation of TCITY, the Twin City Institute for Talented Youth. In R. H. P. Kraft et al. (Eds.), *AERA Monograph Series on Curriculum Evaluation* (Vol. 7).

Stake, R., & Mabry, L. (1997, April). *Ethics in program evaluation.* Paper presented at a conference on Evaluation as a Tool in the Development of Social Work Discourse, Stockholm.

Stake, R. E., Michael, N., Tres, M. P., Lichtenstein, S. & Kennedy, M. (1985). An evaluation of The Joint Educational Specialist Program. Urbana: University of Illinois, CIRCE.

Stake, R., Migotsky, C., Davis, R., Cisneros, E., DePaul, G., Dunbar, C., Farmer, R., Feltovich, J., Johnson, E., Williams, B., Zurita, M., & Chaves, I. (1997). The evolving syntheses of program value. *Evaluation Practice, 18*(2), 89–103.

Stake, R. E., Raths, J., Denny, T., Stenzel, N., & Hoke, G. (1986). *Evaluation study of the Indiana Department of Education Gifted and Talented Program: Final report.* Urbana: University of Illinois, CIRCE.

Stake, R. E., & Theobald, P. (1991). Teachers' views of testing's impact on classrooms. In R. G. O'Sullivan, (Ed.), *Effects of mandated assessment on teaching. Advances in Program Evaluation, 1,* Part B, 189–202.

Stake, R. E., & Trumbull, D. (1982). Naturalistic generalization. *Review Journal of Philosophy and Social Science, 7*(1–2), 1–12.

Steele, C. M. (2003). Expert report. Grutter, et al., Bollinger, et al., No. 97–75928 (E.D. Mich.)

Stokes, D. E. (1997). Pasteur's quadrant. Basic science and technological innovation. Washington, DC: Brookings Institution.

Stufflebeam, D. L. (2003). Personnel evaluation. In T. Kellaghan & D. L. Stufflebeam (Eds.), *International handbook of educational evaluation* (pp. 603–608). Dordrecht, Netherlands: Kluwer.

Stufflebeam, D. L., Madaus, G. F., & Kellaghan, T. (Eds.). (2000). *Evaluation models: Viewpoints on educational and human services evaluation* (2nd ed.). Boston: Kluwer.

Stufflebeam, D. L., & Shinkfield, A. J. (1985). *Systematic evaluation: A self-instructional guide to theory and practice.* Boston: Kluwer-Nijhoff.

Teese, R. (2000). *Academic success and social power.* Melbourne: Melbourne University Press.

Terkel, S. (1972). *Working.* New York: The New Press

Themessl-Huber, M. G., & Grutsch, M. A. (2003). The shifting locus of control in participatory evaluations. *Evaluation, 9*(1), 88–107.

Tolstoy, L. (1876, 19077). *Anna Karenin.* Bungay, England: The Chaucer Press.

Torres, R. T., Preskill, H. S., & Piontek, M. F. (1996). *Evaluation strategies for communicating and reporting: Enhancing learning in organizations.* Thousand Oaks, CA: Sage.

Trochim, W. M. K. (2000). Introduction to evaluation. http://trochim.huma.cornell.edi/kb/intreval.htm

Tsang, M. C. (1997). Cost analysis for improved educational policymaking and evaluation. *Educational Evaluation and Policy Analysis, 19,* 318–324.

von Wright, G. H. (1971). *Explanation and understanding.* Ithaca, NY: Cornell University Press.

Weiss, C. H. (1977). *Using social research in public policy making.* Lexington, MA: Lexington Books.

Weiss, C. H. (1995). Nothing as practical as good theory: Exploring theory-based evaluation for comprehensive community initiatives for children and families. In J. Connel, A. Kubisch, L. B. Schorr, & C. H. Weiss (Eds.), *New approaches to evaluating community initiatives.* Aspen, CO: Aspen Institute.

The Wellness Encyclopedia. (1991). Berkeley: University of California Wellness Letter.

Whewell, W. (1819). The equilibrium of forces on a point. (an elementary treatise on Mechanics) Quotation included in *Bartlett's Familiar Quotations* (14th ed.). John Bartlett, (Ed.). New York: Little, Brown.

Whitehurst, G.J. (2003). The Institute of Educational Sciences: New wine and new bottles. Paper presented at the annual meeting of the American Educational Research Association, Chicago.

Wise, A. E., & Darling-Hammond, L. (1985). Teacher evaluation and professionalism. *Educational Leadership, 42*(4), 28–33.

Worthen, B. R. (1999). A stewardship report to AEA members. *American Journal of Evaluation, 20*(2), xi–xix.

Yin, R. K. (1994). *Case study research: Design and methods* (2nd ed.). Thousand Oaks, CA: Sage.

Young, M. (1959/1999). *The rise of the meritocracy: The new elite of our social revolution.* New York: Random House.

Bibliography

Chelimsky, E., & Shadish, W. R. (Eds.). (1997). *Evaluation for the 21st century.* Thousand Oaks, CA: Sage.

Cook, T. D., Appleton, H., Conner, R. F., Shaffer, A., Tamkin, G., & Weber, S. J. (1975). *"Sesame Street" revisited.* New York: Russell Sage Foundation.

Cook, T. D., & Reichardt, C. S. (Eds.). (1979). *Qualitative and quantitative methods in evaluation research.* Beverly Hills, CA: Sage.

Council for Evidence-Based Policy. (2002). *Bringing evidence-driven progress to education: A recommended strategy for the U.S. Department of Education.* New York: William T. Grant Foundation.

Cronbach, L. J., & Snow, R. E. (1981). *Aptitudes and instructional methods* (2nd ed.). New York: Irvington.

Daloz, L. (1999). *Mentor: Guiding the journey of adult learners.* New York: Wiley.

Darling-Hammond, L., & Hudson, L. (1989). Teachers and teaching. In R. J. Shavelson, L. M. McDonnell, & J. Oakes (Eds.), *Indicators for monitoring mathematics and science education* (R-3742-NSF/RC). Santa Monica, CA: Rand Corporation.

Davis, R., Stake, R. E., Ryan, K. E., Heck, D., Hinn, D. M., & Guynn, S. (1999). *Evaluation of the VBA Appeals Training Module: Certify a case to the Board of Veterans Appeals.* Urbana: University of Illinois, CIRCE.

Dewey, J. (1939). *Freedom and culture.* Chicago: University of Chicago Press, p. 147.

Elliott, J. (1977). Democratic evaluation as social criticism, or putting the judgment back into evaluation. In N. Norris (Ed.), *Safari theory in practice.* Norwich, England: University of East Anglia, Center for Applied Research in Education.

Elliott, J. (1991). *Action research for educational change.* Buckingham, England: Open University Press.

Feuer, M. J., Towne, L., & Shavelson, R. J. (2002). Scientific culture and educational research. *Educational Researcher, 31*(8), pp. 4–29.

Finn, J. D, & Achilles, C. M. (1999). Tennessee's class size study: Findings, implications, misconceptions. *Educational Evaluation and Policy Analysis, 21*(2), 97–109.

Flanders, N. A. (1960). *Analyzing teacher behavior.* Reading, MA: Addison-Wesley.

Fuhrman, S., & Elmore, R. (in press). *Redesigning accountability systems.* New York: Teachers College Press.

Gadamer, H.-G. (1992). Notes on planning for the future. In D. Misgeld & G. Nicholson (Eds.), L. Schmidt & M. Reuss (Trans.), *Hans-Georg Gadamer on education, poetry,* and history: Applied hermeneutics (pp. 165–180). Albany: SUNY Press. (Originally published 1965 in Daedalus: Journal of the American Academy of Science, 95, 572–589)

Glaser, G., & Strauss, A. (1967). The discovery of grounded theory. Chicago: Aldine.

Greene, J. C. (2000). Meta-evaluation: Evaluation of the VBA Appeals Training Module. In R. Davis, R. Stake, M. Chandler, D. Heck,. & G. Hoke, Evaluation of the VBA Appeals Training Module, Phase II Report. Urbana: CIRCE, University of Illinois. http://www.sagepub.com/stake/evaluation/webappendix.

Guba, E., & Lincoln, Y. (1981). Effective evaluation. San Francisco: Jossey-Bass.

Habermas, J. (1974). Theory and practice (J. Viertel, Trans.). London: Heinemann. (Abridged version of Theorie und Praxis, 4th ed., Frankfurt am Main: Suhrkamp Verlag, 1971)

Haertel, E. H., & Wiley, D. E. (1990). Post and lattice representations of ability structures: Implications for test theory. Paper presented at the annual meeting of the American Educational Research Association, Boston.

Harnisch, D., Gierl, M., & Migotsky, (1995). An evaluation of Synergistic Systems in classroom settings. Pittsburg, KS: Synergistic Systems.

Hastings, J. T. (1976). A portrayal of the changing evaluation scene. Keynote speech at the annual meeting of the Evaluation Network, St. Louis.

Havel, V. (1992). The end of the modern era. The New York Times, March 1, 1992.

House, E. R. (1990). An ethics of qualitative field studies. In E. Guba (Ed.), The paradigm dialogue (2nd ed.). London: Sage.

Kellaghan, T., & Stufflebeam, D. L. (2003). The international handbook of educational evaluation. Dordrecht, Netherlands: Kluwer.

Kemmis, S. (1998). RFW meta-evaluation. http://www.ed.uiuc.edu/circe/RFW/Index.html.

Lincoln, Y., & Guba, E. (1985). Naturalistic inquiry. Beverly Hills, CA: Sage.

Linn, R. L. (2000). Assessments and accountability. Educational Researcher 29(2), 4–16.

Linn, R. L., Baker, E. L., & Betebenner, D. W. (2002). Accountability systems: Implications of requirements of the No Child Left Behind Act of 2001. Educational Researcher, 31(6), 3–16.

Mabry, L. (1990). Nicole, seeking attention. In D. B. Strother (Ed.), Learning to fail: Case studies of students at risk. Bloomington, IN: Phi Delta Kappa.

MacDonald, B., Jenkins, D., Kemmis, S., & Tawney, D. (1975). The programme at two. Norwich, England: University of East Anglia, Centre for Applied Research in Education.

Madaus, G. F., & Raczek, A. E. (1996). The extent and growth of educational testing in the United States 1956–1994. In H. Goldstein & T. Lewis (Eds.), Assessment: Problems, developments and statistical issues (pp. 145–165). New York: Wiley.

McLaughlin, M. W., & Thomas, M. A. (1984). Art history, art criticism, and art production: An examination of art education in selected school districts: Vol. 1. Comparing the process of change across districts. Santa Monica, CA: Rand Corporation.

Nave, B., Miech, E. J., & Mosteller, F. (2000). The role of field trials in evaluating school practices: A rare design. In D. L. Stufflebeam, G. F Madaus, & T. Kelleghan (Eds.), Evaluation models: Viewpoints on educational and human services evaluation (2nd ed., pp. 145–162). Boston: Kluwer.

Popham, W. J. (1989, September). Recertification tests for teachers: A defensible safeguard for society, Phi Delta Kappan, 69(1), 45–49.

Postman, N. (1995). *The end of education: Redefining the value of school*. United Kingdom: Vintage.

Romberg, T. A., & Carpenter, T. P. (1986). Research on teaching and learning mathematics: Two disciplines of scientific inquiry. In M. C. Wittrock (Ed.), *Handbook of research on teaching*. New York: Macmillan.

Rosenshine, B. (1997). Advances in research on instruction. In J. W. Lloyd, E. J. Kameanui, & D. Chard (Eds.), *Issues in educating students with disabilities* (pp. 197–221). Mahwah, NJ: Erlbaum.

Rubin, H. J. & Rubin, I. S. (1995). *Qualitative interviewing: The art of hearing data*. Thousand Oaks, CA: Sage.

Ryan, K. E., & DeStefano, L. (2000). Evaluation as a democratic process: Promoting inclusion, dialogue and deliberation. *New Directions for Evaluation, 85*.

Schwandt, T. A. (1998). The interpretive review of educational matters: Is there any other kind? *Review of Educational Research, 68*(4), 405–408.

Schwandt, T. A. (2000). Meta-analysis and everyday life: The good, the bad, and the ugly. A debate with Mark Lipsey. *American Journal of Evaluation, 21*(2), 207–212.

Schwandt, T. A. (2001). Responsive evaluation. In J. C. Greene, & T. A. Abma (Eds.), *Responsive evaluation. New Directions for Evaluation, 92*. San Francisco: Jossey-Bass.

Scriven, M. (1994c). Product evaluation: The state of the art. *Evaluation Practice, 15*(1), 45–62.

Scriven, M., & Kramer, J. (1994). Risks, rights, and responsibilities in evaluation. *Australian Journal of Evaluation, 6*(2), 3–16.

Scriven, M., & Roth, J. E. (1978). Needs assessment: Concept and practice. *New Directions for Program Evaluation, 1*, 1–11.

Simons, H. (Ed.). (1980). *Toward a science of the singular*. Norwich, England: University of East Anglia, Centre for Applied Research in Education.

Simons, H. (2002) School self-evaluation in a democracy. In D. Nevo (Ed.), *School-based evaluation: An international perspective. Advances in Program Evaluation, 8*.

Slavin, R. (1988). *Student team learning: An overview*. Washington, DC: National Education Association

Smith, N. L. (2002). International students' reflections on the cultural embeddedness of evaluation. *American Journal of Evaluation, 23*(4), 481–492.

Stake, R. E. (1979). Should educational evaluation be more objective or more subjective? More subjective! (A debate with E. B. Page). *Educational Evaluation and Policy Analysis, 1*(1), 45.

Stake, R. E., Brown, C., Hoke, G., Maxwell, G., & Friedman, J. (1979). *Evaluating a regional environmental learning system*. Urbana: University of Illinois, CIRCE.

Stake, R. E., Davis, R., & Guynn, S. (1997). *Evaluation of Reader Focused Writing*. http://www.ed.uiuc.edu/circe/RFW/Index.html

Stake, R. E., & Migotsky, C. (2001). An evaluation of an evaluation: CIRCE's meta-evaluation of the site visits and issue papers of the ATE program evaluation. Urbana: University of Illinois, CIRCE.

Stake, R. E., Trumbull, D., Brown, C., Dawson-Saunders, B., Gold, N., Hoke, G., Hutchins, B., House, E., Jones, J., Kelly, E., Leean, C., Reinhard, D., Rugg, D., & Secolsky, C. (1982). *Vitalization of humanities teaching: An evaluation report of PDHDS*. Urbana: University of Illinois, CIRCE.

Stufflebeam, D. L. (1968). *Evaluation as enlightenment for decision making*. Columbus: Ohio State University, Evaluation Center.

Stufflebeam, D. L. (1981). Meta-evaluation: Concepts, standards, and uses. In R. A. Berk (Ed.), *Educational evaluation methodology: The state of the art.* Baltimore: Johns Hopkins University Press.

Stufflebeam, D.L., Gullickson, A., & Wingate, L. (2002). *The spirit of Consuelo: An evaluation of Ke Aka Ho'ona.* Kalamazoo: The Evaluation Center, Western Michigan University. http://www.sagepub.com/stake/evaluation/webappendix

Weiss, C. H. (1998). *Evaluation* (2nd ed.). Englewood Cliffs, NJ: Prentice Hall.

Wholey, J. S. (2001). Managing for results: Roles for evaluators in a new management era. *American Journal of Evaluation, 22*(3), 409–418.

Index

Abma, T. A., 101, 102
Accountability
    democratic evaluation, 199–203
    evaluator disposition, 30
    standards, 164
Accreditation, 177*n. 10*
    goal attainment evaluation, 35
    self-study report, 198–199, 198*n. 6*
Accuracy, program evaluation
        standard, 265
Acompensatory weighted score
        model, 14
Action research
    evaluation role of, 27–29, 28*n. 1*, 38, 186
    example of, 194
    participatory evaluation, 193*n. 2*
Adams, E., 240
Adams, John, 245
Advanced Technology Education
        program, 146, 146*n. 7*, 147–148*fig.*
Advocacy, 249
    bias, 253–254
    case example, 48–49
    in classroom, social advocacy, 87, 127
    democratic evaluation, 199, 201
    education politics, 47, 47*n. 6*
    in evaluation contracts, 219
    for experimental design, 250–251
    participatory evaluation, 198
    for program participants, 47
    role of in evaluation, 46–50, 52
    shortcomings downplay, 49
    See also Roles of evaluation
AEA. *See* American Evaluation
        Association

AERA. *See* American Educational
        Research Association
Aggregative data
    coding system, 100, 129–130
    evidence-based evaluation, 247
    gathering of, 117, 148
    vs. interpretive, 82
Alice's Adventures in Wonderland, from
        (Carroll), 161*n. 2*
Alvik, T., 199*n. 7*
American Educational Research
        Association (AERA), xii, 114,
        115–116*fig.*, 305
American Evaluation Association (AEA),
        xii, 19*n. 7*, 36, 58, 305
American Journal of Evaluation, xvi
American Psychological Association,
        113*n. 2*, 276
Amultiple cutoff weighted score model,
        14–15
Analysis, 2
    accountability systems standards, 164
    aggregative *vs.* interpretive, 82
    attribution and generalization, 163
    communication issues, 167, 168*fig.*
    conceptual structures, 164
    defined, 159, 160–164
    false negatives, positives,
        163*n. 4*
    patterns, issues, 162, 162*n. 3,* 165
    perceptions of merit, 163
    program factors, 160
    program value representation, 161,
        161*fig.,* 161*n. 2*
    project logs, 165, 160*fig.*

project management/evaluation diary
example, 166*fig.*
rational thinking from, 170–171*fig.*
routines, 164–165
single performance criterion,
163–164, 163*n. 4*
statistical analysis, 164
vs. synthesis, 160
Anna Karenina, from (Tolstoy), 248
Anonymity, 268–270, 269*n. 2*
Antecedent data, 109, 109*fig.*, 174
Aróstegui, José Louis, 276
The Art of Case Study Research
(Stake), 305
Artifacts
activity, context of program,
156–159
defined, 142
documentation search, 156
ethnographers, cultural
anthropologists, 157
program history, 155
Ashdown, Jane, 78
Assertions
analysis, synthesis, meta-evaluation,
161, 163, 165
naturalistic generalization, 174
triangulation, 182, 185
Assignment, personnel, 272
Atkin, Mike, 101
Attribution, 5
defined, 251
explication, 177, 177*n. 10*
program analysis, 163
Audience, 21, 258
defined, 195–196
experiential inferences, 175–177
full disclosure to, 264–265
information *vs.* anonymity, 269
investigative reason, 248
quality of work as ethical issue, 261
report read by, 208
vicarious experiences, 175
Autocratic evaluation, 201

Baker, Eva, 164
Baruch, Robert, 75*n. 7*

Becker, H. S., 200*n. 8*
Behavioral objectives, 72, 73–74*fig.*
staff training, 239
Bell, Daniel, 230
Beneficiaries
data from, 113, 117, 138
democratic evaluation, 199–203,
199*n. 7*, 200*nn. 8–10*, 201*n. 11*
evaluand representations, 212–213,
214*fig.*
well-being of, 191
See also Clients; Readers; Stakeholders
Berlak, H., 240
Bernstein, Basil, 237
Beschloss, M., 42
Betebenner, D. W., 164
Bewster, Elizabeth, 271
Bhola, H. S., 197*n. 3*, 224, 281
Bias, 38
advocacy as, 254
explication to deal with, 60
goal attainment evaluation, 35
minimization of, 171
prevalence of, 59–60
probative inference, 176
randomization control of, 250,
253–255
in standards-based evaluation, 178
Bickman, L., 195
The Big Test (Lemann), 235
Bloom, Benjamin, 228
Blue ribbon panels, 23, 99–100, 173, 240
Bohr, Niels, 247
Boruch, Robert, 92*n. 5*
Brandt, Ron, 31*n. 3*
Braskamp, L. A, 197*n. 3*, 276
Bresler, Liora, xxxvii, 187
Brewster, Elizabeth, 271–272
Briggs, Katherine, 216
Broadfoot, P., 240
Brown, J. S., 240
Brown, R., 262
Brown, R. D., 197*n. 3*
Burckhardt, Jacob, 159
Bureaucratic evaluation, 201
Burgess, T., 240
Burke, Marya, 273, 275

Business of evaluation, 279–272
Butterfly
    metaphor of, 286
    of "value realization," 179

Cambridge manifesto, 200–201, 201*n. 11*
Campbell, Don, 75*n. 7*, 92*n. 5*, 250, 251
"Campbell Collaboration," xxii*n. 2*
Caracelli, V. J., 94
Carlyle, T., 124
Carroll, Lewis, 161*n. 2*
Case examples
    action research, 194
    Advanced Technology Education
        program, 146, 146*n. 7*, 147–148*fig.*
    advocacy, 48–49
    behavioral objectives, 72, 73–74*fig.*
    Central America nutrition study, 75
    Chicago Teacher Academy for
        Mathematics and Science, 48–49
    community college organizational
        development, 37
    community social services, 194
    contract renegotiation, 204,
        205–206*fig.*
    Corporate Responsibility, 192, 192*n. 1*
    cost estimation, 77–78, 79–80*fig.*
    County College of Morris,
        New Jersey, 261
    data gathering, 114, 115–116*fig.*
    democratic evaluation, 45
    Design of Comparative Experiments
        example, 114, 115–116*fig.*
    estimating case example, 77, 79–80*fig.*
    explicit criteria standards, 58–59
    gender-equity program, 55–56*fig.*
    holistic quality evaluation, 38–39
    of human subjects protection, 268
    Illinois Gifted Education Program,
        144–145, 145*fig.*
    Indiana Gifted and Talented
        Education Program, 77–78,
        79–80*fig.*
    Instructional Information Exchange,
        73–74*fig.*
    interviewing, 153–155, 153–156*figs.*,
        153*fig.*, 153*n. 8*

Milwaukee Alternative Teacher
    Training, 172
National Development Programme in
    Computer Assisted Learning
    (U.K.), 71–72
National Youth Sports Program
    evaluation, 204, 205–206*fig.*, 231
NCTM Standards, Coding Examples,
    130, 131–132*fig.*
New York State public school
    mathematics standards, 66,
    67–70*fig.*
participatory evaluation, 45–46
personnel evaluation, 273–274
political context, 278–279
Regents testing vs.alternative
    assessment, 278–279
of responsive evaluation, 86–88
school testing survey, 125, 126*fig.*
self-study, 194
site visitation team summaries, 146,
    147–148*fig.*
situational questionnaire use, 139,
    140–142*fig.*
stakeholder and public data sources,
    127, 128*fig.*
stakeholder data gathering, 127, 128*fig.*
stakeholder-oriented
    meta-evaluation, 181
standards-based evaluation, criterion
    for, 55–56*fig.*
State of Illinois Learning
    Standards, 64
Survey on School testing, 128*fig.*
teachers reading English
    standards, 7
Texas teachers literacy evaluation,
    163, 163*n. 4*
UTOS version of standards-based
    evaluation, 75
Veterans Benefits Administration
    letter writing, 38–39, 182
Veterans Benefits Administration
    training, 235–236
Youth Network News, 127, 128*fig.*
Case Studies in Science Education
    (CSSE), 139, 140–142*fig.*

Case Studies in Science Education (Stake and Easley), 174, 305
Case study methodology
  data gathering, 139
  democratic evaluation method, 200nn. 9, 10, 200–201
  evaluator disposition, 30
  in program evaluation, xii, 96, 173
Causal modeling evaluation, 43
Center for Instructional Research and Curriculum Evaluation (CIRCE), University of Illinois, 48, 48nn. 7, 8, 146n. 7, 198, 198n. 4, 305
  Illinois Gifted Education Program, 144–145, 145fig.
  Milwaukee alternative teacher training program evaluation, 172
  National Youth Sports Program evaluation study, xiv, 204, 204n. 12, 205–206fig., 231
  stakeholder-oriented meta-evaluation, xi–xii
  Veterans Benefits Administration professional development evaluation, 235–236
Chandler, M., 172, 235
Chauncey, Henry, 216
Checklist
  in evaluation, 15, 58, 84, 164, 169, 180n. 11, 216
  Key Evaluation Checklist, 276–277
  in observation schedule, 142, 144, 146
  performance criteria, 274
Chen, Harvey, 198
Cherish, defined, 286
Chicago Teacher Academy for Mathematics and Science, 48–49
Chrysalis, 179, 286
CIPP Model of evaluation, 29, 29n. 2, 177n. 8
CIRCE (Center for Instructional Research and Curriculum Evaluation, University of Illinois), xi–xii, 48, 48nn. 7, 8, 146n. 7, 181, 198, 198n. 4, 305
  Illinois Gifted Education Program, 144–145, 145fig.

Cisneros-Cohernour, E., 275
Client-centered evaluation, 38, 101
Clients
  compromises, 192
  contract negotiation, 203–206, 204n. 12, 205–206fig.
  defined, 34
  evaluator contract negotiation, 190–191
  report relevance and comprehensibility, 192, 208
  well-being of, 191
  See also Beneficiaries; Readers; Stakeholders
Cluster evaluation, xxiv
Cochrane Collaboration, xxiin. 2
Coding and records processing, 129–136
  aggregative *vs.* interpretive data, 129–130
  coding, defined, 130
  elaborate categories of coded observation, 130, 131–132fig.
  evaluation project logs, 135, 165, 166fig.
  interpretations, 130
  note taking, 135, 134–136fig.
  in responsive evaluation, 100
Collaborative evaluation, 45–46
  See also Participatory evaluation
Communication
  in analysis, 167, 168fig.
  social action and, 43–44
  in utilization-based evaluation, 198
Community colleges program evaluation, 37
Comparison group, 13–14, 53, 91–92, 198
Compensatory weighted score model, 14, 175
Complexity of program, 102, 110, 156, 177, 224–225, 266–267
Concept mapping, 224, 224n. 4
Conceptual organization
  of an evaluation, 72–73, 72n. 6, 109, 226, 228
  of goal-based evaluation, 71–72
  issues as, 89–90
Confidence
  assurance, xix, xx
  meta-evaluation, 181n. 12

quality-assurance, 186
    validity, 82
data gathering, 216
meta-evaluation and, 180, 183*n. 14*
in standards-based evaluation, 92, 113
triangulation methods, 185–186
Confidentiality issues, 46, 268–269,
    269*n. 2*
Connoisseurship evaluation, 101,
    174, 174*n. 6*
    evaluator disposition, 30
Constructivism, 39, 49, 131*fig.*, 161*n. 2*,
    196, 286
Consumer Reports, 9
Consumer Reports ice cream brand
    comparisons, 9–12*table*
Content. *See* Training content, staff
    development
Context, Inputs, Process, and Product
    model. *See* CIPP Model of
    evaluation
Contexts, 37
    cultural, 20–22, 22*n. 9*, 278–284
    of data gathering, 156–157
    defined, 281
    holistic quality search, 39
    issue complexity, 225–226
    political, 50–51, 278–284
    social, 50–51
    synthesis, 172–174
Contingency coefficient of pattern
    strength, 162*fig.*, 162*n. 3*
Contract negotiation. *See* Negotiation
Control group concept, 88, 252
    for comparison, 13
    in human services evaluation, 91
    in policy studies, 92*n. 5*
    in responsive evaluation, 91–92
    as technical term, 215
Cook, T., 51, 63–64, 75*n. 7*, 92*n. 5*, 99*n.*
    7, 246, 250
Corporate evaluators, 20
Corporate Responsibility project, 192
Correlates as criteria, 272–274, 273*n. 3*,
    274*n. 4*
Costs
    cost-benefit ratio, 77–78, 79–80*fig.*

cost of evaluation, 24, 52–53, 79, 94,
    208, 209–210*fig.*, 290
    effectiveness of, 33
    of program, 76–78
Countenance Matrix, 109–110, 109*fig.*
Countenance Model of evaluation,
    4*n. 1*, 30
Cousins, Brad, 202
Criteria
    criteria of merit, 170
    defined, 61
    explicit, 284
    personnel evaluation, 272, 2273*n. 3*,
        274*n. 4*, 275*n. 5*
    product evaluation, 276–278
    vs. standards, 5–6
    See also Criterial-based evaluation;
        Criterial data gathering;
        Criterial thinking
Criterial-based evaluation, xi
    explanation of, xv, xvi, 2
    See also Standards-based evaluation
Criterial data gathering
    vs. interpretive data gathering, 108
    See also Data gathering
Criterial thinking, 15–16, 169
    cultural context, 283–284
    defined, 2
    observation schedules, 142
    probative inference, 176
    responsive *vs.* standards-based
        evaluation, xiv, xv, 6, 57, 90, 90*n.*
        2, 164
Critical review procedures, 163
Critical studies evaluation, 46, 81,
    226–227
Critical thinking, in responsive
    evaluation, 94
Cronbach, Lee, xi, xii, 64, 74, 101, 108,
    173, 175, 198, 230, 246, 250–251,
    272, 278
CSSE (Case Studies in Science
    Education), 139, 140–142*fig.*
Cultural conflict, 20, 253
Cultural context, of program
    evaluation, 86
    cultural sensitivity issue, 266

domination, empowerment, 283
experience as knowledge, 95
of program evaluation, 280–284
weighting of standards, 283
*Custom and Cherishing: The Arts in
American Elementary Schools*
(Stake, Bresler and Mabry), 305
Cutting scores, 8, 13, 61, 72, 164, 188

Darling-Hammond, Linda, 112, 276
Darwin, Charles, 165
Data Categories, Flanders Interaction
Analysis, 143*fig.*
Data gathering, data sources, 78, 95, 188
analysis, 82
antecedents, transactions, outcomes,
109, 109*fig.*
bias, 254, 255
choosing data sources, 110–111
asking those who know, 110–111
cooperation factor, 111
confidentiality, 206
Countenance Matrix, 109–110, 109*fig.*
criterial *vs.* interpretive, 108
data coding and records processing,
129–136
aggregative *vs.* interpretive data,
129–130
coding, defined, 130
elaborate categories of coded
observation, 130, 131–132*fig.*
evaluation project logs,
107–108*fig.*, 133, 165, 166*fig.*
interpretations, 130
note taking, 133, 134–136*fig.*
evaluation evolution, 88
histories and artifacts, 155–157
activity, context of program,
156–157
documentation search, 156
ethnographers, cultural
anthropologists, 157
program history, 155
instrumentation
indicator variables, 112–113,
112*n. 1*
validity of variables, 113, 113*n. 2*

interviewing
casual *vs.* structured, 148
description of experience, 147
interpretive, 148–149
of parents about art teachers,
149, 153–155, 153–156*fig.*,
153*n. 8*
quotations, 149
skill improvement, 149
tape recording, 149, 150–152*fig.*
uses of, 146–147
vs. issue statements, 102
narrative regarding, 157–158
observation schedules, 142–143, 143*n. 6*
Classroom Observation Report,
144–145, 145*fig.*
classroom social processes,
143–144
Flanders Interaction Analysis,
143–144, 143*fig.*
site visitation team summaries,
144, 146, 147–148*fig.*
outcomes, 109*fig.*, 110
participatory evaluation, 193
quality
of the evaluand, 109
search for, 108–109
recipient responses, 113–123
changes over time measures,
122–123, 123*fig.*
conference feedback evaluation
sheet, 113–114, 115–116*fig.*,
117, 118–120*fig.*
Design of Comparative
Experiments example, 114
item sampling, 120, 122, 122*n. 3*
staff and management responses,
123–126
directors, problems with, 123
identifying with evaluand, 124
informal conversations, 124
response from everyone, 124
school testing survey example,
125, 125*n. 5*, 126*fig.*
written notes, 124
stakeholder and public responses,
126–129

multiple questions, 127, 129
Youth Network News example,
    127, 128*fig.*
surveys, 137–142
    costliness of, 137
    return rate factors, 138
    simple questions issue, 138–139
    situational questionnaire example,
        139, 140–142*fig.*
    transactions, 109–110, 109*fig.*
    types of, 109*fig.*
    validity issues, 83
Data sources. *See* Data gathering, data
    sources
Datta, Lois-ellin, 182
Davis, R., 182, 204, 235, 240
Day, M, 162*fig.*
Decision-based evaluation, 38
Democratic evaluation, 199
    accountability, 197
    Cambridge manifesto precursor to,
        200–201, 201*n. 11*
    case study method, 200*nn. 9, 10,*
        200–201
    contextual factors, 281
    evaluator disposition, 30
    evaluator factor, 201, 202, 283
    social action, 43, 44–46, 99, 201–202
    standards, 283
    status quo challenged, 199–200
Demographics, 41, 114, 142
Denzin, Norman, 184
Denny, T., 78, 144, 149
Design of Comparative Experiments,
    114, 115–116*fig.*
Designs. *See* Evaluation designs
DeStefano, L., 64, 204, 231
Dewey, John, 5
Dialectic
    criterial and interpretive thinking, 94
    critical and episodic thinking, 15–16
    defined, 256
    serving stakeholders, 196
Diary project, 166*fig.*
Discrepancy evaluation, 35
Discrimination, 229*n. 6,* 231, 235
Dispositions of evaluators

bias, 59, 175, 176
    defined, 29
    evaluator preferences, 30–31, 35, 38,
        39, 43–44, 46, 224, 254
    goal-free evaluation and, 35
Diversity
    evaluating merit and worth, 19, 93,
        235, 256
    of evaluator, 19
    in meta-evaluation, 255
Duguid, P., 129, 240
Dunne, J., xxvii, xxxi
Dwyer, Dave, 100*n. 8*

Earl, Lorna, 202
Easley, Jack, 64, 83, 101, 102, 139,
    174, 305
Ecker, Larry, 162*fig.,* 164*n. 3*
Eder, R. W., 276
Edison, Thomas, 247
Eisner, Elliot, 7, 101, 162*fig.*
Eliot, T. S., 104
Empowerment evaluation, 38, 46
Episodic thinking, 15–16
Epistomology
    constructivism, 49
    defined, 170
    of goodness concept, 170, 170*n. 5*
    perception of quality, 6
    as study of knowledge, 47, 172, 179
Equal opportunity for children
    customizing equals discrimination, 235
    fairness doctrine concept, 233
    learning differences, 232–233
    performance and progress
        comparisons, 233, 234
    purposes of education, 232, 232*n. 9,*
        234*fig.*
    rising to potential concept, 232,
        232*n. 8*
    separate and equal impossibility,
        233, 235
    skills identification, 232
Ethical issues
    assessment, complete and fair, 191, 268
    balancing competing principles,
        262–263

bias, 100n. 9, 226, 256
confidentiality and anonymity, 102,
    206, 268–270, 279n. 2
conflict of interest, 266
contract standards, 207fig.
cultural sensitivity, 266
evaluation as discerning good, 260
fiscal responsibility, 266
full disclosure standard, 187, 190,
    264, 266
human subjects protection, 266,
    267–268
in indicator systems, 191
meta-evaluation, 187
personal standards, 263–265
political and cultural contexts,
    278–284
professional standards, 265–267,
    265n. 1
quality work is ethical work, 261–265
resources allocation, expenditure, 206
service obligation, 190
See also Business of evaluation;
    Personnel evaluation; Political
    context, of program evaluation;
    Product evaluation
Ethnography, 123
evaluation aid, xiv, 95, 157
evaluation disposition, 30
participant observation, 22n. 9
EVALTALK, 53, 271
Evaluand
contract negotiation, 203–206,
    205–206fig.
defined, 4–5
representations of, 212–213
in ultization-focused evaluation, 197
Evaluating the Arts in Education
    (Stake), 305
Evaluating with Validity (House), 52
Evaluation, 24–26
Countenance model of, 4n. 1
criterial thinking, 15–16
episodic thinking, 16
evaluand
    defined, 4–5, 19–20
    role of, 18–19
evaluator, 19–20
    culture context, 20–22, 22n. 9
    diversity, 19
    meta-evaluation concept, 23
    mistakes made by, 22–23
    program understanding, 21–22,
        21n. 8
    rewards to, 23
    technical expertise, 22
formal vs. informal, 1–2
formative and summative evaluation,
    17–18, 24–26
function of, 32–33
history of, 42, 74–78, 95, 101–102,
    262–267, 278
investigative reason, 248, 285
knowledge and, 1, 16
merit determination, 16–17
political, cultural contexts, 278–284
quality
    search for, 3–7, 4n. 1, 6n. 3
quality concept, 5–7, 285
    epistemological perception of, 6
    as goodness, merit, worth, 5–6, 6n. 3
    human experience origin of, 6–7
    as nature of something, 5
roles and styles of, 16–17, 32–33
Scripture quotes, 1
situational nature of, xiv
stakeholders, 4, 4n. 2
standards
    acompensatory weighted score
        model, 14
    amultiple cutoff weighted score
        model, 14–15
    beginning and end comparison
        design, 13–14
    control group design, 13
    vs. criteria, 5–6, 6fig., 24–25
    criterial cutting scores, 13
    definition of, 5, 13
    explanation of, 7
    as expressive objectives, 7–8, 7n. 4
    ideal standard, 8, 13
    performance measurement
        compared to, 14–15, 14n. 5,
        15n. 6

previous group comparison
design, 13
for product comparisons, 8,
9–12*table*
setting of, 5
teachers reading English, example, 7
stimulus error, 18, 105*n. 12*, 283
See also Business of evaluation;
Criterial-based evaluation;
Dispositions of evaluators;
Ethical issues; Evidence-based
evaluation; Goal-based evaluation;
Interpretive-based evaluation;
Models of evaluation;
Participatory evaluation;
Personnel evaluation; Product
evaluation; Responsive evaluation;
Roles of evaluation; Social
science-based evaluation;
Standards-based evaluation;
Theory-based evaluation;
Utilization-based evaluation
Evaluation designs, examples, vii-viii
Evaluation Models: Viewpoints on
*Educational and Human Services
Evaluation* (Stufflebeam, et al.), 52
Evaluation Network, xii
Evaluation research, 42–43, 250–253
Evaluation Research Society, xii, 262
Evaluation Thesaurus (Scriven), 224, 276
Evaluators
contract negotiation, 203–206,
205–206*fig.*
dispositions of, 30–31, 224, 254
report writing, 206–220
reporting styles, 211–212
Evidence-based evaluation
bias
advocacies of evaluators, 253–254
control *vs.* removal of, 254–255
reflective practitioner, 255
dialectic, defined, 256
generalizations
investigative reason, 248
naturalistic generalizations, 248
propositional generalizations, 248
narrative regarding, 256–257

policy evaluation, 250–253, 250*n. 3*
attribution, defined, 251
bias control by randomization,
250–251, 253
generalizations, grand *vs.* small,
251–252, 252*n. 4*
generalizations, grand *vs.* small,
248–249
standards-based evaluation, 252
research
defined, 246
vs. science, 246–247
science, defined, 246
science
generalizations search, 247,
247*n. 1*
interpretation of evidence, 246–247
standards-based evaluations, 248–249
scientific principles, 245
skepticism as commitment, 255–256
Experience-oriented evaluation, xi
Experiential inferences
of audience, 175–176
least reliance on judgment, 176
naturalistic generalization, 175, 176
vicarious experiences, 175
Experimental disposition, 30
Experimental studies, 43
Explanation and Understanding (von
Wright), xvi
Explication
attribution, 177, 177*n. 10*
bias and, 60
in evaluation, 50, 170, 286
explicit criteria, 6, 282
goals of evaluation, 58
limitations of, 177–179, 177*n. 8*,
177*n. 9*
of standards of merit, xv, 14*n. 5*
Expressive objectives, 7–8, 7*n. 4*

Face validity, 222
Factors, of programs, xix, 160
analysis, 160
definition of, 58, 58*n. 1*, 64*n. 2*,
61–62*fig.*
democratic evaluation contexts, 281

formative evaluation, 63
  as phases, 62, 62*n. 3*, 63*fig.*
socioeconomic factors, student
    learning, 275
standards, 195
standards-based evaluation, xv, 6,
    60–64, 195, 211
  definition of, 60*n. 2*, 61–62*fig.*
  as phases, 62, 62*n. 3*, 63*fig.*
  synthesis context, 174–176
Fairness issue, 100*n. 9*
  differentiation reference, 229*n. 6*
  equal opportunity for children,
    232–235
      customizing equals
        discrimination, 235
      fairness doctrine concept, 233
      learning differences, 232–233
      performance and progress com-
        parisons, 233, 235
      purposes of education, 233, 233*n.
        9*, 234*fig.*
      rising to potential concept, 232,
        232*n. 8*
      separate and equal impossibility,
        233, 235
      skills identification, 232
    giving special consideration, 229
    meritocracy, 229, 230–231
    personnel evaluation, 272
False negatives, 163*n. 4*
False positives, 163*n. 4*
Fay, B., xxiv
Feasibility, program evaluation
    standard, 265
Federal Education Bill (U.S.), 249
Ferris, G. R., 276
Fetterman, David, 46, 202
Fiscal responsibility, 266
Fitzgibbon, Carol, 191
Flanders, N. A., 143*fig.*
Flanders Interaction Analysis, 143*fig.*
Flick, U., 182
Focus groups, 155
Formative evaluation, 17–18, 24–26
  factors, 62
  organizing and reporting, responsive
    evaluation, 101

Foucault's methods, xxiv
Foundations of Program Evaluation
    (Shadish, et al.), 51
Fournier, Deborah, 170
Fowles, John, 215
Freud, Sigmund, 28
Full disclosure standard, 264

Gadamer, H. G., xxviii
Gagné, Robert, 240
Galileo, xii
Gender-equity program, standards-based
    evaluation, 55–56*fig.*
Generalizations, xvii
  generalization studies, 42–43
  investigative reason, 248
  naturalistic generalizations, 248
  policy evaluation, 248–249, 251–252,
    252*n. 4*
  program analysis, 163
  propositional generalizations, 248
  search for, 247, 247*n. 1*
  See also Naturalistic generalization;
    Propositional generalizations
Geoffrey, W., 95
Gettysburg Address, from (Lincoln), 27
Gierl, M. J., 130
Gilborn, David, 230*n. 7*
Gjerde, Craig, 122
Glass, Gene, 114, 246
Gleser, Goldene, 230, 272
Goal attainment evaluation, 33–35,
    33*n. 3*
  client, defined, 34
  goal-free evaluation concept, 35,
    35*n. 4*, 177*n. 9*
  independence of evaluator, 34–35
  Input and process goals, 35
  outcome data, 35, 35*n. 5*
  priorities negotiation, 34
  sponsor and staff goals, 34
  stakeholder goals, 34
  unstated goals, 34
Goal-based evaluation, 33
Goal-free evaluation, 35, 35*n. 4*, 124,
    177*n. 9*
Goals of program evaluation, 71–76
  behavioral objectives, 72, 73–74*fig.*

CET Programme, 71–72
conceptual organizers, 72, 72*n. 6*, 74
goal-free evaluation, 76, 177*n. 9*
transformation of, 75, 76*fig.*
UTOS version of, 75, 75*n. 7*
Gone native concept, 123
Good, goodness
epistomology of goodness concept,
170–171, 170*n. 5*
evaluation discerning of good, 1, 89,
92, 99, 109, 112, 218, 245, 260
as merit, worth, 5–6, 6*n. 3*
program costs *vs.*, 77
quality search, 285
Goodness grief concept, 170*n. 5*
Gowin, Robert, 224*n. 4*
Grasso, Patrick, 182
Greene, J., xviii, 47, 95, 101, 197, 202
Gross, Terry, 149
Gruber, H. E., 165
Grutsch, Markus, 46
Guba, Egon, 101, 177*n. 8*
Gubrium, J. F., xxiv
Guiding Principles (American Evaluation
Association), 193
Gullickson, Arlen, 37, 146, 174

Habermas, J., xxvi, xxvii, 192, 197
Halberstam, D., 42, 112
Hallinger, P., 125*n. 5*
Hamilton, David, 101, 200, 225
Handbook of Qualitative Research
(House), 278
Haney, W., 240
Hannum, W. H., 239
Harding, S., 281
Harnisch, D., 204, 231
Harris, M., 281
Hastings, Thomas, xi, 198, 228
Havel, Vaclav, ix, x, x*fig.*
HCP (Humanities Curriculum Project),
200, 200*n. 8*
Heck, D., 235
Heck, R. H., 125*n. 5*
Herman, J. L., 164
Hill, Jacquetta, 162*fig.*
Hodder, I., 157
Hoke, G., 78, 149, 235

Hoke, Gordon, 144
Holistic quality, 8, 276
qualitative evaluation, 2
See also Roles of evaluation, holistic
quality search
Holstein, J. A., xxiv
Hooper, R., 72
Hopkins, Ken, 114
House, Ernest, 45, 50, 52, 101, 144, 199,
201–202, 213, 218, 250, 252*n. 4*, 278
Howe, K., 202
Huberman, Michael, 102*n. 10*,
130, 132*fig.*
Hudson, Lisa, 112
Human subjects protection, 266,
267–268
Humanities Curriculum Project (HCP),
200, 200*n. 8*
Hummel-Rossi, Barbara, 78
Hypotheses, 72*n. 6*, 185, 246, 247, 285
analysis testing of, 160
issues *vs.*, 89
ruling out rival hypotheses, 185

Ice cream brand comparisons, *Consumer
Reports,* 9–12*table*
Illinois Gifted Education Program,
144–145, 145*fig.*, 209–210*fig.*
Illuminitive disposition of evaluator, 30
Impact evaluation, 35
Implicit standard, 14, 66, 84, 110
Indebro, A., 201*n. 7*
Independent evaluation, 34–35
Indiana Gifted and Talented Education
Program, 77–78, 79–80*fig.*
Indianapolis elementary schools, viii
Indicators
client well-being, 191
in criterial, interpretive thinking, 169
data gathering, 112–113, 112*n. 1*
in standards-based evaluation,
252, 270
Inferences, 174–179, 177*n. 10*
statistical inference testing, 188
See also Experiential inferences;
Probative inferences
Informal evaluation, 1–2
Ingvarson, L., 172

Institute for Nutrition of Central
America and Panama (INCAP), 75
Institute of Educational Sciences, 249
Institution Review Boards, 267–268
Institutional accreditation, 38
self-study report, 198–199, 199*n. 6*
Instructional Information Exchange,
73–74*fig.*
Instrumentalist evaluation, 35
Instrumentation. *See* Data gathering
Integrative research review, xxiv
Internal evaluator, 17, 20, 22, 124, 177,
177*n. 10*, 187
*International Handbook of Educational
Evaluation* (Bhola), 224
International studies, xiv
Interpretive-based evaluation, xi, 39
case study method, 200
explanation of, xv
"Meta-Analysis and Everyday Life:
The Good, the Bad, and the
Ugly" (Schwandt), xxii–xxxii,
xxii*n. 3*
standards, implicitness of, 58
See also Interpretive data; Interpretive
thinking; Issues needing
interpretation; Responsive
evaluation
Interpretive data, 82
vs. aggregative data, 129–130
vs. criterial data, 108
See also Interpretive-based evaluation;
Interpretive thinking; Issues
needing interpretation
Interpretive thinking, 2, 57, 169
vs. criterial thinking, xiv–xvi
cultural context, 283–284
limitations of, 82–85
in responsive evaluation, 90, 90*n. 2*, 94
See also Interpretive-based evaluation;
Interpretive data; Issues needing
interpretation
Interviewing, 96–98, 97–98*fig.*
See also Data gathering
Intuitive thinking, 97–98*fig.*
cultural context, 284
examples of, 65–66

investigative reasoning, 247–248
responsive evaluation, 101
Investigative reason
in evaluation, 248, 285
issues needing interpretation, 224
responsive evaluation, xii
Irwin-Sweeny-Miller Foundation, 192
Issues
competition, conflict, 192, 192*n. 1*
conceptual structure of, 89–90
examples of, 162*fig.*
review of, 165
Issues needing interpretation
blackboard layout for, 224*nn. 3, 4,*
224–225, 225*fig.*, 229*fig.*, 242
complexity
context, 226
critical study issues, 226–227
evaluator views, 226
investigative inquiry evolution, 224,
224*n. 2*
investigative reason, 224
issue origination, 225–226
narrative regarding, 242–244
differentiation reference, 229*n. 6*
equal opportunity for children,
232–235
giving special consideration, 229
meritocracy, 229, 230–231
program standardization issue,
227–228
benefits, limitations of, 227–228
blackboard layout for, 225*fig.*,
229*fig.*
examples of, 227
meta-evaluation, 228
stimulus error, 228
staff development issue
importance of, 235–236
personal *vs.* management
responsibility, 235
training assessment, 240–242
training content, 237–239
training strategies, 239–240
Veterans Benefits Administration
example, 236
topic collaboration step, 224

topic identification step, 224n. 2
topic research step, 224
wrangle, defined, 224
wrangling, 223–224, 223n. 1
Item sampling, 117, 120, 122, 122n. 3

Jaeger, Richard, 4, 124n. 3
Jenkins, D., 200
Johnassen, D. H., 239
Johnson, David, 239
Johnson, Roger, 239
Johnson (L.) administration, 42
Joint Committee on Standards for
    Educational Evaluations, 43, 58n. 1,
    62, 180, 207fig., 264, 265, 272
Joint Standards, 58n. 1, 62, 182, 206, 207fig.
    Program Evaluation Standards,
        264, 265
    Propriety for Evaluators, 265–266
Judgment, x
Judicial disposition of evaluator, 30
Jung, Karl, 216
Juvenile delinquency program evaluation
    critical factors, xix
    effects, xx–xxi
    generalizability, xix–xx
    variables, xix

Ke Aka Ho'ona WMU evaluation, viii
Keiser, N., 37
Kellaghan, T., 177n. 8, 275
Kelligan, Thomas, 29n. 2, 52
Kemmis, S., 28n. 1, 101, 192, 193, 197
Kennedy, M., 115, 120
Kerins, T., 144
Kidder, Tracy, 162fig.
Kilpatrick, J., 42
King, C., 200
King, Jean, 194, 197
Kinochloe, J. L., 226n. 5
Klein, Robert, 75
Knowledge, 1
Knox, Alan, 114, 239
Koretz, D., 164
Kramer, Jane, 49
Kuhn, Thomas, 253
Kushner, Saville, 38, 46, 102

LaPan, Steve, 144
Laxness, Halldór, 31
Legitimation role of evaluation, 33,
    50–51, 99, 200, 203
Lehmann, I. J., 181n. 13
Lemann, N., 216, 235
Letters of recommendation, 275n.5
Levin, Henry, 78
Leviton, L., 51, 63, 99n. 7
Lichtenstein, S., 117
Lifeworld concept, 192–193, 197
Lincoln, Abraham, 27
Lincoln, Yvonna, xv, 94, 101
Linn, R. L., 164
Linnaeus, Carolus, 104, 104n. 11
Lipsey, Mark W., xvi–xxiii, xvin. 1, xxiiin.
    3, 42, 221, 252, 253, 285
Little, J. W., 48n. 8
Logic-model evaluation, 35
Logic of evaluation, 170
Logs
    coding and records processing,
        107–108fig., 133, 165, 166fig.
Lorenz, F., 37, 146
Losing Ground (Murray), 181

Mabry, Linda, 47, 102, 153n. 8, 182, 187,
    200n. 8, 240, 262, 305
MacDonald, Barry, 45, 72, 101, 102, 133,
    134–136fig., 200, 200n. 8, 201–202,
    202, 213n. 13, 255
MacNamara, Robert, 42
Madaus, George, 29n. 2, 52, 177n. 8,
    228, 275
Marton, Ference, 102n. 10
Mastery learning training concept, 240
Mathison, Sandra, xv, 94
McDonnell, L. M., 112
McEwan, P. J., 78
McKee, A., 58, 59, 102, 200n. 8
McKnight, C. C., 275
McLaren, P., 226n. 5
McLaughlin, M. W., 199
McLean, Leslie, 127
McLeod, D. B., 130
McTaggart, R., 28n. 1
McWilliams, Joyce, 181

Measurements-oriented evaluation, xi
Mehrens, W. A., 181*n. 13*
Mellissinos, M., 13
Member check
   interviewing, 149
   meta-evaluation, 23, 186–187, 255
   validity issues, standards-based
      evaluation, 83
   See also Meta-evaluation
Meritocracy
   fairness, unfairness in, 229, 230
   genetics and intelligence, 230
   role of chance, 230
   selection *vs.* placement, 230–231
   social class, 230
Mertens, Donna, xv, 94
Messick, Sam, 176
Meta-analysis, xvi, xxiii, 285
"Meta-Analysis and Everyday Life: The
   Good, the Bad, and the Ugly"
   (Schwandt), xxiii–xxxii, xxiii*n. 1*,
   xxiii*n. 3*
"Meta-Analysis and the Learning Curve
   in Evaluation Practice" (Lipsey),
   xvi–xxxiii, xvi*n. 1,* xvi*n. 2* Schwandt
   response to, xxiii–xxxii, xxiii*n. 3*
Meta-evaluation
   in analysis, 163
   bias control, 255
   case example, 37, 39, 222
   cultural context, 284
   data validity, 216
   defined, 23, 180
   ethical issues, 187
   how evaluation was conducted,
      180–181
   improving confidence, 180
   Joint Standards example, 181
   member check, 23, 28, 36, 63, 113,
      186–187, 216, 224, 228, 255,
      284, 286
   narrative, 188–189
   process standards, 180
   in program standardization, 228
   project logs, 133
   quality assurance, defined, 186
   quality control, 186–187
   questions to guide, 182, 183*fig.*
   reflection, 186–187, 186*n. 15*
   reliability, 180
   responsive evaluation, 181
   skepticism as commitment, 255–256
   stakeholder-oriented, xi–xii, 181
   test validity estimation, 180, 181*nn.*
      12, 13
   of training, reports example, ix
   triangulation, 182–186, 183*n. 14*
   Veterans Benefits Administration,
      writing, 182
   web index report, 39, 146*n. 7,* 182
Metamorphosis, 180
Metcalf, Stephen, 47*n. 6*
Methods statement, examples, viii
Michael, N., 117
Middle School Technical Education,
   methods example, viii
Migotsky, Chris, 37, 95
Miles, Matthew, 130
Millman, Jason, 114
Milwaukee Alternative Teacher Training
   CIRCE evaluation, 172
   proposals example, vii
Mixed methods concept, 94
Models of evaluation
   alternative approaches, 29
   CIPP Model, 29, 29*n. 2,* 177*n. 8*
   Countenance Model, 30
   defined, 28–29
   experimental model, 29
   Responsive Model, 30
Modus operandi, 92, 101
Moffitt, John, 146
Monsen, L., 199*n. 7*
Morgan, Laura, 97
Moynihan, Daniel Patrick, 159
Multiple cutoff model, 14, 174
Murray, Charles, 113, 181
Myers, Isabel, 216

Names and labels
   data-gathering procedures, 216
   explanations of meaning, 213, 215
   technical terms, 215
   validity issues, 216

Narratives, 86–88, 101, 175
National Board of Professional teaching
    Standards, 275
National Council of Teachers of
    Mathematics (NCTM), 130,
    131–132fig., 263
National Development Programme in
    Computer Assisted Learning
    (U.K.), 71–72
National Institute of Education, 181
National Institute of Standards and
    Technology, 58
National Research Council, 249–250
National Science Foundation, 139
    Advanced Technology Education
        program, 146, 146n. 7,
        147–148fig.
    organizational development
        evaluation, 37
    situational questionnaire, 140–142fig.
    Sputnik evaluation study, 42
    User-Friendly Handbook for Project
        Evaluation, 225
National Youth Sports Program
    evaluation study, xvii, 204, 204n.
    12, 205–206fig., 231
Native, to go, 123
Naturalistic evaluation, 30
Naturalistic generalization
    defined, 174
    evaluator disposition, 39
    as grounds for action taken, 174,
        175n. 7
    vs. propositional generalization, 248
    responsive evaluation and, 102, 211
    standards-based evaluation, 248
NCTM (National Council of Teachers of
    Mathematics), 130, 131–132fig.
Negotiation
    client and evaluator contract,
        190–191, 203–206, 268, 269–270
    in goal attainment evaluation, 34
    issues, evaluation design, 195–196,
        202, 211
    renegotiation, 205–206fig.
    responsive evaluation procedures, 34
    standards regarding, 207fig., 266

Nevo, David, 199, 240
New York State public school
    mathematics standards, 70
Newman, D., 262
Newman, D. L., 193, 197n. 3, 265
Newmann, F. M., 48n. 8, 240
Niemi, Hannele, 197
Noel-Levitz Student Satisfaction
    Inventory, 261
Nomological explanation, xxiv
Note taking, 133, 134–136fig.
Nowakowski, Jeri, 43
Nyberg, D., 194, 275n. 5

Oakes, J., 112
Oakes, Jeannie, 270
Objectives, 72
    See also Goal-based evaluation; Goals
        of program evaluation; Roles of
        evaluation
Objectivity
    in analysis, synthesis, 180
    importance of, 2, 42, 52, 95
    lack of and bias, 59–60, 189
Observation schedules. See Data gathering
Opportunity costs, 76
Organization self-study, 38
Organizational development, 125n. 5
    evaluation conceptual organization,
        24, 72–73, 72n. 6, 89–90, 109,
        226, 228
    evaluation role of, 32, 38, 235
    See also Roles of evaluation,
        organizational development
Ory, J. C., 276
O'Shea, Joe, 74
Outcome data, outcome evaluation, 35,
    35n. 5, 109, 109fig.

Page, Ellis, 42
Panels. See Blue ribbon panels
Parlett, Malcolm, 101, 202, 225
Participatory evaluation, 198
    action research, 193n. 2, 194
    advocacy, 198
    democratic evaluation, 199–203,
        199n7, 200nn. 8–10, 201n. 11

vs. democratic evaluation, 45–47,
    101, 206
evaluator goal, 44
external, 193
factors of evaluation, 195
institutional accreditation, 198–199,
    198*n. 6*
organizational benefits
    maximization, 20
participant critique, 114,
    115–116*fig.*, 246
school-based evaluation, 199, 199*n. 7*
self-study, 193, 194, 221
by stakeholders, 202
See also Utilization-based evaluation
Participatory observation, 22*n. 9*, 46
Particularity
    of evaluand, 251, 286
    vs. generalizability, 174, 248
    of issues, 93, 263
    uniqueness, xxiv, 186
Pasteur, Louis, 247
Patterns
    examples of, 162*fig.*
    recognition of, 162, 162*n. 3*
Patton, Michael, 38, 52*n. 9*, 199, 202
Payne, D. A., 181*n. 13*
Performance representation, 78, 81–82,
    117, 129, 138, 212–213
    aggregative *vs.* interpretive
        analysis, 82
    asking questions, 78, 81–82
    descriptive analysis, 82
    performance measurement, 170
    statistical inference, 82
    See also Personnel evaluation; Staff
        development
Persig, Robert, 6*n. 3*, 108–109
Personalistic evaluation, 46
Personnel evaluation, 8, 272–276, 273*n.*
    3, 274*n. 4*, 275*n. 5*, 277
    assignment focus, 272
    correlates as criteria, 272–274, 273*n.*
        3, 274*n. 4*
    letters of recommendation, 275*n.5*
    performance focus, 275, 275*n.5*
    selection focus, 272

standards-based, 272
teachers, student performance, 275
Peshkin, Alan, 95
Phronesis, xxix
Piontek, Mary, 44
Placement decisions, 230–231
*Planning Ethically Responsible Research: A
    Guide for Students and Internal
    Review Boards* (Sieber), 273*n. 1*
Platt, William, 235
Pohland, Paul, 102
Policy evaluation, 250–253, 250*n. 3*
    advocacy, 198
    attribution, defined, 251
    bias control by randomization,
        250–251, 253
    control group concept, 92*n. 5*
    as evidence-based evaluation, 42–43,
        250–251, 250*n. 3*
    generalizations, grand *vs.* small,
        248–249, 251–252, 252*n. 4*
    standards-based evaluation, 252
    See also Business of evaluation
Political context, of program evaluation,
    50–51, 278–280, 280*fig.*
    change *vs.* status quo, 279
    education advocacy, 47, 47*n. 6*
    ethical issues and, 190
    stakeholder issues, 99
Popham, James, 72, 163
Popham, W. J., 7
Portrayals
    of case example, 86–88
    of evaluand, 38, 41, 95–96, 175,
        200, 213
    full disclosure, 186
    meta-evaluation, 180, 256
    unbiased, x
Possible Bias in Committee Work,
    RELS, vii
Practical knowing, experience as
    knowledge, xxviii, 6, 95–99
    case study method, 96
    empirical study of human activity, 86,
        98, 103–104
    instrumentation of reform,
        99–100, 99*n. 7*

vs. open-ended questionnaire, 97–98*fig.*, 98
vs. pre-ordinate evaluation, 95, 95*n. 6*
subjective data, 96, 98
Praxis, xxviii, 93
Pre-ordinate evaluation, 95, 95*n. 6*
Preskill, Hallie, 44
Prime facie case, 176, 181, 187
Principal's Interview, ix
Pring, R., 247
Probative inferences, 175–179
    attribution, 177, 177*n. 10*
    bias minimization, 176
    criterial evaluation, 175–176
    explication, 177, 177*n. 8*
    prima facie case, 176
Probing, holistic quality search, 38–43
Process data evaluation, 110
Product evaluation, 8, 9–12*fig.*, 42–43, 276–278
    criterial approach to, 277
    Key Evaluation Checklist for, 276–277
Professional development. *See* Staff development
Professional standards, 50
Program costs
    defined, 61–62
    importance of, 76–78
Program standardization. *See* Standardization issue
Progressive focusing, 90, 225
Project management/evaluation diary example, 166*fig.*
Proposals, examples, vii
Propositional generalizations, 250
Proppé, Olafur, 43, 199, 258
Propriety, 265–266
    bias and, 254
    complexity, 226
    report writing, 220
Psychometrics, 229*n. 6*, 278
Purposive evaluation, 35

Qualitative evaluation, 5
    See also Interpretive-based evaluation
Quality, 5–7
    epistemological perception of, 6

as goodness, merit, worth, 5–6, 6*n. 3*
human experience origin of, 6–7
as nature of something, 5
search for, 3–7, 4*n. 1, 6n. 3*, 294
Quality assurance, 186–188
    standardization, 234
Quality representation, 161, 161*fig.*, 161*n. 2*
    See also Roles of evaluation, holistic quality search
Quantitative evaluation. *See* Standards-based evaluation
Questionnaire, survey, 55–56*fig.*, 79–80*fig.*, 94–95, 97–98*fig.*, 98, 137–138, 140–142*fig.*
Quieting Reform (Stake), 181, 305

Ragin, C. C., 200*n. 8*
Rallis, S. F., 94
Randomization, 29, 250–251
    meritocracy and, 230
    in meta-evaluation, 181
    of patterns, 162
    in standards-based evaluation, 24, 75*n. 7*, 212
Raths, J., 78
Rational thinking, 43–44, 50, 58–59, 171–172*fig.*
    Darwin, Bacon, 165
Raven, J., 240
Readers
    names and labels, 211, 215–218
    system *vs.* lifeworld concepts, 192–193
    See also Clients
Recipient needs, defined, 61
Records processing. *See* Data gathering
Reflective practitioner, 186–187, 186*n. 15*, 255
    cultural context, 284
    ethical deliberation, 262
The Reflective Practitioner (Schön), 185
Regression-equation evaluation, 35
Reichardt, C. S., xv, 75*n. 7*, 94
Reliability, 181
Remediation, 49
Reports

evaluand representations, 212–213,
  214*fig.*
evaluation feedback, 213
names and labels, 213, 215–216
styles of reporting, 211–212
Web appendix examples, vii–viii
writing of, 159, 159*n. 1,* 206–210
  confidentiality, 210
  contract fulfillment detail, 210
  costs, 208, 209–210*fig.,* 210
  criticism strength, 218–219
  narrative, 220–222
  offering recommendations, 219–220
  See also Analysis; Meta-evaluation;
    Synthesis
Representation of quality, 161, 161*fig.,*
  161*n. 2*
  See also Roles of evaluation, holistic
    quality search
Research
  defined, 246
  generalization research, 42–43
  See also Evaluation research;
    Evidence-based evaluation
The Research Act (Denzin), 182–184
Responsive evaluation, xii, 39, 305
  activity, context of program, 156–157
  analysis, 160–161
  coding interpretation, 130
  evaluand representations, 212–213,
    214*fig.*
  example of, 86–88
  experience as knowledge, 95–99
    case study method, 96
    empirical study of human activity,
      98, 104
    instrumentation of reform,
      99–100, 99*n. 7*
    vs. open-ended questionnaire,
      97–98*fig.,* 98
    vs. pre-ordinate evaluation, 95,
      95*n. 6*
    subjective data, 96, 98
  explanation of, xiv, xvi, 86–88
  final report, 213
  generalizations, small, 252, 252*n. 4*
  interpretation factor, 6

investigative reason, xii
issues as conceptual structure, 89–90
  examples of, 89
  issues, defined, 89
  power of negative thinking
    concept, 90
  limitations of, 91, 105–106
  meta-evaluation, 181
  multiple sources, grounds for
    valuing, 93
  narrative regarding, 105–107
  naturalistic generalization, 102, 248
  observations and judgments,
    90–92, 178
    control group concept,
      91–92, 92*n. 5*
    criterial *vs.* interpretive thinking,
      90, 90*n. 2*
    vs. scientific evaluation, 91, 91*n. 4*
  organizing and reporting, 100–102
    coding system, 100, 100*n. 8*
    fairness as an issue, 100, 100*n. 9*
    feedback format, language, 100–101
    formal program monitoring, 101
    historic influences, 101–102,
      102*n. 10*
    stakeholder concerns focus, 101
    subjective focus, 101
  perceptions, 92–95
  personal interpretation, 86, 88–89
  vs. pre-ordinate evaluation, 95, 95*n. 6*
  procedures, 102–104, 103*fig.*
    data sources and types, 102–103
    issue statements, 102
    language, 104, 104*n. 11*
    stimulus error, 103
  program history, 155–156
  sampling, 88
  stakeholders *vs.* audience, 196
  standards-based evaluation
    with, 94–95
    critical and interpretive
      thinking, 94
    "here and now" methods, 94
    mixed methods concept, 94
  stimulus error, 105*n. 12,* 283
  styles of reporting, 211

synthesis, 178–179
understanding focus of, 89, 89*n. 1*
    mixed with judgment, 90
    See also Ethical issues
Responsive Model of evaluation, 30
Reston, James, 190
Restructuring (Stake, et al.), 48
Return rate factors, 138
Review panels, 23, 99–100, 174, 240
Ridings, Jeri, 43
Rog, D. J., 195
Rogers, Patricia, 198
Roles of evaluation
    action research, 27–29, 28*n. 1*, 38, 186
    advocacy, 47–50
        case example, 48–49
        education politics, 47, 47*n. 6*
        for program participants, 47
        shortcomings downplay, 49
    data collection only, 31–32
    defined, 28
    goal attainment evaluation, 33–35,
        33*n. 3*
        client, defined, 34
        goal-free evaluation concept, 35,
            35*n. 4*, 177*n. 9*
        independence of evaluator, 34–35
        Input and process goals, 35
        outcome data, 35, 35*n. 5*
        priorities negotiation, 34
        sponsor and staff goals, 34
        stakeholder goals, 34
        unstated goals, 34
    holistic quality search, 38–42
        contextual focus of, 39
        human qualities focus, 38
        qualitative, subjective
            measurements, 41, 42
        telephone interview of veterans,
            40–41*fig.*
        types of, 39
        variability focus, 41
        Veterans Administration case
            example, 38–39
    legitimation and protection, 50–51
        funding focus, 50
        professional standards, 50

social and political context, 50–51
organizational development, 35–38
    case example, 37
    frequency issue, 36
    functional improvement, 38
    internal operation focus, 36–37, 38
    types of, 38
policy and generalization studies,
    42–43
social action, aid to
    communication focus, 43–44
    critical studies, 46
    democratic evaluation, 44–45
    empowerment evaluation, 46
    participatory evaluation, 45–46
    personalistic evaluation, 46
    summary regarding, 51–52
Rombert, T. A., 2242
Rose, Charlie, 149
Rosenshine, B., 238, 240
Rossi, P. H., 262
Routines, 164–168
Rural School Program (Brazil), proposals
    example, ix
Ryan, Kathryn, xv, 94, 276

Sacks, Peter, 230*n. 7*
Sagredo, Giovanfrancesco, xii
Salviati, Filippo, xii
Sanders, James, 36
Santayana, George, xvi
Sarason, S. B., 199
Schappelle, B. P., 130
Scheirer, M. A., 193, 265
Schmidt, W. H., 275
Schön, Donald, 186, 240, 255
School-based evaluation, 199,
    199*n. 7*, 242
School to work transition evaluation,
    reports example, ix
Schudson, M., 281
Schwab, Joseph, 238
Schwandt, Thomas A., xxiii–xxxii, xxiii*n.*
    3, 42, 101, 112*n. 1*, 182, 200,
    253, 285
Science
    generalizations search, 247, 247*n. 1*

interpretation of evidence, 246–247
research *vs.,* 246–247
standards-based evaluations, 249–250
See also Evidence-based evaluation
Scripture quotes
Genesis, 1
Scriven, Michael, xii, 14*n. 5,* 17, 47,
49, 70*n. 5,* 76, 101, 124, 171, 175,
177*n. 9,* 180, 224, 253, 254, 264,
270, 272, 276
on bias, 59–60
goal-free evaluation concept, 35, 35*n.
4,* 177*n. 9*
Secolsky, Charles, 261
Segerholm, C., 232
Selden, Steven, 235
Selection decisions, 230–231, 272
Self-challenge, 255
Service ethic, 190
Shadish, William, 51, 63, 75*n. 7,* 99*n. 7,*
193, 265
Shavelson, R. J., 112
Shinkfield, Anthony, 101
Sieber, J. E., 265*n. 1,* 267
Simons, H., 199*n. 7,* 200, 200*n.
8,* 201, 242
Site-visits, 144, 146, 147–148*fig.,* 198,
198*n. 6*
Situationality, 6, 42
situational questionnaire, 139,
140–142*fig.*
Sloane, K., 204, 231
Smith, Louis, 95, 100*n. 8,* 102, 165
Smith, N. L., 101, 170, 224, 248, 276, 284
Sobel, Dava, xii
Social action. *See* Roles of evaluation,
social action
Social science-based evaluation, 43
Socioeconomic factors, student
learning, 275
Spark, Muriel, 167, 168
Specification error, 65, 65*n. 4,* 71
Spring, Joel, 232
Staff and participant performances,
defined, 61–62
Staff development, 235
importance of, 235–236

personal *vs.* management
responsibility, 236
training assessment
evaluator visits, 241
performance testing, 240–242
qualitative techniques, 240–242
training content, 237–239
change in, 238
participant critique, 115–116*fig.,*
212, 238
simplification and
standardization, 239
social, political, economic
perceptions, 238–239
task analysis, 239
training strategies, 239–240
direct instruction, 239–240
mastery learning concept, 240
task analysis, 239
Veterans Benefits Administration
example, 236
Stake, Bernadine, 99
Stake, Robert, 42, 78, 83, 89*n. 1,* 93, 95,
102, 103*fig.,* 109, 113, 117, 122, 125,
130, 139, 153*n. 8,* 162*fig.,* 173, 181,
182, 187, 200*n. 8,* 204, 231, 233,
248, 253, 262, 275, 305
Stakeholders in evaluation, 4, 4*n. 2*
audience, defined, 195–196
criteria and comparisons standards, 66
data gathering, 127, 128*fig.*
defined, 195
democratic evaluation, 199–203,
199*n7,* 200*nn. 8–10,* 201*n. 11,* 202
evaluand representations,
212–213, 214*fig.*
factors of, 195
goal attainment evaluation, 34
issue selection, data gathering, 196–197
participatory evaluation, 45–46,
193–194, 193*n. 2*
responsive evaluation, 101
staff training content, 239
surveys from, 138
See also Clients; Participatory evaluation; Participatory observation;
Readers

Standardization issue, 227–228
    benefits, limitations of, 227–228
    blackboard layout for, 225*fig.*, 229*fig.*
    examples of, 227
    meta-evaluation, 228
    stimulus error, 228
    See also Standards; Standards-based
        evaluation
Standardized Student Achievement, vii, 8
Standards
    acompensatory weighted score
        model, 14
    amultiple cutoff weighted score
        model, 14–15
    beginning and end comparison
        design, 13–14
    contract negotiation, 213*fig.*
    control group design, 13
    vs. criteria, 5–6, 6*fig.*
    criterial cutting scores, 13
    defined, 5, 7, 13, 65
    in evaluation, 5
    as expressive objectives, 7–8, 7*n. 4*
    ideal standard, 8, 13
    performance measurement compared
        to, 14–15, 14*n. 5*, 15*n. 6*
    personal standards, 271–273
    previous group comparison
        design, 13
    for product comparisons, 8, 9–12*table*
    professional standards, 273–275
    setting of, 5
    teachers reading English, example, 7
    weighting of, 6, 65, 74, 127, 164,
        258, 283
    See also Ethical issues; Standards-
        based evaluation
Standards-based evaluation, xi, 64–66
    analysis, 160
    bias
        explication to deal with, 60
        prevalence of, 59–60
    biased impressions, 179
    conclusions regarding, xxii
    costs
        cost-benefit ratio, 77–78, 79–80*fig.*
        division of work and costs, 77

criteria and standards for
    comparisons, 64–66
    decision-making, 65
    multiple criteria, 65–68
    public school mathematics
        standards, 67–70*fig.*
    specification error, 65, 68*n. 4*
    stakeholder group differences, 66
    subjectivity, 64–65
criterial factors, 6
criterial thinking, 57, 58, 58*n. 1*
criterion instrument for, gender
    equity program, 54,
    55–56*fig.*, 57
criterion instrument for, veterans
    telephone interview,
    40–41*fig.*, 57
effects of, xx–xxi
explanation of, xix–xv
factors, xxii–xxiii, 60–64, 195
    definition of, 60*n. 2*, 61–62*fig.*
    as phases, 62, 62*n. 3*, 63*fig.*
generalizability, xxiii–xxiv
goals of program, 71–76
    behavioral objectives, 72, 73–74*fig.*
    CET Programme, 71–72
    conceptual organizers, 72,
        72*n. 6*, 74
    goal-free evaluation, 76, 177*n. 9*
    transformation of, 75, 76*fig.*
    UTOS version of, 75, 75*n. 7*
investigative reason, 248
limitations
    cooperation issues, 83
    time constraints, 82
    validity issues, 82–83
"Meta-Analysis and the Learning
    Curve in Evaluation Practice"
    (Lipsey), xvi–xxiii, xvi*n. 1*, xxii*n. 2*
method, procedure, xxi–xxii
naturalistic generalization, 250
needs assessment, 66, 71
performance measurement compared
    to standards, 14, 14*n. 5*
performance representations
    aggregative *vs.* interpretive
        analysis, 82

asking questions, 78, 81–82
descriptive analysis, 82
statistical inference, 82
policy evaluation, 254
program development function, 64
rational *vs.* intuitive thinking, 58–59
vs. responsive evaluation, 94–95
stakeholders *vs.* audience, 196
synthesis, 179
taxonomy and terminology, xviii
See also Criterial-based evaluation;
Data gathering; Ethical issues
*Standards for Educational and
Psychological Testing* (American
Psychological Association), 113*n. 2*
Standards for Evaluation Practice
(Rossi), 262
Stanic, G. M. A., 42
Stanley, Julian, 250
State standards, 70, 72
See also Standards-based evaluation
Steele, J. M., 144
Stenhouse, Lawrence, 200
Stenzel, N., 78
Stimulus error, 18, 102, 240
in names and labels, 215
in program standardization, 228
in responsive evaluation, 105*n.
12,* 283
Stokes, D. E., 249
Story telling, 101, 176
Student testing issue, 223
Stufflebeam, Daniel, xv, 29, 29*n. 2,* 52,
52*n. 9,* 101, 177*n. 8,* 180, 180*n. 11,*
275, 276
Styles, of evaluation, 16–18
See also Roles of evaluation
Summative evaluation, 17–18, 24–26, 101
Surveys. *See* Data gathering
Surveys, questionnaires, 55–56*fig.,*
79–80*fig.,* 94–95, 97–98*fig.,* 98,
137–138, 140–144*fig.*
Synthesis, 169, 170*n. 5*
vs. analysis, 160
bias difficulties, 171
connoisseurship evaluation concept,
174, 174*n. 6*

contextual factors, 172–174
defined, 160, 169
epistomology of goodness concept,
170, 170*n. 5*
expert perceptions, 174, 174*n. 6*
finalizing realization of quality,
174–175
logic of evaluators, 170
merit and weakness statement,
174–175
Milwaukee Alternative Teacher
Training example, 172
particularity *vs.* generalizability, 173
program evaluation as case study, 173
in responsive evaluation, 172,
179–180
setting standards in advance, 170–171
in standards-based evaluation, 180
See also Synthesis weights
Synthesis weights, 61, 160, 174, 179,
195, 281

Tape recorded interview, 149, 150–152*fig.*
Task analysis in training, 239
Teachers
performance, student test scores, 275
Texas teacher literacy evaluation,
163, 163*n. 4*

Teachers Academy for Mathematics and
Science, vii
Teachers evaluation
reading English example, 7
Teachers' evaluations, ix
Techne, xxix
Technical rationality, xxvii
Teese, Richard, 228*n. 7*
Telephone interview, 38, 40–41*fig.,*
57, 149
Terkel, Studs, 149
Tessmer, M., 239
Themessl-Huber, Markus, 46
Theobald, Paul, 125
Theory-based evaluation, 43, 198,
198*n. 5*
Thomas, G., 245
Tolstoy, Leo, 248

Tomkins, Silvan, 247*n. 1*
Torres, Rosalie, 44
Training content, staff development, 237–239
    change in, 238
    participant critique, 115–116*fig.*, 212, 238
    simplification and standardization, 239
    social, political, economic perceptions, 236–237
    task analysis, 237
Transactional evaluation, 39, 213
    data, 109–110, 109*fig.*
Tres, Penha, 117
Triangulation, 99, 102, 163
    confirmation, 182, 183*n. 14*, 255
    interpretation statements, 184–188
    ruling out rival hypotheses, 184
    search for alternative meanings, 185–186
Trochim, William, 224*n. 4*
Trumbull, D., 250
Tsang, Mun C., 78
Tyler, Ralph, 74–75, 198
Tymms, Peter, 191

Unamuno, Miguel de, 260
Under the Glacier, from (Laxness), 31–32
Understanding, xi
University of Illinois, xi, 305
Urban School Problem Solving project, 100, 100*n. 8*
User-Friendly Handbook for Project Evaluation (National Science Foundation), 225
Users, treatments, observations, and specifics of time and culture. *See* UTOS evaluation
Utility, program evaluation standard, 265
Utilization-based evaluation, 38, 52*n. 9*
    communication focus, 198
    facilitation focus, 197
    findings being used factor, 197, 197*n. 3*
    institutional accreditation, 198, 198*n. 6*

vs. theory-based evaluation, 198, 198*n. 5*
    unimportance of evaluand, 197
UTOS evaluation, 75, 75*n. 7*, 250–251

Validity, 82–83, 181, 181*nn. 12, 13*
    data gathering, 113, 113*n. 2*
    data sources, 103
    face validity, 216
    member check, 83
    meta-evaluation of data, 181, 181*nn. 12, 13*, 216
    program value representation, 161, 161*fig.*
Value
    perceptions of, 161*n. 2*
    representation of, 161*fig.*
    ubiquitous nature of, x
The Varnished Truth (Nyberg), 275*n.5*
Veterans Benefits Administration
    criterion instrument for, 40–41*fig.*, 58
    holistic quality evaluation, 38–39
    meta-evaluation, 182
    reports example, web appendix, viii, 39
Vietnam War, 42
Vignettes, 90, 110, 157, 162*n. 3*, 165, 167, 169, 211
von Wright, Georg Henrik, xi, xvi

War on Poverty, 42
Watts, M., 59, 102
Web appendix, vii–viii
    Assessment of Student Achievement in Program Evaluation, 242
    CIPP Model, 29*n. 2*
    meta-evaluation, 180
    student achievement issue, 225
    topics, ix
Wehlage, G. G., 48*n. 8*
Weighting
    stakeholder goals, 75
    of standards, 6, 41, 65, 74, 127, 164, 258, 283
    synthesis weights, 61, 160, 174, 178, 195, 281
    weighted score models, 14–15, 174, 278
Weiss, Carol, 75*n. 7*, 197*n. 3*, 198

Whewell, William, 223
Where the Truth Lies (House), 223
Whistle-blowing, 46, 278
Whitehurst, George, 251, 251*n. 2*, 253
Wilde, Oscar, 54
Wilson, B., 162*fig.*
Wilson, D. B., xix, xxi
Wilson, M., 162*fig.*
Wilson, S. J., xix
Wise, A. E., 276
Wolf, Robert, 149
World Economic Forum, 1992, x

Worldview concept, xvi, xxxii, 192–193, 197
Worthen, Blaine, 182
Wrangling, of issues, 223–224, 223*n. 1*
Wye, C., 193, 265

Yin, R. K., 173, 200
Youdell, Deborah, 230*n. 7*
Young, Michael, 230*n. 7*

Zen and the Art of Motorcycle Maintenance (Persig), 6*n. 3*, 108–109

About the Author

Robert Stake is a Professor of Education and Director of the Center for Instructional Research and Curriculum Evaluation (CIRCE) at the University of Illinois. He is a specialist in the evaluation of educational programs, an author, and a researcher.

Since coming to Illinois in 1963, he has been active in program evaluation and has promoted an approach to evaluation methods called "responsive evaluation." He took up a qualitative perspective, particularly case study methods, in order to represent the complexity of evaluation study. He assisted in the founding of CIRCE, a site for the innovative designing of program evaluation, and in 1975 became its director.

Stake is also active in the American Educational Research Association and the American Evaluation Association. In 1988, he received the Lazarfeld Award from the AEA and, in 1994, an honorary doctorate from the University of Uppsala.

Stake is the author of *Quieting Reform, Evaluating the Arts in Education,* and *The Art of Case Study Research,* and coauthor of both *Case Studies in Science Education* (with Jack Easley) and *Custom and Cherishing: The Arts in American Elementary Schools* (with Liora Bresler and Linda Mabry).